Francis A. Drexel
LIBRARY

Books For College Libraries
Third Edition

Core Collection

SAINT JOSEPH'S UNIVERSITY

MONEY CREDIT AND COMMERCE

MONEY CREDIT
& COMMERCE

BY

ALFRED MARSHALL

Reprints of Economic Classics
Augustus M. Kelley
New York 1960

PREFACE

THE present volume is the third of a group, the main purpose of which is to study the direction of man's efforts for the attainment of material ends: and to search for possibilities of improvements in that procedure which may increase the command of the peoples of the world over their resources; and enable them to develop their higher faculties.

The first volume of the group, *Principles of Economics*, published in 1890, emphasized the continuity of the main work of economic studies. "As, in spite of great differences in form between birds and quadrupeds, there is one Fundamental Idea running through all their frames, so the general theory of the equilibrium of demand and supply is a Fundamental Idea running through the frames of all the various parts of the central problem of Distribution and Exchange....The theories of the values of labour and of the things made by it cannot be separated...What differences there are between them even in matters of detail, turn out on inquiry to be for the most part differences of degree rather than of kind[1]."

Various causes delayed my work; and nearly thirty years elapsed before the appearance of *Industry and Trade*, of which the motto is: *The many in the one, the one in the many.* "Several tendencies have gone to the making of each industry and each economic institution: therefore a thorough realistic study of any part of the economic field, calls for some reference to the inter-action of many diverse tendencies, and gives occasion for some care in analysis. And, conversely, almost every important tendency is so far modified by the conditions under which it operates, that an exhaustive study of it may need to range over many fields of work. This motto supplements the motto of my *Principles*, which is:—*Natura non facit saltum*: *i.e.* economic evolution is gradual and continuous on each of its numberless routes[2]."

Industry and Trade is "a study of industrial technique, and business organization, and of their influences on the conditions of various classes and nations." It was designed to be followed

[1] From the Preface to the first edition of *Principles of Economics,* 1890.
[2] From the Preface to *Industry and Trade.*

by a study of the influences on the conditions of man's life and work, which are "exerted by the resources available for employment; by money and credit; by international trade and by social endeavour." But that task is heavy, and achievement has been slow: therefore it has seemed best to publish without further delay the present volume, which aims at accomplishing one-half of the task. A little progress has been made in regard to the second half: and, although old age presses on me, I am not without hopes that some of the notions, which I have formed as to the possibilities of social advance, may yet be published.

A. M.

BALLIOL CROFT,
   CAMBRIDGE
      August, 1922

CONTENTS

BOOK II

BUSINESS CREDIT

BOOK III

INTERNATIONAL TRADE

BOOK IV

FLUCTUATIONS OF INDUSTRY, TRADE AND CREDIT

"bank-money." 3. Various functions of banks in the later Middle Ages.
4. Beginnings of the Bank of England. 5. Expansion of the scope of
English banking. 6. Relations of the Bank of England with the British
Government during the Napoleonic wars . . . pp. 295—307

INTRODUCTION

1. *The modern notion of economic nationality, which found some place in the aspirations of many small States in early times, was developed by Mediaeval City-States; and was passed on by them through Holland to England and other countries*[1].

"International trade," in the strict sense of the term, seems to suggest trade between various nations in their corporate capacity. But as commonly used, it refers to what is primarily only the aggregate of the trade of individuals in one country with individuals belonging to other countries.

The main courses of trade are governed by relations among the surrounding industries in the same way as water courses are governed by the contours of the hills; though trade reacts on industries as the streams react on the hills. Further, a nation's industries and her trade alike imply national ideals and national unity: both are parts of her life and embody much of her character.

List pointed out that a true national spirit could arise in a country, only when she had attained to some degree of unity by common interests in industry and trade. Her ruling classes could indeed develop common political and military aims, by means of those facilities for communication which they alone possessed in early times; but more is required for the development of a national spirit in industry and trade. Therefore a full conception of the notion of international trade waited until the spirit of Bruges or Antwerp, of Venice, Florence or Milan had spread over a whole country. Holland led the way: she absorbed many cities which had already attained high repute. Her waterways contributed greatly to her unity: and they helped her defence against that violence of great military powers, which had subdued the southern half of the "Low Countries." She was forced to give much of her

---

[1] The present volume and that on *Industry and Trade* are designed to supplement one another. Nevertheless it seems best to introduce here a sketch of some leading antecedents of present international relations.

energy to self-defence: but she yet maintained the spirit of national unity in industry and trade. In her case, it would perhaps be better to say "trade and industry."

In England local liberties, though often on a generous scale, were never absolute. But her chief cities had, in effect, the power and the will to develop their own idiosyncrasies with much freedom: and so great were, till recent times, the difficulties which opposed long distance heavy traffic except by water, that each of them was able to develop her own methods of life and work very nearly as she would have done, if she had been wholly free. The relations of each town to the surrounding country-folk resembled in many respects those of some European countries to their colonies in later times: the country-folk looked to the neighbouring town as the chief market for the produce of their farms: and in return they purchased from the town nearly all manufactures, except those which they could make in their own cottages during the winter.

The West-countryman's pride in the maritime vigour of the counties that bore the first brunt of the conflict with the Spanish Armada, was long prominent and approved by the whole nation. Even in the present age men of Lancashire, Yorkshire and other counties, though not directly concerned in industry, have shown a zeal for the economic excellences of their several counties, which indicates a survival to the present times of an earlier ardent affection for local industries. That affection expanded into a patriotic pride in national industry and trade, when the Middle Ages passed into the Modern; and Englishmen could claim a place in the first rank of the business men of the world. Several causes contributed to this expansion: but most of them are connected with the increase of migration, and of communication by travel, by post and by printed news throughout England; though her more distant parts had had not very much direct knowledge of one another before the railway age.

Now-a-days many an artisan and unskilled working man has found employment in more than one county: and what has been called "local patriotism," is necessarily being weakened by modern facilities of travel, and the tendency of organized public education to soften the peculiarities of local dialects. But even now a man is often proud of the past history and the present energy of his own county. A Devonshire man still rejoices that the enterprise of the Spanish Armada had been much lowered before it had passed out of direct touch with Devonshire. Again, even now, an artisan takes a wholesome pride in the reputation which his county has won in the production of some high-class products, or in open-air games.

2. *In Adam Smith's time settled political conditions, good roads, and the printing press had gone far towards welding together the educated classes of the British nation: but local interests were still often more prominent than national.*

When Adam Smith wrote, movements of workers, and migrations of particular branches of industry within Britain had progressed a considerable way—perhaps about half the way—from their mediaeval phase towards that of the present time. Local obstructions opposed to national interests, had diminished: travelling was almost free from dangers. Roads were moderately good. The upper and middle classes together with some few of the manual labour classes could read. Newspapers were already a power in the land, though they seldom gave much information that would help an artisan, who was half inclined to migrate in order to improve his condition: and Adam Smith insisted that "a man is of all sorts of luggage the most difficult to be transported[1]."

It is to be hoped that light will be thrown on the history of internal migrations in England during the Middle Ages by philological and other studies. When these are accompanied by statistics of variations of local wages and of the price of the staple grain consumed by the ordinary labourer, the foundations will have been laid for conclusions as to the development of the modern influences

[1] He said that the common price of labour was eighteen pence in and near London: at a few miles distance it fell to fourteen or fifteen pence. Ten pence in Edinburgh fell to eight pence at a few miles distance. McCulloch, annotating this passage in 1838, said that "roads, canals, railways and steam navigation" have much diminished these inequalities. [At that date the influence of canals was of course greater than that of railways.] He put the wages of labour as "at a rough average all over the country...from 20*d.* to 2*s.* a day." But these and all similar estimates relating to times, when England commonly fed her people herself, must be interpreted, for comparison with present figures, by reflecting that flour was then generally much cheaper in the country than in the cities: and that a much larger part of the wages of ordinary labour was spent on flour and bread then than now.

of economic causes on migration: but at present we do not seem able to see far back at all clearly[1].

It is a general rule that local particular interests (*Sonderinteressen*) are seldom advanced in the long run by action which is inimical to national interests. For illiberal policing in one locality provokes similar policing in others in its neighbourhood: and hindrances to internal migration prevent the best use of the nation's faculties from being made. In the long run the advance of each locality depends much on the richness of the markets which neighbouring districts afford to its buyers and its sellers, and on the suggestions that it derives from the rest of the country, as well as on its power of attracting from outside any men of special attainments, whose aid may be helpful to it. Therefore a selfish policy is generally a foolish policy.

In this connection it may be noted that the influences of customary rates of wages are not wholly adverse to migration, whether within a country or beyond its frontiers. If custom stereotypes the wages for (say) agricultural labour in a village, a man who is stronger and more energetic than his neighbours will be underpaid, if he stays at home: he has therefore more to gain by migrating to a town, or to a more highly waged agricultural district, than he would have had, if his wages at home had been more nearly appropriate to his value.

Adam Smith tells us that "more than fifty years ago some of the counties in the neighbourhood of London petitioned the parliament against the extension of the turnpike roads into the remoter counties. These remoter counties, they pretended, from the cheapness of labour would be able to sell their grass and corn cheaper in the London market than themselves, and would thereby reduce their rents and ruin their cultivation. Their rents have however risen, and their cultivation has been improved since that time."

[1] If the material available to the economic historian were adequate, a history of wages in England should be based on separate consecutive records of variations in each of many representative localities; with statements (or at least reasoned estimates) as to the allowances in regard to free grazing ground and other privileges, which were allowed in each district. Rogers did noble work in this direction; and he seems to have been aware of the difficulties, which must be overcome before a trustworthy estimate can be formed, of general, or average, rates of real remuneration for labour of various sorts throughout England in early times. In so far as wages were paid in kind, the grain selected for the purpose was not likely to be in very good condition: and modern appliances for reaping and bringing the grain under shelter were not accessible.

He, however, appears to have made insufficient allowance for the influence of natural selection in equalizing the earnings of a given order of efficiency; at the same time that it increased the differences among the standard wages of different localities. We shall find this matter to be of great importance in the application of the general doctrine of international values to the real problems of the present time. The migration of men, women and children from rural districts in the south of England to Lancashire textile districts was artificially promoted early in last century: and this tended to equalize average wages by lessening the excess of the vigour of the workers of the north over that of the southern population. On the other hand, "natural selection," while tending to equalize the earnings of work of each order of efficiency, often increases the inequalities of average earnings in different places. For able men tend to quit places where high wages are not to be earned; and thereby to put those, who stay behind, in a rather better position for maintaining or even advancing their wages. This migration at the same time tends to lessen the relative scarcity of operatives in progressive districts and prevent a disproportionate rise in the average wages of those districts; and their own earnings are more nearly proportional to their efficiency, than if they had stayed at home.

3. *The growth of a strong spirit of nationality has been promoted in recent times by cheap, easy and rapid locomotion; by the development of popular newspapers and by universal education.*

The improvement of roads and stage coaches facilitated intercourse among the leaders of trade and industry during the two generations that followed: but they were of relatively small direct service to the working classes: canal boat traffic was however cheap. Similarly, successive advances in the arts of printing, and in postal organization, helped the well-to-do and the business classes throughout the country to keep touch with one another: but they were of little service to the masses of the people, who could neither read nor write. It is true that the spirit of economic nationality spread down from the well-informed classes to others: but meanwhile the pressure of population on the means of subsistence, not yet relieved by the free and cheap importation of food from a distance, tended to generate class hostility; so the people were divided into two nations, the rich and the poor. That cruel abuse of political power by the classes that chiefly controlled the legislature, spread its dark shadow far into the nineteenth century; and its influence in retarding the growth of national unity may be traced even now: but at last the manual labour classes have attained so marked a predominance that, if wisely guided, they can control policy in the interests of the nation as a whole; and they can afford to forget injuries of the long ago.

Universal education, cheap and efficient popular newspapers, combined with the commodious and relatively cheap facilities of railway travel have at last removed almost every trace of the difficulties, which formerly prevented the attainment by a whole country of that full economic unity, which used to be regarded as belonging only to compact trading and industrial cities. In the old trading cities, intercourse went by word of mouth; and an advocate of any economic policy could often make his voice reach the ears of nearly all those who were most deeply interested in the matter: to-day an important utterance on any large issue is made available through the press to the whole of the working classes: it is likely to be read carefully by perhaps a million of those who think for themselves, and influence the opinions of others. Thus the drift towards full economic unity is nearly complete in all matters, in regard to which there are no fundamental differences of interest among different classes. Discussion is clearing away clouds of misconception and hollow spectres of conflicting interests, having no solid substance. It is, however, directing attention to some discords that are not very prominent. The recent European war and the disquiets which have followed it, have reopened and enlarged many grave questions. In particular, they have brought to the front in several countries, and perhaps most prominently in Britain, working class minds, capable of hard thought and resolute in following its conclusions, whithersoever it may tend. These facts afford a strong argument in favour of aiding the working classes to make thorough studies of the causes, and especially the obscure causes that make for or against economic progress[1].

----

[1] It seems that the first Parliamentary grant in favour of education was for £20,000, made in the year following the great Reform Bill. Another con-

In particular it is essential to emphasize the fact that Britain no longer possesses in quite as full degree as formerly a preponderant advantage over nearly all other countries in the individuality and resolution of her people; in her easy maintenance of liberty in conjunction with firm order and the rigid enforcement of equal laws; in the abundance of her capital, and in the resourceful inventiveness of the leaders of her industry. In all these matters several countries have gained ground on her. In some of them she has been surpassed by others, beyond the seas, who speak her own language: this change is in part due to increased facilities for crossing the ocean, of which avail has been taken by many of the strongest and most enterprising of her own sons, and of her continental rivals.

4. *Migration within a country is facilitated and its adjustments are rendered efficient by various influences, which do not favour emigration beyond its boundaries in like degree: and therefore problems of "international values" require a different treatment from that which is appropriate to the relative values of things produced in the same country.*

Movements of population within a country are generally by small stages: and therefore the tendency of work of the same efficiency to obtain about equal wages under like conditions throughout a large country is not effected to a very great extent by migration at single steps over long distances. But districts in which employment is offered on favourable terms draw labour from neighbouring districts; and they in turn replenish their supplies of labour from districts on the other sides of them; and so on. Thus a very small force will effect a gradual movement of labour sufficient to obliterate any disturbance in the relative wages in different districts: though even a small resistance, if concentrated at one point, might have delayed the movement greatly. The case is similar to that of a number of tanks of water connected by pipes. If, when the water is at rest at the same level throughout, a little additional water is poured into one of them, a readjustment

siderable advance was a grant of money for the maintenance of elementary schools: it was made in 1846, in the early stages of a great popular ferment which was spreading throughout Europe, and culminated in 1848. Further progress was made by Lowe's Revised Code, 1862. Forster's Act of 1870 was the first of a series, which have brought the education of the children of the working classes to a higher efficiency than was to be found in many middle class schools half a century ago.

of level will be made quickly throughout the whole system, though the impellent force is small and no water passes from any tank, except to its immediate neighbour. Similarly, the earnings of like faculties tend to equality throughout a whole country under the impulse of numerous small forces. It is seldom necessary to induce individual men, and still less whole families to migrate over large distances; thus moving beyond the range of relatives and friends. For districts where employment is rich and population relatively scanty, draw easily from others near at hand: and these draw, if need be, from others near to them. Thus a level is approximately maintained over a wide area; though the greater part of the migration necessary to maintain it has been over only short distances, and has been set in movement by comparatively small forces. No doubt it is sometimes easier to migrate a small distance across a frontier than a long distance within the same country. But this does not show that frontiers have little effect in hindering the adjustment of labour to the demand for it: for, if there were no frontiers, gradual readjustments, mainly in small stages, would be effected by forces too slight to move many people across a frontier.

Some of the difficulties which ordinarily confront an individual or a family on migrating into a strange country, are indeed absent or easily surmounted in exceptional cases. An Englishman meets his own language in the United States: and in every British possession he finds himself under laws closely resembling, if not identical with, those familiar to him. A German, a Pole, or a Hungarian can emigrate to an industrial district in America, where a group of compatriots are already settled: and indeed he often starts under the guidance of others, who are already working there in the same branch of industry as his own. This inclination of immigrants from the same country to herd together tends in some degree to maintain their previous habits of consumption; and therefore to modify in a very small degree the character of the imports of their adopted country: but the immigrants generally fall in with the industrial methods of their new home, and exert but little direct influence on the character of her exports[1].

[1] The case was different when immigrant artisans were frequently people of highly specialized skill, who generally left their own homes in order to escape from persecution on religious or political grounds; except when they were selected by emissaries of another country, as fit teachers of their crafts to her

The emigration of capital, with or without its owner, is obstructed by difficulties partly similar to and partly different from those which obstruct the emigration of individuals or families in search of employment. The owner of any considerable capital, especially if he is himself a business man, is likely to be more self-reliant, and less dependent on the society of relations and old acquaintances, than are the greater part of those who carry most of their possessions in their luggage: he may for instance be able easily to set up a branch of his business in a distant land; and perhaps he may ere long concentrate his chief energies on it. In any case, he can pass over to leading subordinates the greater part of the personal communications, which he needs to make with his new fellow-countrymen: and his experiences of two countries give him some little advantage over those who know only one. He may have some difficulty in deciding whether to give large credit to particular customers; and, conversely, in obtaining large credit to meet special occasions. These are small matters: but the tendency of capitalists in general to prefer investments at home to investments abroad, other things being equal, has far reaching results and is a considerable contributory cause of the need for a broad study of international trade on lines somewhat different from those appropriate to domestic trade.

If the emergencies of war be left out of account, it is indeed constantly becoming easier and safer than formerly to invest capital in foreign countries; but of two investments of equal intrinsic merits, one at home and the other abroad, the former has still a great balance of pecuniary advantage as well as of sentimental attractiveness. For information with regard to it is more easily obtained and more easily tested: the income from the investment is drawn with less trouble and expense; and if any hitch arise with regard to the recovery of the capital itself in due time, the commercial and the legal difficulties of the task are likely to be much greater if the capital is invested abroad than if it is invested at home.

Causes deep set in human nature underlie the facts that national currency has been a chief symbol of national unity; that the right

people: then the immigration of foreign artisans generally opened out new possibilities of high grade exportation to the country of their adoption. Now the immigrant generally moves towards a country where the standard of popular education is higher than in his old home: and his children are thereby assimilated.

of coinage has been among the choicest prerogatives of sovereignty; that, as metallic money has yielded precedence to modern instruments of credit, national trade has focussed itself around the national banking system; that national money market statistics have grown up together with national import and export statistics; and that all have been associated with the national purse filled by common effort and devoted to the attainment of national ideals through united effort in peace and in war.

No doubt migration across, as well as within, national frontiers is being rendered easier and more attractive by modern developments of the means of communication. But it remains true now for the same reasons, though not to the same degree, as it was a hundred years ago, that national solidarity is mainly caused by the two facts: first, a capitalist has, as a rule, a slight preference for an investment in his own country over one that holds out equal prospects of success and high profits in another; and secondly, a smaller expectation of an increase in earnings and other material advantages, in return for equally difficult and arduous work, will generally suffice to induce a man to migrate from one part to another of his own country, rather than to emigrate to another country.

To conclude: local interests are more constructive and less constrictive than they were in Adam Smith's time. They are less constrictive, because migration, education, the printing-press and the telegraph have tended to merge local interests in national. And thus they become more constructive, because they can not often work effectively for their own ends, save by throwing in their lot with broad movements for the advance of national industry and trade.

These changes have tended to bring facts into closer correspondence with assumptions, adopted by Adam Smith as the starting point of his argument, and developed, with sharper outlines, by his followers. They were to the effect that the movements of labour between different parts of a western country and different occupations in it, are sufficiently easy and quick to justify the assumptions that—as a general rule—the earnings in occupations of equal difficulty, and incidental advantages and disadvantages, are approximately equal throughout the country: and further that each western country's banking and credit organization secures a prompt flow of capital into any industry in the country, which yields profits higher than are required to compensate for the risks and difficulties of that industry; with the result that *net* profits are kept nearly uniform throughout the country.

These two dominant facts afford the basis of the doctrine of domestic values, that is of things produced in the same country; provided, of course, that none of them are under monopolistic control. The facts imply that an increased home demand for one set of home products will, as a rule, be met gradually by a diversion of labour and capital from other work to the industries connected with those products: so that after a time it will again be approximately true that the exchange values of those products will bear the same relation as before to the quantities and qualities of the labour, aided by appropriate capital, needed for their production. A special study of international values is needed, because a similar statement cannot be made in regard to them.

It cannot be made in regard to international values; because a sustained greatly increased demand by one country for the goods of other countries, other things being equal, will cause her goods to fall in exchange value relatively to those of other countries. There may in consequence arise some impulse to increased emigration to other countries, whose products have risen relatively to hers in international demand; but the influence will be slight: therefore the labour and capital employed in her industries will receive less reward than formerly, relatively to the faculties, emotions and sacrifices demanded of them.

The values of the precious metals in any country are in great measure governed by the courses of her foreign trade in them. But these courses are themselves governed by her demand for general purchasing power in the form of metallic money: and that side of the problem of the value of metallic money may conveniently be studied by itself. That being done, a study of the causes that govern the international distribution of the precious metals, and the consequent general level of metallic-prices in each country, will follow easily in the course of an investigation of the effective demand by each country for imported goods. An effective demand is of course one which includes an offer of equivalent goods, delivered at once, or deferred under arrangements of international credit. The details of some of these provisions are complex: but the general principle, which underlies them, is simple and definite.

BOOK I

MONEY

CHAPTER I[1]

FUNCTIONS OF MONEY

1. *Various uses of the term "money."*

I, I, 1. The terms "money" and "currency" are used sometimes narrowly, sometimes broadly. They consist, in the first place, of those media of exchange, which pass freely from hand to hand, even among persons who are strangers to one another; and thus transfer the command of amounts of general purchasing power, which are set out in clear type on their faces. Under this head are included, in the first place, all coined moneys, issued by competent authority, and free from injury by "clipping" or otherwise. Next in order come notes printed on paper, and issued by Government or other competent authority: under the latter head may be included notes issued by banks under official supervision; notes issued by other banks which are in good repute, serve the same purpose in ordinary times. In times of disturbed credit, however, the only bank notes which can be regarded as money, in the full sense of the term, are those which are "legal tender"; that is, notes which cannot be refused in payment of a debt: Bank of England notes enjoy this prerogative in an exceptional degree.

The term "legal tender" points to a broad contrast between the amounts of currency that are needed for the efficient discharge of business in times of good credit and bad credit respectively. When credit is good, people generally are in no hurry to call in all the money that is owing to them, and they are not very critical of the manner in which payments are made: a private cheque, as well as a note of an ordinary bank, is commonly accepted. But when credit is disturbed, they scan with some care payments in other forms than currency and legal tender notes. That is to say, the effective stock of the means of discharging monetary obliga-

---

[1] Appendix A is attached to this chapter.

tions are in danger of being curtailed at those times, at which the amount of work set for them is greatest.

These considerations indicate that the need for elasticity in the use of the term "money" is somewhat greater than in most other economic terms[1]. There are some inquiries in which it may with advantage be used narrowly, and others in which a broad use of it is appropriate. There is, however, a general, though not universal agreement that, when nothing is implied to the contrary, "money" is to be taken to be convertible with "currency," and therefore to consist of all those things which are (at any time and place) generally "current," without doubt or special inquiry, as means of purchasing commodities and services, and of defraying commercial obligations. Thus, in an advanced modern society, it includes all the coin and notes issued by Government.

Almost in the same class are the notes issued by banks which are in good repute: for such notes are in fact accepted at their full value, at all events locally, without hesitation under all ordinary circumstances: and therefore we may proceed on the understanding that they are reckoned as money, unless something is said to the contrary in the context[2].

At the same time it must be admitted that the solvency of the private issues of bank notes is a matter of degree: and especially in reference to times when commercial credit is violently shaken, it seems expedient to draw a distinction between those notes which rest on the mere credit of a private institution and those of which the solvency in terms of standard money is effectively guaranteed by stringent Government control[3].

The above remarks imply that the value of each element of a

[1] Some observations on the need for elasticity in the use of economic terms are made in *Industry and Trade*, Appendix A, § 2.

[2] This is substantially the definition for which F. A. Walker argued with great force in 1878: and which has won its way to general acceptance.

[3] There are even some inquiries in which it is best to reckon in only those notes which are full "legal tender"; that is, the tender of which is a full legal answer by a debtor to a charge that he has failed to meet his obligation. No responsible Government concedes legal tender privilege to a note issue without taking full precautions for securing that the note shall be convertible into currency, for the credit of which the Government is directly responsible: and therefore such notes are on almost the same footing as that currency. But an ordinary bank-note may be refused if tendered by a debtor in payment of an obligation; and, even when accepted by the creditor, it does not discharge the obligation, if the bank by which it is issued fails before the creditor has had time, with reasonable diligence, to present it for payment.

I, I, 2. good system of metallic currency is definitely fixed and universally
recognized as a certain proportion of a *standard* coin. This term
is somewhat ambiguous: but, in its fullest sense, it means the coin,
to which the mint of the country in question is open without charge
or at a low charge, and the value of which is therefore tied firmly
to that of the metal of which it is made. As a rule, every element
of an inconvertible paper currency rests on one and the same
foundation of credit, whether that be solid or not[1].

2. *The "money-market" is the market for command over
money: "the value of money" in it at any time is the rate of
discount, or of interest for short period loans charged in it.*

The "money market" is not now occupied to any considerable
extent with dealings in diverse currencies; though much of the
early business of banks was connected with money-changing. It
is in effect the market for loans, or advances of money; and in
this connection the "value of money" is in effect the proportionate
excess of a certain sum in hand over the (secured) promise to pay
that sum at a later date. The date most commonly in view is three
months from the present time: and the "value of money" is then
that annual rate which corresponds to the discount of a good bill
with three months to run[2].

The chief means of payment (sometimes even spoken of as
"currency") in English manufacturing districts early in last century, consisted of bills of exchange; some of which had a hundred
names on their backs by the time they became due. The only other
considerable currency easily accessible consisted of notes issued by
local banks; so many of which had got into trouble, that people
often felt themselves able to judge the security given by the names
on the back of a bill, better than that offered by a neighbouring

[1] As Dana Horton has pointed out (Introduction to *The Silver Pound*) "the
standard currency" refers sometimes to a standard of fineness of the dominant
coins; sometimes merely to the coin, in which accounts are commonly kept,
whether it is full legal tender or not; sometimes to the money which is full legal
tender, whatever its constitution.

[2] But sometimes the annual rate, or value of money, quoted is for "short
loans" for a few days, or again for "money at call," that is liable to be demanded
for payment during the day, or for a loan "over-night"; *i.e.* from near the end
of business hours on one day to near the beginning on the next. The context
shows in each case which period is meant; and it is convenient for the purposes
of the Money Market to speak of the amount of ready command over money
that bankers and others are inclined to lend on any of these terms, as the
"amount of money" that is available for it.

bank. But since a bill of exchange cannot pass freely from hand to hand, unless everyone to whom it is tendered, knows at least one of the signatures on it; and since there is no easy means of ascertaining whether this condition is satisfied in any particular case, even such bills of exchange are better described as substitutes for currency than as money or currency.

It is further to be noted that a bill of exchange grows in value during each day of its approach to maturity in which it is held by any one: that is to say, it is a source of income while held, as well as a means of discharging a monetary obligation when occasion arises. In this respect it is even less properly to be classed as pure money than is a good cheque: for there is no similar gain to be got from holding a cheque.

A bank is bound to pay currency, when demanded on presentation of a cheque: but the holder seldom desires to draw any considerable quantity of currency, unless in order to pay wages. A considerable cheque is almost sure to be handed, as a business or other transaction, to some one else; with the effect that its amount is added to the credit of that person at his bank, and deducted from that standing to the account of the drawer of the cheque: there has been no transfer of cash, but payment has been made by the transfer of command over cash; and this is commonly expressed by saying that it is paid in bank money[1].

3. *The functions of money can be efficiently discharged only when its general purchasing power is secured against violent changes*[2].

For immediate (current) business money needs only to be a clearly defined, easily handled, and generally acceptable medium of exchange. These conditions can be satisfied by anything which has obtained adequate prestige from custom, or from the edict of a public authority, even though it is not capable of performing

---

[1] A bank of deposit originally was the house of a goldsmith or other banking house with whom valuables were deposited for safe custody: and when, for instance, the famous Bank of Amsterdam issued transferable certificates of ownership of any such deposits of cash, the deposits were not unjustly called "money" so long as the bank was faithful.

[2] The present section is reproduced from an article on "Remedies for fluctuations in general prices" in *The Contemporary Review*, March, 1887: some of it is also included in the remarks on the measurement of interest on capital in my *Principles*, VI, VI, 7.

I, I, 3.   any other direct service, and would be valueless but for this
prestige. The credit derived from prestige is sometimes rather
frail: partly because it is liable to be undermined by an undue
increase in its quantity: and, for this reason, nothing has been a
perfectly satisfactory medium even for immediate business, unless
its supply has been controlled more or less closely by its cost of
production, or by some other cause less unstable than custom or
public ordinance. Of course no hard and fast line can be drawn
between that stability of value which is required to make a currency
act as a satisfactory medium of exchange for immediate business,
and that which is required to enable it to act fairly well as a
standard or as a store of value for long period contracts and
deferred payments. The difference is one of degree; but its general
character is definite[1].

As has just been indicated, the chief functions of money fall
under two heads. Money is, firstly, a *medium of exchange* for
bargains that are completed almost as soon as they are begun;
it is a "currency"; it is a material thing carried in purses, and
"current" from hand to hand, because its value can be read at a
glance. This first function of money is admirably discharged by
gold and silver and paper based on them.

The second function of money is to act as a *standard of value*, or
standard for deferred payments—that is, to indicate the amount of
general purchasing power, the payment of which is sufficient to
discharge a contract, or other commercial obligation, that extends
over a considerable period of time: and for this purpose stability of
value is the one essential condition. The term "stability of value"
is indeed incapable of exact definition. For when some prices
have risen and others have fallen, the resultant change in the
purchasing power of money cannot be ascertained exactly. This
matter will be further considered in the following two chapters.

Much of the importance of having a good standard of deferred
payments is peculiar to modern times. In early stages of civiliza-

---

[1] It may be noted that a medium of exchange is the concrete form of a *common
denominator* of value for immediate business; and the function of a store of value
is most efficiently performed by a concrete thing, which sets a good *standard* of
value for deferred payments: these two pairs, concrete and abstract, may be
regarded as the counterparts of one another in regard to short-period and long-
period transactions respectively. Money has served minor functions, more or
less akin to these four: full accounts of the whole are given by Prof. Carl Menger
under the head "Geld" in the *Handwörterbuch der Staatswissenschaften.*

I, I, 3.

tion business arrangements seldom looked far ahead; contracts to make definite payments at distant times were rare and unimportant. But a great deal of our modern business life is made up of such contracts. Much of the income of the nation goes to its ultimate recipients in the form of fixed money payments on Government bonds, on the debentures of private companies, on mortgages and on long leases. Another larger part consists of salaries and wages, any change in the nominal value of which involves great friction; so that as a rule the nominal rate remains unchanged, while the real rate is constantly fluctuating with every change in the purchasing power of money.

And, lastly, the complex nature of modern trade and industry puts the management of business into the hands of a comparatively small number of men with special ability for it, and most people lend the greater part of their wealth to others instead of using it themselves. It is therefore a great evil that whenever a man borrows money to be invested in his business, he speculates doubly. In the first place he runs the risk that the things which he handles will fall in value relatively to others—this risk is inevitable; it must be endured. But in addition he runs the risk that the standard in which he has to pay back what he has borrowed will be a different one from that by which his borrowing was measured.

We are vaguely conscious that an element of speculation is thus unnecessarily introduced into life, but few of us, perhaps, realize how great it is. We often talk of borrowing or lending on good security, at say 5 per cent. If we had a real standard of value that could be done; but, as things are, it is a feat which no one performs except by accident. Suppose, for instance, a man borrows £100 under contract to pay back £105 at the end of the year. If the purchasing power of money has meanwhile risen 10 per cent. (or, which is the same thing, general prices have fallen in the ratio of ten to eleven), he cannot get the £105 which he has to pay back without selling one-tenth more commodities than would have been sufficient for the purpose at the beginning of the year. Assuming, that is, that the things which he handles have not changed in value relatively to things in general, he must sell commodities which would have then cost him £115. 10s. in order to pay back with interest his loan of £100; he has lost ground unless the commodities have increased under his hands $15\frac{1}{2}$ per cent. While nominally

I, I, 3.   paying 5 per cent. for the use of his money, he has really been
paying $15\frac{1}{2}$ per cent.

On the other hand, if prices had risen so much that the purchasing
power of money had fallen 10 per cent. during the year, so that
he could get £10 for things which cost him £9 at the beginning of
the year—that is, £105 for things which cost him £94. 10s. at the
beginning of the year; then, instead of paying 5 per cent. for the
loan, he would really be paid $5\frac{1}{2}$ per cent. for taking charge of the
money.

The consequence of this uncertainty is that when prices are
likely to rise, people rush to borrow money and buy goods, and
thus help prices to rise; business is inflated, it is managed recklessly and wastefully; those working on borrowed capital pay back
less real value than they borrowed, and enrich themselves at the
expense of the community.

Salaries and wages, unless when governed by a sliding scale,
generally retain their nominal value more or less fixed, in spite of
trade fluctuations; they can seldom be changed without much
friction and worry and loss of time. And for the very reason that
their nominal or money value is fixed, their real value varies, and
varies in the wrong direction. It falls when prices are rising, and
the purchasing power of money is falling; so that the employer
pays smaller real salaries and wages than usual at the very time
when his profits are largest in other ways, and is thus prompted
to over-estimate his strength, and engage in ventures which he
will not be able to pull through after the tide begins to turn.

When afterwards credit is shaken and prices begin to fall, every
one wants to get rid of commodities and get hold of money which
is rapidly rising in value; this makes prices fall all the faster, and
the further fall makes credit shrink even more, and thus for a long
time prices fall because prices have fallen. At such a time employers
cease their production because they fear that when they come to
sell their finished product general prices will be even lower than
when they buy their materials; and at such times it would often
be well for both sides and for the community at large that the
employés should take rather less real wages than in times of prosperity. But, in fact, since wages and salaries are reckoned in money
which is rising in value, the employer pays higher real wages than
usual at such a time unless he can get money wages reduced. This

is a difficult task, partly because the employés, not altogether un-reasonably, fear that when nominal wages are once let down they will not be easily raised. So they are inclined to stop work rather than accept a nominal reduction even though it would not be a real one. The employer, on his part, finds a stoppage his easiest course; at all events, by diminishing production he will help to improve the market for his own goods. He may not happen to remember that every stoppage of work in any one trade diminishes the demand for the work of others; and that if all trades tried to improve the market by stopping their work together, the only result would be that every one would have less of everything to consume. He may even think that there is a fear of general over-production, not because he is prepared to say that we could have too much of everything at once; but because he knows that when a long period of peace and invention has increased production in every trade, the volume of goods rises relatively to that of money, prices fall, and borrowers, that is, men of business, generally lose.

A distinction must be made between fluctuation of general prices which come and go quickly and those whose period is long. Short-period fluctuations practically efface themselves when we compare the mean prices of successive decades, but are conspicuous when we compare prices in successive years. Long-period fluctuations do not show themselves clearly from year to year, but stand out prominently when the mean prices of one decade are contrasted with those of other decades. They are chiefly caused by changes in the amounts of the precious metals relatively to the business which has to be transacted by them, allowance being of course made for changes in the extent to which the precious metals are able at any time to delegate their functions to bank-notes, cheques, bills of exchange, and other substitutes. And they would certainly be much mitigated if each decade's supply of the metallic basis of our currency could be made uniform—*i.e.*, to grow proportion-ately to our commercial wants. Some tendency in this direction would be exercised by the addition of silver to gold as the basis of currency: but there is no security that the yield of the silver mines will be great when that of the gold mines is small. History indeed indicates that the probability is the other way, for, when a new country is prospected, silver mines are often found in one part and gold in another, while some mines produce both gold and silver[1].

It has often been suggested that the supply of a nation's currency itself might ultimately be so adjusted as to fix the purchasing power of each unit of the currency closely to an absolute standard. In spite of the severe criticism to which this suggestion has been subjected, there seems no good ground for regarding it as wholly impracticable: but many long and tedious studies, stretching perhaps over several generations; and many tentative experiments moving cautiously towards the ideal goal, would need to be taken before any large venture in this direction could properly be made. We are at present concerned only with the main idea which underlies such suggestions.

That idea is that there are some long term engagements in which both sides might desire to avoid dangers, which inevitably attach to a gold standard. It might be to the advantage of all that governments, when borrowing funds, should give to investors the choice between an income of a certain quantity of gold coin: and an income of gold coin (or other currency), which would give command over fixed quantities of specified chief representative commodities.

[1] This statement is illustrated in the *Contemporary Review*, March, 1887, by a diagram which shows that the great variations in general prices between 1782 and 1885, which were recorded in the standard tables of Jevons and Sauerbeck, would not have been much diminished if prices had been reckoned half in silver and half in gold, instead of in gold alone.

Something is said in Appendix A as to the inconveniences of barter and the services rendered by even crude forms of money.

CHAPTER II

THE MEASUREMENT OF GENERAL
PURCHASING POWER

1. *The term "general purchasing power" is elastic: its context must indicate whether it is to be interpreted broadly or narrowly. In regard to distant times or places, its best measure is often in terms of unskilled labour, or of a staple grain.*

The term "the general purchasing power of money" is usually and reasonably taken to mean the power which money has of purchasing commodities in a country (or other place) in those proportions in which they are in fact consumed there. An increase in the price of wool would greatly diminish the purchasing power of money if it occurred near either of the Poles, but not if it occurred near the Equator.

It is of course impossible to reach even approximate measures of the extreme changes in the relative values of things, which are met as one passes from a cold to a hot climate, or from a backward to a highly civilized country. Such changes alter fundamentally the character of man's requirements. Few of the things, which a well-to-do Londoner buys now, could have been had at any price by a primitive monarch; and not very many of the others would have been fully appreciated by him[1].

Therefore comparisons of the purchasing powers of money in widely different phases of civilization have often been based on the earnings of unskilled labour, on the price of a staple food-grain; or, though more rarely, on a combination of the two. Records of prices of staple grain have a double significance. They are the most important among the records of the prices of commodities, and they tell much of the value of human life. For in every age except our own, by far the greater part of the wages of ordinary labour has been generally taken out in these grains: and by far the greater part of that produce of the fields, which

---

[1] A few observations bearing on some of these matters will be found in my *Principles of Economics*, II, ii, 6; III, iv and vi.

I, II, 1.   the actual cultivators in past times have retained for themselves, has consisted of them. Further, the methods of raising grain have remained nearly constant throughout the ages: and, though power generated by steam is now being used to control the movements of multiple ploughs and other heavy machinery over the fields, yet the work of the agricultural labourer still sets the standard of value for muscular effort controlled by ordinary intelligence and not requiring any rare manual skill[1].

Hence it arises that the wages of ordinary labour and the price of the standard grain in the country, or district, under observation were commonly taken as representatives of value in general. Such a course would be wholly unreasonable now in regard to any country of the western world, and especially in regard to Anglo-Saxon countries. But it was reasonable in the times of Adam Smith and Ricardo: and it is necessary to interpret "classical" doctrines as to value by reference to it[2].

Ricardo defended the provisional adoption of gold as the measure of value, on the ground that its production called for the services of capital and labour in about equal proportions[3]. And advances were made a little later towards a statistical measure of general purchasing power by Joseph Lowe, 1822; and by G. Poulett Scrope, 1833. Both of them wrote before the shadow of the great French war had passed away: they prepared the way for Tooke's great *History of Prices* published in the middle of last century[4].

---

[1] Of course many agricultural labourers, still working for low pay, have more intelligence and power of initiative than is required in the simpler parts of some of the tasks of building; and some other industries which rank as artisan work, and receive higher remuneration. But these parts cannot be conveniently separated from others for which skill is wanted. A medical man reasonably charges full fees for visits, in which he has no occasion for more recondite knowledge than is possessed by an experienced nurse.

[2] Locke, writing two generations earlier had said "That grain which is the constant general food of any country is the fittest measure to judge of the altered value of things in any long tract of time: and therefore wheat here, rice in Turkey, etc., is the fittest thing to reserve a rent in, which is designed to be constantly the same for all future ages. But money is the best measure of the altered value of things in a few years; because its vent is the same and its quantity alters slowly." See *Considerations of the lowering of interest and raising the value of money*, Works, Vol. v, p. 47.

[3] *Principles of Political Economy*, A.D. 1817, Chap. I, Sect. VI; and Chap. III.

[4] Reference may be made also to Rogers' well known *History of Agriculture and Prices in England*, covering the thirteenth, and three succeeding centuries;

2. *Further difficulties in comparisons of the purchasing power of money at distant places and at distant times.*

It must be admitted that histories of prices are of little service in attempts to compare the economic conditions of the people in a modern western country with those which prevailed in earlier times. The careful statistical inquiries of Rogers and others in this direction do not, and indeed cannot, reckon with such facts as that a fairly good watch can now be bought for four shillings; that a newspaper containing several thousands of words of matter (other than advertisements) can be bought for a half-penny; and that an excursion ticket costing but a few shillings will enable a working man to spend a holiday at a distant seaside resort. Indeed they throw but little light on the influences which mechanical and other inventions have exercised on the purchasing power of wages, since the time when mediaeval conditions gave way to the general freedom of life and work[1].

Measures of general purchasing power are indeed of little use in comparing the benefits which the possession of much property or a large income confers on its possessor in advanced and in backward countries. So far as social prestige is concerned, the benefit which anyone gets from an income ten times as large as the average, depends but very little on the purchasing power of money. And, in so far as a large income is regarded as the means of obtaining direct personal benefits, its influences have changed greatly in recent times.

and to d'Avenel's masterly *Histoire économique de la propriété...et de tous les prix en général*, 1200–1800. A long list of similar histories is given in the article on "Prices (History)" by Prof. Flux in Palgrave's *Dictionary of Political Economy*. See also Appendix B, below.

[1] It may however be worth while to quote a statement by an exceptionally acute observer of the sufferings caused by war a century ago. Lowe, *State of England, 1822*, pp. 271–3, says "War enhances commodities in various ways: First by the addition of a tax to the price of an article; next by a general rise in labour from the demand for men for Government Service, whether in the field or in the preparation of clothes, arms and other warlike stores; and lastly by the interruption of international intercourse. If these causes had a serious operation on prices in the sixteenth and seventeenth centuries their effect has been greatly increased by the adoption of the funding system, since which the scale of military expenditure has been enlarged in every country of Europe." He insists that any anticipation of the future of prices must be difficult and uncertain. For "on the one hand what a prospect of fall is held out by the application of improved machinery to the American mines, and the introduction of bank paper on the Continent of Europe. On the other what a counterpoise from the prospect of increased population, or the recurrence of a state of war."

In short, a complete solution of the difficulties involved in attempts to measure changes in the value (*i.e.* the purchasing power) of money at a given place is not in sight. Even when the problem is narrowed to changes ranging over but short periods of time, and confined to a single district, it seems to defy all efforts, whether coming from expert statisticians, or from expert mathematicians[1].

3. *Broad and well organized information as to prices is confined for the greater part to wholesale dealings. But much information as to their relations to retail prices in ordinary household goods is diffused by the experiences of working-men's co-operative societies.*

From the point of view of the general consumer, measures of the purchasing power of money should be based on retail prices: and it is possible that the printed lists of large "co-operative" and other stores may ere long be used for this purpose. But lists of prices adjusted to the inclinations of inexpert buyers would in any case be liable to difficulties of interpretation on account of vagueness and other defects. Therefore the best sources of information for our present purpose are records of wholesale prices of standardized commodities: and these are, from the nature of the case, almost exclusively either raw materials, or elementary manufactures, few of which are suitable for the needs of ultimate consumers. Nevertheless these wholesale statistics afford, with few exceptions, the best indications available of changes in the general trend of retail prices: and they are generally used for that purpose.

There are however a few retail prices of goods sufficiently standardized for use in this connection: and they have the advantages of being free from ambiguities, and of being open to the direct observation of the general public. There are also a few raw and half finished products, which are sold in open market: such are cotton, wool, iron, grain, etc. Moreover the extension

[1] Those who would follow its mathematical intricacies are referred to three *Memoranda* written in 1887–9 by Prof. Edgeworth, acting as Secretary to Committees of the British Association: also to *The purchasing power of money*, 1911, and *Stabilizing the dollar*, by Prof. Fisher of Yale University; and to *Money and Prices*, 1907, by Prof. Kemmerer of Cornell. Note may also be made of an article on "Modes of constructing index numbers," by Prof. Flux in the *Quarterly Journal of Economics*, 1907.

of "Co-operative Stores" has disseminated much information
among the working classes as to the relations between wholesale
and retail prices: the common arrangement that official positions
in them circulate at least as rapidly as is consistent with efficiency,
tends to diffuse some knowledge of the relations among (i) actual
costs, (ii) wholesale prices, and (iii) retail prices.

The general public already has access to fairly trustworthy and
definite information as to movements of the retail prices of (1) the
more elementary kinds of food and drink (except in so far as they
may be affected by special imposts); (2) house-room; (3) boots
and simple manufactures of wool, cotton and linen; and (4) means
of locomotion. In coming times the number of trustworthy general
price-lists of partially standardized commodities may probably
be much larger than now. But of course the larger the number
is, the less trustworthy will be inferences drawn from the list as to
changes in general prices: for the simpler a commodity is, the
more likely is its name to represent nearly the same thing at
distant times. A complex product, that was commonly used in
one age, is likely to differ greatly from the thing that passes by
the same name in another age[1].

4. *The average changes of prices, starting from a rather
distant date, are shown by "index numbers" representing
the percentage proportions of particular prices in each successive year to the prices at that date. "Weighted" index
numbers.*

The purpose of an "index number" is to use authoritative lists
of wholesale prices of certain leading commodities as representative
of all prices; and the average of their changes. The results thus
obtained may be interpreted, and perhaps modified, by means of
a special inquiry: and thus may be constructed index numbers
representing the general purchasing power of money from the
point of view of agricultural labour, or of unskilled labour
generally, or of skilled artisan labour; or again of any particular
class of Government officials.

The purpose of the list being to show the percentage changes

---

[1] Even now the oxen, that supply most of the meat (other than bacon) which
is eaten by the people in central Europe, would not find a ready sale in a London
market: and mutton is not eaten by the well-to-do-classes: but bacon of fairly
good quality is generally accessible.

from year to year in the selected prices, a particular year, say, 1850, is chosen as the basis, it is called the "basal year." The price in that year of each commodity (or group of commodities) to be considered is set at 100: the price of the commodity in each subsequent year is translated into its percentage of the price in the basal year; and this percentage is entered in the price-list against that year. Simple averages of these percentages for each successive year constitute a list of "arithmetical index numbers."

But, unless care is taken in the selection of prices to be thus treated, the result may be misleading: for an increase by one-half in the price of an unimportant commodity, may be of less importance than an increase by a hundredth part in the price of, say, steel. Therefore wholesale prices of leading commodities, either raw materials, or elementary manufactures (such as staple yarns), are taken as representative of all others. The further task of estimating the costs of working them up into complex finished commodites is not at present capable of treatment by any simple rule: though in some cases, as for instance in that of elementary cotton goods, that can be done.

On this plan everything, which has a separate column in the list, counts on equal terms with every other: the list is therefore said to be "simple" or "unweighted." So a further step is often taken: the figures in every column are each multiplied by a number which represents approximately the importance, or "weight" of the commodity with which it is concerned: and the average of these for any year is called a "weighted arithmetical index number."

A weighted arithmetical index number shows the amount of money which would need to be spent in each year of the period to which it relates, in order to purchase the amounts of the several products entered on its lists, that could have been purchased for a given sum, say £100, in the basal year. That is one of its great merits; its second chief merit is the relative simplicity of the calculations required for it: by virtue of them it retains its place as the dominant measure of purchasing power. But a mere change in the basal year changes its details, and may even modify its general character.

In spite therefore of the simplicity of the Arithmetical Mean,

Jevons and some others have preferred the Geometrical Mean, I, II, 4.
which represents ratios of prices and not their amount. It is always
consistent with itself: but it is not in close touch with reality[1].

[1] The geometrical index number is constructed nearly in the same manner
as the arithmetical. The price of each thing (or group of things) is set at 100
for the basal year. But the corresponding figure for a subsequent year is not
the ordinary ("arithmetical") mean of these numbers. It is their geometrical
mean: that is it represents the average of their proportionate changes. This
may be illustrated by a special instance:—The arithmetical mean of 2 and 32
is one half of 34; that is 17. But their geometrical mean is the square root of
the number, 64, which is obtained by multiplying them together: that is, it is 8.

It is however to be noted that there is no great difference between the arithmetic and the geometrical means of two numbers whose proportions are not
very different. For instance the arithmetical mean of 900 and 1024 is 962:
while their geometrical mean is the product of 30 (the square root of 900) and
32 (the square root of 1024): that is 960. A third mean the "Harmonic" is not
suited for the purpose of measuring general changes in the prices of commodities.

CHAPTER III

MEASUREMENT OF VARIATIONS IN THE PURCHASING POWER OF MONEY

1. *Difficulties in the construction of an index number which will truly represent the purchasing power of money even at a single time and for a single place.*

An ideally perfect unit of general purchasing power is not merely unattainable: it is unthinkable. For the effective value of money to each individual depends partly on the nature of his wants. A rise in the price of meat, accompanied by an equivalent fall in that of bread, adds to the purchasing power of the wages of those who are unable to buy much meat in any case. To a well-to-do bachelor the price of the necessaries of life is of very little importance: though, if with the same income, he had to find food and clothing for a large family, he might regard a fall in the price of luxuries, accompanied by even a small rise in that of necessaries, as a diminution in the purchasing power of money. What we must mean by a unit of purchasing power for, say, the United Kingdom, is merely that which will give an approximately uniform means of satisfying his wants to the average consumer. [To fix the ideas, the average consumer may be taken to be a family of five persons, which consumes a ten millionth part of everything that is consumed by the fifty million inhabitants of the country in question.]

The simplest plan as we have seen is to select a number of representative wholesale articles and to add together their prices at different times. The next step in advance is to estimate the importance of each commodity by the mean of the amount spent on it at the different periods under investigation. This importance or *weight* is then multiplied into the change in price of the commodity. For instance, if the value of the pepper consumed in an average year in England is £500,000, and that of the tea is £20,000,000, then a rise in the price of tea by 1 per cent. counts for as much as a rise in the price of pepper by 40 per cent. If the weight of pepper is taken as equal to 1, that of tea must be 40.

A third step is to allow in the weights of particular commodities   I, III, 1.
for the values of things whose prices are governed in the main
by the same causes, but which change in character so that there
can be no continuous record of their prices. Thus, for instance,
the weight allowed for cloth of a standard quality might well
include the values of many woollen and worsted manufactures,
which change their forms with every breath of fashion. Alter-
natively wool might be counted instead of the things made of it,
and the change in the cost of weaving a yard of standard cloth
might be taken as typical of changes in the cost of other branches
of manufacture[1].

It is however to be remembered that the weights thus assigned
are relative to ordinary conditions; and do not represent the
absolute importance of the several commodities. Thus the cost of
drinking water is almost negligible as a rule: but on rare occasions its value rises nearly to the level of the value of life. A rise
in an index number, in which agricultural products are prominent,
may indicate a considerable fall in the purchasing power of money
from the point of view of the artisan, and even of the agricultural
labourer; though it brings great gain to the farmer in the first
instance, and the landowner in the second.

To take another illustration:—If one-fifth of the wages of an
artisan family will produce an adequate supply of their staple
food at its normal price, a rise of 300 per cent. in the price of

---

[1] A method frequently used is intermediate between these two. No attempt
is indeed made to assign exact weights to the several commodities: but small
commodities are reduced somewhat in importance relatively to large by the
method of grouping. That is, several small commodities, whose prices are
subject to somewhat similar influences, are grouped together: the average of
their prices is taken, and is entered in the table as a single price for a compound
commodity. If the group is still not sufficiently weighty to be reckoned on an
equality with very important things, such as wheat and cotton, then the prices
of each several varieties of wheat, cotton, etc., may be entered in a separate
column; and the index number so obtained will show what may be called an
adjusted mean. This course has been followed in the standard index number
of Jevons and Sauerbeck for English prices, as well as in many of the chief
index numbers of other countries. See Jevons, *Investigations in Currency and
Finance*; and Sauerbeck's articles in the *Statistical Journal*, 1886, and in the
Economic Journal, 1895. The "unweighted" mean corresponds to a suffrage
in which every man has one vote and only one. The "weighted" mean to one
in which each votes in proportion to his supposed interest in the state, on the
so-called joint-stock company principle. The method just described corresponds
to that of the old Prussian suffrage in which every citizen had one vote; but if
his contribution to the public revenue was small he was put into a class whose
collective vote counted for little in proportion to its numbers.

that food will still leave them a margin beyond the bare necessaries of life. But if its price had been so high relatively to their wages that they needed to spend four-fifths of their wages on it in normal times, then a rise of 30 per cent. in its price would inflict on them grievous hunger followed by weakness, if not by illness, and anyhow by incapacity to do full work and earn full wages.

There is of course no comparison between the evils inflicted on the unskilled labourer by a rise in the price of his food at the beginning of last century and now. Even if we look at the skilled labourer, whose wages have generally shown some margin above necessaries, we should regard the social equivalent of a rise in the price of the staple grain as under-estimated, when it is measured by the percentage of the worker's income which the rise takes from him. On this plan fluctuations of 10s. in the price of a quarter of wheat now, would be regarded as an evil about equal to fluctuations of 5s. in that price at the beginning of last century; and not of about 25s., as they would be on the plan of reckoning the evil as varying with the percentage of the normal price involved in the change.

2. The same set of price changes may affect different classes of a nation in very different ways. "Index numbers," weighted in accordance with the shares held by various goods in working-men's consumption, are of special significance in connection with "working-men's budgets."

The general purchasing power of money should properly be measured by reference to the retail prices paid by the ultimate consumers of finished commodities. But this course would be difficult in nearly every case, and impossible in many. Consequently recourse is generally had to trade-price-lists of leading raw commodities, together with a few staple elementary manufactures. This method makes for simplicity: and indeed its use is almost inevitable[1].

---

[1] The wholesale prices of important, fairly well standardized, raw products are recorded from time to time (in some cases from day to day) in trade journals and in some others: but there is not and there cannot be any corresponding exact knowledge as to retail prices. There are several reasons for this; which fall into two groups.

One group is related to the enormous variety and complexity of finished products. The other is related to differences among the services which are rendered by retailers who cater for different classes of trade: in fact the services

I, III, 2.

This difficulty is in some degree met by the collection of numerous "working-men's budgets," each of which represents the details of the expenditure of a careful family. On this basis it is possible to set up a special measure of the purchasing power of money in terms of the *retail* prices of ordinary inexpensive commodities: which may afford a useful check on inferences drawn from wholesale prices. If however it is used as a substitute for such inferences, and not merely as a subsidiary check to them, it is apt to mislead[1].

In such budgets, rates are commonly taken with rents: and, so interpreted, rent now includes as a rule charges for a practically continuous and unlimited supply of water delivered to the consumer almost without effort on his part, for the removal of sewage, etc., and for very expensive lighting and paving of streets. If the working-men's dwellings had been supplied with these advantages even a few generations ago, when iron pipes and light of a given candle power cost very many times as much as now, the cost of these neglected trifles might have more than doubled the rent required of them for each thousand cubic feet of room[2].

of one retailer may be rendered more cheaply than those of another, though his prices are lower. A well-informed customer, whose tastes are critical, and scorns crude display, will often deliberately elect a shop in which high prices prevail, because he has reason to expect that he will there be afforded an opportunity to select things exactly adapted to his individual needs and tastes.

[1] A working man is sometimes tempted to understate his wages, sometimes to overstate them. But he is almost always under some inducement to overstate the prices which he pays for his household goods, and especially for meat. Anyone who has watched the prices at which meat is sold in the working-class quarters of large towns, especially on Saturday night, will not believe that the average price per pound is nearly as high as is commonly entered in working class budgets. No doubt much of the meat is of kinds which no one would be proud to say that he had bought. But it is wholesome, and probably much better on the average than meat which the same classes used to buy, in earlier times, if they bought fresh meat at all.

[2] The following statement is taken from *The Month's Work* of the Department of Labour, March 1920, as to the measurements of changes in the cost of living published in the *Labour Gazette*:

The statistics definitely relate to working-class conditions, and include the prices of food, clothing, fuel and light, as well as rent and other items.

The figures relating to the prices of the principal articles of food are based on information collected from representative retailers including Co-operative Societies, large multiple firms and private shopkeepers conducting working-class trade in 630 towns and villages. The total number of retailers, including Co-operative Societies, applied to is about 5500, but this number is not a full indication of the basis of the Returns. In many cases the prices given by a retailer relate to several shops; in many cases, too, prices are so regulated by

I, III, 2.   We may conclude then that estimates of the general purchasing power of money from the point of view of any class of society should in the main be derived from a list of wholesale prices of things which are consumed by that class, or which contribute, as steel rails do, towards services which it needs. On this foundation there may be built a superstructure of inferences as to the

Food Control Orders or by voluntary understandings on the part of retailers, that an article is sold at a uniform price throughout a locality.

The foodstuffs included in this list of principal articles are beef, mutton, bacon, fish, flour, bread, potatoes, tea, sugar, milk, butter, margarine, cheese, and eggs. These normally account for over three-fourths of the total family expenditure on food, and the inclusion of a greater number of articles of relatively minor importance would not materially affect the average percentage increase. The most important omission is that of fruit and vegetables (other than potatoes), which it is impracticable to include in a series of retail prices index numbers.

The percentage increases for the separate articles are combined into a general figure to represent the average increase in the level of retail prices by multiplying each percentage by a "weight" based on the relative importance of the several articles in pre-war working-class budgets, and dividing the product by the sum of these "weights."

*   *   *   *   *   *

Returns as to the retail prices of articles of clothing and clothing materials are collected through the post from representative retailers (some with many branch establishments) in large towns. It is, however, very difficult to estimate with close accuracy the movements which have occurred in the prices of articles of clothing. The primary difficulty is that arising from the necessity of obtaining prices at different dates for articles of the same or similar quality. The figures are designed to relate to the same qualities of articles or corresponding qualities, so far as possible, and to those ordinarily purchased by the working classes.

Statements as to the prices of coal and gas are obtained regularly each month from local correspondents of the Department in 30 of the principal towns. The figures obtained in this way are checked, from time to time, by information obtained from a larger number of towns, and it is found that they satisfactorily represent the general position.

Estimates are also obtained from various sources—retailers, public announcements, etc.—as to the increase in prices of other items of smaller importance from an expenditure point of view, including soap, soda, oil, candles, matches, brushes, ironmongery and pottery, newspapers, fares, and tobacco, sufficient to enable the Department to judge what would be the effect of the increase in prices of these items, taken as a whole, on the general percentage increase for all items.

In order to arrive at a single figure representing the increase in the prices of all the items taken together, the percentage increases under each of the main groups of expenditure are combined in accordance with their relative importance. In this operation, certain "weights" are used. The sum of these "weights" is 12¼, and the "weight" employed in the case of each main group of expenditure is as follows:—Food 7½, rent (including rates) 2, clothing 1½, fuel and light 1, and domestic sundries (soap, soda, domestic ironmongery, brushes and pottery, tobacco, fares and newspapers) ½. The effect of using these weights is to obtain the average percentage increase in the cost of maintaining the pre-war standard of living.

additional charges for finishing the process of production, in case the wholesale prices are available only for the earlier stages of the production; and, in any case for the costs of retail distribution. The same foundation will serve, in the main, for all classes of consumers. It will serve also for many problems connected with trade, industry, and employment, as well as consumption. And it will lend itself to international comparisons, which are fruitful themselves, and which are valuable also as checks on the accuracy of national estimates.

3. *The interpretation of index numbers is impeded by variations in the character of goods and services, which continue to bear the same names; and by variations in the exchange value of a thing from one season of the year to another.*

Passing then to comparisons of the purchasing power of money in places under similar climatic influences, and in times sufficiently near together to enable us to assume a general similarity in the technique of their industries, we have yet to make considerable allowance for changes in things which at first sight appear to have remained unchanged. An ox or sheep weighs now twice as much as it did not very long ago: of that weight a larger percentage is meat; of the meat a larger percentage is prime meat: and of all the meat a larger percentage is solid food, and a smaller percentage is water. Again, an average ten-roomed house is, perhaps, twice as large in volume as it used to be; and a great part of its cost goes for water, gas, and other appliances which were not in the older house. For these and similar reasons we ought to strike off a great deal from the ordinary estimates of the purchasing power of money in backward countries, and in the earlier history of our own country. Again, modern facilities for transport have not only lowered the cost of each kind of transport: they have also effected rapid and commodious transport of persons by land, air and sea at moderate or low prices.

Even statistics professing to compare the prices of bread in England at different times and places are generally untrustworthy. Those who were born in the first half of the nineteenth century will recollect how the bakers' bread, though more tasty than home-made bread when new, would frequently develop an evil savour

I, III, 3. if kept for a few days: how it was seldom of full weight: and how the flour was adulterated with potatoes, alum and other things, in order to lessen its cost, or to improve its colour, or to cover the flavour of mildew. In 1836 indeed Jacob, asked by a Committee of the Lords, whether much of the bread called wheaten was not made of potato flour, replied, "I believe that it is, a very good bread too"—an answer which compresses together much history[1].

If the quality of a thing is improved much and its price rises a little, the change is properly to be regarded as making for cheapness: but statistics are likely to treat it as contributing to a rise in general prices. Errors of this kind are capable of correction by care and thought: and, though no diligence will avail much, if we attempt to compare two distant periods without access to the detailed statistics of intermediate times; a little can be done by systematic analysis of statistics. A new commodity almost always appears at first at something like a scarcity price; and its gradual fall in price can be made to enter year by year into readjustments of the unit of purchasing power; and thus to represent fairly well the increased power of satisfying our wants which we derive from the new commodity. No notice of the new commodity would be taken in fixing the unit on the first occasion of its appearance in the price list. Suppose this to be on the first of January, 1920; then the unit for 1920 would be made up so as to give the same purchasing power of commodities, other than the new one, at these prices as the last unit did at the prices of a year ago. But before making up the unit for 1921, the weights in the unit for 1920 would be shifted a little, so as to allow for the new commodity; and then the unit for 1921 would be made to give the same purchasing power of all commodities, including the new one, as did that for 1920.

A somewhat similar difficulty arises, when a thing is supplied at a time of the year at which it used not to be available. The best plan seems to be to regard it as a new commodity when it first appears out of its old season. Suppose that at one time strawberries were to be had only in June, their average price being 6d. Suppose further that by improved methods they are

---

[1] He added that bread was cheaper in Paris than in London, because the London millers have a monopoly: "the bakers are poor and the millers are rich and they compel the poor bakers, by giving them credit or something or other, to buy their flour of them." (Q. 281; 301–314.)

supplied at 3d. in June, at rather higher prices in May and July; and at high prices during several other months. A crude reckoning of average monthly prices would show a rise; whereas in fact a great fall would have been effected.

This class of consideration is perhaps more important than it appears at first sight: for a considerable part of the work of agricultural and transport industries is now devoted to increasing the periods of time during which different kinds of food are available. Neglect of these facts has vitiated some of the statistics of the purchasing power of money in mediaeval times, with regard to nearly all kinds of food except grain, when even the well-to-do would hardly get so simple a thing as fresh meat in winter. In backward parts of England now each fruit is often cheap when in its full season; but very dear, if procurable at all, at other times. A dealer who makes the supply accommodate itself to our wants really sells a superior commodity, and his price, though nominally higher, may really be lower; just as a coat which fits well and costs £4 may be cheaper than a similar coat that fits badly and costs only £3[1].

Several of these cases of divergence between apparent and real cheapness of supply are in effect illustrations of the general rule, that a true comparison of price levels at different times or places must take account of the extent to which the times of supply are adjusted to the convenience of the seller or of the buyer. If the sellers in effect adjust supply to their own convenience, and leave the market bare, when supply is difficult; they may make good profits on prices below the direct expenses to which they would be put, if they arranged to keep an adequate supply on hand at favourable seasons to meet all requirements and to maintain prices at fairly steady levels.

It is therefore doubtful whether any index number has been, or can be constructed, which gives a tolerably correct presentation of changes in the general purchasing power of money for universal use. But each, if carefully constructed, is likely to be

---

[1] In earlier times fresh sea-fish could seldom be obtained far from the sea: so their prices included but little costs of carriage: now costs of carriage, including allowance for risks of spoiling, and the expenses of widespread distribution, often exceed by far the prices received by the fishermen. This source of error would be much more than corrected if statistics of early fish prices, took account of the costs of sea-fish carried alive in sea-water to luxurious Roman and mediaeval magnates.

I, III, 4. of use for one or more special uses. Therefore the methods on
which it has been obtained should be made clear: a transparent
index number can be applied constructively by a careful worker.
This consideration is specially important in view of modern tendencies to venture boldly on estimates and calculations of high
significance, in which index numbers play a part: such a venture
may be fairly safe if based on an appropriate index number; but
perilous if based on another, which may perhaps be superior to
it in regard to a different purpose. Unless so guarded, the indications of a good index number may be less trustworthy than
those reached by mere commonsense, working on facts generally
known.

It is true, then, that we cannot hope to get a standard of purchasing power which is free from great imperfections. But it is
equally true that a perfect standard of length baffles all the
resources of science; and though the best standard of value that
we can get is not nearly so good for its purposes as an ordinary
yard measure is for its purposes, yet it is an advance on using
as our standard the value of gold, or even the mean between the
values of gold and silver, of the same kind, though not nearly
as great, as the advance of substituting a yard measure for the
length of the foot of one judge or even for the mean between the
lengths of the feet of two.

4. *An official unit of general purchasing power might be
of service in connection with long-period obligations.*

An official index number, representing average movements of
the prices of important commodities, might well afford the basis
for a *Unit* of general purchasing power, in terms of which long-
period obligations might be expressed: and in this matter the
State might advantageously lead. The Unit would be derived from
an official price list by adding together the prices of certain
quantities of wheat, barley, oats, hops, beef, mutton, tea, coffee;
together with staple timbers, minerals, textile materials and
fabrics and so on. A new contract for interest on loans and other
long-standing obligations might then be arranged by free consent
of both parties to it in terms of the standard unit, instead of money.

There might also be gradually set up special Units, each adapted
to the conditions of particular classes of industries and trades:

and any of these might be adopted, by consent of both parties, I, III, 4.
as the basis of a loan or other engagement: such bargains could
be enforced without difficulty by Courts of Law.

Government should also arrange conditions on which its own
securities might, at the option of any holder, be converted from
terms of money to terms of "Units." Government securities
already command rather high prices relatively to the incomes
which they yield, partly because they meet the needs of those
who desire to be as certain as possible of an income that will
command a given quantity of the necessaries and comforts of life.
But the certainty which they thus obtain is far from being complete. Shrinkages of the purchasing power of the sovereign after
1850, and after 1863, brought some privations to many who had
thought themselves secure of adequate supplies of necessaries,
together with a few cherished comforts. Such people could have
made themselves safe against this trouble if they had been able to
purchase Government, or other sound, stock-exchange securities
in terms of Units[1].

[1] See also Appendix B.

CHAPTER IV

THE TOTAL VALUE OF THE CURRENCY NEEDED BY A COUNTRY

1. *Functions of a currency.*

Money or "currency" is desired as a means to an end; but yet it does not conform to the general rule that, the larger the means toward a certain end, the better will that end be attained. It may indeed be compared to oil used to enable a machine to run smoothly. A machine will not run well unless oiled; and a novice may infer that the more oil he supplies, the better the machine will run: but in fact oil in excess will clog the machine. In like manner an excessive increase of currency, causes it to lose credit, and perhaps even to cease to be "current."

This analogy may seem at first sight to be rather forced. But it is to be observed that:

A. Money is not desired mainly for its own sake, but because its possession gives a ready command of general purchasing power, in a convenient form. A railway ticket is desired for the sake of the journey over which it gives control. If a railway company adjusted its tickets to the lengths of the corresponding journeys, a long ticket might be more desirable than a short one: but if the lengths of all the tickets were doubled, the increase of lengths would merely cause a little inconvenience. In like manner an increase in the volume of a country's currency, other things being equal, will lower proportionately the value of each unit. In fact, if that increase threatens to be repeated, the value of each unit may fall more than in proportion to the increase already made.

B. As a railway ticket is valued in accordance with the length of the journey to which it gives access, so currency is valued in accordance with the amount of ready purchasing power over which it gives command. If an extension of the advantage thus gained could be acquired without cost, everyone would keep a large command of ready purchasing power on hand in the form of currency. But currency held in the hand yields no income: there-fore everyone balances (more or less automatically and instinctively) the benefits, which he would get by enlarging his stock of currency in the hand, against those which he would get by investing some of it either in a commodity—say a coat or a piano—from which he would derive a direct benefit; or in some business plant or stock exchange security, which would yield him a money income. Thus the total value of the currency which a nation holds is kept from falling considerably below, or rising considerably above, the amount of ready purchasing power, which its members care to hold in hand. If then the discovery of new mines, or any other cause, increases considerably the stock of currency, its value must fall, until its fall makes the acquisition of increased supplies of gold unprofitable. That is, the value of a gold coin, freely minted, will tend to be held rather close to the cost of attainment of the gold which it contains.

A country's demand is not for a certain amount of metallic (or other) currency; but for an amount of currency which has a certain purchasing power. Her stock of gold at any time tends to be equal to the amount, which (at that value) equals the purchasing power that the people care to keep in the form of gold either in their own custody or in their banks; together with the amount that the industrial arts of the country will absorb at that value.

If she has gold mines of her own, her stock of gold is governed by cost of production, subject to indirect influences of changes in demand for exportation, etc. If she has no gold mines, her stock tends to be such that she can absorb it at about the rate of cost at which she can make and export commodities which gold-producing countries will accept in exchange for it: the manner in which this adjustment is effected will be considered later on.

If her stock of gold were fixed by nature's decree, gold being used by her only for currency, all her other media of exchange being in effect orders for certain quantities of gold; then the total value of that gold would be the same whatever its amount. But gold generally passes from one country to another with perfect freedom; and therefore the stock of it, which each country holds, adjusts itself to her demand for it as currency and in other uses.

Its purchasing power within her territory must bear such a relation to its purchasing power in other countries, that neither her importers nor her exporters find a considerable advantage in substituting gold on a large scale for other goods. Therefore her

IV, 2.   stock of gold never diverges for any considerable time far from that amount which keeps her general level of prices in accord with that of other countries, allowance being made where necessary for costs of transport and frontier taxes.

Of course the total demand for each precious metal is made up of the demand for it for use in currency, and the demand for it in industrial and personal uses. These uses include for instance the service of silver in spoons and silver-plated spoons; and the service of gold in watch-chains and in gilding picture frames and so on. Each of these various demands has its own law of variation. The more difficult of attainment the silver is, the less use of it is likely to be made in each industry; but its power of enabling a person to make considerable purchases would be increased by a rise in its value. Many people habitually carry on their persons and keep in store at home a greater weight of silver than of bronze coin, because not many of their needs can be satisfied by the expenditure of only a few bronze coins[1].

2. *In early times it was commonly said that the values of gold and silver are " artificial." But in fact they are governed on the side of supply by cost of attainment, and on the side of demand by the needs of people for ready purchasing power based on gold and silver, together with the demand for these metals for the purposes of industry and display.*

Observations that the value of a coin often rose above that of the metal contained in it, suggested the notion that the value of currency generally is "artificial"; that is, due to convention, custom, or other inclination of the mind. Many centuries passed before general attention was given to the dependence of the value of each unit of a currency of given volume on the quantity of work which the currency had to do. But a little progress of thought in this direction was often made, when either the inconstancy of nature's supply of the precious metals, or exceptional recklessness on the part of those responsible for the quality of the currency, had caused or threatened great changes in general prices. Dis-

---

[1] These matters are discussed in some detail in the present writer's *Principles of Economics*, III, VI; and the Notes in the Mathematical Appendix, attached to it: also in Appendix C.

cussions on the value of money were eager, though not well-informed, in England when Henry VIII debased the currency; and again when the mines of the New World sent their first large deliveries to Europe: and they rose again to a high level in the seventeenth century, when commerce was demanding more exact systems of coinage than before, and thought was becoming more patient and solid.

At last it was seen that the conditions of the country at any time governed the amount of ready purchasing power, which was then required for the convenient discharge of the country's business. To use a shorter phrase, the general conditions of the country imposed a certain amount of work on her currency. Therefore the greater the quantity of her currency the less work there would be for each part of it to perform: the less therefore would be the effective demand for each coin, and the lower its value. The next step was to take account also of the way in which the work to be done by money itself could be lightened by the aid of credit[1].

It was not, however, till the beginning of the last century that the study of the causes which govern the value of money was taken quite seriously. Men's thoughts were then much occupied with the economic basis of political security as well as of general well-being. Again, the violent disturbances of public credit and prices, which were caused by the devastations and the alarms of the Napoleonic wars, set a singularly able and well-informed group of students and men of affairs at work on the problem; and they left very little to be added as regards fundamentals by their successors[2].

Ricardo was one of the powerful thinkers, who wrote the great

---

[1] Thus Petty (*Taxes and Contributions*, A.D. 1667), considered how the title deeds of land, under a good system of registry, and warrants issued by "Depositories of Metals, Cloth, Linen, Leather and other Usefuls" together with "credit in Lombards or Money-Banks" will make "less money necessary to drive the Trade." He meant of course less money at its previous purchasing power; and equal money at a lower purchasing power. Good work was done by Locke; and by that reckless, and unbalanced but most fascinating genius, John Law. Harris, and the acute though little known Cantillon, together with others, led the way up to Hume and Adam Smith.

[2] Ricardo held a chief place among them: and his high prestige has perhaps tended to throw the work of others into the shade. Prof. Hollander (*Quarterly Journal of Economics*, 1911) has shown that nearly every part of Ricardo's doctrine was anticipated by some one or other of his predecessors: but his masterly genius, like that of Adam Smith, was largely occupied with the supreme task of building up a number of fragmentary truths into coherent doctrine. Such a doctrine has constructive force, because it is an organic whole.

I, IV, 2.   *Bullion Report* of 1810. It states that "the effective currency of
the country depends upon the quickness of circulation, and the
number of exchanges performed in a given time, as well as upon
its numerical amount; and all the circumstances, which have a
tendency to quicken or to retard the rate of circulation, render
the same amount of currency more or less adequate to the wants
of trade. A much smaller amount is required in a high state of
public credit, than when alarms make individuals call in their
advances, and provide against accidents by hoarding; and in a
period of commercial security and private confidence, than when
mutual distrust discourages pecuniary arrangements for any
distant time. But, above all, the same amount of currency will
be more or less adequate, in proportion to the skill which the great
money-lenders possess in managing and economising the use of
the circulating medium....The improvements, which have taken
place of late years in this country and particularly in the District
of London with regard to the use and economy of money among
Bankers, and in the mode of adjusting commercial payments...
consist principally in the increased use of Bankers' drafts in the
common payments of London; the contrivance of bringing all such
drafts daily to a common receptacle, where they are balanced
against each other; the intermediate agency of Bill-brokers; and
several other changes in the practice of London Bankers, are to
the same effect, of rendering it unnecessary for them to keep so
large a deposit of money as formerly." This terse statement carries
far.

The stocks of gold and silver in the western world are known
to have increased rapidly during recent decades, though no definite
statistics in regard to them are available. But it seems that the
annual production of silver increased about tenfold since the
middle of last century. The stock of gold increased nearly tenfold
between 1840 and 1855: but slowly for the next forty years:
latterly its increase has been rapid[1].

Meanwhile the use of gold in the arts of production has increased
fast; and that considerable part of it which takes the form of
gilding unfits the gold used for further employment. It is possible

---

[1] Prof. Lexis says, in the article on "Gold" in the *Handwörterbuch der Staatswissenschaften*, that four-fifths of the production of gold between the years 1801
and 1908 belongs to the last sixty years of the period.

therefore that, in the course of a few centuries the stock of gold may become small and its purchasing power may be liable to great changes from small causes. In that case there may be strong arguments in favour of basing all long term obligations on authoritative standards of general purchasing power.

In England a large purchase is generally effected, not by transfer of currency itself, but by transfer of a cheque (or other document) that gives command over currency. For that reason the demand for currency in England is not representative of general conditions even in the western world: but we may ignore for the present the influences on prices which are exerted by cheques and other private documents: something will be said about them later.

3. *The total value of a country's currency, multiplied into the average number of times of its changing hands for business purposes in a year, is of course equal to the total amount of business transacted in that country by direct payments of currency in that year. But this identical statement does not indicate the causes that govern the rapidity of circulation of currency: to discover them we must look to the amounts of purchasing power which the people of that country elect to keep in the form of currency.*

The main facts are then: (1) every change in the rapidity of circulation of goods tends to cause a corresponding change in the rapidity of circulation of currency, and substitutes for currency; and (2) the chief of these substitutes are cheques, and—in some cases—bills of exchange. But the motives that govern the rapidity of circulation of money are not obvious: let us look for them.

It will appear, on consideration, that changes in the rapidity of circulation of money are themselves incidental to changes in the amount of ready purchasing power which the people of a country find it advantageous to keep in their own holding. This amount is governed by causes, the chief of which can be seen with but little trouble. It is true that comparatively few people analyse their own motives in such matters: but implicit suggestions of their motives are contained in such observations as: "I have kept a larger stock of money than I really need: I might have used some of it in purchases for personal use, or invested it." Opposite

I, IV, 3. reflections occur, when a man has spent or invested nearly all the money which he commands; and has in consequence failed to take advantage of a good bargain which came within his reach. Or he may have been forced to buy from retailers who charged him high prices and delivered inferior goods, being fortified by the knowledge that if he raised objections, he could be brought into subjection by a hint that he must pay up quickly. The customer might indeed obtain leave to overdraw his account at a bank: but this resource is not always available[1].

This preliminary statement indicates the general nature of a country's demand for ready purchasing power in the form of currency: or, at least, of immediate command over currency, such as is derived from keeping a considerable sum of money on current account in a bank.

To give definiteness to this notion, let us suppose that the inhabitants of a country, taken one with another (and including therefore all varieties of character and of occupation) find it just worth their while to keep by them on the average ready purchasing power to the extent of a tenth part of their annual income, together with a fiftieth part of their property; then the aggregate value of the currency of the country will tend to be equal to the sum of these amounts. Let us suppose that their incomes aggregate in value to five million quarters of wheat (in a normal year), and their property to twenty-five millions. Then the total value of the currency will be a million quarters of wheat: for, at that rate, everyone will be able to have as much ready purchasing power at command as he cares to have; after balancing one against another the advantages of a further ready command, and the disadvantages of putting more of his resources into a form in which they yield him no direct income or other benefit. If then the currency contains a million units, each will be worth a quarter

---

[1] It is obvious that a private person, who buys on long credit without special cause, must pay dearly for his purchases in one way or another: for the trader looks to get profit on his capital, and the private person can seldom get more than a rather low rate of interest on his. It is not always to traders' advantage to have attention called to this fact; partly because, when customers are much in arrears, they are not in a position to complain against faults in the things sent to them. The total costs which they thus throw upon traders, in addition to those incurred in dealings for cash, vary with the amount of extra book-keeping involved, the risk of bad debts, and other circumstances. In some cases the workman, who is but a single week behind with his payment, is in effect mulcted in interest at the rate of at least a halfpenny in the shilling for that week; that is, at 200 per cent. per annum, counting simple interest only.

of wheat; if it contains two million, each will be worth half a I, IV, 3.
quarter.

Thus the position is this. In every state of society there is some
fraction of their income which people find it worth while to keep
in the form of currency; it may be a fifth, or a tenth, or a twentieth.
A large command of resources in the form of currency renders their
business easy and smooth, and puts them at an advantage in
bargaining; but, on the other hand, it locks up in a barren form
resources that might yield an income of gratification if invested,
say, in extra furniture; or a money income, if invested in extra
machinery or cattle. In a primitive state of society, even in one
as far advanced as that of India, only the rich care to have much
of their resources in the form of currency. In England all but the
very poor keep a good deal; the lower middle classes keep a
relatively very large quantity; while the very rich who pay all
their tradesmen by cheques use relatively little. But, whatever
the state of society, there is a certain volume of their resources
which people of different classes, taken one with another, care to
keep in the form of currency; and, if everything else remains the
same, then there is this direct relation between the volume of
currency and the level of prices, that, if one is increased by ten
per cent., the other also will be increased by ten per cent. Of course,
the less the proportion of their resources which people care to keep
in the form of currency, the lower will be the aggregate value of
the currency, that is, the higher will prices be with a given volume
of currency.

This relation between the volume of the currency and the general
level of prices may be changed permanently by changes in, first,
population and wealth, which change the aggregate income;
secondly, by the growth of credit agencies, which substitute other
means of payment for currency; thirdly, by changes in the methods
of transport, production, and business generally, which affect the
number of hands through which commodities pass in the processes
of making and dealing, and it may be temporarily modified by
fluctuations of general commercial confidence and activity[1].

[1] The above statement is reproduced from my answers to Questions 11,759–
11,761 put by the Indian Currency Committee in 1899. In fact a considerable
part of the present discussion of the problems of money and credit may be found
in my answers to Questions 11,757–11,850 put by that Committee: and my
answers to Questions 9623–10,014 and 10,121–10,126 put by the Gold and Silver
Commission in 1887–8.

I, IV, 4.   Of course the total value of currency needed by the business
of England is relatively small. For her middle and upper classes
discharge most of their considerable obligations by cheques; and
but few of these cheques are presented for payment in cash: most
of them merely transfer command over currency from one banking
account to another.

As has already been noted, the precious metals (whether in bulk
or in the form of coin) used to be commonly hoarded in order to
make provision against the needs of the future, known and unknown: this practice still prevails among the peasants of a large
part of the world. But in "western" countries even peasants, if
well to do, incline to invest the greater part of their savings in
Government, or other familiar stock exchange securities, or to
commit them to the charge of a bank: and especially among
Anglo-Saxon peoples, by far the greater part of the currency,
which is held in private hands, is designed as provision against
some occasion for its use as direct purchasing power in the not
very distant future.

4. *Influences exerted by occupation and temperament on
the amounts of currency, which people with similar incomes
are likely to keep under their immediate control.*

The improvidence of a particular weekly wage receiver may
cause the gold and silver coins which come into his possession to
circulate on the average quickly away from him: but as, unless
he is exceptionally reckless, he keeps on hand at least a shilling
to the end, he probably does not pay away his bronze coins much
more quickly than other people. In like manner the improvidence
of one whose salary is paid quarterly may raise the average rapidity
of circulation of the gold coins which come into his possession:
but, as he will seldom be without a pound's worth of money, it
will not materially affect the rapidity with which silver and bronze
coins pass in and out of his possession.

The large trader holds relatively little currency in a modern
country in which nearly all considerable payments are made by
cheques. But, in the absence of any credit auxiliaries to currency,
every trader is dependent on the stock of purchasing power which
he holds in the form of money, for the means of making good
bargains when they offer. By instinct and experience he balances

he benefit against the loss of a large holding: he knows that, if he keeps too little purchasing power at his command, he will be frequently brought into straits; and that if he keeps an inordinate quantity, he will diminish the material sources of his income, and yet may find but few occasions on which he can turn the whole of his ready purchasing power to any great advantage.

To sum up:—the rule for one man may not serve well for another in similar conditions: but, as Petty said, "The most thriving men keep little...money by them, but turn and wind it into various commodities to their great profit[1]."

5. *Although the purchasing power of a unit of a currency varies, other things being equal, inversely with the number of the units ; yet an increased issue of inconvertible paper currency may lower its credit, and therefore lessen the amount of ready purchasing which the people care to hold. That is, it may lower the value of each of the units more than in proportion to the increase of their number.*

So far no account has been taken of the influence which the credit of a currency exerts on the willingness of the population to hold much of their resources, either directly in the form of cash in hand and at a bank; or indirectly in the form of debentures and other stock exchange securities, which yield fixed incomes in terms of currency. But this influence may become important, if the credit of the currency is impaired. In fact an ill-considered increase in the volume of an inconvertible currency is likely to lower the value of each unit more than in proportion to the increase: for it will lower the credit of the currency; and incline everyone to

---

[1] Petty thought that the money "sufficient for" the nation is "so much as will pay half a year's rent for all the lands of England and a quarter's rent of the Houseing, for a week's expense of all the people, and about a quarter of the value of all the exported commodities" (*Quantulumcunque*, Queries 23 and 25: see also his *Political Arithmetic*, ch. IX and *Verbum Sapienti*, ch. VI). Locke estimated that "one-fiftieth of wages and one-fourth of the landowner's income and one-twentieth part of the broker's yearly returns in ready money will be enough to drive the trade of any country." Cantillon (A.D. 1755), after a long and subtle study, concludes that the value needed is a ninth of the total produce of the country; or, what he takes to be the same thing, a third of the rent of the land. Adam Smith has more of the scepticism of the modern age and says: "it is impossible to determine the proportion," though "it has been computed by different authors at a fifth, at a tenth, at a twentieth and at a thirtieth part of the whole value of the annual produce."

I, IV, 5. hold a rather smaller share of his resources in that form than he otherwise would. Each unit of the increased currency will therefore command a smaller part of that smaller share of his resources and its value will thus suffer a double diminution. The total value of an inconvertible paper currency therefore cannot be increased by increasing its quantity: *an increase in its quantity, which seems likely to be repeated, will lower the value of each unit more than in proportion to the increase.*

This notion that the amount of ready purchasing power, required by the population of a country at any time, is a definite quantity, in any given state of her industry and trade, is implied even when not explicitly stated, in the now familiar doctrine that the value of a unit of a currency varies, other things being equal inversely with the number of the units and their average rapidity of circulation.

This "Quantity doctrine" is helpful as far as it goes: but it does not indicate what are the "other things" which must be assumed to be equal in order to justify the proposition: and it does not explain the causes which govern "rapidity of circulation."

It is almost a truism: for, if one column of a ledger recorded accurately all the transactions for money in a year with their values; while another column specified the number of the units of money employed in each transaction; then the two columns when added up would balance. The second column would of course represent the aggregate value of the total number of changes of ownership of all the units of money: and that is the same thing in other words as the total value of the money multiplied by the average changes of ownership (otherwise than by free gift, theft etc.) of each unit.

The other things, that must remain equal for the purposes of this statement, include (*a*) the population; (*b*) the amount of business transacted per head of the population; (*c*) the percentage of that business which is effected directly by money; and (*d*) the efficiency (or average rapidity of circulation) of money. Only if these conditions are reckoned in, can the doctrine come under investigation: and if they are reckoned in the doctrine is almost a truism.

6. *Currency differs from other things in that an increase in its quantity exerts no direct influence on the amount of the service it renders. Inconvertible paper currencies.*

The exceptional character of this "Quantity" statement in regard to the value of currency has been described in many ways. But the central fact in the account now submitted is that *an increase in the amount of money in a country does not increase the total services which it performs.* This statement is not inconsistent with the fact that an increase in amount of gold in a country's currency increases her means of obtaining goods by exporting gold; and also gives her a power of converting some of her currency into articles of ornament. It merely means that the purpose of a currency is firstly to facilitate business transactions; and for this purpose, it needs to be clearly defined and generally acceptable. Next, it needs to command a stable purchasing power: such stability can be attained by an inconvertible paper currency, so long as the Government (1) can prevent forged notes from getting into circulation, and (2) can make the people absolutely certain that genuine notes will not be issued in excess. Gold coins may indeed be regarded as currency based on the belief that Nature will not countenance a violent increase in the currency drawn from her stores. If there were discovered (in spite of the opinion of geologists and mineralogists that no such thing is physically possible) a mine of gold ore with contents as large in volume as those of a vast coal mine, then gold coins would cease to serve any good purpose[1].

Of course the stability of value of a gold coinage owes something to the stability of the demand for gold for ornament and for some industrial uses: but the discovery—*if it were possible*—of a vast deposit of gold would make it difficult to find good uses for it. We can conceive a planet, of different construction from ours, in which enough iron ore to make a good saw has a higher exchange value than a pound of gold[2].

---

[1] The elaborate and careful printing of paper currencies, makes plausible imitations of them very expensive, and yet liable to prompt detection. Forgery of Bank of England notes is well known to be prevented by exceptional arrangements and methods.

[2] This consideration can be extended. If diamonds became abundant, they would revolutionize and extend branches of industry in which hard steel is not hard enough: but they would need to be used with great caution for personal

I, iv, 6.   If an inconvertible currency is controlled by a strong Government, its amount can be so regulated that the value of a unit of it is maintained at a fixed level. That level may be such that (1) the average level of prices, as evidenced by a trustworthy index number, remains unchanged: or (2) that this average level adjusts itself to general changes of prices, in countries whose currencies are firmly based on the precious metals: or (3) that the Government of the country in question sets up a carefully framed list of general prices within its territory; and so adjusts the amount of her currency, that (say) a thousand units of it command, on the average, uniform amounts of commodities in general, on some plan of the kind suggested in Chapter III above.

"Convertible" notes—that is, notes for which gold (or other standard metallic) currency will *certainly* be given in exchange on demand—exert nearly the same influence on national price levels, as would be exerted by standard coins of equal nominal value. Of course, if even a small doubt arises as to their full convertibility into standard coins, men will be shy in regard to them: and if they cease to be fully convertible they will fall in value below the amounts of the gold (or silver) which they profess to represent.

It will be noted that this chapter is concerned with the demand for currency only when general credit is in a normal condition. When credit is shaken, it may be advisable to adopt abnormal, and (so to speak) medicinal measures in regard to the supply of currency. Something will be said on this matter in connection with fluctuations of credit in Book IV.

ornament. On the other hand, if a fall in the price of wool, or almost any other serviceable commodity, caused a greater quantity of it to be consumed at a less aggregate cost, there would be a nearly proportional increase in the real wealth of the world: the rich would gain only a little: but the poor would be more warmly clad.

CHAPTER V

METALLIC CURRENCIES

1. *Gold and silver have always been highly esteemed, because their brilliancy and durability adapt them for many decorative and other uses.*

Gold and silver are described as the "precious metals": but they are less costly than some others that hold important places in modern industry. They appear, however, to be the only metals, which have the brilliancy and the power of resistance to the atmosphere, which are required for the purposes of personal adornment; and yet have been obtained, even by elementary processes of mining, in considerable quantities and in many places. The search for them has been eager in nearly all ages: and such of Nature's stores of them as were easily accessible, have been quickly appropriated. They were chief promoters of the voyages and explorations, which discovered and gradually opened out the "New World." They have promoted travel: and they have themselves travelled ceaselessly and far.

When agricultural machinery was unknown, the gleaners, who responded promptly to an invitation to follow the reapers, were well rewarded for their labour; while those who arrived late obtained but little. So it might have been supposed *a priori* that. as gold and silver have been highly esteemed in every age of which a record survives, they would have been cheap in terms of human labour in the early stages of man's life on this planet; and that they would gradually have reached a very high scarcity value. But the older seats of civilization lay in a rather compact group in South-East Europe, North-East Africa and Southern Asia: and therefore large stores of gold and silver awaited those who first brought advanced industrial methods to bear on the treasures that had been stored up by Nature in Mexico, South America and Australia. When the great empire, which was centred in Rome, followed its predecessor's paths to decay, colonizing influences ceased: the civilized world had to be content with stocks of the

4—2

I, v, 2.   precious metals, which were being wasted by use, and were not
replenished: therefore prices generally fell to very low levels.

Later on, gold became so scarce that it ceased to be the material
of money in common use: and the diminution in the stock of
silver, relatively to the demand for it, caused prices in Europe
to decline generally, until traffic with Asia and Africa and with
Mexico and Peru contributed considerable fresh supplies of silver.
For a long while silver and money were almost synonymous terms[1].

Silver had thus been the dominant basis of currency over the
greater part of the world till the nineteenth century discoveries
of gold, chiefly in Australia and California, enabled several
countries, following in the wake of Britain, to take gold as the basis
of their currencies; either singly, or in combination with silver[2].

*2. Gold and silver, separately or conjointly, can set good
standards of general purchasing power, in regard to obligations and business transactions, which do not range over
more than a few years: but obligations, which range over
long periods, call for standards that are not dependent on
the hazards of mining.*

At some periods in the world's history the volume of "the
precious metals" has diminished relatively to the purposes for which
they are required; and at other periods it has increased faster than
they. This balance has been sufficiently even to give rise to a half-
unconscious expectation that their purchasing power is likely to
remain almost uniform; and that they may therefore reasonably

---

[1] Note the transition from the use of the Latin word *æs* (which means brass)
to the French word *argent* (which means silver).

[2] Note should be taken of the habit, common some centuries ago, of embodying
stores of purchasing power, available against a time of stress, in silver plate. This
habit had a considerable effect in steadying the purchasing power of silver. The
aristocracy of the Teutonic races were country folk with but little interest in
commerce; and they often lacked facilities for lending out their money with
profit and safety: but their accumulations of silver plate served the purpose of
yielding a steady income of gratification similar to that, which a rich man of to-
day derives from more varied and subtle forms of display.

Charles I of England owed much to the silver plate, which his adherents melted
down to meet his needs: whereas even well-to-do people now are for the greater
part content to share with all but the poorest classes the services, which a thin
deposit of silver on spoons and forks can render in protecting the mouth from
the taste of inferior metals. But, while the domestic uses of solid silver have
shrunk, those of gold have expanded; both in the form of "gilding" by layers
of microscopic thickness; and in that of watch-chains and other ornaments.

A little more is said in Appendix A on various early forms of currency.

be taken as standards of value. But this assumption calls for the inquiry:—Is this approximate equality of two opposing sets of forces, the one tending to raise general prices, and the other tending to lower them, the result of accident?

The answer appears to be in the negative, for less than half the world's surface has been thoroughly explored by skilled miners, equipped with large funds: and the mechanical and other appliances, available for gold and silver mining, appear to advance from decade to decade at about the same rate as the appliances used in other heavy industries. Therefore the cost of production of a hundred-weight of gold and silver seems likely to keep, for a considerable time, nearly the same position as formerly relatively to other raw products. The values of many sorts of fine manufactures will probably continue to fall relatively to those of the materials of which they are made. But, partly for that reason, the prices of raw materials tend increasingly to dominate those of the products made of them: and on the whole there seems to be no good reason for supposing that the cost of obtaining gold and silver will rise considerably in the near future relatively to general prices. Attention has already been called to the fact that the ever-growing power and celerity of the means of transport tends to diminish the inequalities in the relative values of different things throughout the world: and the mobility of gold and silver is so great that their values, in terms of other commodities generally, tend to equality in different places more effectively than do the relative values of most other things for which different places have unequal advantages. This nearly even balance may probably be maintained for a considerable time. But it seems impossible at present to peer into the distant future; though we can conceive that the united efforts of the several sciences, which bear on the question, may ultimately go far towards explaining the genesis of those gases and liquids, which cool down into metals.

The sway of gold and silver has, on the whole, been widened and strengthened throughout the ages: but it is in some danger of being partially superseded by an even more exact standard. For, as the arts of life progress (and indeed as a condition of that progress) man must demand a constantly increasing precision from the instruments which he uses, and from money among others: and he is beginning to doubt whether either gold or silver, or even

I, v, 3.   gold and silver combined, give him a sufficiently stable standard
of value for the ever widening range of space and time over which
his undertakings and contracts extend. It is no doubt true that
the durability of gold and silver gives security that the stock
of them will not vary very rapidly: that their general purchasing
power will not be liable to sharp and sudden fluctuations; and
that they will therefore afford fairly good standards of value for
deferred payments and contracts lasting over several years: "a
stream makes little difference to the volume of a great lake, though
it may itself be changed from a rill into a torrent." But that
supposes the torrent to be short-lived or the lake to have a broad
outflow; if not, the volume of the lake may increase more than
that of the torrent can: and gold and silver have had a less stable
value during the history of the world, than has accrued to those
staple grains, which have supplied the chief means of supporting
life to the great mass of the people in every age.

3. *Silver coins have set the standards of value in most
civilized countries: but these standards have been lowered by
successive curtailments and debasements of silver coins.*

It is an easy matter to keep the composition of gold and silver
coins true to specification as regards quantity and quality. But
every country, which has a long history, shows an almost continuous lowering of the metallic content of its standard coin.
Occasionally the evils, which followed a period of reckless debase-
ment, lead to a partial reform: but the making of good resolutions
seldom out-lived the next strong temptation[1].

But though improvident monarchs could reap small temporary
gains at the cost of loss of credit by depreciating their currency,
they had no desire that the depreciation should be carried further
through the pilfering of parts of the coins by private persons.

---

[1] In England the process of degradation was comparatively slow. The shilling
was reduced only from 270 grains of silver in the shilling in William I's time to
93 from the end of the sixteenth century onwards: though it had fallen much
lower under Henry VIII. It was practically debased again at the end of the
seventeenth century through carelessness rather than wilfully: but Montague
and William III, Newton and Locke repaired it in 1696. For details, see Shaw's
History of the Currency, and *Writers on English Monetary History*, 1626–1730;
also Lord Liverpool's *Coins of the Realm*, and Tooke and Newmarch's *History*,
Vol. VI.

The depreciation of German currencies went much further, and that of the
French livre further still: see d'Avenel, *Histoire des Prix*, I, II; and Beissel,
Geldwerth und Arbeitslohn im Mittelalter.

There was therefore nothing but the *vis inertiae* to hinder them from adopting such mechanical improvements in the art of coinage as were gradually invented: and they learnt to regulate exactly the sizes and circular shapes of the discs which were to be coined; to make the stamp fit the discs accurately; and by the aid of powerful machinery either to mill the edges, or to draw out from the side of the coin a short legend in raised letters. Next, the coins were made very hard and tough, so as to bear a clearly defined impress in low relief. Coins in low relief wear well: they cannot be sweated safely; and they cannot be imitated, without expensive appliances.

It is well known that many beautiful coins, and some which were technically exact, were made by artists and highly skilled artisans without the aid of machinery. But such work could not have supplied any considerable part of the vast number of coins that are needed for modern commerce. Even if it could, so large a part of their cost would have been due, not to the material of which they were made, but to the work spent on them, that the element of hazardous credit in their value would have been very large: the modern aim of fastening the values of gold coins close to that of the gold itself could not have been attained[1].

Silver is by nature better suited than gold to be the chief material of current money in any but very rich populations; and, until recently, it was generally used as a standard metal either alone or in some sort of association with gold: the English monetary term "pound," originally meant a pound's weight of silver pennies of more or less varying shapes and weights: and so in regard to the livre.

It is easy to keep in circulation Government notes printed on silver for a certain number of grains of gold; for the silver tokens are designed only for use at home: they are not required to be

---

[1] The first important step towards the massive production of accurate coins was made by Boulton late in the eighteenth century. His ideas have been greatly developed: and the plant required for good modern coinage is too expensive to be within the reach of any but those, who have a good deal to lose and are unwilling to run great risks except in the hope of very high gains. The bulkiness of the plant, and the large number of men required to work it, are likely to attract the attention of the authorities; while the increased resources of Governments and improved communications by telegraph and otherwise make it difficult to put into circulation in any country false coins made outside her jurisdiction. Lastly, the officers of different Governments are more willing than formerly to co-operate promptly for the suppression of crime.

I, v, 3. acceptable abroad in large payments. But when the shadows of the Dark Ages passed away, and European commerce settled down again to large, solid, and relatively safe operations, merchants organized their dealings with no more regard than they could avoid to the fussy regulations of monarchs as to the values at which their several coins were to be taken. So gold was long ago recognized as the "natural standard of merchants[1]"; and many of those Governments, which were largely under the influence of merchants, went as far as they could towards keeping their coinage in close touch with gold. For this and other reasons, ordinances fixing the rate at which gold coins should be current in terms of the standard silver money were made and re-made at frequent intervals[2].

Silver, in a more or less stable partnership with gold, has been the basis of most national currencies during the greater part of modern history: but nearly all the great currencies of the world were based, more or less effectively, on gold before the recent great war. Gold has not indeed been largely handled by the common people except in a few countries, mostly Anglo-Saxon; but adequate provisions were generally made before the war, in the countries of western Europe and in a rapidly increasing number of other countries, to keep every part of the currency fixed close to that gold value at which it was rated.

[1] Harris, *On Coins*, A.D. 1758, pp. 89, 90.
[2] Neighbouring countries fixed rates without agreement with, and often in opposition to one another. Such discrepancies, in so far as the ordinances were effective, caused constant shiftings of gold between different countries: the trade was often prohibited, but it was profitable to individuals, while it cost great national loss. The ordinances could not, however, be strictly enforced as long as the gold coins were in so bad repair that even in their own country they were often taken by weight and not by tale.

In comparatively recent times the (silver) price of the English Guinea was frequently altered by proclamation; and yet not fast enough to keep pace with changes in the market, which would often cause the Guinea to be taken in exchange by common consent at a price corresponding to its value as merchandise, and not that at which it had been rated by the last proclamation. And in Prussia before 1873, when the silver "Thaler" was the standard coin, there remained in use a great many gold "Krone." Their market price was published every day in the newspapers, and they passed from hand to hand with tolerable freedom at about that rate: but of course there would be a little bargaining if the person to whom the coin was tendered thought its price would be a trifle lower on the morrow. That is to say, gold and silver were used as media of exchange, but silver alone was used as money in the proper sense of the word: there was no thorough system of currency, based on gold and silver equally.

Lord Liverpool's Treatise, A.D. 1805, and especially his chapter "Of the great inconvenience and expense arising from the fluctuations of the relative values of gold to silver," contains much information on these points.

4. *British sovereigns (in ordinary times) are coined from*   I, v, 4
appropriate material without charge. They are in effect gold
ingots whose quantity and quality are certified at public
expense. British shillings have been in like manner, Govern-
ment notes for certain quantities of gold printed on silver.

Jevons well said, "A coin is an ingot of which the weight and
the fineness are certified by the integrity of the designs impressed
on the surfaces of the metal." This is true of all coins in some
degree; but it is especially true of those gold coins that have set
the standard of value for the British currency. The opportunities
of unauthorized coiners would be too great, if the gold contained
in a coin could be obtained much more easily than the coin
itself.

Gold coins need to be supplemented by "surrogates" in silver
and bronze: so called because their value (or "authority") is
derived from that of the sovereigns. So long as they are current,
their purchasing power is dependent on that of the sovereign:
that is, in effect, on the value of gold; subject only to the practically
negligible indirect seignorage levied on the coinage of gold. The
distinctive feature of a sound currency *system* is that, the value
of every part of the currency is so firmly fixed to that of standard
coins, that no one has any reason, beyond his own immediate
convenience, for preferring one sort to another: and therefore
everyone distributes his holdings of currency among gold, paper
notes, silver and other coins, according to the scale of his transactions. Thus the economic conditions of the people, their habits
and temperaments, govern the amounts of the various surrogates,
by which each hundred sovereigns is accompanied[1].

The British sovereign (in ordinary times) is an exceptionally
good standard of value: because no charge is made by the Government for coining gold, of appropriate quality, into sovereigns of
equal aggregate wealth. [It is true that the return is only made

---

[1] The nature of a trader's business must in great measure govern his action
in such matters. But, for other people a shilling's worth of bronze coins, and a
pound's worth of silver coins are generally more than sufficient. The holdings of
bronze coin are probably about as high among the self-respecting members of
the working classes as among any others (it is said to have been considerably
increased generally by automatic machines for sales at a penny): and those held
in the form of silver coin are fairly high among self-respecting members of the
lower middle classes.

I. v, 4.   after the few days that are required for testing, coining, etc.: the
indirect charge made by this delay is practically negligible, except
in so far as it makes bar gold a more fitting material for exportation to foreign countries than sovereigns would be.]

Of course no gold coins can fall in exchange value appreciably
below the gold that is in them: for as soon as gold in coined form
becomes cheaper than other gold, it would go into the melting
pot fast: but gold coin, other than the sovereign, can be minted
only when coined gold is worth more than uncoined gold by the
equivalent of that charge. Inconvertible paper bears in effect a
seignorage of nearly 100 per cent.: and conversely a coin that bears
a seignorage of two per cent., may be said to have the weakness
of an inconvertible currency to the extent of two per cent. of its
value. The sovereign, alone among coins, is a gold ingot ever
available for all uses without appreciable loss: and it thus has
an advantage over any other coin as the unit of international
finance; and England (in ordinary times) puts no hindrance in
the way of anyone who wishes to export gold. For these reasons,
among others but more perhaps than others, London acquired and
retained a dominant position as the central office of the Money
Markets of the world: which was not even threatened till the
emergencies of the world war compelled London to borrow largely
in New York. In short, the sovereign was such good merchandize
everywhere, at the value of the gold which it professed to contain,
that it might almost be said to be internationally current. The only
considerable element of hazardous credit in its value was that which
attached to the value of gold itself; and that is governed, not by
national, but by cosmopolitan influences. The shilling was really
a credit-note in Britain for a twentieth part of the value of a
sovereign, or nearly five and a half grains of gold: and abroad its
value was its credit value after deducting the expenses direct or
indirect of marketing it in some place in which it had that value:
(if it could be so marketed, its value in ordinary times would be
a good deal less than that of three grains of gold).

Under normal conditions, therefore, the British Government was
responsible for the quality of the gold coinage; but not for its
quantity: that was governed by the world supply of gold and the
demand of the nation for gold coins. On the other hand private
persons could not take silver or bronze metal to the mint, and

demand coins in return: so that the supply of "surrogates" was controlled by the Government, under information from banks and other businesses as to the needs of the public. Thus, these coins were only inconvertible notes for various quantities of gold, printed on common metals: but they were kept at their nominal values, by making them legal tender up to certain amounts, and adjusting their supply to the needs of the people.

I, v, 4.

CHAPTER VI

METALLIC CURRENCIES, CONTINUED

    1. *Gresham's law that an inferior currency, if not limited in amount, will drive out a superior currency.*

Petty expressed a common opinion, when he said:—"The world measures things by gold and silver, but principally the latter; for there may not be two measures, and consequently the better of many must be the only of all[1]."

The principle that surrogates cannot advantageously be printed on material of superior value to that of the standard coins is closely allied to another, which is known as *Gresham's Law*. It is to the effect that bad coins tend to drive good coins out of the field: the terms "good" and "bad" refer of course not to the technical excellence of the coinage, but to the metallic value of the ingot of which the coin is made.

The law is based on the fact that, whenever the specie value of a certain class of coins exceeds their currency value, the coins will begin to go into the melting-pot, or be exported. As when the level surface of the sea falls it is the highest rocks that first stand out, so when there is a gradual fall of the level surface of the currency value of all coins which have the same rating, it is the specie value of these that will first stand out above that level: these will be the first to be taken to the melting-pot. The best will go first, and then the next best; it is the worst that will remain. This is the substance of Gresham's Law[2].

---

[1] *Taxes and Contributions*, p. 17 of the second edition, 1667. The dictum "bad money drives out good," appears to have been first used in the proclamation of 1560, in which Gresham took a prominent part. See Palgrave's *Dictionary of Political Economy, s.v.* "Gresham's Law" and a Note by Giffen in the first volume of *The Economic Journal.*

[2] Gresham enunciated it in 1558: but its principle had long been known. In particular it was indicated by Oresmius in 1382, and stated clearly by Copernicus in 1526. John Hales, in 1549, writes:—"Was there not made proclamations that the olde coyne, specially of golde, should not be currant here above such a price: was not that the rediest way to dryve away our golde from us. Everything will go where it is most esteemed, and therefore our treasure went over in heapes." And he quaintly adds: "There be searchers that might let that matter well ynough, if they be true,...but there be many wayes to deceave the searchers,

Gresham's Law has often been represented as a paradox. But
in fact it is a representative of a large class of laws that are
operative in ordinary affairs, though they seldom attract special
notice. Even a man building a house for himself would be careful
not to put expensive red bricks in party walls where they would
not be seen, when cheaper white bricks equally strong could be
got. And a man building a house on contract for a stranger would
go further; he would not supply a better quality either of white
or red brick than was called for by the specifications: the worst
bricks that satisfied the specifications would drive out the better,
provided he had another good use to which to turn them.

The tendency indicated by Gresham's Law is strong but not
irresistible. If specifications for building were so drawn, that
easily made bricks were included with those of better quality,
then the coarse bricks would drive out the better, *provided that
there were enough of them to satisfy all needs*. If not, then good
bricks would be used together with inferior bricks: and the makers
of inferior bricks might perhaps combine to put their prices to
a level with those of good bricks.

Similarly, if the cost of production of an ounce of gold were
equal to that of only ten ounces of silver, and mints were open to
receive an ounce of gold on the same terms as fifteen and a half
ounces of silver, then, gold would tend to drive silver out of
circulation; because gold would be the inferior metal according to
the mint's regulations. If, on the other hand, the cost of production
of an ounce of gold were equal to that of twenty ounces of silver,
then, under the same regulations, silver would appear as the inferior metal; and it would tend to drive out gold.

Gresham's Law has been considered generally in relation to
metallic currencies: it represents a tendency to take good coins
out of the currency. The opposite tendency prevails in regard to

if they were never so true, as by putting of the sayde coyne in their shippes
balast, or in some vesselles of wyne, or other lyquor transported either unto us
or from us: then every creake in this Realme hath not searchers: And if they had,
they bee not such saintes as would not be corrupted for money."

Coin can be so easily melted down without detection, that when there has been
much to gain by it, it has always been done, whatever penalties have been set
against it. Sometimes a penalty on melting down current coin has been supplemented by requiring those who wanted to export bullion to swear that it
had not been obtained by this means. "Sworn off" bullion, as it was called, had
an extra high market price; and this additional value was commonly spoken of
as the market value of perjury, with its attendant risks.

I, VI, 2. notes issued by banks, without effective Government control: for any, that are not legal tender and fall into disrepute, cease to circulate[1].

2. *Difficulties in the way of the permanent maintenance of currencies based on gold and silver at a fixed ratio.*

The recent great war has set aside many arrangements for the coinage of the precious metals. The most interesting and important of these was the scheme of the "Latin Union," which in effect meant the group of European nations in whose language the Latin element predominates over the Teutonic. Under it the mints of the associated countries were kept open to gold and silver equally, on the plan of treating one ounce of gold as equivalent to fifteen and a half ounces of silver. It was called "bimetallic": but it appears to have always been open to the danger of becoming, and did in fact become, one for "alternative-metallism." Nature has not yielded an ounce of gold continuously at about the same cost in labour and outlay as fifteen and a half ounces of silver. She yielded it at less than that cost when rich gold deposits were opened out in Australia and California: and later on she yielded more than fifteen and a half ounces of silver from South American mines at the cost of obtaining an ounce of gold. When the advantage of superior cheapness of supply lay with gold, the basis of the currencies of the Latin Union came almost wholly from gold; but afterwards mainly from silver. That is to say, changes in the purchasing power of the currencies of the Latin Union were governed—in so far as they depended on their metallic basis— almost exclusively by the cost of producing silver. After a time the pendulum swung in the opposite direction: new gold deposits were opened out; and yielded more than an ounce of gold to labour and outlay equivalent to those needed for obtaining fifteen and a half ounces of silver: so additions to the basis of the Latin

---

[1] The famous *Bullion Report* of 1810 (p. 61 of Cannan's reprint) argued that under these conditions any local excess issue will raise local prices: therefore people will return some of the notes to the issuing bank, and demand Bank of England notes or Bills upon London; in order that they may make many of their purchases in London, where prices are moderate because the London currency is not inflated. Forecasting the future it argued that, if Bank of England paper should be issued to excess, the foundation of the whole currency of the country would be enlarged in similar proportions: and the total addition to the country's currency would be much greater than that caused by the direct action of the Bank.

I, vi, 2.

currencies came almost exclusively from gold, and Latin prices—in so far as they depended on those bases—were governed almost exclusively by the cost of producing gold. Thus the so-called "bimetallic" system was really under *alternate* metallic influences.

It may be admitted that an agreement, entered into by all the commercial countries of the world to keep their mints open to gold and silver at almost any reasonable ratio, would tie the values of metals to that ratio, so long as the agreement lasted, unless indeed one of the two metals were driven absolutely out of circulation. (Silver could not of course be used directly as a medium of exchange in large transactions: but it might ultimately serve as the sole basis of Government notes.) But it seems probable that—as human nature is constituted—such an agreement would not endure very long after changes in the conditions of mining had made the relative costs of production of the two metals differ widely from their relative ratings in the agreement. Especially, if gold were the metal which the change had caused to be underrated, the knowledge that the demand for it in the arts of production was large and urgent, would induce some Governments to manipulate their stocks in favour of gold: for they would know that if the agreement were broken up, they would gain much more advantage from the possession of a large stock of gold, than from the possession of a stock of silver which, though equivalent to it under the rating, would be of much lower value after the rating had ceased to be effective. The scramble for gold would probably be further intensified by its special fitness for the modern service of military chests in time of war.

An agreement which embraced nearly all the leading countries of the world—a "World-union" as we may call it—would be liable to nearly all those troubles which overthrew the Latin Union; and to many others. For the members of the Latin Union were a homogeneous group of countries with long commercial experience and similar economic needs and resources: in particular none of them had a strong direct interest in either gold or silver mining. But among the members of a World-union must necessarily be some without settled economic traditions, some with strong special interests in either silver or gold; while many possibilities of war could be latent among them. If then the productiveness of the mines threatened to move away from the rating agreed upon, rumours would quickly spread that it was in danger of being broken: suggestions would be put about for a change in the rating: and these being perhaps subsidized by wealthy persons having a strong pecuniary interest in the matter, would cause a general disturbance of credit; which might perhaps exceed in breadth and intensity anything that the world has yet known.

It is of course true that international agreements are now spreading over all fields of commerce and politics, to an extent which would have been thought impossible even a generation ago: and a few generations hence the psychological force of international opinion may be sufficient to support almost any agreement which is generally approved. But, on the other hand, the advantages of basing the currencies of the world on two metals rather than one seem to be estimated by careful thinkers now at a lower value than formerly: it is getting clearly to be recognized that the scheme of "fixed-ratio mintage" which is commonly called "bimetallism," can at least as fitly be described as "alternative-metallism." And there certainly exists another route by which it would be possible, if desirable, to base every national currency on gold and silver conjointly.

There was indeed felt a general sense of relief throughout the western world, when it became practicable to make gold alone in effect the international standard unit for by far the greater part of the civilized world. The changes which made this possible, without a great dislocation of general prices, were a great increase in the supply of gold; and an extensive development of the plan by which Holland had fastened the value of the silver currency of her Asiatic possessions to that of gold, for all purposes of international trade, by fixing the rate at which drafts on Holland, and therefore in currency on a gold basis, would be bought and sold in terms of the local currency for the purposes of the external trade of the Dutch East Indies.

3. *Although coinage of gold and silver at a fixed ratio causes movements of prices to be governed chiefly by the production of gold and silver alternately, a plan can be devised which would make the two metals work together: it may be called Symmetallism.*

A scheme for setting up an international currency on a solid basis of gold and silver *together*, was submitted by the present

writer to the Gold and Silver Commission in 1888[1]. It was set out   I, vi, 3.
as follows:

Ricardo suggested that we should use a paper currency resting
on a basis, not of coin, but of stamped gold bars weighing 20 ounces
each. If, he argued, the currency were in excess and showed signs
of falling below its gold value, it would be taken to the Mint and
exchanged for gold bars for exportation; if it were deficient, gold
bars would be brought to the Mint and currency demanded. Within
the country the paper would be a perfect medium of exchange,
while for the payment of the balances of foreign trade stamped
gold bars are better suited than coins.

The currency scheme now submitted for consideration differs
from his only by being bimetallic instead of monometallic. I
propose that currency should be exchangeable at the Mint or
Issue Department, not for gold, but for gold and silver, at the rate
of not £1 for 113 grains of gold, but £1 for 56½ grains of gold, together with, say, 20 times as many grains of silver. I would make
up the gold and silver bars in gramme weights, so as to be useful
for international trade. A gold bar of 100 grammes, together with
a silver bar, say, 20 times as heavy, would be exchangeable at the
Issue Department for an amount of the currency which would be
calculated and fixed once for all when the scheme was introduced.
(This number 20, or whatever it might be, would be fixed on
arbitrarily once for all. If we wished the value of the currency
to be regulated chiefly by gold we should have only a small bar
of silver; if chiefly by silver we should have, perhaps, 50 or 100
times as heavy a bar of silver as that of gold. But if we wished
the two metals to have about equal influence we should, taking
account of the existing stocks of the two metals, probably choose
our silver bar about 20 times as heavy as that of gold.)

Anyone who wanted to buy or sell gold or silver alone in exchange for currency could get what he wanted by exchanging
gold for silver, or silver for gold, at the market rate. Government
fixing its own rates from day to day, so as to keep its reserves of
the two metals in about the right proportion, might safely under-

---

[1] See the *Appendix to its Final Report* [C. 5512–7]; especially answer to
Question 9837. Much of its substance is contained in an article on "Remedies
for fluctuations of general prices" in the *Contemporary Review* for March, 1887;
where some matters kindred to these currency policies are discussed.

I, vi, 3.   take this exchange itself, and then anyone could buy or sell either gold or silver for currency in one operation.

To ensure convertibility the currency would not be allowed to exceed, say, twice the bullion reserve in the Issue Department, except in times of emergency, when the minimum rate of discount was, say, 10 per cent.; and then the rule might be broken, either as now, by the authority of the government, or, which I think would be better, by a self-acting rule. The country would save so much on the cost of its currency that it could well afford to keep, as a normal reserve, bullion worth, say, £20,000,000 in excess of this limit, and thus prevent the sudden stringencies which we now suffer whenever there is even a small foreign drain of bullion. There would be, as now, token coins of silver and bronze; but, since even a small percentage on the value of a gold coin is sufficient to pay the illicit coiner, it is doubtful whether it would be worth while to have token coins of gold.

Ricardo's proposal was made at a time when the mismanagement of paper issues at home and abroad had made the notion of a paper currency repugnant to all prudent people. But now there is a greater tendency to discriminate between paper money which has no sound basis, and which may fairly be called soft money, and paper whose convertibility into hard metal is properly secured. The strangeness of the scheme will make many refuse to examine it closely; but those who can overcome their natural repugnance to the use of paper money will, I think, find that it has the following advantages:—(1) it would be economical and secure; (2) though economical, the largeness of its reserve would obviate the sharp twinges, that now frequently occur in the money market; (3) it would vary in value with the mean of the values of gold and silver; (4) as it would in no way attempt to control the relative values of gold and silver, and would not be affected even if an ounce of gold became worth 50 ounces of silver, it could be begun at once and without risk by any one nation, and it would be specially suitable to the circumstances of the Anglo-Indian Empire; (5) if adopted by several nations it would constitute at once a perfect international basis of currency and prices. France could, if it chose, still reckon in francs, England in pounds, and America in dollars; but every 20 franc note would state on its face how many francs were exchangeable for a standard pair of

bars of 100 grammes of gold and 200 grammes of silver; and 1, vi, 3.
therefore the equivalent in £ s. d. of 100 francs would be settled
once for all. There would be nothing to be allowed as now for
seignorage or for wear and tear of coins. Francs, pounds, or dollars
would alike give a definite command over bars of gold and silver,
which would form a perfect medium for international payments.

It may be added that proposals to tie the value of currency to
that of gold or silver or both, without the use of gold and silver
coins, occupied a good deal of attention rather more than a hundred
years ago; partly under influences similar to, but stronger than,
those which spread over Europe after the recent great war. This may
be seen clearly in the evidence of Alexander Baring and Ricardo
before a Secret Committee of the House of Lords in 1819. They
approved proposals that "the Bank" should "deliver uncoined
Gold or Silver at the Mint Standard and Price in exchange for
their Notes, instead of the Delivery of Coin"; while the bank
should buy bullion offered to them at rather lower prices[1].

[1] The quantities of these transactions were indeed not to be unlimited; and
the mint was to remain open for the coinage of gold money: the precedent of
the bank at Hamburg was quoted. Minor conditions were added: the bank was
not to be troubled by small transactions. Reference was made to difficulties
arising from probable variations in the relative values of gold and silver: experience indicated that they would not be great. Baring would prefer that gold
should be the fixed standard; silver being treated as equivalent at rates which
"should be adjusted every ten years, or at some other given period."

It may be added that there seems to be no good ground for an opinion, which
was much in vogue some time ago, that "bimetallism" (in the sense of fixed-
ratio-mintage) would necessarily cause a great rise of prices. It would probably
have that effect if the proportion in which the two metals were combined in the
basis of the currency (say 16 to 1) made it easier to increase the currency by
adding to its basis sixteen ounces of silver than by adding one ounce of gold. But
Nature has been secretive in regard to her stores of the two metals. This point
was raised by the present writer in evidence before the Gold and Silver Commission in December, 1888, and the following January, QQ. 9623–10226; and
before the Indian Currency Committee in January 1899, QQ. 11757–11850.

BOOK II

BUSINESS CREDIT

CHAPTER I

THE DEVELOPMENT OF MODERN MARKETS FOR CAPITAL

1. *Private capital—other than that which consisted of the ownership of land, buildings, and slaves—was not of great volume till recent times.*

The chief capital employed in early stages of large-scale industry consisted of slaves, or, at least, of serfs. But merchants had large capitals invested in stocks of goods; and, sometimes, in ships or in long trains of mules or other beasts of burden.

Rome dug out wealth with the sword; but she developed it by business energy. She became the centre of large industry for a great part of Europe: and during her decline Constantinople was rising to take her place. All the while the chief capitalistic investments were in ships and in slaves; and goods ready for sale came next: the implements of production were not costly.

Later on the productive capabilities of the energy of falling water and of wind developed factories, each of which absorbed a considerable quantity of capital: and, yet a few centuries later factories and railways worked by steam power became chief embodiments of capital on the land: while steam-propelled ships made a powerful contribution towards the capitalistic unification of the trade of the world.

In the earlier stages of capitalistic development the first place was held by individuals, or by small groups of men, each possessing much wealth. In the modern age, many railways and other undertakings are owned in great part by multitudes of small capitalists. The main effect of this development is to strengthen the position of the middle classes relatively to the working classes on the one II, I, 2. hand and to the wealthy classes on the other.

The term "capital" has been supposed to refer to the number of heads of cattle which constituted the chief wealth of pastoral tribes: and again to the number of heads of slaves employed in cultivation of the land; or in "manufacture"; in the original sense of the word, in which it suggested direct manual labour. During the Middle Ages feudal-tenure of land gave "landholders" certain rights over the services of those who lived on their land. They themselves "held" the land indirectly from the Sovereign (or State): but in effect they owned it subject to certain claims, which successive generations of lawyers have defined and limited; until the land of the country has become private property, and is regarded as an exceptionally stable form of capital.

Landowners might therefore have set up strong banks, which would have supplied industry and trade with the funds needed for that rapid increase in their activities, which was caused by the development of world-trade, and by the continual increase in the costliness, as well as the efficiency, of the appliances of manufacture and of transport by land and sea. But in fact trade and industry, have been the chief sources of the great volume of capital, which has enabled the present age almost to defy the severity of Nature's law, to the effect that increased applications of effort to land, already fairly well cultivated, will yield a continually "diminishing return."

2. *Early phases of business credit: the chief capitalists were traders; the largest borrowers were sovereigns and republican governments.*

The work of credit in the modern age differs from that of earlier times in two chief ways. Formerly a great part of it was given by professional money-lenders to spendthrift heirs: now it is chiefly given by people who are living within their incomes to States which do not spend recklessly; and to strong businesses, in the hands either of private persons or joint stock companies. Again, formerly those who received it, were generally hard-pressed by those to whom they had incurred obligations: now they are, for the greater part, powerful businesses engaged in production, transport or commerce.

Monarchs used to be large borrowers: chiefly for the purposes of war; largely to support extravagance on the part of themselves and their favourites; and occasionally for financing expenditure on good roads and other requisites of national well-being. Sometimes indeed professions that a loan was needed for purposes of urgent public concern, were used as decoys for bringing a good deal of the national capital to the aid of the personal extravagance of a sovereign and his courtiers. In such cases loans were invited by bankers and other financiers in their own name: the lenders could appeal to Courts of Law against the nominal borrowers; and they were able to put pressure on a monarch to whom the proceeds of a loan were transferred: they could threaten to refuse help in his need at a future time; and they could often force him to give into their hands a material guarantee for their good faith.

But, after all, the most massive loans have been those which were believed to be necessary to ward off national disaster. Such were the loans by aid of which England financed the Napoleonic wars; those arising out of the American Civil War, and the recent great European War.

The motives of subscribers to such loans have always been, in part at least, patriotic and unselfish: and the respect, which they have earned, contributed to the complete disappearance of the notion, which long prevailed, that dealings in credit are unworthy of a man of high character[1].

---

[1] It was indeed long maintained by Patristic writers, that a loan of money (as distinguished from the letting out of a house, an implement, or other valuable commodity) rendered no real service that could rightly demand a reward. That opinion derived support from the fact that the borrower was frequently in distress: the practice of borrowing additional funds in order to develop a strong business was then not very common.

The hardships that might otherwise have resulted from the wholesale condemnation of "usury" were, however, mitigated by the pious fraud of arranging that the person in need should sell something at one price and engage to buy it back after a time at a higher price. It might have been observed that the loan of money and its repayment constituted a similar double exchange: but no one was inclined to perceive a thing, which authority declared not to exist.

The literature of the subject is large, and sometimes trivial. But attention may be directed to Knies, *Der Credit*; and to the description by Laspeyres of the epoch-making conflict in the Netherlands between old prejudices against all interest on loans, and the rising tendency towards a discriminating transference of the command over capital to those who could turn it to good account (*Geschichte der volkswirtschaftlichen der Holländer*) Book VI. The chapters on Usury in Beawes' *Lex Mercatoria*, 1761, give a long list of devices, reaching up to the middle of the eighteenth century, for evading the law that prohibited interest at more than five per cent.

3. *At one time merchants were the chief dealers in credit*   II, I, 3.
in England. But the capital employed in manufacture has
increased fast and steadily.

During the Middle Ages merchants were the chief dealers in
credit on a large scale, and on reasonable terms: while millers
gave a good deal of credit on a rather small scale. Petty loans
were often made to persons in distress on terms which went
some way towards justifying the popular prejudice against
"usury[1]."

Consequently merchants could make good profits by lending
considerable sums at rates which would be unreasonable in the
present age of abundant capital, but were moderate relatively to
the conditions of the time: and many banks of the highest standing
now can trace their origin back to merchants.

Great merchants stood high in general esteem: many of them
had inherited the reputation earned by several generations of
honourable dealing in large affairs. But manufactures had passed
by almost imperceptible steps from work done in cottages by rude
men, who received their wool or flax material from a trader, and
were paid by him on return of the cloth or linen made therefrom.
Merchants were thus trained by their own business in the chief
functions of a banker.

But the relations of banking to industry changed gradually.
Handiwork, on methods inherited from earlier generations, gave
place to massive manufacture; in which tradition was of but
little avail; and changing conditions required an alert mind,
which seldom looked backwards. A manufacturer with a masterful mind became powerful and rich, provided that he looked always
forwards: he needed to study the past indeed; but his main
concern with it was that he might consider how far the future
would differ from the present, as the present differed from the
past.

The rise of manufacture to a chief position in the world of

---

[1] The borrowers did not know that a debt of one pound at 5 per cent. a month
(if left to run) would amount to £10 at the end of four years; to £10,000 at the
end of sixteen years. But usurious lenders knew a good deal about such matters:
and, being aware that they could not obtain the full value of a debt thus accumulated, they contrived to avoid receiving back a loan in full, with the
interest due on it. At the same time they rather encouraged the borrower not
to incommode himself by completely discharging his debt.

finance was partly due to the need of progressive manufacture for a large supply of capital. But it was also in great measure due to the fact that, while in former ages constructive imagination was the task of the merchant, who gave out his orders to handicraftsmen, the modern age requires that task to be shared between the manufacturer and the merchant. In many cases indeed the pioneering effort of constructive imagination comes from the manufacturer; and the trader follows: and this change, in concert with the increase in the capital required by a progressive manufacturing business, has modified, and is modifying, the organization of markets for credit, national and international[1].

When massive manufacture had been well set up, it ceased to be dependent on trade for its supply of capital. It borrowed from bankers; while the bankers supplemented their own resources by others obtained from the general public. In particular, they issued notes: and these passed into general circulation; thus constituting in effect quiet loans from the public to the banks, the loans being thus passed on to the public at large. The ultimate result was that the public lent, almost *gratis*, to banks the power of issuing notes; and the banks used these notes as a chief embodiment of the loans, which they made to particular members of the public in return for agreed interest (or discount) on the loans.

---

[1] Some account is given in *Industry and Trade*, Book I, Chapter IX, of the foundations of modern business in general trust and credit; and of the causes, which have given to the leaders of productive industry much of the prominence and responsibility that formerly belonged almost exclusively to great merchants. Also the first effect of the methods of manufacture, which belong specially to the modern age, was to draw industries away from towns, to quiet places where the power of falling water could be applied in moving textile and other machinery. But that power was seldom sufficiently concentrated at one place to enable it to drive a single giant factory, and a stream was often used to turn in succession the wheels of many rather small factories, all of which were sometimes held in the same hands.

A long time ago I saw a mine being worked by aid of power derived from a waterfall about a quarter of a mile from it. The water turned a huge wheel; each revolution of which pulled a long chain of wooden blocks running on rollers to the pit-head: one-half of a revolution of the wheel pulled the chain down; and when the pull ceased, a counterpoise, weighing several tons, pulled the chain up again. The present easy and inexpensive method of converting mechanical energy into electrical, and conversely, has rendered such devices obsolete: but they are worthy of honour.

4. *Since the rate of interest on a loan is commonly expressed in terms of money, it is liable to be affected in fact, though not in appearance, by changes in the purchasing power of money*[1].

The constructive uses of modern business credit are generally understood; and a good deal has been said about them in previous works by the present writer[2].

"Interest" in the strict sense of the term is the payment, which any one receives during a given period, in return for a loan: whether to a private person, or to a Government, *e.g.* when buying Consols; or to business undertakings, *e.g.* when buying the debentures of a railway. A world can be conceived in which the opportunities for the profitable investment are so small that people are willing to entrust their capital to Governments or other stable recipients, without expecting any reward other than the security of a full return on demand. In such a world interest would be unknown. In stagnant districts even of this world, a man rarely borrows in order to expend either for personal consumption, or for business purposes: and a supply of loanable capital in such a district might fail to earn any considerable interest beyond a mere insurance against the risk of loss of the capital.

As a general rule, interest rises in consequence of a greater willingness of borrowers to borrow, or of a greater unwillingness of lenders to lend: the first generally indicates increased confidence, and perhaps increased prosperity; the latter generally indicates the opposite. Loans to one man make him a good customer for others at good prices, and make them therefore eager to borrow, and that makes them good customers; and so the movement grows. Thus, a fall in the purchasing power of money tends, after a while, to raise the rate of interest on investments, whether for long periods, or short. The large trade in loans for short periods is the chief source of the profits of those banks, which do not issue currency. Much of the credit given by a bank is in the form of giving cash in return for a bill, which contains an undertaking to pay a certain

[1] This Section is in the main reproduced from the present writer's evidence submitted to the Indian Currency Committee, 1899, Q. 11765: and to the Gold and Silver Commission, 1888, Q. 9981.

[2] Especially *Principles of Economics*, II, VI–VIII, on "Interest of Capital, and Profits of Capital and business power"; and *Industry and Trade*, II, IX, on the "Financial basis of business organization." A short abstract of these chapters based on their "Contents" is given below in Appendix D.

II, 1, 4.   sum at a given date—frequently after three months: the deduction thus made is called "discount[1]."

This divergence from technical accuracy in regard to short loans is well understood. It is indeed of very little importance relatively to the influences which changes in the general purchasing power of money exert on the *real* rate of interest for loans, even though the interest, measured in terms of money, remains unchanged. It is, indeed, obvious that any one, who borrows money, stands to gain if there is a general rise of prices before he is called on to repay it: for that rise is a fall in the value of currency, and therefore he can obtain the currency needed for the repayment at less real cost than if prices had remained stationary. Attention has been called above (I, 1, 3) to the facts that, if a man borrows a peck of green peas in April, and returns two pecks in June, and pays no interest at all: he does not even return the corpus of the loan: that if a man borrows £100 under contract to pay back £105 at the end of the year, and meanwhile the purchasing power of money has risen 10 per cent., he cannot get the £105 which he has to pay back without selling one-tenth more commodities than would be sufficient for the purpose at the beginning of the year. On the other hand, if prices had risen so much that the purchasing power of money had fallen 10 per cent. during the year, and he could get £100 for things which cost him £90 at the beginning of the year, then, instead of paying 5 per cent. for the loan, he would really be paid 5½ per cent. for taking charge of the money.

This illustrates the principle that the general rate of interest will be raised by a gradual and anticipated fall in the value of currency relatively to commodities, and that it will be lowered by a rise in that value, even where there is no change in the conditions of general demand and supply; and similar relations hold between fluctuations of general prices and fluctuations of the rate of interest.

Of course a sudden fall in the purchasing power of currency, that is to say, a sudden rise of prices, may be due to a very bad harvest at home, and then it is clearly an evil; or it may be due

----

[1] Thus if the rate of discount is 4 per cent. the bank will pay £99 for a bill due after the lapse of three months. Of course interest on £99 for that period at 4 per cent., would be rather less than £1.

to a bad harvest elsewhere, as the rise in Indian prices in 1891 was caused mainly by the Russian famine, and that was good for India. But, especially in the West, a sudden rise of prices is generally the result of either currency inflation or improvement in credit. In so far as the rise of credit is a revival, after the industrial system has been purged from its impurities by the preceding period of low credit, it is a welcome sign of recovered health. But the movement would be as beneficial for the time if it were accompanied by a more cautious use of credit and more uniform prices; and in the long run it would be more beneficial. As it is, the inflation causes lenders to be careless; all business men seem to be having a large margin of profits; speculative buyers can borrow and become rich by selling for many counters what they have bought for few counters, and their gains, which add nothing to the common stock, are merely the result of successful raids on the common stock; and these gains give to business a fictitious appearance of prosperity. The rate of discount is determined by the average profitableness of different business; that is, determined partly by the amount of capital that is seeking investment as compared with the openings for new docks, new machinery, and so on; and the extent of these openings is itself practically determined to a great extent by the belief that people have that prices will rise or fall, other things being equal, for people are unwilling to borrow if they think that prices will fall. The supply of loans on the one hand and the desire of people to obtain loans on the other, having fixed the rates of discount at anything, 8, 6, 5 or 2 per cent., then the influx of a little extra gold, going as it does into the hands of those who deal in credit, causes the supply to rise relatively to the demand; the rate of discount falls below its equilibrium level, however low that was, and therefore stimulates speculation.

It is true that a fall which had been produced by the thinning out of the field for the investment of capital relatively to the supply of capital, could not increase speculation, because it had itself been caused by the difficulty of finding a profitable opening for speculation. But ere long discount would fall sufficiently low to absorb the capital even in spite of the thinning out of the field for its profitable employment: and then a new equilibrium at the lower rate of discount would be reached between the

II, I, 4. demand for loans and the supply of them. This new rate effects the equilibrium by causing capital to go into the hands of speculators who would not take capital at the old rate, but do take it at the new; and whatever form their speculation may take, it is almost sure, directly or indirectly, to raise prices. This is the main issue.

There is, however, a side issue which may be in some cases more important than the main issue. It is that, when the gold comes to the country its arrival is known, and people expect that prices will rise a little. Now, if a person doubting whether to borrow for speculative purposes has reason to believe that prices will rise, he is willing to take a loan at 3 per cent., which before he would not have taken at more than $2\frac{1}{2}$ per cent. Consequently the influx of gold into the country, by making people believe that prices will rise, increases the demand for command over currency, as a means of buying goods; and thus profiting by the rise in prices. It tends therefore to raise the rate of discount. This matter is further considered below, Book IV, Chapter IV.

CHAPTER II

THE OWNERSHIP OF CAPITAL IN JOINT STOCK[1]

1. *The beginnings of England's experiences in the massive organization of industry and trade.*

In former ages the physical force, required for the purposes of industry and trade, was derived from the muscles of animals and men, with only a little aid from wind and from falling water. Now, by far the greater part of it comes, in some form or another, from coal: the chief tasks of man in the matter have lain in the contrivance of plans for this purpose, and the provision of appropriate mechanism. But those great men, by whom these tasks were set in progress in the eighteenth century, could not foresee the full extent of the influences which they would exert, directly on the technique of industry and trade, and indirectly on their financial organization. It is indeed possible that the later experiences of the Regulated Companies, and the old Joint Stock Companies, which opened up England's trade with distant lands, and developed many industries in them, may have suggested the notion that an increasing share in the development of such industry and trade would fall into the hands of persons who were not directly engaged in them. But that experience could not go very far in suggesting that many industries and trades, which were mainly concerned with the supply of home markets, would soon come in large measure into the ownership of people who took no part in their work.

For indeed the present organization of a great factory was not then foreseen. Many of the implements used in manufacture were so simple and inexpensive, that they could be worked in cottages; and a large factory in any industry could be little more than an aggregation of many small factories. As has already been indicated[2] this method obtains in some branches of the textile

---

[1] The rehearsal of elementary considerations, contained in this chapter, seems necessary for completeness: but some readers may prefer to read only its section headings.

[2] See *Industry and Trade*, Appendix C 4.

II, II, 2. industry now: but in earlier times it was general; and, consequently, a man with small capital could bear the risks of a proportionately small business without much difficulty.

A considerable number of modern industries cannot work to advantage without the aid of very large capital; while those engaged in continuous heavy transport over long distances require vast capitals. In some of these industries, indeed, no business can be started with a small capital. A man of genius may sometimes so develop a business of moderate size, that it can grapple with the difficulties which are generally beyond the grasp of any but giant capitals: but, even in such cases, the business is frequently thrown into joint stock form, either when old age presses on its founder, or after his death.

2. *While loans for short periods are most conveniently obtained from banks and other dealers in credit, permanent loans are invited direct from the public. These commonly take the form of debentures, which are in effect liens on the property of the business concerned.*

There is no fundamental difference between credit for short periods and credit for long periods; as there is no fundamental difference between a sailing boat and a sailing ship: but the methods, appropriate to short and long period credits, have differed widely. It is true that an able and diligent financier could often keep a debtor in tow for a long while, by so managing that the debt with accruing interest should never be paid off in full. But long period credit is mainly effected in the present age by the emission of standardized "securities," which are handled on Stock Exchanges; though banks act as intermediaries between some of their customers and brokers on a Stock Exchange. Short period loans on the other hand are for the greater part obtained by a customer from the bank with which he deals: he may have placed title-deeds or stock exchange securities in the bank's hands, which are pledged in effect, though not in legal form, against the loan; but such loans are often made without any safeguard, other than the personal character of the borrower. In the early days of joint stock banking, when Stock Exchange securities were relatively rare, much stress was laid on the inability of an official of a joint stock bank to grant personal credit of this kind as freely

and fully as it could be granted by a private banker; who risked
only his own capital in doing so.

"A joint stock company is a company or partnership, whose
capital is divided into shares, usually transferable; some of which
are held by each of the members. A limited liability company is
one whose members are individually liable for the companies' debts
only to a specified amount, often not exceeding the amount of
stock that each holds." The shares of such a company are often
divided into two classes, "Ordinary" and "Preferred." The company is likely also to have issued "Debentures." These are in part
acknowledgments of debt paying a fixed rate of interest: they
give no right of control over the affairs of the company so long
as that interest is paid. Thus the property of the company is vested
in its shareholders: debenture holders are in effect creditors of the
company, who cannot demand repayment of their loans so long
as they duly receive interest on them. The risks of the company
fall mainly on the Ordinary shareholders: but, if it is registered
under the "Limited Liability" Act, the utmost that can be
demanded from them by creditors of the company is the full
nominal value of their shares. If that amount is inadequate to
discharge its debts, creditors may demand from Preferred shareholders the full nominal value of their shares. Debenture holders
are liable to the loss of their fully paid up property in the company
in case it fails: but they are under no direct liability to other
creditors of the company.

3. *The normal rate of interest on fairly secured permanent
loans, other than those to Governments, is now set by the
markets for debentures of joint stock companies.*

The assured length of life of a well organized joint stock company is indeed an important factor in the trust with which
investors are inclined to regard its securities. Even a man, who
cannot expect himself to see the full development of a company's
power and prestige, knows that its securities will rise in value as
its future prospects improve: and that it therefore will become a
better property for himself, and for his heirs. Indeed the largest
stores of capital free for investment, which come into a man's
possession, are likely to find him thinking as much of their
probable value to his heirs, as of the direct benefit which he will

II, II, 3.   himself derive from them. For these and similar reasons, debentures of first class commercial undertakings appear frequently to offer at least as good a promise of secure and permanent income as do the securities of even a strong Government. Of course some business, especially such as is connected with inheritance, may have special reasons for selecting securities, which have the authority of Government: and the high price of British consols relatively to their yield is partly due to the advantages which they offer for the investment of trust-funds.

In joint stock enterprises, numerical comparisons of expenditure need to be constantly compared with assets. It is not necessary that the tangible assets should exceed the outlay; for a young business may often advisedly spend a good deal in building up a connection, the chief fruits of which will be reached in later years: but where any considerable claim has to be entered on this ground, the basis of the claim calls for close scrutiny.

Partly for this reason a great venture is often set up by a group of able capitalists, each of whom can form a fairly good judgment as to the value of the intangible assets which it is building up: and, only when its net profits have reached a level which yields a good return on all the outlay, do responsible men see their way clear to invite the public to take shares in the venture.

CHAPTER III

THE DEVELOPMENT OF BRITISH BANKS

1. *Introductory.*

"The word *bank* in the economic sense covers various meanings, which all express one object, a contribution of money for a common purpose." Thus Bacon, in his essay on Usury, while explaining "how the discommodities of it may be best avoided and the commodities retained," uses the word "bank" as a term with which his readers would be familiar. Originally connected with a mound or bank of earth—hence with that of *monte*, an Italian word describing a heap—the term has been gradually applied to several classes of institutions established for the general purpose of dealing with money[1].

The industry of finance has been affected, like others, by the ever-growing volume of business to be handled, by the increasing facilities for standardization, and by the development of rapid communications. Telegraphic messages, sent when necessary in cypher, enable close concert to be maintained among banks and other financial houses; and more particularly between the head office of a financial house and its branches. In fact, in the modern age, the citizens of almost every considerable town have immediate, though indirect, access to the centre of the financial resources of their country.

Thus a bank receives from professional men, and other customers, large quantities of money or command over money. It renders important services to them by safeguarding that command; and by transferring it according to their instructions—generally expressed in the form of cheques—to its several destinations: it pays them a low rate of interest on any considerable sums that are left with it. The details of these arrangements vary of course with the locality, and with the circumstances of particular cases. In return for these services it obtains the power of lending a

---

[1] This statement is reproduced from an article by Palgrave on "Banks and banking" in the current edition of the *Encyclopaedia Britannica*.

II, III, 1. considerable amount of the command over money placed in its
hands: its receipts from this source are very much larger than its
payments of interest to depositors. This excess supplies insurance
against minor losses on loans, remuneration to its officials together
with other costs of its establishment; and lastly, income to its
proprietors.

Nearly all the chief work of an English bank now falls under
one of two heads. The first consists in the transmission of money,
or command over money, from one person or corporation to
another. This task is responsible; but it is a matter of routine: it
calls for intelligence, punctuality and rigid exactness; but it makes
little demand on the relatively rare faculties that are specially
required in the higher work of business.

The second, and more responsible, part of its work consists in
deciding to whom it should afford credit, how large those credits
should be, and on what security they should be based. In the early
days of banking, such credits were chiefly based either on direct
knowledge of the affairs of an applicant for loans; or on the deposit
of documents representing real property or merchantable goods:
now, these bases are enlarged, and in many cases superseded, by
the deposit of stock exchange securities. If, as generally happens,
these are of high quality, their values are publicly recorded from
day to day: and, as a rule, the bank need not make any special
inquiry in order to be assured that their aggregate market value
shows a good margin above the amount for which they are pledged.
When ample security of this kind is pledged, although the task
of the banker still requires alert intelligence, it no longer makes
great calls for independent responsibility.

There are, however, many cases in which a rising trader or
farmer has nothing outside his own business which he can pledge.
A private banker, who has spent all his life in the neighbourhood
of his bank can often safely lend on mere personal security, where
a manager of a branch of a great joint stock bank, who has no
direct personal acquaintance with his clients, could not. It is
to be hoped that the supersession of small banks by branches of
large banks will not leave small farmers and other traders in time
of difficulty with little recourse, save to a class of private money
lenders, whose ways are apt to be dark.

A little more is said about the development of British banking II, III, 2.
in Appendix E.

2. *The Bank of England as the bank of bankers, and in some respects a guardian of national interests.*

The supremacy, partly moral and partly material, which the
Bank of England obtained during the suspension of cash payments, continued after gold had again come into full circulation.
It had become the Bank of bankers as well as of merchants, and
it has retained that position. Indeed, as time went on, its responsibilities were increased by every increase in the economy of
coin which came about with further developments of banking
organization. For, while the general banking business of the
country increased rapidly, the banks whether in London or the
provinces kept a constantly diminishing proportion to their
reserves in cash. They got into the habit of keeping by them little
more than "till money"; *i.e.* enough to meet the ordinary demands
of their customers for cash to pay wages, and for other retail
transactions: this often came to very little in the case of banks
which issued their own notes. Their real reserve was left at the
Bank of England; and their larger transactions were settled among
themselves, partly by various systems of "clearing" or cancelling
obligations against one another, the balances being paid at first
in Bank of England notes, and afterwards in cheques on the Bank[1].

Thus were laid the bases of the two great characteristics of
English banking, firstly, the attenuated reserve of bullion on
which the vast business of the country rests for its immediate
credit in times of panic; and secondly, the anomalous position

---

[1] Charles Bosanquet (1810), after explaining this, adds, "accredited brokers
now hourly walk Lombard Street, take the superfluous cash of one banker and
lend it to another in any sums for any time, a week, a day," or even "at three
o'clock repayable by draft at the clearing at four....The banking houses in
London are like so many cisterns disposed on each side of the street, between
which pipes of communication are introduced."

But it remained in a great measure true that "the Bank of England is the
great regulator of the country paper: when they increase or decrease the amount
of their notes the country bankers do the same." (See Ricardo, *High Price of
Bullion*; compare also his *Reply to Mr Bosanquet's Observations*, ch. v; Thornton,
On Paper Credit, ch. VIII.) There is much evidence of bank directors and others
before the Parliamentary Committees of 1819 to the same effect. Similar remarks
apply in part to the bills of exchange, which were the chief circulating medium
in Lancashire then and for some time later; and which, when drawn by a country
bank, differed little from bank notes: see the evidence of Stuckey and Lewis
Lloyd before the House of Lords Committee in 1819.

II, III, 2. of the central Bank: which in effect acts as trustee for the community in the administration of its ultimate cash reserve; although no formal act of the Government, the Parliament, or the bankers has imposed on it the responsibility of administering that reserve in the general interest[1].

The Bank of England has become not only the Bank of bankers, but also their leader in matters that directly affect the security of general credit in the business of the country. Its Directors include many leading business men: and it has been stated publicly that, as a general rule, their stakes in the Bank itself are so much less than their stakes in the general commercial prosperity of the country, that they cannot be tempted to sacrifice public interests to those of the shareholders of the Bank. They must often reach quickly important decisions on difficult issues; and their wisdom is occasionally called in question by critics: but no suggestion is made that they have sacrificed general to particular interests. In fact, they act with that full sense of responsibility which belongs to public ministers[2].

[1] Inglis Palgrave, a banker and an economist, said (*Bank-rate and the Money-Market*, 1903, p. 23), "the balances, which bankers in London keep with the Bank of England rather represent...their 'Till-Money' than their reserve." For it is in effect "the amount which every banker is bound to keep close at hand to meet the calls of the moment....It is transferred for convenience sake to the Bank of England." On similar lines he contrasts (p. 29) a bank's responsibilities in regard to bills which are based on current transactions, and "turn themselves into money," with those "such as the acceptances of contractors and others, which, though they no doubt will eventually be paid, may require a fresh loan to be made to continue them. '

[2] The troubles of 1837 and 1839 evoked much criticism of the general management of the currency: and the Act of 1844 divided the business of the Bank into two parts. Under it, the Banking Department exercised its discretion as to the granting of credit, and similar matters; just as any other bank does. But the department, which is responsible for the issue of notes, was rigidly bound by the rule that the total face value of its notes might not exceed that of the bullion held against them by the amount of its original loan to the Government; together with certain portions of the rights of issue formerly held by other banks, which it was permitted to purchase from them. The rights of issue retained by other banks were rigidly limited: and, in effect, an increase in the total amount of the currency was limited (subject to the special procedure already noted in regard to silver and copper coins) to the equivalent of certain debts of the Government to the Bank; together with certain still remaining rights of uncovered issues by other banks, and the amounts of gold coin and of gold bullion held for currency uses. But during the recent war these regulations were suspended and the British currency became for the time a paper currency, with an undefined backing of bullion. The position thus reached is complex and transitional. Its development up to 1921 can be seen in a long series of Acts of Parliament, Proclamations and Reports of very strong Committees, which are reproduced as Appendices in Kirkaldy's *British Finance*, 1915–1921.

So far nothing has been said as to the exceptional power and II, III, 3. responsibility of the Bank of England in times of disturbed credit: that matter will be considered later.

3. *The reorganization of private banks as joint stock companies has often been accompanied by a diminution of the personal element in the credits given by them.*

Adam Smith in 1776 had regarded banking as one of the few businesses of which "the operations are capable of being reduced to a routine, or such an uniformity of method as admits of no variation"; and which can therefore safely be intrusted to the divided responsibility and the narrow enterprise of a joint stock company: but he seems to have had chiefly in view the work of the Scottish joint stock banks. On the other hand English bankers at the beginning of the nineteenth century had before their minds a business which was not mainly one of routine: and their evidence before successive Parliamentary Committees up to 1833 was generally against the joint stock principle.

Lord Overstone, writing in 1832, says: "joint stock banks are deficient in everything requisite for the conduct of the banking business, except extended responsibility": it requires constant alert attention to details and prompt, discreet decisions, guided by "a nice reference to degrees of difference in the character of responsibility of parties": and more to the same effect. On this Bagehot observes that the banker of Lord Overstone's time lent much to private individuals, from whom he could obtain no security: and therefore acted on "his judgment of the discretion, the sense and the solvency of those to whom he lent....The joint stock banks were quite unfit for the business Lord Overstone meant, but then that business is quite unfit for the present time." This was written in 1873: the changes which Bagehot saw at work have continued at an increasing rate during the last half-century[1].

It is true that the owners of a private bank have undivided interests in its prosperity; and also perfect freedom to take a risk which is justified by particular considerations within their knowledge, even though it belonged to a class not generally suitable to

---

[1] His *Lombard Street, a description of the money market,* 1873, is a masterpiece, which is likely to be read by successive generations with almost as much interest as by that for which it was written.

II, III, 3. be taken by a bank. It is true also that they are likely to associate intimately, and on even terms, with other leaders of business in the neighbourhood of the bank: and are thus in a position to form good judgments as to the personal qualities and conditions of applicants for loans, and to obtain trustworthy confidential information on matters of local interest.

On the other hand, local disturbances of credit and of economic activity are increasingly associated with, and even dependent on, fluctuations of general confidence and activity in national industry and trade: and in regard to them those in the central control of a great bank have great advantages. The more closely the business interests of a district are united with, and influenced by, those of the country at large, the more important becomes the guidance which the manager of a branch of a great bank receives from its headquarters. He has indeed somewhat less freedom of action than belongs to the heads of a private bank: but yet he may be specially authorized, under suitable conditions, to give large support to a great venture. If the district in which a small private bank is situated offers at any time either a very large or a very small scope for the use of free capital, its manager may draw some command over capital from, or dispose of it to, the central market: but such adjustments are often even more easily made by the central command of a great bank. No doubt the importance of such considerations is less now than formerly: for variations in the demands for prompt payment and for command over capital are passing in great measure beyond the control of local conditions: and a general disturbance of credit throughout the country is likely to press heavily on the resources of banks in nearly all centres of industry and trade.

At such times branches in quiet residentiary districts may indirectly come to the aid of those whose operations are more interesting, though less stable. But, for this and other purposes, some kind of national organization is wanted. The need might have been met by Government intervention, or by a development of existing local arrangements among bankers into a national scheme. It was in fact met by the rise of a London bank to so leading a position, that it could act as a clearing house for that part of the banking business of the country, which had a wider range than was covered by the existing local associations among

bankers. Such local associations would in any case need a central II, III, 4.
clearing house: many of the purposes of such a clearing house
were automatically solved by the rise of the Bank of England to
leadership: every bank soon had a connection, not always direct,
with it: and it became the chief centre for non-local banking
business.

Every bank is likely to receive cheques drawn on other banks:
these are brought to a "clearing house" and set off against one
another, the balances being adjusted by cheques. The chief of
these houses is of course in London; and some time ago the
balances settled there daily exceeded on the average twelve
thousand million pounds.

4. *The partial publicity of the affairs of a joint stock
bank has proved to be less inconvenient, and more helpful
than was formerly anticipated: and this fact has told on the
side of great banks.*

The publicity of the affairs of a joint stock bank is in some
respects a source of strength. Petty said more than two centuries
ago:—"Whereas Credit everywhere, but chiefly in London, is a
mere conceit that a man is responsible or not, without any certain
knowledge of his Wealth and true Estate,...I should prove that,
if every man's Estate could be always read in his forehead, our
trade would be much advanced thereby, although the poorer
man be commonly the more industrious[1]." But it was in the
increasing hurry and multiplicity of English business in the nineteenth century, that people set themselves against the trouble of
guessing the estate of those with whom they were dealing: so they
turned increasingly to joint stock companies, whose estate is
written on the foreheads of their published accounts, in figures
which give some definite information, and which are thought by
some investors to give more information than they really do.

It may be well to look back at the course of this movement during
the last hundred years. The wild crisis of 1826 found many of its
victims among private banks: and the distress caused thereby
among the innocent, as well as among those whose imprudence
or dishonesty had contributed to the disaster, caused a strong
movement of opinion in favour of extending the privilege of joint

[1] *Taxes and Contributions*, 1679, p. 33.

II, III, 4.   stock organization to those who desired to form banks of deposit.
They were indeed denied a right to limit their liability, which was
granted to other companies in 1855: but that right also was
granted to them in 1858, as a result of the grievous failures of the
Western Bank of Scotland and the Borough Bank of Liverpool
in 1857, which induced Parliament to offer that privilege to them
also. Those cases showed that, when a bank failed for a large sum,
the poorer shareholders would be made bankrupt by the first
few "calls" made on them to meet its liabilities: the next few
calls would break a great part of the fairly well-to-do shareholders;
and since by that time there were few remaining among whom the
burden could be divided, the last calls must needs be very large
relatively to each share. These disasters raised doubts in the minds
of thoughtful people as to the wisdom of holding shares in ordinary
banks. In 1878 the great City of Glasgow Bank failed under the
pressure of bad management and adverse conditions: and the
suffering caused thereby was so deep and so widespread, that a
law was passed enabling unlimited banks to register themselves,
subject to certain conditions as "limited." Many banks speedily
availed themselves of the privilege: and the failure in 1890 of
Barings—the greatest of those distinctly English credit agencies,
which were not reckoned as banks—hastened the movement
towards its completion.

Some functions of banks in regard to fluctuations of credit and
prices are considered in Book IV.

CHAPTER IV

STOCK EXCHANGES[1]

1. *Introductory.*

The methods of procedure on stock exchanges differ: but the purposes of all are nearly the same. The present chapter illustrates these purposes by reference to the methods of the London Stock Exchange; though these are in some respects peculiar[2].

An organized market provides for the exact statement of the terms of any agreement made on it, and for the enforcement of that agreement. Stock exchanges are the chief of such markets: they deal in shares of joint stock companies: and in obligations to make definite annual payments by such companies; and by Governments, both central and local. "A stock exchange is an association composed of persons who trade in public stocks and conduct their business in conformity with settled rules and usages, commonly buying and selling for the public on commission."

The aggregate money volume of the transactions, effected on stock exchanges, is very much greater than that of any other set of organized dealings; and the records of their transactions are exceptionally definite, because their material is exactly standardized. A great market of grain can indeed make a near approach to standardization of each class of wheat that it handles: but the standardization of each particular issue of securities handled on a stock exchange is absolute. The rules for the conduct of business on various stock exchanges differ in some respects: but each set is exact and rigid; and the main purposes of all are the same.

Stock exchanges are not merely the chief theatres of large business transactions; they are also barometers which indicate the general conditions of the atmosphere of business. When credit is bad, stock exchanges record a general fall of prices. When

---

[1] This chapter has some ground in common with the fifth chapter of the second book of *Industry and Trade*, which deals with constructive speculation in organized produce markets.

[2] A clear account of the methods of the various stock exchanges is given, under the heading "Fond-verkehr," in an article on "Börsen-wesen" by Ehrenberg in the *Handwörterbuch der Staatswissenschaften*.

II, IV, 1.   credit is good the prices rise. But, when they rise very high,
cheerful expectations are in danger of being clouded by indications
that credit has been pushed too far, and that the atmosphere of
business will become increasingly sultry until it breaks in a storm.
Overcharged hopes are then quenched: and the businesses, which
survive, gradually resume their activities under conditions more
favourable than before; because weak credits have succumbed,
and the strong have been strengthened by being freed from
entanglements in dubious schemes: but these matters will be
considered later on.

Bourses or exchanges arose in the chief trading cities of Europe
towards the end of the Middle Ages. They early lent themselves
to speculation: some of which was mere betting as to events over
which the gamblers could have no control; while some related
to such things as the coming rates of exchange which they might
conceivably control to some slight extent. On these exchanges
men dealt in the loan of capital; official market rates of discount
as well as rates for the exchange of moneys of different places
were established and gave form and force to speculation.

The chief financial transactions were for long connected with
the loans, not always voluntary loans, obtained by princes for
their wars. Supplies of gold and silver, then as now, served to
make capital more fluid: they increased largely not indeed the
stock of capital in the world, but the stock which the agencie
of credit could collect in driblets from the people and turn in large
streams to great enterprises, taking their own profit as it passed [1]

----

[1] Some of these great enterprises were industrial, but most were military
For as Ehrenberg says, the bearing of arms, which in the feudal times had bee
a natural occupation of all, became in the thirteenth and fourteenth centurie
a skilled handicraft followed for wages; and in the fifteenth it became a capitalist
industry requiring a large outfit of cannons and muskets. But the capital was no
that of the princes, it was supplied by private financiers, partly from their own
resources and partly from those of other people. The enterprises did not alway
turn out well for borrower or lender: the great crises on the exchanges of th
sixteenth century arose from the failure of princes to meet their obligation
Meanwhile the shares of the great trading companies were rising into prominenc
and became the subject of wild speculation at the end of the seventeenth centur
and the beginning of the eighteenth.

For a full description of early stock exchanges see Ehrenberg's *Zeitalter d
Fugger*, Vol. II, from which some of the above statements are reproduced. The
is interest in the references to early stock exchanges in Anderson's and Ma
pherson's histories of Commerce, and in Rogers' *First nine years of the Bank
England*; while Francis' *Chronicles and characters of the Stock Exchange*, 184
reproduces a characteristic pamphlet of 1719, *The Anatomy of Exchange Alle*

2. *For a long while stock exchanges were concerned chiefly* II, IV, 2.
with the obligations of Governments: but much of their atten-
tion is now given to the securities of joint stock companies.

A stock exchange is an organized market for dealing in certain
standardized rights. For a long while the chief of these were
portions of debts due by Sovereigns and other Public Authorities:
the purchaser of one of these rights generally obtained a claim to
a specified annual income, which was to continue till the time
came—if it ever came—for the debt to be discharged. But the
growth of powerful companies, among which railway companies
took the first place, has overshadowed the growth of Government
securities, rapid as that has been in many countries[1].

The purchaser of almost any "security," of which considerable
quantities are habitually bought and sold on a stock exchange, is
generally fortified by the knowledge that expert and well-informed
capitalists regard its price as fairly representing its real value.
Therefore, although stock exchange machinations may occasionally
set for a time, an unduly high value, or an unduly low value on a
particular "security," yet, in the main, the judgment of well-
informed, capable men protects the general public from grave errors
of judgment in their investments, so long as these are conducted
with reasonable caution.

"Debentures" generally give prior claims to specified annual
payments. "Preferred" stocks generally give claims to similar
payments, which rank next in order to those due on Debentures.
Each group of each class of these securities is "standardized";
that is, two securities of the same group, issued by a company,
have the same value.

Here something is to be said as to the stimulus which the variety
of stock exchange investments offers to saving. Some investors,
being perhaps timid or conscious of ignorance of business, put

---

or a system of stock jobbing, proving that scandalous trade, as it is now carried on,
to be knavish in its private practice and treason in its public. So grave and able a
writer as the author of the *Considerations on the East India Trade,* 1701 (reprinted
in M'Culloch's *Select Tracts on Commerce*) finds in the evils of stock jobbing a
strong argument for the abolition of the companies whose shares afford the chief
material to it.

[1] Britain incurred the greater part of her debt during the Napoleonic war;
and she borrowed again in each subsequent considerable war: but during each
intervening peace she has set herself to pay off her debt. Therefore she can borrow
on exceptionally easy terms.

II, IV, 3. perfect safety above all other considerations; and provision is made by first class Debentures, and—though in a less degree—by good Government securities for their needs. Some desire temporary investments, which they can make and unmake, with certainty and at small expense, as occasion arises: their needs are met by Consols. The price to buyers is always near to that which sellers obtain; stock exchange charges being low, because the market for Consols is large and active. Those who are not averse to some risks, and hold the opinion—which is often mistaken—that they are fairly good judges of the merits of a security, select Ordinary stock of strong undertakings or Preferred stock of others. Lastly those who know, or think they know, the financial, technical, commercial and personal strength and weakness of particular undertakings, will invest a part at least of their capital in the Ordinary stock of companies which they believe to have solid foundations, and to be in the hands of able, upright men. Investors who have strong advantages of this kind, can probably get half as much again on the average as if they had invested in Consols: in reckoning these gains account is to be taken of the permanent rise in the market value of some of their investments and of the fall in that of others.

Trust funds are commonly, and sometimes compulsorily, invested in Government securities. Next in order to these are Debentures of strong, well-established undertakings, among which railways have been prominent: next come the Preferred stock of strong companies. Mortgages are often available for this purpose: but there are some mortgages on which a man may be willing to invest his own money, but not willing to take the responsibility of lending the money of another.

3. *The methods of stock exchanges vary: but the results obtained by the London Stock Exchange may be taken as fairly representative.*

Stock exchanges in all western countries, by whatever names they are called, are in effect media for the circulation of command over capital from those who hold it in a ready form to those who desire to invest it as a source of income: but the New York Stock Exchange seems to afford the only close parallel to that of London in regard to its methods of working. It will be convenient to

describe the functions of stock exchanges generally in terms of II, IV, 3.
the practice of London.

Every person occupied in the business of the stock exchange
is commonly called a "stock broker": but, within the stock
exchange itself, only those of its members who act as intermediaries
between the general public and the actual traders are called
"brokers": the actual traders are called "dealers."

It is impossible for any one dealer to be fully acquainted with
the conditions of all the many securities which are handled on
the London Stock Exchange: and each particular class of securities
is apt to become localized in a particular part of the room; and
a security, whose conditions are peculiar, is likely to be avoided
by all except one or two dealers: they must be sought by a broker
who desires to obtain them, or to dispose of them.

A broker is willing to buy a stock exchange security for any
who instruct him to that effect: (if the transaction is large, he may
require his client to guarantee him sufficiently against a speedy
fall in the value of the stock, in spite of his client's expectation
that it will rise: and *vice versâ* in case of an order to sell[1]).

Suppose that three per cent. is a sufficient "margin" to cover
any of the effects of any probable reversal of his expectations
(allowance being made for expenses); then £300 will secure the
purchase of stock of the current value of £10,000. If the stock
rises, the speculator gains the excess of that rise over the charges
involved in the transaction. If the value of the stock remains
unchanged, the speculator loses those expenses: and, if it falls,
he loses, in addition, an amount corresponding to the fall in the
nominal value of the securities concerned.

With that proviso the stock broker will carry out his instructions:
if the stock does rise, the broker will hand to the speculator the
increase in the value of the stock thus purchased, after deducting
the appropriate charges for the work. If it falls, the speculator
will lose the amount by which the stock purchased has fallen in
value, together with the sum of those charges: therefore the
amateur speculator is nearly sure to lose in the long run.

On the other hand speculators sometimes work in groups. Each

---

[1] On the English Stock Exchange the term "broker" has a narrow significa-
tion. He is an intermediary between the general public and those who operate
on the stock exchange. The latter are technically known as "jobbers."

II, IV, 4. brings to the common stock some information that is not generally
accessible: and each may be able to exercise influence, direct or
indirect, on the course of those particular securities, in the prices
of which the group takes, for the time, a particular interest. Such
manoeuvres occasionally afford much private gain: but their net
results are, as a rule, detrimental to the public interest. In earlier
times public opinion condemned nearly all forms of speculation
in coming prices. Now it is recognized that on the balance freedom
to speculate is greatly to the public interest. But, when speculation
is associated with manipulation of prices by any means, and
especially by putting false rumours into circulation, it is a crime
against the public. Unfortunately the facts necessary to establish
a charge against the offenders are not easily ascertained: they
can generally command excellent forensic skill in proving that
suspicious actions are capable of innocent interpretation.

Almost every important business operation involves a considerable amount of speculation. The agriculturist runs great risks from
uncertain weather: even bounteous harvests do not secure him
against the risk that markets will be over-stocked.

Again, the manufacturer who lays in a great stock of raw material
may find that he has to sell his products in competition with others
of like kind, the materials for which were bought at much lower
prices: he runs also the risk of failing to obtain the necessary labour
for his work on terms favourable to himself. To be in business is
to be faced at every turn by speculative risks.

The relations between stock exchange activities and fluctuations of general credit, industrial output and trade expansion are
close and intricate: something will be said about them a little later.

4. *In times when general credit is fairly stable, the methods
of the stock exchange give considerable protection to buyers
for investment who are not specially expert.*

An investment locks up the command over capital out of the
reach of its owner; and, in many cases, the risk that that command
cannot be recovered, except by forced sale at a heavy loss, is a more
important consideration than the risk that it will not yield the
full income which it appears to promise. This first risk is almost
abolished by the stock exchange. Of course the investment may have
altered in value: but, if not, its owner can sell it for almost the same

price as he paid for it. In contrast with this case, if anyone who is not a professional dealer in horses buys a young horse for £80, and next year a change of plans makes him desire to sell the horse, which is in good condition, he will be lucky if he gets £70 net for it: and in a few days he may find that a friend of his has bought it from a dealer for £80 or more. The stock exchange almost abolishes this source of loss; and it even reduces very much the chance that an uninstructed investor will pay a good price for a bond or share which better informed people know to be worth but little: for its machinery enables anyone who has reasons to suspect a security, to sell it whether he has it or not; and if it falls as quickly as he expects, he will make his profit by doing so.

The private purchaser of railway shares, may know nothing of the latent causes that are tending to increase or diminish the prosperity of the line concerned; he may not know whether its management is becoming less able than before or more able; he may be unable to tell whether any set of accounts were hollow, and whether large expenses had been charged to capital that ought to have been charged to revenue: but he buys with the confidence that all such points have been scrutinized by many keen men with special knowledge; who are able and ready remorselessly to "bear" the stock if they find in it any weak spot, which had not been noticed by the general public, and had not been allowed for in making up its value. Also the narrowness of the turn between the jobbers' buying and selling prices for such securities gives a further economy and security to the uninstructed investor.

Thus stock exchanges are necessary auxiliaries of modern industry and commerce; and the services which they render to the public probably outweigh many times the evils which they cause to it. But the magnitude of the real services which they render by no means varies with the volume of operations on them, and amateur speculators are likely to lose their own fortunes, with no gain to the public.

5. *Some contrasts between causes which exert only temporary influences on the values of stock exchange securities, and those whose effects are likely to endure.*

The unskilled investor is apt to attribute too great importance to passing changes in the earning power of a business, whose

II, IV, 6. securities are quoted on the stock exchange: the shrewd speculator profits by this lack of insight, and sells when it is unduly raising the price of any security. For instance, he takes prompt account of the fact that, if unusually fine weather during holidays has raised the net receipts of a railway that is largely engaged in passenger traffic, uninformed speculation may have raised its price unduly; and so he is more likely to sell than to buy the stock of that railway at the time. He may even turn his attention to a local line in a coal-and-iron district, whose traffic has suffered a little from an excess in holiday-making over the average; or to another, that has been the scene of a disastrous accident, by which it has been involved in heavy compensation for damages. Uninstructed investors, perhaps not realizing how promptly the full effect of any passing misfortune is discounted on the stock exchange, are not unlikely to sell just when he buys; and thus to play into his hands. It may indeed be said that shrewd, far-seeing speculators sometimes govern their own action, not so much by forecasts of the distant future, as by forecasts of the inaccuracy of the forecasts of that future.

6. *The growing importance of the part played by stock exchange securities in national and international markets for capital.*

Until recently a country could not very greatly anticipate in a single year much of the income that belonged to future years: for the pressure of war or other emergency that inclined her to anticipate her future income, lowered her credit in all the markets of the world. But this position has been changed in great measure by the rapid expansion of stock exchange securities, which are habitually handled and quoted on the stock exchanges of several countries. These "international securities," as they are sometimes called, exercise a powerful influence—at all events in the absence of wars and grave rumours of war—in tending to equalize the rates of interest obtainable for long loans on good security throughout the western world: for they cannot be marketed, permanently and in large quantities, at much higher prices, measured in like units, in one country than in another.

If the currencies in question are all firmly based on gold, this statement is self contained. If they are based on different metals, or if either of them is not firmly attached to any metal, a more complex statement is needed, the general nature of which will be suggested in the course of the following study of international trade. It may, however, be appropriate here to note that debentures, expressed in terms of an inconvertible foreign paper currency, are liable to great fluctuations of real value. The ordinary shares of a company, which has issued a great quantity of debentures, may be raised in real, as well as in nominal value, by a currency change, which lowers the real value of the income yielded by its debentures. The interests of preferred shareholders in such case are likely to vary with the circumstances of the company.

So far we have been occupied with the organization of national credit, exemplified by reference to the case of Britain. The next task might appropriately be to make some study of the causes and effects of disturbances of national credit. But, in the present age, national credit is closely interwoven with international credit; and therefore it seems best to consider international trade relations, before inquiring into fluctuations of credit. It may, however, be added here that many first-class stock exchange securities are eminently exportable. It might almost be said that electric wires and electric cables have enabled them to act as instantaneous adjusters of passing disturbances in the balance of trade. If A, in one country, has occasion to make a prompt remittance to B in another country, he can—directly or indirectly—deposit stock exchange securities (perhaps international) with a suitable bank; and request the bank to telegraph to a bank in the second country a request to place to the account of B a sum corresponding to their value. The details of such action lie within the province of dealers in finance: our present concern with them is that they hold a considerable place among the causes that justify the use of the term "the world market for capital," at all events in time of peace. We are thus brought near to the problems of International Trade: and it will be well to say something about them before considering fluctuations of credit, in which international influences are already strong, and are rapidly growing in strength. The subject of this book is continued in Book IV.

BOOK III

INTERNATIONAL TRADE

CHAPTER I

INFLUENCES OF TRANSPORT FACILITIES
ON TRADE

1. *Some characteristics of long-distance trade.*

Stephenson's locomotive facilitated the transport of goods from one part of a country to another. But the superiority of the long luggage train over the cart drawn by horses or oxen is perhaps not greater than the superiority of a first rate steamship over the best sailing vessel as a carrier of cargo. And in recent years freight charges by sea for many kinds of traffic, and especially for coal, have again been falling relatively to those by land: partly because the economies of building and working ships have been increasing faster than those of building and working railways; while electric and other appliances for handling bulky cargoes have reduced the terminal charges for maritime transport relatively to those for land transport.

Almost in the same class are mechanical facilities for communication between buyer and seller by word of mouth and otherwise. With the advent of railways, the human wear and tear, the fatigue and discomfort of long journeys fell very rapidly: and the costs of some kinds of long distance trade are being lowered fast by improvements of this kind on sea and land. A similar influence in many kinds of trade is being exerted by the telephone and by aerial messages.

Facilities for long distance trade were provided early by bills of exchange and other elementary machinery of world money markets: and the extension of these by aid of a quick post and telegraph was brought nearly up to its present limit more than

III, I, 1.

a generation ago. It is true that changes of this class are helping domestic trade as well as international trade: but they are generally more important in regard to long distances than to short.

Lardner's *Law of Squares in transport and trade* is to the effect that, provided the routes of trade from any place spread out in several directions, an increase in the distance over which goods can be carried at a given expense is likely to increase the area over which they can be profitably marketed, as the square of that distance (since the area of a circle increases as the square of its radius). The position of Britain is exceptionally advantageous for maritime traffic, and especially for that of the Atlantic ocean: most of her industrial districts have grown up near the sea. Her Continental rivals have less advantages in this respect: but they often benefit by through railway traffic, from producer to ultimate purchaser, without break of bulk. Japan's position in regard to the Pacific resembles Britain's in regard to the Atlantic[1].

If gold and silver mines had been discovered in the north of America, the United States and Canada might have attracted the Spaniards and Portuguese; who, disdaining hard manual work, might perhaps have turned them to but poor account, even by aid of forced labour. As it was, those races annexed the tropical and semi-tropical regions of North and South America; while the parts of North America, which had the greatest power of developing strong character, were peopled by Dutch, English and French, Later on the English predominated, largely under the influence of a desire for freedom in religious creed and observances. For, while the "orthodox" and relatively rich and cultured royalists gave their tone to the southern states, where wealth could be acquired easily by aid of negro labour, the sturdy and resolute Puritans settled in the more bracing north.

The history of the Eurasian continent reproduced itself in America with great speed. Those districts, which yield wealth least easily, are now the richest: the northern states are richer than the southern; and the southern are much richer than those, still nearer the Equator, which are peopled by races from southern Europe. This stratification of human energy from north to south

---

[1] Something is said on these subjects in *Industry and Trade*, Book I, Chap. II.

III, I, 1. in the two Continents largely influences the present courses of trade: but it is itself effect, rather than ultimate cause. For, in the long run, national wealth is governed by the character of the population more than by the bounty of nature. Invigorating climates have attracted and developed strong characters; and wealth has come to them.

The economist must look to students of vegetable life for a great part of the explanation of the strange fact that the chief staple foods of the world are grown in temperate zones: as in this direction insufficient suggestion seems to be afforded by the influences of climate on human energy. Perhaps something may be attributed to the sustained industry, with which the breeds of the staple grains of temperate climates have been improved by artificial selection and appropriate nutriment[1].

Mere physical conditions might, of course, have been expected to make the chief courses of trade in animal and vegetable products run north and south between temperate and tropical regions. Carey, an influential advocate of a Protective policy for America, complained that free trade caused them to run east and west: but he seems to have overlooked the fact that climatic conditions have controlled the nature of man almost as much as that of vegetables: he did not consider that trade runs east and west in the north temperate zone, partly because the configuration of the globe makes that zone much more important than the south temperate zone; and partly because climatic conditions have opposed the highest development of human energy in other zones[2].

---

[1] The main exceptions to the general rule, that the staple foods of the world come from temperate zones, appear to be found in rice, sugar, some maize and some wheat from tropical uplands, sago and bananas. Energy has forced ever-increasing supplies of sugar out of the recalcitrant beetroot in Europe and America: while lassitude has, in some places, acquiesced in a relative decadence of output from the more generous sugar cane. Buckle pointed to the unkindness of nature, shown in her too lavish gifts to the tropical peoples, in that she had given to them the prolific maize, which he believed to be "rarely seen beyond the fortieth parallel of latitude"; together with the banana, an acre of which "will support more than fifty persons, whereas the same amount of land sown with wheat in Europe will only support two" (*History of Civilization*, A.D. 1851–61, ch. II). But maize is now raised largely in temperate zones.

[2] See R. E. Smith, *Wheatfields of the world* (Saint Louis, 1908); especially ch. XXIX. The predominance in energy of the Northern States over the Southern has tended to send some traffic to Atlantic ports; though it has at least as good access, so far as purely geographical conditions go, to the Gulf of Mexico.

2. *The Mediterranean Sea was during many centuries the centre of the greater part of the advanced industries, the far-reaching credit and the massive trade of the world.*

Constructive uses of credit have grown with the use of artificial power in manufacture and transport: the two growths have been in great measure dependent on one another. No doubt the industry and commerce of southern Europe, southern Asia and northern Africa made great advances without the aid of steam: the connections between western Europe and eastern America, which were established by sailing vessels, absorbed a considerable amount of capital. But giant developments of heavy traffic and trade required vast supplies of capital, organized by great markets for constructive credit.

No doubt the way was prepared for modern expansions of enterprise by bold men, who were but ill-provided with material resources. A few small vessels carrying but little capital sufficed for the Portuguese, Corilham, who reached Calicut in the southwest of India in 1486; and was followed twelve years later by his better known fellow-countryman, Vasco da Gama. And the same is true of Columbus, who reached the eastern coast of North America about the same time. These events were not only the beginning of the economic unification of the world. Incidentally they prepared the way for massive sea-borne trade between Europe and other Continents: the goods exported in that trade gave a new impetus to the already strong tendency towards massive production by large aggregations of capital. Water power and steam power enabled north-western Europe to develop massive manufacture of simple goods for consumption near home and in other parts of the world: and rapid strides were made towards the modern vast uses of capital, and the modern development of a world-market for it.

Western Europe might not have been able to find highly remunerative work for all her recent accumulations within her own territory: but the steam power, which was at first used mainly in manufacture, is now in large measure occupied with facilitating the interchange of products of "western" manufacture for food and raw materials received from countries whose industries are more nearly akin to those of mediaeval Europe[1].

[1] It is conceivable that inhabitants of some other planet, whose civilization is of earlier date than that of this world, may have made a full study of the

3. *Causes which have influenced the main courses of trade
at various stages in the evolution of industry.*

Progress in the industrial arts has depended largely on the
increasing facilities, which accrue to manufacturers and other
producers, for getting just those materials, and implements, and
services which, account being taken of their costs, are most conducive to each particular purpose in hand. This perpetual "substitution" of the more efficient agent (or material), relatively to
its cost, is a chief occupation of the alert business man; and a
chief means by which he promotes material well-being, while
building up a rich business. It is a relatively simple task, when
he can draw suitable materials from sources near at hand, which
are controlled by those with whom he is in personal contact; but
its difficulties increase with distance, especially when good means
of communication are lacking.

Before modern methods of transport had been developed, the
mineral and vegetable resources of those districts, which bore a
dense progressive population, were applied not only to uses, for
which they were well fitted, but also to many, for which other
resources might with advantage have been substituted, if they
had been better known and more accessible. For instance, poor

changes wrought in the surface of this earth by the development of railroads
and in other ways. They may have surmized that our civilization had its origin
not far from the equator; but that its strongest forms have been developed
rather far from the heats of the equator. Aided by telescopes superior to ours,
they may have noted the large and varied physical conditions of that northern
continent, which has been artificially divided into Europe and Asia. They may
have laid stress on the fact that easy communications by water suffice for many
of the purposes of a great trading city. Finally, when their telescopes, more
subtle than ours, revealed innumerable roads, straightened out and levelled
almost regardless of expense, they may have anticipated that these railways
may have effected the concentrated unity of great industrial regions of this
world, which are not either archipelagos or deltas of great rivers. Thus they may
have conjectured that the civilizations of Europe and southern Asia dominated
the world for a long while: America having been kept a little in the background
by her lack of islands and small peninsulas, whose populations had easy communications over relatively smooth waters. They may have understood better
than the inhabitants of this world did till recent times, the causes of the fertility
of Egypt: as well as of the backwardness of Australia; and of those parts of
Asia, which are not in close touch with either the Pacific or the Indian Ocean.
They may probably have guessed that social inequalities began in very early
phases of civilization; and that they increased in all parts of the world, as
civilization progressed; partly because growing wealth would give an ever increasing advantage in education and material resources to those strains of the
population who had already obtained some wealth and some predominating
influence.

strata of iron and other ores were worked in Europe, while far richer strata slumbered undisturbed in other Continents, even within easy reach of good communications: and, great as has been the recent extension of railways in backward countries, it is possible that not a half of the richest mines in the world have yet been tapped.

The main courses of international trade, in so far as they depend on mineral products, lie therefore beyond the range of human prediction: and nearly the same is true of some vegetable products, especially of a tropical character, which have not yet been largely cultivated by alert and strenuous races. But the temperate regions of the world have been sufficiently explored to enable agricultural experts to form a fairly good judgment of their capacity for producing grain, meat, dairy produce and other staple products by the best methods now known. Of course, certain methods are more effective in some districts than in others: this is the case, for instance, with methods now on their trial for "dry cultivation" in arid regions; and again, with schemes for obtaining nitrates to fertilize the soil from the atmosphere, by means of electricity, in places that are rich in water power.

The human factor is also uncertain; the sudden rise of Japan suggests caution: but population in the modern age drifts rapidly and cumulatively to districts to which it is invited by nature; and the most powerful industries are nearly sure to be settled, before many generations are past, in those places in which the supply of power is most abundant, whether derived from coal, or water, or any other source. Facilities for long distance transport and personal communication may continue to advance and to be diffused with increasing rapidity, until they have unified the whole of the habitable globe.

Until recently, nearly all long distance trade made the greater part of its travel by water: spices and other light goods travelled far by land: and very few households could show many bulky goods which had not been produced in its near neighbourhood. But now, every British cottager buys tea, sugar, tobacco and other comforts which have come from distant lands: and the greater part even of his clothing is made of material which has travelled some hundreds of miles by land, and some thousands of miles by

III, i, 3. water. Formerly, nearly all the materials used in construction came from woods, quarries or mines close at hand. But now, Brazilian, Norwegian and other distant forests supply timber for all purposes, and choice woods for tables and other furniture in general use. Even the jobbing carpenter in industrial districts will now select, from many various kinds of pine and deal wood, brought together from different parts of the earth, that which is best for each separate use, taking account of its lightness and its strength, its cheapness, its durability, etc. In a large factory, twenty different kinds of woods will sometimes be in use at once; and nearly the same is true of different kinds of wool and leather.

A country often exports a commodity over one frontier, while she imports practically the same over another. Thus Germany has imported English coal along the North Sea and the lower Rhine; while she exported it over nearly every inland frontier. New England imports coal from Nova Scotia, while Pennsylvania exports it to Ontario. Pennsylvania imports soft wood from Canada, while Maine and the Pacific States export it in large quantities. But, more commonly, the commodities which enter into trade of this kind differ a little from one another, though called by the same name. Thus Belgian steel on its way to England, often crosses English steel on its way to Belgium; but the consignments are likely to be of different qualities, and to be used for different purposes[1].

Again, if two sorts of the same commodity are of unequal usefulness, but cost the same for carriage, the better sort is likely to be chosen for long distance transport. Where wood is plentiful, thick beams of quick-growing inferior wood may be preferred to thin beams of better wood, which perhaps cost twice as much: but if both have been imported from afar, the cost of carrying the thick beams may cause preference to be given to thin beams of superior wood. Similarly, all sorts of British coal are sold to consumers who live near tidal water throughout most of northern Europe; while the best kinds of gas coal penetrate by land into the heart of the Continent.

Again, the commoner sorts of wine are generally consumed near

---

[1] The cause of this may, however, be that the producers in each country have agreed to restrict their home sales in order to maintain home prices; while looking with some disapproval on the "dumping" of home products in foreign countries, whose rival industries give them some cause for jealousy.

home, while the better travel far: and a district which produces only the better sorts is likely to import the commoner sorts for ordinary use. France is the largest producer, the largest exporter and the second largest importer of wine in the world; though it is true that some of her imported wine is re-exported, as French wine, after being treated with a skill which is almost unrivalled. Venetia buys coarse olive oil from southern Italy, and exports fine oil to the north. Guernsey exports very early potatoes at high prices: and later in the year buys potatoes for her own consumption at low prices. Some English pastoral districts sell fresh milk at high prices to industrial centres; and buy their cheese and even butter from distant lands, and so on.

The percentage of the world's trade which is governed by differences in natural resources is increasing, while that which is governed by differences of industrial phase, and of aptitude for particular sorts and grades of manufacture, is less now than formerly; but yet its absolute volume is increasing. This increase is specially great in the case of central Europe. Almost every place is developing new means of communication with neighbours on either side of her in widely different industrial phases. Much of the trade, which passes over the Eastern borders of Germany, has its origin in the present backwardness of Slavonic Europe as much as in her own advance. She imports some fine manufactures for herself from the West; and exports manufactures, some fine and some coarse, towards the East. Russia also exports manufactures across her Asiatic frontier, while still largely dependent on the West in regard to fine manufactures for her own use.

It seems probable that advantages, which any particular country has gained from an early start in the industrial race, will diminish: for nearly every place will gradually develop her resources up to a fairly high level. Each industry will then be worked almost exclusively with the material, the mechanical appliances, and the human resources best adapted to its purposes, account being taken of their necessary cost. If they are easy of transport, they will come to the industry: if they are not, and the ultimate products of the industry are portable, it will go to them.

An alert industry, well aided by natural advantages, will gener-

III, I, 3. ally have the whole world for its market, except where stayed by restrictive regulation; and thus the courses of all trade, which has a solid basis, will be broadened. But backward countries will gain on those that are more advanced: and therefore those local inequalities of human faculty, which now afford a solid basis for such trade, seem likely on the whole to diminish: and this, in spite of the tendency towards the concentration of some classes of industries which can derive great economies from production on a vast scale. For the equalizing tendencies, which arise from improved means of communication and increased human plasticity, seem not yet to have reached their full development: while the increased economies, which arise from mere enlargements of the scale of production, have already occupied the greater part of the territory of industry in which they are of much importance.

The conflict between these two tendencies, the one strengthening many weak industrial nations, and the other strengthening the strong, will afford an interesting retrospect to the economic historian a hundred years hence. He will certainly find that some forecasts of the present generation are falsified by new developments, such as that of aviation, which are already becoming prominent; and by others of which we have as yet no inkling. And he will probably find that we have misjudged many influences which are no longer new, and the true interpretation of which will seem obvious to any one who looks back on its record.

A great part of the world's resources is wasted through the unhealthiness of a large part of its surface. But there are reasons for hoping that this evil will be gradually remedied; and, if so, then the rate of migration, which has prevailed in the last century, may probably continue for at least another: meanwhile, the energies of those races, which were civilized while Europe was still barbarous, may be aroused and trained in modern methods. Should these changes come to pass, the economic forces of western Europe may be over-matched by those of each of at least two other Continents: the main courses of the world's trade will probably then be governed by climatic conditions, and pass between north and south more generally than ever before.

CHAPTER II

CHARACTERISTICS OF INTERNATIONAL TRADE

1. *The special features of international trade did not* *become prominent until the partial solidarity of national interests in industry and trade had been recognized. Its full significance was made manifest by Ricardo.*

It has already been noticed[1] that in early times local interests bore a relation to national interests, somewhat similar to those which national interests bear to cosmopolitan interests (in times of peace). Political economy is sometimes described in Germany and elsewhere as "National economy": and, in its early stages, it was much concerned with the material interests of individual nations; especially in regard to the importation and exportation of the precious metals. But, later on, it became more and more a part of the study of human well being: its spirit approached to that of Plato's dialogues, and its various methods approached to those of Bacon, Newton and Darwin.

The discussion of "some general relations between industry and trade," in the second chapter of *Industry and Trade,* is in effect an introduction to this volume as well as to that in which it is placed. But it seems advisable to reproduce part of its substance, occasionally even without verbal change, in the present chapter. The point of view in *Industry and Trade* is mainly that of industry; but in the present volume the affairs of industry come into view only in so far as they affect the courses of trade[2].

The study of the economy of nations could not be carried far in early times, when few people knew much, or even cared much, about any business affairs other than those of their own neighbourhood. In fact, "Political Economy," in its original sense of the economy of a city, was a more appropriate description than it is

[1] Introduction, § 1.

[2] Something is said in regard to international trade in various passages of *Industry and Trade.* These may be found in its First Book, Chap. I, §§ 4–6; Chap. III, §§ 3, 4; Chap. IV, § 6; Chap. V, § 1: also in its Second Book, Chap. IX, §§ 3–5: in its Third Book, Chap. XIII, §§ 4, 5: and in its Appendix B.

III, II, 1. now. "An inquiry into the nature and causes of the Wealth of Nations" was the title under which Adam Smith described the purpose of the most important study of it that has been made. And yet its first Book is entitled: "Of the Causes of the Improvement in the productive Powers of Labour, and of the Order according to which its Produce is naturally distributed among the different Ranks of the People": and this foreshadowed the present drift of the work of Adam Smith's disciples[1].

Problems of international trade had come into prominence in the economic writings of many nations during the seventeenth and eighteenth centuries; and a mastery of their leading principles was achieved by a brilliant group of Englishmen, who were impelled by the troubles of the great French war to the study of the national currency, finances and trade. Ricardo was a chief leader in all these matters, and especially in relation to international trade. He based himself in part on much similar work that had been done, especially in England and France, during the eighteenth century, as to the causes that govern value: and he proceeded to emphasize and explain the divergence of the relations between money values and *real* costs in places between which the migration of labour and capital is not easy. Such divergencies are not peculiar to international trade: but they are exceptionally prominent in it; because the migration of labour and capital is more difficult between different countries than between different places in the same country[2].

A national spirit, of which the closely watched frontiers of a country are outward signs, is the chief cause of the public interest taken in the only kind of trade of which systematic statistics are recorded. Hopes and fears, ambitions and anxieties, ideals and disappointments, which are common to the whole, call for a large common purse; out of which to defray the expenses not only of

---

[1] The general relations of Adam Smith's position to that of his immediate predecessors and contemporaries the "Physiocrats"—that is, advocates of a free course for "the rule of Nature"—are well known. Something is said about them in my *Principles of Economics*, Appendix B, § 2.

[2] In this connection it may be noted that most of the cities of Europe once levied, and many still levy, frontier duties—commonly described as *octroi*—on peasants bringing their produce to market. The cessation of that trade might have caused even greater harm to the townspeople than to the peasants: but the townspeople could afford to wear expensive armour; and the country people often could not.

defence against external foes, but also the costs of national movements connected with religion, education, and provision against infirmity. They call for, and they help to sustain, a common Money Market, with a unified currency, and an almost perfectly free movement of capital from one part of the country to another. Common habits, common systems of law and administration, and a common language, further facilitate internal migrations of the people: and though, as Adam Smith said, "Man is of all sorts of luggage the most difficult to be transported," yet it still takes much less force to move a man within his own country than away from it.

2. *Benefits which a country derives from her external trade in general.*

The real income of every family is governed by its own energy and ability combined with the resources at its disposal: and in a primitive society, in which the family is nearly self-sufficing, these causes alone are of importance. But the real income of an artisan family consists for the greater part of things which it obtains in exchange for its own products and services. A large country with ample natural resources, and simple manners, such as Russia or China, resembles a self-sufficing family: her real income consists mainly of her own products; and it is not very greatly affected by the terms on which she exports a small part of them in exchange for foreign goods. Nearly the same may be said of the United States: for, though her economic life is very complex, and though her people are alert to discover, and resolute to obtain, any foreign product that will meet their needs or their fancies; yet her area is so large, her mineral resources are so various, and the range of climate between her northern and southern States is so wide: therefore her consumption of foreign products is relatively small; and it is not a matter of vital importance to her whether the terms on which she obtains her imports in exchange for her exports are very favourable. But the case is different for a country, whose natural resources are small; especially if her people have accustomed themselves to somewhat luxurious habits of life, in which a great part is played by imported products.

In broad terms it may be said that the *primâ facie* and direct gain which a country derives from her foreign trade consists in

III, II, 3. the excess of the value to her of the things which she imports over the value to her of the things which she could have made for herself with the capital and labour devoted to producing the things which she exported in exchange for them; the costs of working the trade being of course reckoned in.

No statistics are, however, available for making a near estimate of this excess: and consequently the gain which a country derives from her foreign trade is often stated on another plan, which suggests more definite ideas: it is not strictly correct; but it serves fairly well for some purposes. On this plan, it is tacitly assumed that the country would make for herself those things which she imports, if she could not get them by trade: and accordingly her gains from her trade are taken to be the excess of the cost to which she would be put if she made her imports herself, over that to which she is put by making other things and exporting them in exchange for her imports. This result is of course very far from the truth in regard to such things as Britain's imports of tropical foods: for she could not produce any great quantities of these herself; and, if she could not import them, she would have very little of them. If, on the other hand, her imports of wheat and other staple grains were arrested, she would be forced to make up the deficiency by her own production; even though that would require poor crops to be wrung by very great labour from unsuitable soils, and climates. If her imports of French woollens were arrested, she would probably make up the greater part of the deficiency by her own products, which would be pushed into uses for which French products are still preferred.

3. *Part of a country's external trade is often caused by some weakness in her resources or in her energies: but, as a general rule, a large trade indicates high national efficiency*

When a country's exports are large relatively to her area, they are almost certain to consist mainly of manufactures. Some of the West Indian Islands, which have such exceptional advantage for the production of sugar and other products, are so densely populated that they import much of their own food; and again a small country, containing large rich mineral resources, might do likewise. But these cases are not representative.

More interest attaches to the trade of some British Dependencies

and other places, which are sparsely peopled by energetic races. III, II, 3.
They export almost exclusively raw produce: and in return they
obtain manufactured and other goods, which they have no special
facilities for producing. But their imports often represent borrowed
capital in addition to returns for their exports: such borrowing
has sometimes represented self-indulgent idleness and extravagance, but in general it indicates confidence, which the capitalists
of the old world feel in the energy and probity of the colonists.
Good business is done by borrowers and by lenders when goods
go from the old world to the new, in order to provide vigorous
colonists with the means of developing large natural resources,
from which borrowers and lenders will alike derive good profit;
while the rest of the world will also derive some benefit from an increase in the supply of raw materials and food from the new world.

Thus it may be difficult to decide whether some particular
increase in a country's trade indicates an increase of her strength:
but, in fact, no country has attained a very large trade save by
energy. There have, indeed, been several cases of large trade per
head of a thin population, which exploits the resources of a rich
new country, without devoting much energy to developing those
resources; but such cases have not been frequent or on a large
scale. A great national trade has always been an evidence of
high industrial energy. It is true that easily worked rich mines,
or exceptionally advantageous soil and climate, have sometimes
yielded a large *per capita* external trade for a small population:
but they have never yielded a very large *aggregate* trade. That
has always belonged to a great energetic people, who export a
considerable part of the raw or the manufactured products of their
industries.

There is indeed some solid foundation for the suggestion that
the existence of a very large external trade indicates a high degree
of efficiency in industry. For the same energy of character, that
makes a nation eminent in industry, is likely to make her traders
alert to seize every opportunity of bringing the products in which
she excels, to the notice of countries that cannot produce those
things with as much relative ease and efficiency as they can other
products, which are in demand in her own markets but cannot
be produced there with as much ease. The case is specially strong
when the exports consist largely of high grade products.

III, II, 3.   A densely peopled country is indeed likely to export chiefly manufactures: and several causes combine to increase her foreign trade rapidly. In the first place, she is likely to import a considerable part of the material which she re-exports in a manufactured state: and the value of such material enters twice into her foreign trade. Britain was once the chief exporter of wool: later on she used up all her own wool; and now a considerable part of her exports consists of manufactured goods made of imported wool: the value of that wool appears twice in her foreign trade.

In the second place, an extension of any national manufacture as a general rule increases its efficiency and economy. Skill is increased in quantity, in quality and in variety: each sort and degree of skill is set to the work for which it is specially adapted: plant is improved rapidly; and that which is no longer the best of its kind, is quickly thrown out, often to be exported to countries whose industries are still backward.

These considerations have long been prominent; and they scarcely need to be mentioned save for the sake of completeness: but there is a kindred group of considerations, which have perhaps hardly received sufficient attention. They are connected with the broad facts that the expansion of a country's foreign trade depends largely on her facilities for internal transport; and that these facilities, in so far as they do not proceed from natural waterways, are generally indications of a highly developed internal trade. The chief exceptions to this general rule are found when colonists from an advanced industrial country take up mineral, pastoral, or agricultural land in a new country; for then they obtain, chiefly from their own home, the capital required for building railways from the interior to convenient ports. This is one of many ways, in which developments of external trade anticipate varied industrial activities, and prepare the way for them.

During the process of development of a new country, her imports habitually exceed her exports; because she does not pay at once for the capital devoted to her railways and other developments. After a time she may become rich enough to provide the capital needed for most of her own enterprises: and then the payment of interest on the capital, borrowed in her early phase, will tend to increase her exports relatively to her imports.

4. *Statistics relating to international trade have been col-* III, II, 4.
lected more generally and regularly than any others: and,
partly for this reason they are sometimes used to suggest
variations in national energy and prosperity. But they are
not well adapted for that purpose.

The statistics of a country's foreign trade are more promptly
and exactly ascertained than almost any others, which can be
easily applied to measure a side of her economic progress; and the
indications supplied by them are generally in the right direction:
but they sometimes mislead. Of course nominal increases in
imports and exports may be caused by an inflation of prices,
while there has been no substantial change: but this kind of
misinterpretation is easily checked. There remains however another,
which is more subtle; and therefore calls for fuller notice. Its
general character may be indicated by an illustration.

Britain's foreign trade consists in great measure of an exchange
of manufactures for grain and meat. Let us then suppose that the
methods of intensive cultivation are vastly improved: so that the
produce of British farms can be greatly increased; since farmers
obtain as good a return to much larger applications of labour and
capital than before the change. The result would be a considerable
addition to Britain's wealth. But her imports of grain and meat
would have diminished and her exports would have diminished
in like degree (unless indeed she were taking the opportunity of
bringing home some of her capital).

The consequent increase in the prosperity of her people might
accelerate marriages among them, and lessen their inclination to
emigrate, so that her imports of grain and meat might reach their
old level ere long. But, meanwhile, this increase in the efficiency
of her people would have checked the expansion of her foreign
trade, because it had lessened their dependence on external
supplies.

So far our attention has been directed mainly to the quantity
of the exports of a country: but in some respects their quality
is of even greater significance for her future. The test of national
leadership is the doing of things which others, with similar economic

III, II, 4. problems, will be doing later on, but are not yet able to do: and a good measure of a country's leadership is supplied by the character of the manufactures and other goods which she exports, and of those which she imports.

As a rule, the exports of a country consist of things which she can produce with greater ease, than the countries to which she sends them can: but this rule is not universal. Obviously a gardener may "export" products or deliver services to a highly capable botanist, who happens to be stronger than he is in body as well as in mind. The faculties of him who receives or "imports" the services find full scope in studies, which are of higher value, partly because they are scarcer, than mere expert manual work. Similarly, the Channel Islands buy much grain, part of which is produced on soil less suitable for it than their own: for their land has exceptional facilities for growing early vegetables, fruit and flowers, which sell at high prices. To speak more generally, it is likely to be to the advantage of a particular locality, whether a village or a country, to devote as much as possible of her energies to producing things as to which she has the greatest relative advantage, while she imports others. This is true, even if she is on the whole as strong as those who trade with her; or is either superior to them, or inferior to them, in every industry. In short, places whose advantages are distributed in unequal proportions among different industries, may carry on a trade that is profitable to both, even though one of them is the stronger all round.

It may be observed that *other things being equal* a small country will have less varied industries, and therefore will need to import more in proportion to her population, than a large one will. Also, though this is a minor point, her frontiers are likely to be long relatively to her area. But other things are seldom equal. A large country often has superior advantages for the development of great concentrations of highly specialized industries, and she has the better chance of obtaining exceptional genius capable of developing new openings that may occur[1].

---

[1] If two countries are of similar shape and one has four times as large an area, her frontier will be only twice as long: if her area is nine times as large, her frontier will be only three times as long.

5. No measure can be obtained of changes in the aggregate III, II, 5.
volume—as distinguished from the aggregate value—of a
country's imports or exports.

It is of course possible to measure the tonnage of a country's
imports or exports, a ton of coals being reckoned as equivalent
of a ton of linen: but such reckonings are of no service, except in
connection with statistics of the volume of traffic by land or water:
and they are not of much service even in that use. Therefore
aggregates of imports or exports must generally be expressed in
terms of money value. But the general level of prices is liable to
gradual changes in consequence of varying yields of gold mines,
and other causes: and it is liable to sharp, quick changes in consequence of fluctuations of general credit, etc.: and a remedy is
needed for the disturbing effects which these changes exert on the
measurement of the volume of trade. For this purpose it is usual
to take the prices of a single year as standard; to reckon, for
instance, the value of each ton of coal in each year as the price
for the standard year, and to do the same with each yard of cloth,
each gallon of oil, and so on. The aggregate of the values thus
obtained represents roughly the aggregate of those changes in the
trade, during the period under view, which are independent of
changes in prices[1].

On this plan, there is some tendency to exaggerate the importance
of those steel and other goods, whether imports or exports, in the
production of which great improvements have been made recently;
or of which very large rich sources of supply have been recently
opened up. It under-rates the relative importance of those which,
like coal and dairy produce, are at least as difficult to procure
now as they were long ago; and even of plain textile goods, and
others, which are not very much easier to procure. If these
statistics show that the quantity of a country's imports is on the

---

[1] This method of measuring quantities, by reducing the actual prices of each
year to those of a standard year and then adding up the entries, was introduced in
British official statistics, under the control of the late Sir R. Giffen; see [Cd. 5386]
of 1888. Many articles are entered in the detailed returns by value only and not
by quantity: but the change in their total value which would have resulted, if
priced as at the basal level, is guessed by "assimilating them to some sufficiently
allied group" for which total value and quantity are known.

The crude "official" statistics of British trade during the eighteenth and part
of the nineteenth century ignored this difficulty.

III, II, 6. whole increasing much faster than their value, while the quantity of her exports is not, then there is reason for thinking that her foreign trade is conferring increasing benefits on her. But this *primâ facie* impression must be checked by inquiring firstly, whether her exports are more difficult to produce than they were; and, secondly, whether recent improvements in the production of her imports have been such that she could make them for herself with less difficulty than before[1].

6. *Statistics representing value per head, and percentage changes in that value, are generally the best adapted for studies of international trade in relation to the internal economy of a country. But total values, and percentage changes in them, are the more important in relation to world economics and world politics. Percentages of increase are specially misleading, when a powerful country is cultivating a trade which she had previously neglected.*

We may next consider the chief purposes for which statistical tables dealing with absolute and relative amounts are severally the more serviceable. Speaking generally, when we want to study the internal conditions of any country, or to compare the internal conditions of several, the most appropriate statistics are those which represent trade, income, taxes, etc., at so much per head. If we want to infer from the past some augury as to the future, we must subdivide further: we must consider not only the actual growth, or shrinkage, of each quantity per head, but also the *rate of growth*; that is, we must show the percentage of each total quantity per head, which corresponds to its increase in a year (or any other period). But these percentages must never be studied alone. For differences in quantity almost always bring with them differences in quality: and, unless we know the quality, we cannot tell the true significance of an increase of, say, 10 per cent. in it. Again, an increase of 10 per cent. in the food allowance of an

---

[1] It was shown by Prof. Bowley (*Economic Journal*, 1903, p. 632), when comparing British and German trade, 1881–1900, that the prices of imports (in bond) had fallen in both countries fast and in about the like proportion: but the prices of Germany's exports had fallen more slowly and those of England's exports more slowly still; so that, so far as mere prices were concerned (without taking account of changes in real difficulty of production), Germany had obtained her imports about one-tenth cheaper at the end of the twenty years than at the beginning, while England obtained hers one-fifth cheaper.

under-fed population implies a great change in their physical, III, II, 6. mental and moral vitality; but it has no such significance with regard to a well-fed population. Increases of 10 per cent. in the commercial class of Russia and England would signify very different changes[1].

A fourfold increase of the industrial population and trade of a new suburb of a large city is of less significance from every point of view than an increase of one quarter of the population of the whole city: and a doubling of the trade of New Zealand has less significance than an increase by one half of that of Russia. A relatively small check to commercial activity in one of the leading industrial nations is of greater consequence than a panic in a small state; and so on.

Again, suppose that a great industrial country develops direct steamship communication with some large markets, to which her merchants send well-chosen goods; her exports thither may then increase many times as fast, measured in percentages, as those of another country which has cultivated the trade longer; while yet their actual increase is perhaps but a quarter as large as that of the exports of her older rival. In that case it is probable that she has not devoted to the trade nearly as much energy and resource as her rival; for she has dealt with smaller difficulties. It is of course possible that she may ultimately overtake her rival: but the percentages of growth do not by themselves give good reason for believing that she will. And if the percentages are given alone, without the totals, no indication is afforded that the much greater difficulties, which lie before her, are probably much greater than those which she has yet overcome.

Aggregates and percentages must then be studied together, and not separately. Practice will enable anyone, while reading down columns of aggregate values for successive years, to interpolate as he goes fairly accurate estimates of percentage changes and *vice versâ*.

---

[1] This class of consideration suggests that the uses of logarithmic diagrams, and similar devices for concentrating attention on changes in *percentages* of economic quantities, have but narrow uses.

CHAPTER III

BRITAIN'S EXTERNAL TRADE[1]

1. *England's external trade in the seventeenth and eighteenth centuries.*

The history of England's trade has been described in two sets of simple annals: one by Anderson, published in 1787, and the other by Macpherson, published in 1805. Both made large use of the official records of trade which date from 1698[2]. But the modern history of Britain's external trade may be taken to begin about a century later, when her great American colonies broke away from her. For about that time massive production established its claim to dominate manufacture: and the Independence of the United States of America gave a great impetus to the inclination of her people towards that massive production, to which their genius is specially inclined. Their demands for mechanical appliances covered so large a portion of the whole field of industry, and were so powerful, that Britain's trade must have become many times greater than it actually did, had its course been free: but it was still shackled by relics of mediaeval regulation.

Let us look at her chief rivals. France was hindered by a protective policy of a very obstructive and unscientific character, which was partly responsible for her supineness in the construction of railways: and, as has happened again since then, those of her industries prospered most which lent upon protection least. The industries of Belgium were nearly as advanced as those of Britain; and therefore she was ready to buy many British products for which there was little use elsewhere. Switzerland and Saxony also turned their rather narrow resources to good account. Germany was hampered by poverty, by internal barriers, and by the dis-

[1] Appendix F is attached to this chapter.
[2] Both Anderson and Macpherson begin with some speculations as to prehistoric times and take the whole world as their field in a few all embracing sketches of early history. But when they settle down to serious work, they pay little attention to any history save that of England, and later on of the United Kingdom. Among later histories reference may be made to those of Ashley, Cunningham and Levi.

taste of her ruling classes for industry. The tariff policy of her several States was indeed not very narrow: and the Zollverein gave her so much internal freedom and stability as to compensate for the restrictions imposed on trade external to the Zollverein[1].

2. *Changes in the volume of Britain's external trade since 1850.*

The liberation of Britain's energies from obstructive regulations at home and abroad, which came about the middle of last century, added much to her productive force: it increased the amount of goods which she could get in exchange for each bale of her own and diminished the charges incurred in the double transport. Trade went quicker: intercourse, which used to occupy many months, could now be put through in a few weeks by aid of steam, telegraph and post. The last cumbrous relics of mediaeval usury laws disappeared in 1854; and capital was further prompted to large and bold ventures (conducted sometimes with even too feverish energy) by the concession of Limited Liability to Joint Stock Companies, which was begun in 1855 and completed in 1862.

Whatever the task to which Britain then turned, she found in it fresh opportunities, in which she met but little effective competition. New channels of commerce were constantly opened out,

---

[1] Belgium had a low tariff; and like Britain she seized the opportunity which the new age gave her to develop her rich resources in coal and iron. Her navigation of the Scheldt was obstructed after her separation from Holland in 1830; and this set her on making two railways, connecting her ports with the French and the German frontiers, and crossing one another at Malines, which were worked with greater vigour than any others on the Continent.

Macgregor's *Commercial Statistics* (more aptly described on its title page as a *Digest of the productive resources of all nations*), 1847, shows Belgium and the United States as far ahead of all other countries, other than Britain, as regards the variety and elasticity of their energies. Here, and in his evidence before the Committee on Import Duties, 1840, he lays great stress on Belgium's freedom from restrictive taxation; though he himself was not ready for a complete abolition of the British corn laws, and advocated a fixed duty of eight shillings on the quarter.

Symons' *Arts and Artisans at home and abroad*, 1833, gives a short, but vivid, account of the position. He, however, regards tariffs as the almost exclusive causes of some national differences, which now seem to have had their chief roots in far deeper soil. But his well-informed inductive argument, to the effect that protective tariffs as then worked in Europe did not make for national prosperity, must count for much in any historical treatment of the problems of trade policy.

III, III, 2. along which she could sell her own goods on more profitable terms than before; and along which she could bring back things to meet her wants more easily, safely and cheaply than before. The war with Russia passed quickly: much of the commerce between the two countries had indeed been continued quietly during the war by a not very roundabout route through Prussia. That and the Indian Mutiny being past, she found her chief potential rivals occupied in wars, which made them eager to buy, almost regardless of price, just those products which she could most easily produce. So the quantity of her exports, and the power which they gave her of importing such things as she needed, increased faster still. We may take the statistics broadly for the present: some difficulties in their interpretation are considered in Appendix F.

British net imports (that is, imports after deducting *palpable* re-exports) appear at £m133 in 1854, the first year in which Real values were recorded; in 1873 they were £m315: the rise had been nearly continuous; such small unevennesses as showed themselves being largely due to fluctuations of the prices of harvest products, especially grain and cotton; to war; and to fluctuations of credit. But a great part of this rise had been due to an inflation of prices caused by the new supplies of gold; and by attempts, which proved somewhat premature, to introduce Anglo-Saxon methods of economizing currency on the Continent.

After 1873 the reversal of some of these influences caused prices to fall; and therefore, though the aggregate volume of imports continued to rise rapidly, their money value oscillated about the 1873 level for fifteen years, after which it began to move upwards almost steadily till it reached a maximum of £m553 in 1907, followed by a decline and a subsequent rise to £m693 in 1913 and to £m1321 in 1920. The value of British Special exports moved more irregularly. It rose indeed fast and almost steadily from £m51 in 1840 to £m256 in 1873. But then it fell, partly in consequence of the fall in prices just mentioned; and it only once (in 1890) reached that level again till 1900; when it rose rapidly and reached a maximum of £m426 in 1907; followed first by a decline, and later by a rise to £m525 in 1913 and to £m827 in 1920[1].

[1] The European war which began in 1914 set up a series of disturbances in the courses of trade, which have not ceased at the time of writing: and the interpretation of international trade statistics during this period belongs almost as much to the military expert as to the economist. The dominant facts are that

3. *Changes in the character of Britain's export trade since* III, III, 3.
1800.

The shadow of the Napoleonic wars spread over the years that
followed the battles of Leipzig and Waterloo. But Britain was
active: and in 1830 she had more railways than all the rest of the
world. In 1840 both the Continent of Europe and the United
States had passed her. In 1860 each of them had three times as
many miles as she: and now the Continent of Europe has about
nine times, and the United States more than ten times as many
as she has. Of course her railways have a larger percentage of
double, treble and quadruple tracks than those of any other large
country: but, allowance being made for that, it remains clear that
her own resources, however intensely worked, could not have held
for long the dominant position, which had resulted from her
enterprise, and the ravages of the Continental wars. The wars came
to an end for the time in 1815: and it is not matter for wonder
that enlightened men about 1840, when urging on the British
Parliament and nation a more liberal handling of foreign commercial relations, laid stress on the proved futility of restriction.
It is impossible, they urged, for Britain to keep other countries
in leading-strings: manufactures are growing up in all directions
around her: her prohibitions of the exportation of machinery are
evaded; and the more she refuses to take from them the wheat
and other things which they are able to supply to her, the more
will they yearn for manufactures that will make them independent
of her: it may be that by restrictive taxes and regulations she
delays their progress for a while: but she thereby puts an artificial
premium on their efforts to rival her.

Early in the nineteenth century Continental weavers were
dependent on British spinners for all cotton yarns except the
coarsest (those of less than two shanks to the pound): but ere
long it was lamented that they had got up to forties, and in
Switzerland even to seventies[1]. These movements have continued

during the war Britain lent 568 million pounds to Russia, 508 to France, 467 to
Italy, and smaller sums to other countries, making 1740 millions in all, and that
she herself borrowed 842 million pounds from America. These and other relevant
facts are noted in *The economic consequences of the peace*, by J. M. Keynes, C.B.,
1919.

[1] *Report of Committee on Manufactures*, 1833, Q. 5368. American competition
was at that time much feared; partly because the advantage which it had in
the cost of carriage of raw cotton was a little more important than now; partly

III, III, 3. without ceasing. Almost all Britain's exports of cotton yarn and goods to the Continent are now of very fine quality: one cause of this is that her coarser goods now meet with severe competition in many markets and are excluded from some by heavy duties; while her finer products, having something of a monopoly value can force their way over tariff walls; and another cause is that the demand for the more elegant and more tasteful cotton fabrics continually increases.

In 1820 four-fifths of Britain's exports of cotton products went to Europe and North America; and, though she exported a good deal to Asia, she brought back an almost equal value of cotton stuffs finer than that she could herself make: but the position is now almost inverted. Europe now buys her fine yarns and fancy stuffs. Before the war their value per pound was about twice as high as that of purchases of yarns by those countries in Asia, Africa and South America which buy the greater part of her exports of calico; India now takes the first place among these.

In 1840 Britain was still so much ahead of other countries in many large branches of industry that if they had been rich, and transport had been cheap and unimpeded, she might have found a highly profitable market for more than ten times her actual exports of manufactures; provided at least that she could have increased her supply of plant and of skilled workers fast enough.

It is true that Saxon hosiery, Silesian linens, French silks, and some other manufactures held their own against British competition; and that the iron works, founded by the Englishman Cockerill in Belgium, were larger than any in Britain and were excellently equipped. But capital and skilled labour were scarce: Britain had not nearly enough for her own needs; and yet almost every enterprise on new lines was helped by British capital, and managed by British foremen superintending British machines.

Passing to woollen (and worsted) exports, we find a history similar in fundamentals, but differing much in details. For primitive appliances have never been at as great a disadvantage in common wool fabrics as in cotton: and even a very backward

because some great improvements in machinery had been made in America, and not immediately adopted in England; and partly because, as the cotton industry was almost alone in offering occupation to American women, their labour could be had on relatively low terms.

industrial district can work up its own wool into substantial stuffs, III, III, 3.
that have a certain rude charm of their own. Consequently
British exports of woollen stuffs have never been nearly so large
a part of the world's output of similar goods as her exports of
cotton products. She has, however, long led the fashions for the
world, and she seems to be supreme in production in regard to
the best cloths for men; though somewhat backward in regard
to the fashions and stuffs of women's dress. Her best cloths leap
even over the very high barriers of the American tariff.

Many of the finest and most expensive products of French woollen
and worsted looms are marketed in England; together with flimsy
worsted tissues, which attain excellent effects for the time by the
use of inexpensive materials combined with judgment, and with,
of course, a prophetic knowledge of the fashions which England
is about to import together with the tissues from France. France
seems to be the only country from whom Britain buys any considerable quantity of goods of as high quality and price as those
which she sells in return.

It is noteworthy that Britain's trade statistics show an extra-
ordinary increase in the exports of clothing just after 1846. For
a great rush of British emigrants to new countries was caused
by the potato famine, the gold fever, and as after effects of the
excitements which collapsed in 1848: the emigrants all wanted,
and many of them could afford to pay well for, clothing from home.
This was the beginning of large exportations of Britain's ready-
made clothing, almost exclusively to her Colonies. A great part
of her Colonial trade has always consisted of articles of food,
clothing, etc., which her sons and daughters preferred to have after
the fashion of the old home: and nearly the same may be said of
her exports for the personal consumption of British residents in
India. This suggests one cause of the commonly observed fact that
"trade follows the flag."

Among other influences, tending in the same direction, are her
setting up frequent sailings, and, in the course of time, regular
mail services with her colonies. Also she lends them capital; and
her merchants supply their shopkeepers, etc., with goods on credit.
Again, those in charge of her railways and other undertakings can
buy plant, etc., from British producers with more certainty and
ease than from any other source. These causes are heightened by

III, III, 3.] sentiments, of which the common flag is the symbol. But for the most part they are not dependent on the flag. A great trade has sprung up between Argentina and Italy, because there are many Italians in Argentina, though the two countries are not under the same flag.

The influence of custom and sentiments is, however, apt to be weakened by the lapse of time. Those who have a direct memory of a British home are now a rather small part of the whole population in nearly every British Dependency, and, of course, the problems of agriculture and mining and in a less degree of many other industries, which call for solution in new countries, have more in common with those of the United States than they have where land is so scarce relatively to population and capital as in Britain.

Thus the percentage of the inhabitants of Canada, Australia and other British Colonies who are personally intimate with Britain, has diminished: that of Germans, Americans and others who are less intimate with her than with their own homes has increased, though it is still relatively small. She still supplies her colonies with by far the greater part of the capital which they need; and her "invisible" exports of services to them are considerable. But Germany and other countries now run excellent lines of steamers to them, which, though rather thin, carry well chosen specialities; while the United States has a geographical advantage, amounting to supremacy, in the trade with the north-west of the Canadian Dominion. Consequently there has been some slight decline in the percentage of the trade of Britain's colonies, which is carried on with herself.

In the middle of last century Britain was indeed more mature industrially than other countries; and therefore her imports consisted of food and raw materials, which her own soil and climate did not readily supply, together with a few manufactures and appliances for production, which other countries yielded of better make or cheaper than her own. One or other of them might outrun her for a while in some new industry or in some improved machinery and process for an old one: but, if she chose, she always could be quick on their heels, because she already possessed the capital and the chief elements in the skill and aptitude needed for the work. In recent years, on the other hand, the chief western countries have been so nearly in the same industrial phase that each buys from the other at short notice improved machinery and half products of many kinds.

But backward countries on the other hand seldom have much demand for such things. They may be ready to buy calico, when spinning machinery is useless to them; and when they are not eager for machine spun yarn. They import bicycles before they import component parts of bicycles, and long before they import automatic turret lathes to make the hubs of cycle wheels: and so on. The demands for British goods therefore, which come from a backward country, are constantly changing their shapes as that country makes her way upwards. Most of these changes proceed on the same lines, but there are many varieties in detail. In fact, the same country may be shifting her demand from finished to half-finished British goods in some branches of production; while in others she is shifting it from half-finished ordinary goods to completely finished goods of exceptionally fine quality.

A "new" country (that is, one which is being rapidly developed by immigrants from an advanced country) may be backward in all but a few industries, while leading in those for which she is specially suited. A new mining district—the Transvaal or Western Australia—may be quicker than almost any industrial centre of the western world in adopting electrical appliances for saving labour in transport and milling; and yet it may have no use for spinning or weaving machinery, and not very much use for simple cloth, etc.: it may prefer to import the greater part of its clothing ready made. As numbers increase, strata of population will begin to put in an appearance, who are prepared to do the ordinary work of manufacture for a moderate remuneration: they generally develop first those manufacturing industries in which alertness and vigour count for much, and highly specialized skill is not greatly needed; in which the capital outlay per head is not exceptionally large; and in which the physical resources of the country will be most helpful. The changes in their selections of British half manufactures and finished manufactures will show as many cross currents as those of a backward country. The cross currents will be different in character, because the backward country will need to avoid tasks that involve great strain; and the new country will need to avoid those which do not afford a rich return to high

III, III, 4. applications of energy. But in the one case, as in the other, the cross currents will render untrustworthy any simple inferences from crude aggregate statistics.

4. *Britain's foreign trade is somewhat smaller and less important than it appears; inasmuch as it includes many latent re-exports, and a considerable oscillatory or return trade of similar commodities travelling in opposite directions on the same route.*

The opening of the Suez Canal in 1869 tended to lessen Britain's entrepôt trade in Oriental goods. Her power of equipping rapidly vessels suitable for it, combined with her financial and commerical prestige and the foreign connections of her central markets, have enabled her to hold her own fairly well. Time, however, has been on the side of a direct trade to all places which had good railway communication with the chief ports on the Mediterranean: and the rapid extension of Continental railways, while increasing Britain's facilities for trade with the centre of Europe, has increased even more the facilities for trade with other Continents *via* Marseilles, Genoa, Trieste, Havre, Antwerp, Hamburg, etc. Consequently dealings in wool and other raw material, for which London was once the world's market, have tended inevitably to be diffused over many markets. But the richness and variety of British demand for the finer products; the unrivalled specialization, promptitude, and directness of action of her merchants and brokers; the ease and elasticity of her banking system; and the consequent preference for a bill on London over a bill on any other place, have tended to strengthen the re-export trade of London.

Meanwhile, there has been a rapid increase of Britain's exports of manufactures, more or less finished, which are largely made of imported material. The main reason for this is that her area is small, and her population is so large and so rich that there is scarcely any important raw material of which she can supply enough for her own needs: therefore only a small part of her Special exports are true exports of her own produce to their full extent. Some of her iron and steel exports are indeed made from her own ores by use of her own coal; and they are truly and wholly hers. But a great part of the value of her exports of calico is derived from the raw cotton which she has imported: and her III, III, 4. exports of woollen goods contain so much imported material that we may say that she has no true net exports of wool, as distinguished from the work spent on wool by manufacturers and others. Similarly, though a little wheat and wheaten biscuits are included among the Special exports of her own produce, it may be said that she has no true net export of wheat. It appears, indeed, that her net exports of native material contain nothing important except coal, salt, fish, glass and earthenware[1].

The character of Britain's re-exports is, of course, much influenced by her position on the highway between Europe and other Continents; and by her intimate relations with Australia, South Africa and other gold producing countries. She re-exports on the balance a great quantity of gold, which goes chiefly to the Continent of Europe; and a great quantity of silver from America, which goes chiefly to India: and, as gold and silver are not included in the ordinary statistics of her imports and exports, she appears to be exporting a good deal less to the Continent and to India than she really does. Conversely she appears to import less from Australia and South Africa and America than she really does.

Again, her re-exports of raw material, both in its original form, and latent in her own manufactures, have come to her chiefly from other Continents, and go in a great measure eastwards to Europe. And, on the other hand, the things which she receives in a more or less manufactured state, and which she re-exports with or without the expenditure of some additional labour on them, come chiefly from the Continent of Europe, and go chiefly to more distant Continents. These facts are vital to any effective comparison of the trade, which she carries on with different countries.

[1] It is true that the statistics of other European countries contain considerable entries of raw material imported from Britain: but this is explained by their counting as imported from Britain, a great part and in some cases the whole of the raw material which she has imported and re-exports to them. Most of this is entered in her official statistics as "re-exports": though any of it that gets at all far from her docks is apt to be classed as a Special export. Under that head are entered some beef, milk, cotton seed and other foreign oils, sugar, timber, flax, silk, cotton and other seeds, raw hides, furs, and other things of which her own production, if any, is small relatively to her consumption. British statistics are, however, less inaccurate than those of most other European countries in this respect; partly because nearly all her re-export trade is handled in seaports.

She carries on much "cross trade": the exportation of goods that are very nearly alike in opposite directions on the same line of travel. Such trade is often due to market fluctuations and other accidents: an instance of this is found in the constant exports of the precious metals from every western country to others which are nearer the mines than she is; but whose money market happens to demand gold for a time. Again, if the supply of a product has risen relatively to the demand in one country, and especially in the neighbourhood of a convenient port, it is often exported, in order that it may be sold at less than its normal price without injuring the market in which its owners are specially interested: and it is likely to pass on its way some similar commodity which is going from its own home to be slaughtered in like manner; or perhaps sent under a contract of some standing. But, independently of such irregularities in the relations of supply and demand, there is a constant oscillatory flow of things that differ a little in quality or suitability for special purposes. Sometimes the differences which cause such apparent oscillations of traffic are so slight, as to be obvious only to experts: a considerable part of Britain's trade with her industrial neighbours is of this kind, especially in regard to woollens, silks and metals.

Britain is a more fastidious buyer than almost any other country: a given quantity of meat or butter, or fruit, or tobacco, or cotton or wine which appears in her imports is likely to be worth more than similar quantities which appear in the import lists of most other countries. And again her exports are, speaking generally, becoming finer in quality. Thus a million pounds of cotton yarn, or even a million yards of calico, appearing in her export list, are likely to represent a higher real value than similar entries in her own lists twenty years ago, or in the lists of most other countries now. And a similar distortion arises from the vagueness of the terms manufacture, or "mainly manufactured." But of course the quantity of her exports is swollen by her large exports of coal, the volume and weight of which are large relatively to their value.

Britain's exports of "articles wholly or mainly manufactured" include some bulky raw materials and other things, on which relatively little labour has been spent, such as ingots of tin and other metals, leather, thrown silk, etc. But, with no considerable exception, these, together with her re-exports of the same things, III, III, 4, are less than the imports of similar things, which are entered among her imports as "wholly or mainly manufactured." That is to say her net exports of the cruder manufactures are a negative quantity. Yarns are not included here, because, as has already been remarked, the tasks of spinning those fine cotton yarns and combing those fine and even woollen tops which she alone exports in large quantity, are more difficult than ordinary weaving.

If both imports and exports of manufactures were minutely classified according to quality, the net export of any one quality could be deduced by simple subtraction of the corresponding import. But, as things are, no useful meaning can be attached to the phrase—Britain's net exports of manufactures: for the greater part of her imports of so-called manufactures are of low quality; and the greater part of her exports, which are similarly classed, are of high quality.

Britain's "invisible" exports of shipping services may seem to be of a different order from her exports of material commodities. The difference is in truth merely superficial. And, if it were worth while, stress might be laid on the facts that ships' stores and bunker coal are clearly exports of material commodities: that if a British ship wears herself out in the carrying trade between, say, Australasia and the western coast of the Pacific, she is a material commodity, exported for the benefit of other countries, and in effect is gradually sold to them; and lastly, that the same is true in regard to the services of a British ship trading between British and foreign ports, in so far as the benefits of her work accrue to foreigners[1].

---

[1] The *Economist* index number for general prices showed a maximum of 325 in March 1920 starting from the basis of 100 in July 1914. In January 1922 (the latest date for which figures are available) it had fallen to 167.

CHAPTER IV

THE BALANCE OF IMPORTS AND EXPORTS

1. *The phrase "a favourable" balance of trade.*

This chapter is required for completeness. But it is concerned only with matters that are familiar to many business men: its Section headings may suffice to indicate to them the part which it is designed to play in the present Book.

In discussions of international trade, a "nation" is to be regarded as consisting of the inhabitants of a country which has definite frontiers. Some taxes are generally levied on goods passing over these frontiers and, for this and other reasons, the traffic over them is watched by "Customs" officers—that is, by the successors of those who used to collect the "customary" tolls which every Government collected at the frontiers of its special dominion.

In earlier times men's minds were much occupied with the desire to retain in their country as large a stock of the precious metals as they conveniently could. This desire, as has already been indicated, arose in part from a mistaken notion that the precious metals constitute wealth in a special use of the term: but it had some solid foundation in the fact that gold and silver alone afforded ready command over the means of supporting military forces in some of the emergencies of a great war. If a country was buying from abroad things of greater value, in terms of the precious metals, than those which she was selling abroad, she was taking a step towards a condition when "the balance of trade" would be against her: and, in case of war, she might find it difficult to support armies abroad, even if her own people were full of patriotic ardour. Of course war was not then regarded as a national concern, in the same full sense as it is now. In some cases it was waged in the special interests of a dynasty, or a ruling class, rather than of the nation as a whole; and then payment in silver (or, in rare cases, in gold) would lead many a shrewd dealer into the courses desired by the King or the ruling classes.

But the unscrupulous genius of Napoleon taught Englishmen and others to recognize the superiority of the interests of the nation as a whole over those of particular sections of the nation: and III, IV, 2. during the nineteenth century national trade has attained a high place among the interests of every nation of the Western World.

The trade of a country is taken to consist of her exports of goods on the one side and her imports of goods on the other: and the aggregate values of these two groups tend to be equal. But this tendency is apt to be in some measure disturbed by the exportation of capital, and the importation of the equivalent of the interest (or, in some cases, the profits) derived from the use of the capital abroad. And, further, the goods consumed in country A by a person who derives his means from country B, are in effect exports from B to A: but they are not represented, unless incidentally, in the list of B's exports or of A's imports.

There is, moreover, no means of knowing how much of the expenditure of (say) a Belgian domiciled in France is drawn from his property in Belgium, and how much from his work and property in France. For our present purposes it is best to raise no question as to the ultimate destination of the imports of France into Belgium; but to consider only their aggregates.

2. *A country's recorded imports tend to exceed her recorded exports, other things being equal, by all the expenses incurred at home in carrying goods between herself and any foreign country, or between two foreign countries; and in carrying foreign passengers: and also by all the net profits of her ship-owners, merchants, commission agents and bankers, in so far as they arise out of her foreign trade and are brought home.*

In the early Middle Ages silver and gold were regarded as the measure, and even sometimes as the substance, of national prosperity: and penalties were imposed on any private person who exported them. But the Mercantilists relaxed this rule: they allowed any trader to export treasure, if it could be shown that re-exports of part of his imports would lead to the return of at least an equivalent amount of treasure. An equally important, though less prominent, advance was made by their insistence that commerce is an industry and that "The Labor of Seamen and the Freight of Ships is always of the nature of an Exported Com-

III, IV, 2. modity, the over-plus whereof, above what is imported, brings back Money, etc.[1]"

Let us work out this hint. If a farmer undertakes to supply straw to a fly proprietor in return for manure, doing all the carting himself, he will perhaps send straw that is worth £10 in the town but only £6 on the farm and take back manure that is worth £10 in the town but £14 on the farm. If the carriage necessitates forty journeys, each of which may be valued at 4s., the bargain will be a fair one. But while the fly proprietor's *visible* imports and exports will be of equal value, viz. £10 each; the *visible* exports of the farm will be worth only £6 on the farm and its imports worth £14. The farmer will really have given out eight pounds worth of services in carting. In another year it may be arranged that all the carting shall be done by the fly proprietor, and that the farmer shall deliver to him on the farm, besides the straw, an amount of hay which is worth £8 on the farm, and perhaps £11 in the town. The fly proprietor's imports will now be worth £21 in the town and his visible exports only £10; but in addition he will have given out £11 of cartage. All the farmer's imports and exports will be visible, and therefore they will be equal in value; in fact each of them will be worth £14 on the farm. If part of the carting is done by the fly proprietor, and part by the farmer, a smaller amount of hay will redress the balance.

As it is with the commerce between individuals, so it is with the commerce between any groups of individuals, as for instance between two towns, or a town and the neighbouring agricultural districts. But statistics are available only for the traffic across the frontiers of nations.

Suppose then an Englishman, *i.e.* a man who makes that country the basis of his operations, to send goods in his own ship to Brazil and sell them there; to invest the proceeds in Brazilian goods; to bring those goods home in his ship; and finally to sell them

---

[1] This phrase comes from Petty, who had advanced somewhat beyond the Mercantilists: but its substance is implied in Mun's central argument that "remote trades must be most gainful to the Commonwealth," because the services rendered by English ships in them are of the nature of exports, and tend to bring back treasure ultimately. Something is said as to the relations of the Mercantilists to their predecessors and their successors in *Industry and Trade,* Book I, Chap. III and Appendices C–G.

at home on such terms as give him the normal profits of his trade: III, IV, 2.
his imports will exceed his exports in value by his full expenses
and profits as a trader and merchant. And the result will be the
same, if he pays an Englishman to carry part of his cargoes for
him: he will merely use some part of the excess value of his imports
over his exports in paying that Englishman for the work.

But the result will be different if part of the merchant's work
is done by a foreigner, that is, a person domiciled in another
country. If, for instance, his return cargo is heavy, and he employs
a Norwegian shipper to bring back part of it, he will have to
surrender to the Norwegian some part of his command over
Brazilian goods, or rather over the price of them in England. That
will give the Norwegian the power of drawing out goods from
England without sending any to her in return; and thus it will
diminish the excess of Britain's imports over her exports by the
cost of that part of the carriage which was undertaken by the
Norwegian.

Again, the officers and men of the ship are likely to spend some
money in Brazil, on buying ship's stores and other goods, and on
the services of agents and porters, and so on. The means for their
outlay will be provided directly or indirectly out of the proceeds
of the sale of the ship's cargo in Brazil. This will either diminish
the amount of Brazilian goods which the ship can command for
the homeward voyage, or give Brazil the power of drawing some
additional goods from England without importing anything in
exchange for them.

That is to say, the merchant has the power of bringing back
Brazilian goods, which when sold in Britain will exceed his exports
in value by the full costs of the double voyage. But he may elect
to have some of those goods in the form of ship's stores bought
in Brazil, which will be consumed on the voyage and therefore
will not appear as imports; and a further part of his power is
handed over to his crew, who may spend some of it on local
services, or on goods which also do not appear among British
imports. Accordingly, that excess of Britain's imports over her
exports, which results from the double voyage in question, will
be diminished by the total outlay on behalf of the ship thus
incurred in Brazil.

This result seems to point to the conclusion that a country's

III, IV, 2. nominal imports tend to exceed her nominal exports by all those expenses which are incurred at home on account of her foreign trade, together with the profits of the trade so far as they accrue to her own people.

But no account has yet been taken of the fact that the ship is likely to carry passengers as well as cargo. Such of the passengers, as are foreign, must remit the equivalent of their fares: and the country's imports will be swollen relatively to her exports by the value of those fares; any outlay of the ship on their behalf in foreign ports being of course deducted. But, in so far as the passengers draw their resources from the country itself, the payment of their fares is a mere transference within the country; and therefore it does not affect the balance of imports and exports. Thus, the nominal addition to a country's imports relatively to her exports, due to her shipping industry, is equal to the gross earnings of that industry for goods and passengers, other than those domiciled in her. Deductions must however be made for any outlays on behalf of the shipping industry abroad, and for any part of the profits of the industry which accrues to persons resident abroad[1].

Again, if a merchant or anyone else, who had been reared in one country (A), spent the greater part of his life in another (B), he would perhaps bring home to A some of his savings in the form of the precious metals. The chief benefit of the expense, which had been devoted in A to his early nurture and education, would have accrued to B; and B would probably have gained more from his ability and energy than the equivalent of the wealth which he took away with him; whether that was in the form of precious metals or not. This consideration has some bearing on the present relations between England and India. England exports to India a good many able young men: they do not enter in India's

---

[1] Sir R. Giffen estimated some years ago the charges of the British shipping and merchant services, which must be returned with profits in order to maintain that influx of capital and energy into the trade. He concluded that a sum of from £m100 to £m125, needed to appear in Britain's visible excess of imports over exports, one year with another, in order to defray these charges. Since he wrote, improvements in shipbuilding have greatly lowered the cost of working a ship of given carrying power: but the recent war, followed by increased costs of material and labour, worked strongly in the opposite direction. Several years must elapse before a fairly confident estimate of the future of such charges can be made.

list of imports; but it is claimed that they render to her services whose value exceeds that of her total payments to them. They return to England (if they come back at all) after their best strength has been spent: they are unreckoned exports from England. But that part of their incomes, which they have saved, is likely to come sooner or later in the form of material goods which enter into her imports. On the other hand, India counts these material goods among her exports to England: but of course she makes no entry among her imports for the expensive young men who have been sent to her.

3. *When capital is invested in a country by foreigners, or credit is extended to her from abroad in any other form, then there may be a temporary increase of imports into that country relatively to her exports. This is often more than compensated in the long run by an excess of her exports; for those, who export capital, draw interest or profits on it, and perhaps ultimately bring the capital itself back to their own country.*

The Mercantilists were not impelled by the circumstances of their time to pay much attention to the two groups of invisible imports and exports—those due to international credit and to absenteeism—as they did to the services of commerce and shipping. But, the financial and commercial troubles of the great French war made English statesmen and economists examine the balance of trade with a care and thoroughness never before attempted: and they found that some important matters had been overlooked. This work was continued for another generation; and but little ground of first-rate importance was left to be covered by their successors[1].

A considerable part of international credit is made up of small items, such as the selling of goods on long credit to foreign merchants and shopkeepers, or the sending out goods to be held till sold by a general commission-agent, or a branch of the home firm. But the greater part of it arises out of massive transactions; such as the issue of large loans in the London market on behalf of foreign or colonial governments or private railway and other trading

---

[1] See in particular pp. 28–9 of the epoch-making Report of the "Bullion Committee" of 1810; which inquired into "The cause of the high price of bullion," and into "The state of the circulating medium and of the exchanges between Great Britain and foreign parts."

III, IV, 3. companies. Whether the loans be large or small, documents are likely to be transmitted to the lending nation acknowledging the loans: and receipts for payment of interest, and ultimately of capital value, are likely in due course to be transmitted in the opposite direction. If it were possible to enter these documents in the tables of imports, the balance between imports and exports would not be disturbed either by the loans or by their settlement; but this cannot be done. In short, when a country lends abroad £1,000,000 in any form, she gives foreigners the power of taking from her £1,000,000 of goods; while she herself does not, for the time being get any goods in return: on the other hand, the interest on these loans, and perhaps the capital itself, ultimately are expected to be returned home; and when paid, they increase England's imports relatively to her exports.

This contrast between deferred and immediate claims is of great importance in connection with the Foreign Exchanges. As Goschen well said: "when the relative indebtedness and the balance of trade between the two countries is spoken of, the permanent debts of one country to another do not enter into consideration— at least not till the term of payment has arrived: the balance of trade depends upon the transactions which have to be settled, not upon those which by common consent are held in abeyance for a term of years[1]." The balance of a country's imports and exports in any year has no direct relation to the deferred claims; though, of course, it is affected by interest for the year on loans already made by her, or to her.

On the other hand, there is an intimate connection between the imports and exports in any one year and the claims of all kinds falling due in that year. Coupons for any year, debentures of which the period ends in, say 1922, drafts drawn by tourists for their travelling expenses in 1922, etc.—all these form immediate claims on one side or the other of national indebtedness, which enter into the national account with other countries, on the same footing as do the claims created on the one side and the other by her imports and exports of merchandise respectively in that year[2].

---

[1] *Foreign Exchanges*, Chap. II.

[2] For simplicity it is assumed here that each year's transactions are completed within the year; or, which comes to nearly the same thing, that the outstanding transactions at the end of one year are about equal to those at the end of the next. But, of course, if bad harvests in Europe coincide with good harvests in

If a British bank, or Fire or Life Insurance company or other financial house opens a foreign branch, it generally sends out (besides petty cash) a certain command over British capital for immediate service: this swells British exports. If no more ready command over capital is required, it can bring home all its net profits, and these swell British imports.

Powerful financial houses often make considerable net profits by speculation on foreign Stock and Produce Exchanges; and these, as well as the net profits of Fire and Life Insurance companies or foreign business, swell the imports of the home country. Speculative sales and purchases are, as a rule, settled by the payment of margins, and their capital values do not enter into annual international balances to a considerable extent. It is, however, true that even temporary purchases by foreign houses of stock exchange securities are an important means of rendering international assistance in times of financial disturbance; and they may materially mitigate for some months the pressure to export goods for sale in any markets that are not receptive.

Thus the influences of fluctuations of credit on the balance of imports and exports are diverse. If credit in country A is shaken, her capitalists may desire to bring home command over capital, in spite of the facts that her business activities are declining, and that there is but little scope for investments of capital in new or enlarged enterprises in her industries.

4. *The total earnings of the shipping industry oscillate with changes in commercial credit. But Britain's nominal excess of imports over exports is often high in depressed times, because she is then restricting her foreign investments.*

Since the middle of last century the aggregate tonnage of Britain's shipping has increased fast, and its aggregate carrying

wheat exporting countries, much grain comes to Europe in the autumn and is likely to be valued rather high; so that the imports into Europe for that year are swollen considerably, while some of the exports that are to pay for them follow a little later. Similar inequalities may be caused by sharp temporary disturbances of international credit.

Again, some borrowers make default, and exports to them are never fully compensated. But in all hazardous trades the good returns on some ventures have to make up for losses on others. Lenders require a relatively high rate of interest to induce them to lend on hazardous ventures, especially in foreign countries; and the gains accruing from such of these loans at high interest, as are fully honoured, may be taken to cover the losses on those that make default.

III, IV, 4. power has increased much faster. Consequently the fall of freights, though sometimes interrupted by war and by bursts of commercial activity, has been rapid. The diminution of the cost of building and working cargo ships has been accompanied by an incessant increase in the percentage of bulky goods which travel long distances by sea: and this has again tended to lower the average rate of freight-charge per ton-mile. The gross receipts of Britain's shipping have increased very fast, though unevenly. The ship-owning business has remained profitable, at all events according to the ever diminishing standard of profits, which are afforded by modern conditions to businesses that have no effective monopoly. But its net profits have oscillated more violently than its gross receipts.

During a time of ascending commercial activity and credit, cargoes increase fast: and the gross earnings of ships increase faster still, because freights are very sensitive to every variation of demand. Britain's net "invisible" exports of shipping services are much larger in value than the visible net exports of cotton manufactures, which come next in order on her list of exports: and one might have expected the excess of visible imports over exports to rise during those ascending periods faster than the imports themselves, and much faster than the exports[1].

In fact, however, this has not happened; but rather the reverse; for in ascending periods she exports largely on credit. Her area is so small, relatively to her capital—it is, so to speak, so nearly saturated with capital—as to allow scope for any new enterprise that holds out prospects of high return. Consequently, the activity of her industries depends in an exceptional degree on the confidence and strength of business enterprises in other countries, and especially in new countries. That confidence is sometimes misplaced. But, so long as it lasts, capital flows from her for

[1] Britain's excess of imports over exports was £m36 in 1854: it rose with slight fluctuations to about double that amount in 1868, when trade was depressed. After that year it fell almost without intermission to about its 1854 level till 1872, when the inflation of trade was unprecedented; and thence it jumped up to £m145 in 1877, about four times as much as in 1873: 1877 was a year of extreme industrial depression. It fell again irregularly till 1886, but after that it rose with little intermission to £m182 in 1903, which again was a year of depression; after which it fell to £m128 in 1907, a year of inflation. (It reached £m783 (in paper currency) in 1918.) Its relation to the migration of capital is noted above, § 2.

investment abroad, and especially in new countries: and the only III, IV, 4. way in which this flow can be effected is by a net increase of exports, visible and invisible; that is, by making aggregate exports larger relatively to imports than they otherwise would have been. Of course there is no necessary connection between an increased investment of British capital in any particular country and an increase of her exports to that country[1].

Nearly all advanced industrial countries are creditor countries, because their industries have already provided them with more capital than they have an urgent need to use themselves. This abundant supply of capital gives them a differential advantage for the production of things which cannot well be made without very expensive plant; that is, of those things, which countries that borrow capital, cannot as a rule very easily make for themselves. Meanwhile the aggregate volume of international trade is being increased, in spite of high tariffs, by cheap and rapid transport of goods and news. Telegraphs and telephones are aiding the inter-communication of private and public news among all advanced countries, and enabling them to keep in close touch with their representatives in new and in backward countries: thus, inflations and depressions of industrial activity are becoming increasingly international. Britain is the most distinctively old industrial country, and consequently her industrial activities are influenced by international influences more than are those of any other country.

[1] For instance a railway in Eastern Russia might borrow in London some of the capital needed for increasing its rolling plant: that plant might move on its own wheels from German locomotive works, rather than be shipped via Riga; and Germany might perhaps use the payment, which she received from Russia, in buying goods from China, for which Russia in effect paid; while China was paid by drawing goods from Britain with the money received from Russia. This would of course be effected through the foreign exchanges, which are to be considered at once.

CHAPTER V

INTERNATIONAL EXCHANGES

1. *The nature of the economy effected by bills of exchange in the settlement of obligations between different places.*

The present chapter is an elementary account of matters that are familiar to every business man, and are well understood by a great part of the general public. It may therefore be omitted with advantage by many readers[1].

Norwich was the chief centre of English industry outside of London when the Exchanges first attracted general notice: and she holds her place in the following reproduction of an often-repeated statement of the case. As has been well said, "Commerce, in all its phases except the very rudest, has avoided the sending of money, coin or the precious metals in any other form, on long journeys, when it could be avoided by means of arrangements between neighbours. If *A* in London owed money to *B* in Norwich, and *C* in Norwich owed the same money to *D* in London, the two debts could be extinguished without the expense and cost of sending money by the simple arrangement that *A* should pay *D*, and *C* should pay *B*. Hence arose Bills of Exchange, and the machinery of the Exchanges."

A bill of exchange is generally a written request by the "drawer" of it, addressed to another, "the drawee"; in which he is requested to pay a certain sum of money to a person indicated on the face of the bill and called the payee. This person may be the drawer himself or a third person. It may request the drawee to pay it to anyone, to whom the payee may transfer the bill, subject to certain conditions and formalities. The bill states the time at which it is payable, as for instance at sight, or at three months from date.

---

[1] It is concerned with ordinary conditions: and ignores disturbances which may be caused by war, or a collapse of general credit. War is apt to disturb violently the values of currencies even though they have been firmly based on gold or silver, or both. For under the stress of a great war, even a strong and resolute Government is likely to issue inconvertible paper currency in such quantities, as to reduce its value greatly. In this connection reference may be made to a note on "The Mark Exchange" in *A revision of the Treaty*, by J. M. Keynes, C.B., 1922.

When the bill has been "accepted" by the signature of the drawee written across its face, it then becomes a promissory note from him, its acceptor. For the payee may sell it to a second person, who may sell it to a third, and so on; each seller signing it on the back, or endorsing it, before he passes it on. The selling value of the bill is reached by deducting a "discount" from the value on the face of it. This discount varies, firstly with the time for which the bill has yet to run; secondly with the market rate of discount on short, secure loans; and thirdly, with the risk that it may be difficult, or even impossible, to collect the value of the bill. The demand for payment of it will be made in the first instance on the acceptor of the bill; and, failing him, from the drawer; and, failing him, from its endorsers in the order in which they have signed their names.

Bills of exchange were at first used mainly as a means of transferring debts from one person to another; and thus economising the transference of command over ready purchasing power in *space*. But in doing this they incidentally transferred command over ready purchasing power from one date to another; and this transference in *time* became in some ways more important than the transference in space. Bills drawn by one person on another were sometimes used as a means of borrowing money from a third person: and this use often degenerated into an abuse, against which the term "fictitious" bill is aimed, though not well aimed[1].

Further, every additional name on the back of a bill gives it a new security, without involving any additional formality. When it is further considered that the bill yields interest to its holder for every day that it lies in his hands, and that his capital invested in it has still some life, while yet practically available to give him ready purchasing power whenever he wants it, there is no reason to wonder that good bills of exchange have been readily current

---

[1] The modern use of bills of exchange seems to have had a nearly continuous history from the eleventh century. They were in common use in Venice and throughout Lombardy, and apparently in Hanseatic towns in the twelfth century; and the Papal revenues were remitted from all quarters of the world by bills through the whole of the Middle Ages. The use of Inland bills came later. The Jews of course had always a great share in dealings with both kinds of bills. Holland was supposed to owe a considerable part of her commercial strength to the limpidity given to her capital by the full and wise use of bills of exchange: and Sir Josiah Child (*Discourse of Trade*, A.D. 1751, Chap. v) pleaded for their use in terms that may be read with profit even now.

III, v, 1. and popular among business men. In Lancashire, early in the nineteenth century, bills, chiefly inland, passed from hand to hand covered sometimes with a hundred signatures; and between them nine times as much business was done as by bank notes. Since that time, bills have not become less secure or less convenient: but, in various degrees in different countries, bank notes, cheques, drafts on banks, and telegraphic transfers have increased greatly in volume, trustworthiness and convenience, and bills have receded somewhat into the background. They now play but a small part in internal trade; and the part which they play in foreign trade is steadily diminishing[1].

While commerce was taking on its modern shape, the costs and risks of transport, especially inland, were so great that a merchant would pay a considerable percentage for a bill on a town a hundred miles off, whenever that was required in order to free him from the necessity of sending coin; and quotations were regularly made of the prices to be paid for such bills. The aggregate amount which people wished to remit in the one direction or the other, and the local exchange rates for these inland bills, were for many merchants more important than the foreign exchange rates[2].

The charges made for the transmission of command over money from one part of England to another are now commonly merged in the general charges for banking accommodation: no special rate of exchange between them is publicly quoted. But even

[1] The following quotation from an experienced banker in 1842 may serve to show of how recent growth is the Englishman's confidence in bank notes: "When the origin of bills is *bona fide* and legitimate, I place them, with the security of the drawer, acceptor, and perhaps twenty endorsements on the back, in the first class of our currency, before notes, and next in rank only to gold. I know no purpose of money, except wages, to which bills are not applicable in the provinces throughout this Kingdom, though not seen in London in making payments," J. W. Bosanquet, *Metallic, etc., Currency,* p. 91. See also Lewis Lloyd's evidence before the House of Lords' Committee on the Resumption of Cash Payments, 1819.

[2] Thus Harris, whose work *On Money and Coins,* 1757, contains an acute study of the foreign exchanges (though less profound than that in Hume's Essay of 1753) begins by quoting a careful description of the exchanges between London and Norwich from the *British Merchant,* 1721, the great opponent of trade with France. The attack was based on the ground, abandoned as inadequate by the more enlightened Mercantilists, that she sold much to England and bought little in return: the brilliant Cantillon in like manner commences his study of the exchanges, 1755, with a full account of those between Paris and Châlons.

to-day, and in countries whose monetary traffic is as highly organized as in Germany and the United States, the rates of exchange are quoted between distant towns, as, *e.g.* Hamburg and Frankfort, or New York and Chicago: in more backward countries a charge is generally made for transmitting command over money even for short distances. But so great a part of the financial business between western countries now passes through their commercial capitals, that it is customary to speak of the exchange between any two of them as a single unit—a strong testimony to the consolidation of economic nationality.

The primary function of a bill of exchange has just been illustrated by the economy which might enable two merchants in Norwich and two in London to settle their obligations by transfers of money in London and in Norwich, thus obviating the necessity for sending money backwards and forwards between the two places: the exchanges, when fully developed, effect similar economies in settlements between nations. If England has large payments to make to America, which has large payments to make to China, which has large payments to make to England, England is likely to discharge part of her obligations to America by bills on China: and if she does this her merchants will compete for bills on China, and the exchange with China will tend to become unfavourable to her, though the balance of trade is favourable. This seems obvious now: but Adam Smith and many of his predecessors were forced to spend great pains in arguing it against the narrower sections of the Mercantilists.

These "roundabout" operations are among the chief economies effected by the exchanges. Thus, America has little relative advantage in the production of goods for which there is much demand in Asia: but she is a large consumer of Asiatic goods, and she exports very large quantities of agricultural produce to Britain and other European countries. Were it not for roundabout settlements by bills and other instruments of the world's market, she would need to remit vast quantities of gold and silver to Asia, which would come back to her in the course of time through Europe. As it is, the whole of the country's imports (visible and invisible) from the world at large are set against the whole of her exports (visible and invisible) to the world at large; and that part of the

III, v, 2. total adjustment which is relegated to imports and exports of the precious metals is relatively small.

2. *Limits of variation of the exchanges between countries whose currencies are based on gold.*

At the present time (1922) the international market for gold has only a slight and indirect connection with national levels of general prices; because paper currencies have—for the time at least—superseded gold currencies. But problems of the exchanges between countries, whose currencies are based on gold, have a permanent scientific interest. It is to be hoped that ere long they will have a direct bearing on ordinary practice: for long-period contracts expressed in terms of a standard, which is liable to be altered by any great change in the economic or political conditions of the country concerned, belong to the province of speculation rather than of solid business. And though, as was indicated above (Book I, Chap. iv, § 6), an inconvertible paper currency may be so adjusted as to set a better standard of value for the country concerned, than that which can be set by a gold (or silver) standard; yet the time is apparently not near when such artificial standards can be of service in international trade.

Let us then follow the workings of the exchange between two neighbouring countries, France and Belgium, at a time when the standard of the currency of each country was set by gold twenty-franc pieces. We may, for the present, suppose them to trade only with one another; and neglect the fact that gold cannot generally be obtained for exportation without paying a premium for it. If then the claims for immediate payment held in Belgium on France, on account of goods sold, money borrowed, remittances due, etc., were equal to the total claims held in France against Belgium; then those who had claims to sell on Belgium would just balance those who needed to buy claims. A bill on Belgium for fr. 1000 drawn in France would sell for fr. 1000 (allowance being made for discount for the time it had to run); and so would a bill for fr. 1000 drawn in Belgium on France. Exchanges would be at *par*.

But if the claims held by France against Belgium were greater in the aggregate than those held by Belgium against France, the holders of the former would not easily find purchasers; and a

French bill on Belgium for fr. 1000 would, after allowing for discount for the time it had yet to run, sell for less than fr. 1000; while bills drawn the other way being scarce, would sell for a premium, that is, for more than fr. 1000, after allowing discount in like manner.

This state of the Exchanges is conventionally described as Favourable to France and Unfavourable to Belgium. But really it is favourable to those who bring goods to France from Belgium, whether they are French import merchants or Belgian export merchants; and it is unfavourable to all who send goods in the opposite direction. One of the goods, which may be sent, is gold; and if the exchanges become so unfavourable to Belgium that a bill for fr. 1000 on France in Belgium sells in Belgium at a discount greater than the cost of sending fr. 1000 worth of gold to France (allowance being made for insurance and interest), then the point has been reached at which it pays to send gold from Belgium to France; or, as is said, the Exchanges have reached a *Gold-point*. If, on the other hand, they had become increasingly Favourable to Belgium, and therefore Unfavourable to France, the other Gold-point would have been reached; that is, the point at which gold would begin to flow from France to Belgium[1].

The exchanges between Britain and Australia are in some respects simpler even than those between France and Belgium. For not only are sovereigns coined in either legal tender in the other, but in both countries any amount of them, that may be desired for exportation, can be instantly obtained in ordinary conditions of the money-market; whereas, in many European countries, difficulties of various kinds are put in the way of obtaining gold for exportation. But as Australia produces much

[1] All countries use the term "Favourable Exchange" in the same sense. But a "rise" of a foreign Exchange is Favourable or Unfavourable to a country, according as the terms of the exchange are so quoted as to state the foreign "uncertain" price of a "certain" fixed sum of her currency; or her uncertain price for a fixed sum of foreign currency. England follows the former in regard to nearly all countries. Thus the London exchange on Paris, for instance, is quoted at the price of £1 in French money; the figures given are those of the francs and centimes equivalent to £1, the £1 being taken for granted and not specified. On the other hand, the number mentioned in the quotation of the exchange on Calcutta is the number of pence and farthings that have to be given for a bill for a rupee. A rise of the French exchanges is therefore Favourable to England, that of India is Unfavourable. The account of this given by Harris resembles closely in form and substance that given in modern books on the Foreign Exchanges.

III, v, 2. gold, a bill on Britain is generally worth more than the gold which
it represents, after allowing discount for the time it has to run,
by the cost of transport to Britain: in other words the exchanges
are favourable to England up to about the gold-point.

A further complexity is introduced into the exchanges between
countries which have different currencies, even if they are both
based on gold, especially if either of them levies a seignorage. A
twenty-mark piece, for instance, under normal conditions must
be worth gold of equal weight and fineness with it, together with
the small seignorage charged on it, for otherwise gold would not
be taken to the mint to be coined. But if, in ordinary conditions
of the money market, gold has to be sent from Germany to Britain
and there remains no bullion available, the gold coins on arrival
will be treated at the British mint as mere bullion; (though it is
true that financial houses will in such cases often buy the imported
coins at a little more than their bullion value, with a view to the
chance that it may not be necessary to melt them down at all).
At such times therefore, Germany may be unable to discharge a
debt for £1000, without sending as many twenty-mark pieces as
will contain as much gold as there is in £1000. That is, a bill for
£1000 on Britain can be bought in Germany (neglecting discount)
only for marks weighing as much as the £1000, together with cost
of transport.

When the Exchanges swing to the opposite extreme; when
German currency is relatively scarce, and gold is going to the
German mint; then a bill for £1000 on England can be bought in
Germany for gold which weighs as much as £1000 minus carriage
to Germany: and this gold can be got for twenty-mark pieces
which fall short of it in weight by the amount of the seignorage.
That is to say, the extreme limits of the fluctuations of the
Exchanges between England and Germany are the double cost
of transport together with the seignorage charged in Germany.
And of course the limit of fluctuation between Germany and
France, where also a seignorage is charged, is the double cost of
transport together with the sum of the two seignorages. But even
this limit can be exceeded in disturbed times, such as the breaking
out of war; or when the currency of either country is debased or
mutilated. This last case points towards the exchanges between
countries whose standard money is made of different materials

gold, silver or paper: but we need not stay to discuss such cases III, v, 3.
here[1].

The difficulties, which we have so far considered, relate only
to countries whose currencies are all based on gold. A generation
ago there was a great deal of trade between such countries and
those whose currencies were based on silver; or consisted of paper
notes which were nominally based on silver but were really inconvertible. But now such trade is a comparatively small part
of the whole; and the problems connected with it are relegated
to Appendix G.

3. *The part played by variations in the rate of discount
charged in a country's money market in maintaining the
equilibrium of her commercial obligations.*

So far we have considered bills of exchange as "short"; that is,
as drawn for payment either immediately, or after so short a time
that the rate of discount on deferred claims at the time of drawing

[1] This assumes that there are adequate facilities for obtaining large quantities
of gold coin for exportation in each country. But, in fact, this is not always the
case; and when not, the effective gold-points may be appreciably higher, and
the difference between the extreme lines of the Exchanges may be considerably
greater than indicated in the text.

Further, when coins have to be exported, they may be found to be of less
than full weight, and then the exchange may further vary by the average
deficiency in weight, not indeed of the coins in circulation, but of those which
are least deficient, and which are therefore carefully selected for exportation.
English sovereigns are generally of full weight, though half-sovereigns are often
allowed to be worn down. Nominally, no seignorage is charged in England. But,
in fact, the mintage operations cause a delay, the equivalent of which would be
a seignorage of rather less than a half-penny in the pound.

When coins were in a poor condition the exchanger had a troublesome task.
Harris tells us that: "Those who have made the proper experiments, find that
most of the foreign mints are very inaccurate, and this makes it difficult to
ascertain what are the precise values in respect of one another of the legal
monies of different countries....What the merchant must regard is the amount
in bullion of what he usually receives in consideration of a given sum of money.
If the balance from any country be usually remitted in coins, and those coins
be worn or otherwise diminished below the legal standard,...the exchange will
in appearance be against that country when really it is even." This is no doubt
a cause of the very high exchange charges often recorded, *e.g.* by Cantillon,
which were much above the costs and insurance needed for moving gold, high
as those were. And Adam Smith's famous Digression to show how an order
for "bank-money" on the Bank of Amsterdam, was maintained effectively a
little above the full value of the bullion which it represented, was motived by
the desire to explain how "before the reformation of the [English] silver coin
in King William's time exchange between England and Holland computed in
the usual manner was five and twenty per cent. against England" though "the
real exchange may have been in favour of England."

III, v, 3. is of little importance. But now we have to take account of the influence on the course of international trade exerted by changes in the rates of discount deducted upon "three months" and other "long" bills: this also tends to readjust the machinery of commerce to changed conditions; and it helps to bring about a new position of equilibrium, which in some cases is merely temporary, and in others is more or less permanent.

The value of a bill depends partly on the credit of those whose names it bears; and the "discount," deducted on bills of questionable security, often contains a large element of insurance against risk. But this matter does not specially interest us now: and we may suppose the values of first class bills to govern those of others, the necessary element of insurance being counted separately.

When the rate of discount on a first class bill is high in any country, those, who make advances on it, gain the benefit of the high rates, or at least a part of the benefit: and, therefore, if the credit of the country is sound, foreigners will lend to it for the time as much as they conveniently can, and will borrow little from it. If they have prompt claims against it, they will gladly exchange these for deferred claims with interest added at a high rate, and they will purchase deferred claims on it in every convenient way. If, for instance, the rate is higher in Paris than in London, loans will tend to flow from London to Paris. Londoners who have claims for "money" in Paris, that is the ready command over capital there, will let it stay there for a time, to earn the relatively high interest which is just then to be got there. And Parisians who have claims for money in London, i.e. the ready command over capital there, will bring it home for use: they may discharge their own obligations with it and so escape paying a high rate of interest, or they may lend it out and so earn a high rate. Meanwhile Belgians, Germans and others, if they want to draw any "money" home will bring it from London rather than Paris; if they want to lend money out, they will send it to Paris rather than London. These changes may be made in many different ways; but, however they are made, the ultimate effect will be the same. A little more ready command over the world's capital will be stocked at Paris for the time, and a little less at London than would otherwise have been the case. Paris therefore will be to some extent relieved from the necessity of making prompt payments abroad. Her immediate obligation to make payment to III, v, 4. other countries will be lessened, and the exchange will become more favourable to her.

Again, when an increased demand for foreign goods or any other cause makes the exchanges unfavourable to that country; that is, when it causes bills on foreign countries to be sold at a higher rate than usual, its merchants tend to be in increasing need of loans; and this tends to raise the rate of discount. This tendency may be strong, if there is any fear that gold will be drawn out of the country, and that in consequence bankers and other money dealers will restrict their credit. Meanwhile, the accompanying fall in the price of bills on that country, caused partly by the fall in the rate of exchange on it, and partly by the rise in the rate of discount in it, will tempt foreigners to buy and hold bills on it: this will ease the money market and check the rise in the rate of discount in that country. Thus there is a constant interaction between the rate of discount prevailing in a country and her foreign exchanges.

A sufficiently high rate of discount, if maintained steadily, thus brings gold into the country; and the influx of gold inclines bankers to enlarge their loans. Perhaps little or none of the new gold may go at once into currency: but the substitutes for currency are increased: and prices will be restrained from falling, even if they are not set on a rise.

4. *The parts played in modern adjustments of international commercial obligations by the drafts of exchange banks, and by telegraphic and other stock exchange operations.*

Nearly everything that has been said so far might have been said, and indeed most of it was said, a century or more ago. But a little may be added as to the changes in technique caused by modern uses of steam and electricity, and by the ever growing volume and rapidity of commercial transactions.

Money and fairs enabled the primitive man, having a horse to spare and wanting a canoe, to sell the horse and buy the canoe without waiting for "the double coincidence" of finding another who was in want of a horse and had a canoe to spare. Presently bills of exchange enabled a merchant to specialize on the export trade in, say, cutlery or cloth, without needing to become an adept

III, v, 4. in the wine or the silk or the rice that would ultimately be brought back in exchange for it. Later on the roundabout exchanges enabled merchants of any country collectively to buy from any other country much more than they sold to her, without incurring the expense of sending bullion to pay for it, because they could send to her bills on some third country to which they sold much. And now the modern organization and unification, firstly of national money markets and secondly of the international money market, enable anyone to deal anywhere in things which can be bought or sold at a price that suits him, with the knowledge that the necessary payments can be made quickly, certainly and without any considerable cost or trouble to him.

Some banks and other financial houses in the commercial centre of every great country, devote their energies largely or wholly to handling payments to and from foreign countries, or some group of them, in the old or new world. They are not indeed able on their own responsibility to buy bills and other commercial paper with perfect safety from all classes of producers and other traders, even in the countries with which they are in touch: for the affairs of some of these traders need special and wary study. Therefore such a trader commonly discounts his bills at a relatively high rate to a broker, who gives his whole thought to the material and personal details of that particular market in which that trader moves: and the broker re-discounts them, after endorsement, at a bank or other financial house which does a more general business. But, directly and indirectly, the "Exchange banks" (as they are frequently called) become the centres, to which promises, in one form or another, to pay great masses of the currency of particular foreign countries converge. They can therefore sell an order on such a country for any reasonable sum easily and instantly. For many years they did this chiefly in the form of drafts on their correspondents (perhaps branches of their own) in appropriate foreign marts; and these drafts encroached so much on the business of international remittance as to reduce commercial bills to a secondary position. More recently these drafts are themselves being in a great measure pushed out by telegraphic orders.

Meanwhile a new influence has arisen to cooperate with the Exchanges in the speedy adjustment of international relations, especially in regard to loans and the prompt supply of command

over capital. What are now called stock exchange securities did III, v, 4.
indeed begin to take their place alongside of bills, in some of the
chief trading centres of the Continent more than three centuries
ago: and early in the eighteenth century they became prominent
in England. But recently there has been a great multiplication
of "international securities"; that is, securities for which there
is a good market in several countries. Every international borrowing, whether on public or private account, gives the borrowing
nation a claim on the other for the amount of the loan; and, in
return, every coupon or bond, when it becomes due, acts as a claim
against the borrowing country, just in the same way as a trade bill
of like amount payable at the same date. International money
dealers buy up and sell again all such claims or the proceeds of
them; such business falls more and more into the hands of large
discount firms and international banks; who draw on their correspondents, by letter or by telegram, drafts on behalf of anyone
who may wish to have the means of making a payment abroad.
This is an additional route by which, in case of need, importers
can indirectly pay for their purchases, and exporters can receive
payment.

Thus the world money market has become an agency, at once
firmly unified and highly specialized. It is unified, in that the
different parts of it are so closely connected that claims of any
one kind can be used indirectly to balance claims of any other:
and it is specialized, in that different financial houses give themselves to dealing in particular classes of international drafts, bills
and other claims. A house that holds an excess of claims of whatever kind in a foreign country will, in one way or another, dispose
of drafts on that country to persons who have payments to make
there. Trade bills and financial bills, coupons and telegraphic
transfers, are all ultimately interchangeable; and the whole of the
claims on the one side are set off against those on the other. If
the two sets are exactly equal, there is equilibrium: if not, there
must be further movement.

Thus, the machinery of the foreign exchanges, supplemented
by telegraphic and other stock exchange transactions, enables
debts, owing from one country to another, to be transferred to a
third, so easily and quickly that there is nothing to be gained by
a close balancing of accounts between any two countries: the trade

of each with the world is a coherent whole. The trade of each with any single other country may indeed profitably be studied from many points of view, and especially in order to discover which of the two is the stronger in those industries which make for leadership; but not from the point of view of the balance of trade.

5. *So long as national currencies are effectively based on gold, the wholesale price of each commodity tends to equality everywhere; provided allowance is made for costs of carriage, etc.; for frontier taxes; and for mint charges on the coinage of gold.*

Insufficient attention was paid to the matters now to be discussed, till the exigencies of England's great war with France caused British currency to consist of inconvertible notes. This led to careful studies of currency problems, which continued during two decades, and left but little of first rate importance to be done by later generations.

In particular, Ricardo and others insisted that so long as a country's mint is kept open to all who choose to bring gold to it to be made into standard coins, the value of those coins will adhere closely to the cost of obtaining the gold, together with the mint charge. They agreed that an undischarged balance of obligations is only one of many causes which may tend to increase a country's exportations rather than her importations: and that the question, whether the precious metals are sent, rather than other things, to discharge a balance of obligations, is decided simply by the relative values of the precious metal and other things in the different countries concerned. Account is of course to be taken of the fact that the exportation of a given amount of value is generally more easy and less costly when embodied in the precious metals than in ordinary commodities.

It was recognized that the uses of gold and silver in each country are not those of ordinary commodities, and that, in modern phrase, the "elasticity of the demand" for it is altogether peculiar[1]. But none the less they urged that everything which is in the hands of alert business men, whether as owners or agents for others; and which is held by them for business purposes, is likely to move quickly from its present place to any other, if the terms on which

[1] See above, I, iv, § 1 and Appendix C.

it can be marketed there are so much better than those which can be obtained where it is, as to cover with a profit all the trouble, expenses and risks of transmission, including of course any import or export duties that may be levied on the way.

Let us pursue their argument a little further, taking account of the growth of a great international market for stock exchange securities; which are as much more portable relatively to their value than gold is, as gold is more portable than cheap bulky goods of value equal to it. Let us then suppose that the people of any country are desirous of obtaining command of ready purchasing power abroad; because their imports of some things have been very heavy; or because some of their wonted exports have not been in good demand abroad; or because they want to pay off some old debts; or because they have bought foreign securities, new or old, and must pay for them; or for any other reason. These are the conditions which put command over foreign currencies at a premium relatively to the home currency; and, in the language of the Money Market make the Exchanges Unfavourable to her. If these conditions are continued long enough, the value of gold, as a means of purchasing foreign commodities by being exported in exchange for them, will rise so much that it will be profitably exported for the purpose: and this, even though the country, having no gold mines, imports gold on the balance under ordinary circumstances. But under these conditions merchants are likely to look around them, and see whether there is not some other thing which the country does not produce herself, and therefore does not habitually export; but which could under the circumstances be marketed profitably abroad. Britain, for instance, imports on the balance both lead and Egyptian bonds: but if her merchants were in more urgent need of command over purchasing power in France or elsewhere, the value of lead or Egyptian bonds might have fallen in London relatively to either the French goods which they wanted to purchase, or to the French currency which they had to provide in order to discharge their debts in France. In that case better business might be done by sending to Paris lead or Egyptian bonds, than by sending more coal or other things which are commonly exported from Britain to France; or even by sending gold: and then it might reasonably be said that the exporters "lead-point" or "Egyptian bond-point" had been

III, v, 5. reached, before the gold-point had been reached, because the difference between the excess of the amount of gold or other commodities, which a merchant would obtain in France for lead or for Egyptian bonds, over what he would obtain for lead or Egyptian bonds in England, is such that it is worth his while to export lead or Egyptian bonds.

CHAPTER VI

GENERAL RELATIONS OF DEMAND AND SUPPLY IN INTERNATIONAL TRADE

1. *Introductory*[1].

A small force will cause movement where there is little resistance to it. There is generally but little resistance to movements of capital, and of labour from one occupation to another in the same neighbourhood; provided the resources and faculties required for the two are similar. As a rule the change is easy, if it makes no new demand on faculty, and causes no rupture of the social amenities of life. The son need not follow the occupation of the father: the lapse of a single generation is therefore amply sufficient for a large drift of labour from one industry to another in the same city, and even in the same industrial district. There are indeed still some occupations, entrance to which is in effect confined to the sons of those already in it. But, speaking generally, the son of an English artisan, who prefers an occupation different from that of his father, can obtain admittance to it, provided he is sufficiently alert: his father must of course supplement the small payments which his work is worth, while he is developing the skill and aptitudes required of an adult artisan[2].

Thus a part of the basis of the study of international trade lies in considerations which extend beyond the special province of economic studies; for they are largely concerned with sentiment: sentiments are not always firmly based on reason: but economic reasonings, which ignore them, are likely to mislead. For our present purposes, the chief differences in character between international trade and trade among different places in the same "country"—that is, the same self-controlled economic area—are based on two allied considerations. The first is that labour and capital migrate, between different parts of the same country, more easily and freely than they do between different countries. The second is that every part of a country is called upon to contribute

---

[1] Appendix H, attached to this chapter, discusses divergencies of relative values from relative costs in international trade.

[2] See above, Introduction, § 4.

to the expenses of its central Government, which are incurred for defence against external enemies; as well as for internal administration in regard to order, education, health and some social amenities.

The necessities of internal administration require a clear definition and a firm control of a country's frontiers: and this control can conveniently be applied to taking record of all goods that cross its frontiers, and drawing revenue from taxes on appropriate things. Thus political considerations supply material, which can be turned to account in registering some important features of the economic development of a country; in forming a judgment as to its trade relations with other countries, and in adjusting its fiscal policy to its faculties and its needs.

2. *Though money affords a fairly good measure of the relative real costs of things made in the same country; it does not afford a means of comparison of the real costs of goods made in places, between which there is not a large and free circulation of labour and capital.*

It is reasonable to assume that a cargo for which a merchant paid £100,000 in a country, where prices are reckoned in pounds sterling, is the product of about half as great a real cost to that country of her labour and the use of her capital, as another cargo of a different sort for which twice that sum was paid. And similarly, a cargo bought for 1,000,000 yens in a country which uses yens as money, may be reasonably supposed to be the product of half as great a real cost to that country of her labour and the use of her capital as another for which twice that sum was paid. But, since we are not supposing that labour and capital circulate as freely between the two countries as they do within either of them, we cannot say anything as to the comparative real costs of the £100,000 cargo and the 1,000,000 yen cargo, even if we know that one is exchanged for the other.

If the pound and the yen were merely local currencies, not connected with one another in any way, such a comparison would perhaps not be likely to be made. But, if it were known that the pound and the yen were made of gold, the pound containing (say) ten times as much as the yen, there might be some temptation to suppose that the two cargoes exchanged for one another because they represented equal costs; it being implied that these costs were real costs. In fact, however, equal gold costs in different countries have no general tendency to represent equal real costs in both.

Thus, a great increase in the demand of the second country for the goods of the first would make it profitable to send gold yens, or gold in some other form, from the first country to the second. This flow of gold would continue until there was no longer any profit in it; that is, until a kilogram of gold in either country would buy goods, which (after allowing for costs of transport, etc.) could be sold for about a kilogram of gold in the other. Then a £100,000 cargo would again exchange for a 1,000,000 yen cargo: and, if we looked only at prices, the terms of trade would appear to be unchanged. But in fact the £100,000 cargo would represent less real cost in the first country than before; the 1,000,000 yen cargo would represent more real cost in the second country than before; and the first country would get goods, that represented a fifth as much again of real cost in the second country, for goods that were of a given real cost to herself. Thus money, even when firmly based on gold, does not afford a good measure of international values, and it does not help to explain the changes in those values, which are caused by broad variations in international demand: but on the contrary it disguises and conceals them. For it measures changes in values by standards which are *automatically modified by the very variations in international demand, the effects of which are to be measured.*

The unsuitability of gold as a measure of value in international trade, arises mainly from the fact that gold is itself moved freely from one country to another by the direct action of trade: while the supplies of labour and capital cannot move with equal freedom.

To avoid this difficulty Mill took a yard of cloth as representative of the products of one country and a yard of linen as representative of the products of the other. But it seems better to suppose either country to make up her exports into representative "bales"; that is, bales each of which represents uniform aggregate investments of her labour (of various qualities) and of her capital.

3. *The problem of the trade between two countries, supposed to be isolated from the rest of the world.*

Ricardo approached the complex problem of world trade by way of the relatively simple problem of the exclusive trade between two countries: we may well follow on his lines. We may suppose two countries, E and G, to trade exclusively with one another, no credit being given on either side; and that the balance of imports and exports is not disturbed by foreign investments of capital, or by absenteeism, etc. We may suppose that each country bears the expense of delivering her exports at the other's frontier; and that their values are reckoned on this basis. Or, we may suppose that the conduct of the trade is equally divided between the merchants of the two countries. Either of these suppositions practically enables us to avoid all discussion of the costs of transport: we will adopt the latter course. We will suppose that the currency of each country has no value except in its own home: later on we will take account of the possibility that the currency of each country may have value in the other: and therefore may enter into the trade as an exportable commodity.

Further, we will suppose every merchant to do an all-round trade; and to bring back the goods which are obtained in return for his exports, due allowance being of course made for the expenses of his trade. He draws no bills against his exports, and the difficulties of the foreign exchanges do not arise; they will come into discussion later. He, of course, makes his purchases carefully. Thus, if his basis is in E, he selects for exportation those of E's goods which he thinks can be marketed in G on the best terms, relatively to their cost to him when delivered in G (costs and trouble of handling them being reckoned in): and he lays out the money which he receives for them on those of G's products which he thinks he will be able to market to best advantage at home, after defraying the costs of carrying and handling them. He is primarily interested in a limited number of classes of goods at home and abroad. He watches carefully lest any one class of goods, which he is in the habit of handling, should be exported or imported, by himself or others, in such quantities that it cannot be marketed on terms as favourable as he had anticipated. If that appears probable, he restricts his operations; unless he sees his way to substituting for it goods of some other class, either such as he habitually handles, or such as he has generally left to be handled by others. Of course he is liable to similar invasions of his special territory: and thus every all-round merchant, even though his own peculiar field of operations may be somewhat narrow, bears his share in the collective interests of his country's trade as a whole: and the machinery of the foreign exchanges puts the mere exporter or the mere importer on nearly the same footing as the all-round merchant; except, of course, when credit or currency is much disturbed. Thus, a broad view being taken, the separate interests of particular groups of producers and traders are seen to be in a great measure merged in the collective interests of the population as a whole, regarded in their two-fold aspect as producers and as consumers: and it is not unreasonable to speak of the equilibrium of trade, in regard to imports as a whole and exports as a whole.

On these suppositions the trade between the two countries is pure barter. All that an E merchant wants to know about G's markets, is the quantity and quality of G's goods which he can buy net (i.e. after all necessary deductions), with the proceeds of the cargoes that he sends there. He wants to know whether G's prices for the things, which he has to sell, are high relatively to the things which he looks to bring back from G: and, if they are, he does not care whether the general level of prices there be high or low, either absolutely or relatively to those in his own country. He does not even care whether they are rising or falling, provided there is no appreciable change which elapses between the completion of his sales and the settling of his terms of purchase: for if he receives for his cargo a bag of G's currency, which will give him a certain command over G's goods, it does not matter to him what the size of the bag is. And, in like manner, the dealings of an all-round G merchant in E's market may be mere barter from his point of view, if he invests all his net receipts in fresh purchases.

In the case of trade between individuals, the one side commonly supplies pieces of metal or their representatives, which give general purchasing power, and demands specific commodities; while the other demands general purchasing power and supplies specific commodities: and the practice of describing the first as bringing demand and the other as bringing supply is usual, convenient and, in general, harmless. But in the general trade between two

III, VI, 3. countries neither can be specially associated either with demand or with supply. The demand of each has its origin in the desires of her people to obtain certain goods from abroad; and her supply has its origin in her facilities for producing things which the people of other countries desire. But her demand is, in general, effective in causing trade, only in so far as it is backed by her supply of appropriate goods: and her supply is active, only in so far as she has a demand for foreign goods.

Thus the demand of each stimulates the supply of the other: and the demand of each is made effective by its own supply. Consequently, while the problem of international trade has been correctly described as that of "international demand," it might have been described as that of "international supply." This term may specially be appropriate when a new supply initiates an unwonted demand; as when the advent of a ship laden with European wares, in a quiet bay of America, set its inhabitants on the systematic production of things that could be exchanged for them. Changes in international demand are perhaps the dominant influences on international trade: but supply creates demand almost as certainly as effective demand calls forth supply. The terms of international trade can properly be said to be governed by the relations of international demand: but, with equal correctness they can be said to be governed by the relations of international supply. It seems best to speak of them as governed by international demand and supply.

J. S. Mill emphasized the fact that the "law of International Values is but an extension of the more general law of Value, which we called the Equation of Supply and Demand." The value of a commodity always so adjusts itself as to bring the demand to the exact level of the supply. But all trade, either between nations or individuals, is an interchange of things: those which either side is prepared to part with constitute its means of purchase. Thus the supply brought by the one constitutes its demand for what is brought by the other: "supply and demand" is but another expression for "reciprocal demand," and to say that value will adjust itself so as to equalize demand with supply, is in fact to say that it will adjust itself so as to equalize the demand on the one side with the demand on the other. But Mill sometimes applies the abbreviated title "Equation of International Demand" (the

word Supply being omitted) to this equalization; while the term
"reciprocal" is sometimes substituted (as by Torrens) for "international." Some writers have however laid so much stress on the
word "demand" in this phrase, as to imply that the problem of international trade is one of demand rather than supply: and this is a
reason for emphasizing the interdependence of supply and demand.

4. *Numerical illustration of the demands of each of two
countries which trade together, for the goods of the other: and
the general dependence of the terms of trade on the relative
volumes and intensities of those demands.*

The possible relations of demand and value in the exclusive
trade between two countries are most effectively represented by
diagrams. But diagrams are not effectively assimilated by all
readers; and they are therefore relegated to Appendix J. Numerical
illustrations must suffice here. The numbers refer to representative
units—for definiteness they may, as already stated, be called *bales*
—of either country's imports and exports.

Proceeding on Ricardo's lines, we may suppose that the
following tables represent the amounts to which E and G would
be severally willing to trade at various "terms of trade"; or, to
use a phrase which is more appropriate in some connections, at
various "rates of interchange." (The phrase "rate of exchange"
is avoided; because it is already specialized, in connection with
the Foreign Exchanges, to indicate the rate at which command
over the currency of one country can be obtained in terms of the
currency of another country.)

These tables, which may be called E's and G's "trading
schedules," embody the fact that, if G's specialities generally
were very scarce in E's markets, they would be bought up at
very high costs by wealthy persons who had an urgent desire
for them. If their supply increased greatly some of them would
need to attract other persons, who were less wealthy, or had a
less urgent desire for them; and the purchasing power for which
each hundred of them could be sold in E would fall considerably.
If their quantities became very large, relatively to the population
of E, they would have to be forced at still less advantageous rates
to the importers: and at these low rates it might be possible to
find a market in E for some other goods, for making which G had

III, VI. 4. no very great differential advantage, and which had not been exported previously. When most of G's exports had been brought down to prices within the range of the great mass of the population of E for ordinary consumption, the amount of them which could be marketed in E would be very large: and it would then increase considerably in response to even a very small further reduction in the cost at which they were to be obtained. (If a monopolistic company controlled the whole trade, everything would of course be different: but more of that later on.)

	Schedule of terms on which E is willing to trade		Schedule of terms on which G is willing to trade	
(1)	(2)	(3)	(4)	(5)
Number of E bales	Number of G bales per hundred E bales at which E will part with those in (1)	Total number of G bales for which E is willing to part with those in (1)	Number of G bales per hundred E bales at which G will buy those in (1)	Total number of G bales which G is willing to give for those in (1)
10,000	10	1,000	230	23,000
20,000	20	4,000	175	35,000
30,000	30	9,000	143	42,900
40,000	35	14,000	122	48,800
50,000	40	20,000	108	54,000
60,000	46	27,600	95	57,000
70,000	55	38,500	86	60,200
80,000	68	54,400	$82\frac{1}{2}$	66,000
90,000	78	70,200	78	70,200
100,000	83	83,000	76	76,000
110,000	86	94,600	$74\frac{1}{2}$	81,950
120,000	$88\frac{1}{2}$	106,200	$73\frac{3}{4}$	88,500

[The import of such figures is perhaps best grasped by aid of diagrams which are supplied in Appendix J, § 1.]

The schedules indicate that if 1000 G bales were offered in E markets they could be disposed of at the rate of 10 for each 100 E bales: at that rate, E would be willing to trade to the extent of exporting 10,000 of her bales: or, which is the same thing, to the extent of importing 1000 G bales: but a rate more favourable to her would be required to induce her to extend the scope of her trade. At the rate of 20 G bales for 100 of her own, she would be willing to trade to the extent of importing 4000 bales and exporting 20,000: and so on. Similarly, a small quantity of E's goods could meet with so eager a demand in G's market that 10,000 E bales could be disposed of at the rate of 100 for 230 G bales: and so on.

Adding up, we find that G gets for 70,200 of her bales a number of E bales for which it would be worth her while to pay 125,300 of her bales rather than forego them. The net benefit of the trade to her therefore is 55,100 unit products of her labour and capital.

The arrangement of the figures is rather less convenient for a similar calculation of the gain which E derives from the trade. But they indicate that it would be worth E's while to give 170,000 of her bales for the 70,200 G bales for which she actually gives 90,000: so that her total net benefit by the trade is 80,000 unit products of her labour and capital. The aggregate gain to the world of the trade is thus 135,000 unit products of labour and capital.

It is obvious that G's net benefit from the trade would have been greater if (the equilibrium position of trade remaining as before) the rate of interchange, shown in column (4), at which she was willing to trade for very small amounts, had remained high throughout the greater part of the column; and had come down rapidly only just before the equilibrium level of trade had been reached. On the other hand, the direct net benefit would have been very small, if the first number in column (4) had been 100 instead of 230, and the following numbers had descended gradually to 78 at the equilibrium point.

5. *An increase in a country's demand for imports generally causes a more than proportionate increase in the quantity of her own goods which she must give in exchange for them.*

There is a good deal of interest, *from a purely theoretical point of view*, in tracing the results which may follow from various possible arrangements of the figures in these schedules: but only one general group of arrangements has any considerable importance from a practical point of view.

All others involve assumptions as to the nature of international trade which are not consistent with its ordinary trade; though some traces of them are to be found under exceptional conditions. They appear to be a necessary part of the broad problem which Ricardo and J. S. Mill proposed to themselves: but just at present we may leave them out of view.

Under the actual conditions of trade in the modern world, it is generally true that the greater the amount of imports, which is pushed on a country's markets, the less (other things being

III. vi. 5. equal) will be the value measured in her own goods, at which each
consignment of them can be marketed: and the more favourable
to her will be the terms of interchange: consequently her schedule
must show that every increase in the volume of her imports is
accompanied by an improvement in her rate of interchange.

Conditions may be conceived in which an increase in the
volume of a country's imports may lower the terms at which they
can be sold, so much that the aggregate price received for them
is less than would have been obtained by a smaller volume of
imports. But such conditions occur so rarely, if indeed they occur
at all, that they may be left out of account here[1].

Under ordinary conditions (free competition being assumed),
merchants will tend to push E's goods on G's markets up to the
limit (or margin) at which no more than the common rate of
profit is to be earned by the trade: and similarly, G's goods will
be pushed on E's markets till any further increase would compel
them to be sold on terms that would not yield good profits to the
merchants. A little "trial and error" may be necessary if the
trade is new: but when matters have settled down and experience
has been gained, the amount of E's goods sent to G will be such
that the terms on which G will accept them, will cause just that
amount of G's goods to be returned to E which E is willing to
accept on those terms[2]. Let us suppose, in accordance with the
particular figures chosen for our illustrative tables, that this
point is reached when 90,000 E bales are marketed in G at the
rate of 100 E bales for the price of about 78 G bales (carriage,
etc. paid), the 70,000 G bales finding a market in E at the same
rate, viz. about 78 G bales for 100 E bales. The trade is then in
equilibrium.

And the equilibrium is stable. For, if the trade shot past the
equilibrium point and more than 90,000 E bales were offered in
G, they would so far glut the market that more than 100 of them

---

[1] The intricate relations, to which they might conceivably give rise, cannot
be easily handled without the aid of diagrams. But the matter is of some interest;
and it is considered incidentally to a broader discussion in Appendix J.

[2] An examination of the figures in the tables, which claim to represent normal
conditions of trade, will show that they imply that every increase of the figures
in column (3) will be accompanied by an increase of those in column (2): and
every increase of the figures in column (1) will be accompanied by a decrease of
the figures in column (4). They imply also that every increase in column (3) must
be accompanied by an increase in column (5); and *vice versâ*.

would be needed to enable a merchant to return 78 G bales to E: III, VI, 5. and the E market would be so far glutted by a considerable excess of G bales above 70,000 that more than 78 of them would be needed to enable a merchant to return 100 E bales. The trade would yield no profit, and perhaps show a loss: so it would shrink again till the equilibrium level had been reached: this proves that the equilibrium is stable. Conditions of unstable equilibrium are theoretically conceivable, as will be argued in Appendix J.

Before leaving this subject, a few words may be said as to the relation in which our imaginary schedules stand to the actual statistics which could be obtained in regard to the international trade of a world in which there were only two countries; each of them being in a highly advanced economic stage, but each lacking some important resources which existed in the other. If the terms of trade had been for a long while not very far from the present position, that is, if *about* 90,000 E bales (sometimes rather more and sometimes rather less) had been for a good many years exchanged for *about* 70,000 G bales; then a good deal of experience would have been gained as to the terms on which E and G respectively would be willing to participate in a small or even a considerable expansion of the trade; and the horizontal rows of figures, near to those which correspond to the existing equilibrium position, could be filled in with some rough approximation to accuracy on a statistical basis. But no such experience would be available in regard to the receptivity of either country for amounts of imports, either very much greater or very much less, than those of which there had been fairly recent experience: and therefore no approximation, however rough, could be made to a statistical basis for the figures at the top and the bottom of the schedules.

Difficulties of this kind are of but little importance in regard to the practical applications of economics: for there is seldom much to be gained from speculations as to the results of conditions far removed from those which have already been experienced. On the other hand, speculation as to the results of conditions which have never been experienced has gone, and ought to go on cheerily: for it has often proved to be of service, if not in connection with the problems by which it was

III, vi, 5. set on foot, yet in others relating to matters having no superficial resemblance to those with which it was connected in the
first instance[1].

[1] This difficulty runs through the whole of economics, on its analytical side.
For on that side we naturally suppose, for the purposes of illustration, that all
the requisite data could conceivably be obtained; we ignore the fact that experience throws little or no direct light on the terms at which the imports of a
country, if violently contracted in quantity, could be sold. The experience of
celebrated sieges tells us that, if water is very scarce, a pint of it will sell for
more than a pint of strong wine; because it quenches thirst better; and that if
no one is allowed more than a scanty ration of ordinary meat, the price, in
ordinary times, of many pounds of meat may be obtained for a thing which can
be sold freely, as small and undesirable as a common rat. But no one can guess
what would be the price of leather, if the supply of it remained for a considerable
time at a hundredth part of its normal level.

It is true that guidance as to the probable intensity of demand for some kinds
of commodities, if they had become either very scarce or very plentiful, can
be obtained, by observing the ordinary demands of the poorer classes for commodities which are too costly for their use save on rare occasions, and by the
demand of the rich for commodities the cost of which is barely noticeable by
them. But even this method would be difficult of application to the intensity
of the total demand of a country for her imports, on the supposition that—her
general economic conditions remaining unchanged—their volume is reduced to,
say, a twentieth part of its present amount. Such a reduction has occurred
occasionally in the extremities of war: but all economic relations have been up-
set at the same time by the same cause; and the results, even if known accurately,
would be of little use. For all that we know to the contrary, a country's demand
might be of the "exceptional" order under those conditions: but our present
study does not claim to apply to those conditions.

CHAPTER VII

ELASTICITY OF A COUNTRY'S DEMAND
FOR IMPORTS

1. *Meaning of the term "elasticity of national demand."*

Ricardo, by a single effort, set up an explanation of the causes that govern the broad courses of international trade. But he confined his inquiries in the main to the case of exclusive trade between two countries E and G. We may follow his lead in the present chapter: and afterwards consider the extensions which he knew that the business men, for whom he chiefly wrote, would make for themselves.

The elasticity of a rubber band may be measured by the extent to which it is stretched by a given stress (the size of the band being known). So *the elasticity of a country's demand for imports may be measured by the proportionate increase in that demand, which results from any movement in her favour of the terms on which she can obtain them.*

We start from the position that, when two countries trade exclusively with one another, each of them demands the goods of the other, and supplies her own, by one and the same act; and that, at all events when international credit is left out of account, neither side can be properly described as making a demand, or offering a supply, in any sense in which the other does not. The same is true of a country's total trade with the world, unified as that is now by world markets. The elasticity of her effective demand for foreign goods is governed not only by her wealth and the elasticity of the desires of her population for them; but also by her ability to adjust the supplies of her own goods of various kinds to the demands of foreign markets.

This consideration was very important in early trade; when few goods would bear the expense of distant transport, and when each country had to look to her immediate neighbour for the greater part of her trade. And even now, it is important in regard to the trade of those countries, whose exports owe more to special bounties of nature than to man's energy. A country, whose resources

III, vii, 2. for foreign trade are derived mainly from exceptional natural advantages, may be unable to expand her trade without accepting much less favourable terms to herself: she may have already developed those resources nearly as far as they will reach; or her special products may be such as to command high prices abroad, only when supplied in limited quantities.

2. *Although the great demand of a large and rich country for imports tends to make the terms of her foreign trade unfavourable to her; yet this tendency is opposed, and often overborne, by the variety and resourcefulness of her supply.*

There are great differences in character between the demand of a large country and a small one; an advanced country and a backward one; a country whose land is already cultivated intensely, and one whose difficulties lie rather in the transport than in the production of agricultural produce. For instance, a poor country can seldom afford to buy things from abroad, unless they are intensely serviceable: whereas a rich country buys many things which she could easily forego. Thus, the rich country has less real benefit from the trade than the poor one, for just the same reason that, when a rich man makes a fair exchange with a poor one, giving a thing that is worth a pound for another that is worth a pound, the real serviceableness to the rich man of what he receives is not likely to be nearly as great as the real serviceableness to the poor man of that which is exchanged for it; simply because the real serviceableness of each pound's worth of purchasing power is relatively small to the man who has many pounds. And again, the rich country can with little effort supply a poor country with implements for agriculture or the chase which double the effectiveness of her labour, and which she could not make herself: while the rich country could without great trouble make for herself most of the things which she purchases from the poor nation: or at all events could get fairly good substitutes for them. A stoppage of the trade would therefore generally cause much more real loss to the poor than to the rich nation.

The scope of Ricardo's argument did not require him to take account of such differences. But Mill pushed on further. After stating truly that "the countries which carry on their trade on the most advantageous terms are those whose commodities are III, vii, 2. most in demand by foreign countries, and which have themselves the least demand for foreign commodities," he continued: "From which, among other consequences, it follows that the richest countries are those which *coeteris paribus* gain the least by a given amount of foreign commerce: since, having a greater demand for commodities generally, they are likely to have a greater demand for foreign commodities, and thus modify the terms of interchange to their own disadvantage. Their aggregate gains by foreign trade, doubtless, are generally greater than those of poorer countries, since they carry on a greater amount of such trade, and gain the benefit of cheapness on a larger consumption: but their gain is less on each individual article consumed[1]."

This argument is valid, so far as it goes: but it is incomplete. It is of course true that the foreign trade of a small country is likely to be greater in proportion to her population than that of a large one; because she depends on foreign supplies for many things which a country with more various resources can produce for herself: and her demand for foreign goods is therefore very eager, while a large and rich country can attract foreign purchasers by a great variety of goods, including many choice specialities, the subtler diversities of which are not represented in ordinary tables of statistics.

But this consideration needs to be balanced by others which make for the opposite conclusion. It is, that a great rich country has opportunities for pioneering new sorts of implements and machinery, and new sorts of comforts and luxuries of all kinds: she is likely to have highly organized transport and commercial relations with so many markets that she need not push any one variety of any product on a market which shows signs of being glutted with that variety. The trade of the rich country and of the poor is not with the other alone. It is with all the world; and the rich country has better opportunities for adapting her output to the receptivity of various markets than the poor one is likely to have. If an abstract England exported only cloth, and an abstract Germany exported only linen, the richer either of them became, the less no doubt would she gain by foreign trade. But the real England and Germany, as they have grown in riches,

---

[1] See his *Principles*, III, xviii, 8.

III, VII, 2. have found it more easy, and not more difficult, to curtail particular varieties of exports which were in danger of glutting any foreign market; and to substitute goods which would meet with a good and elastic demand somewhere or other. Before looking into that however, it will be well to develop Mill's proposition a little further.

Let us suppose a country G to be in trade with two countries E and E', which are alike in all respects, except that E is ten times as large as E', and with ten times as large a population: the natural and acquired resources of the two are to be similar in character: the resources of the average inhabitant and his desire for those things which neither country can produce for herself are to be equal in the two countries. Then the elasticity of demand of E' for any given aggregate of imports will be the same as that of E for a tenth part of that aggregate. But G will not be very greatly disturbed by variations in the demand of E', so long as that of E is elastic.

This suggests some considerations, the importance of which will appear when we come to inquire into the incidence of Preferential duties; that is, of duties levied in full measure on the supplier of a thing which comes from one country or group of countries; but which are not levied, at all events in full measure, on the same thing when coming from other sources: (of course Protective duties, which are levied on certain imported goods, but not on similar goods produced at home, are a special form of Preferential duties).

In all such inquiries it is important to remember that the influence which a country exerts on the value of a thing does not depend only on the elasticity or *degree* of the responsiveness of her demand for it or of her supply of it. It would so depend, if all countries were equal in economic force; that is, in population, wealth, energy. But, as things are, it is not even approximately true. The influence which she exerts depends on the *aggregate amount* of her response to more favourable terms of interchange; that is, on the volume of her imports multiplied into elasticity of her demand. If E and E' were both in trade with G, the influence of E would be ten times as great as that of E', because an equal elasticity would be multiplied into a volume of imports ten times as large.

3. *Resourcefulness of supply is one cause of elasticity of* III, VII, 3.
demand.

It is practically certain that the demands of each of Ricardo's
two countries for the goods in general of the other would have
considerable elasticity *under modern industrial conditions*, even if E
and G were single countries whose sole trade was with one another.
And if we take E to be a large and rich commercial country, while
G stands for all foreign countries, this certainty becomes absolute.
For E is quite sure to export a great many things which some at
least of the other countries could forego without much inconvenience: and which would be promptly refused if offered by her
only on terms considerably less favourable to purchasers. And,
on the other hand, E is quite sure to have exports which can find
increased sales in some countries, at least, if she offers them on
more favourable terms to purchasers. Therefore the world's
demand for E's goods, which is practically unified by the machinery
of modern commerce and the modern money market, is sure to
rise largely if E offers her goods generally on terms more advantageous to purchasers; and to shrink largely if E endeavours to
insist on terms more favourable to herself. And E, on her part,
is sure on the one hand to import many things from various parts
of the world, which she can easily forego, if the terms on which
they are sold are raised against her; and on the other to be capable
of turning to fairly good use many things which are offered to
her from various parts of the world, if they were offered on terms
rather more favourable to her than at present.

Also, those human resources of high energy and varied faculty,
aided by a large supply of free capital, to which a great industrial
country owes her prosperity, can be adapted and adjusted with
comparative ease to a very large range of wants in various parts
of the world: and, if she needs more imports, her demand for them
can be quickly made effective by an increase of her exports, which
will give her direct or indirect command over the things which
she needs, without moving the terms of trade considerably against
her. The fact that most of her products have to run the gauntlet
of close competition before they can be sold at all, indicates that
there is probably a large volume of foreign demand, which she
can master, if her own demand for foreign goods rises. And, if,
on the other hand, the reception of her exports by foreign markets

III, VII, 4. should become less favourable to her, she has generally no very great difficulty in turning a part of the resources, with which she had produced her exports, to good account in meeting domestic demand for other products of like character.

Further, the demand of any one country for imports is as a rule small relatively to the world's supply of goods of the same class; and the world can nearly always follow changes in that demand rapidly and easily by a change in supply. There are indeed exceptional cases, as when a war almost quenches for a time the demand of two or more great countries for some classes of goods, while increasing it for others: and a similar dislocation is apt to result from a sudden cessation of war. Again, the export industries of a large part of the world may be distressed by a collapse of the credit and industrial activity of a single very powerful country: or even by a violent change in her tariff system. But such influences are transient: and there are but few exceptions to the general rule that a great industrial country can easily adjust her exports to changes in the amount of imports which she desires to obtain from the rest of the world; and that the exports of the world to any particular country can even more easily be adjusted to changes in the willingness of the customers of that country to accept the terms on which she is willing to trade.

Thus, the elasticity of effective international demand depends on the elasticity of wants, and on responsive adjustments of supply: but yet the demand for imports by an energetic industrial country will generally be elastic. Also the world's demand for her goods will generally be elastic.

4. *Characteristics of the demands of some leading industrial countries for imported goods.*

The imports into New countries depend largely upon the credit in which they stand at the time with Old countries. If that is good, they import large quantities of railway material and other plant and, as they pay the wages of the workers on new undertakings largely out of the funds they have borrowed, their imports of goods for domestic consumption often increase at such times very rapidly. Their credit is governed partly by the prudence of the leaders of their finance; partly by international movements of credit; partly by opening out of new mineral resources; partly III, vii, 4. by the harvest of cereals and the supply of grass for stock, and partly by changes in their tariffs. As a general rule, their peoples are enterprising, eager for novelty, quick to adopt any new form of personal expenditure that may promise to yield large satisfaction in proportion to its cost, and quicker still to adopt any implement or machine the cost of which has fallen so as to make its use remunerative. That is, their demand for foreign goods is elastic.

In New and Old countries alike, consumption and therefore imports are usually large in an ascending phase of general commercial credit; and, at the same time prices are high, and therefore the imports appear larger than they are. But a lending country, like Britain, generally exports capital largely when credit is good, and her working and other classes are spending freely: while a borrowing country is likely to swell her imports by goods obtained on credit, just when her imports would be largest and at the highest prices, even if she were not borrowing.

Japan resembles New countries in that she is eager to adopt western methods that require a larger capital than she yet possesses. And though her people are poor, because what little raw produce they export has to be raised from a crowded land at a high real cost; yet they are so alert, so closely in touch with western thought, and so full of independent enterprise, that her manufactures for export are growing rapidly, to buy rice and cotton and such manufactures as she cannot with advantage provide for herself; and the responsiveness of her demand to change in the terms on which they can be attained is very quick.

India has not yet awakened to follow Japan's example. Her cotton manufactures are indeed mainly in the hands of her own people. But her large exports of tea and jute owe much to western enterprise; and in spite of the denseness of her population, nearly all the remainder are raw products raised with but little aid from advanced appliances. Railway material holds a considerable place among her imports; but their chief characteristic is the predominance of European luxuries for the consumption of her ruling classes, Native and European. A good many of the things, which she is importing in increasing quantities, could, however, be made easily by her own people, if they aroused themselves. She pays for them largely by the exportation of cotton, jute, and tea; and the recent development of these three industries, has been a chief cause of that reduction in the real cost to her of her increased demand for European goods.

China and Russia resemble India in many respects: but high tariffs, and the difficulties connected with their internal traffic keep their trade rather smaller and probably rather less responsive than hers. For the last two hundred years the vast riches of South America have been just on the point of being fully exploited; and the disappointment of extravagant hopes with regard to them has played a great part in many commercial crises from which Britain and other western countries have suffered. Anglo-Saxon, German and Italian energies are, however, gradually making their way against political and other difficulties: the native population, though limp in character, are alert in mind; and, especially in their chief cities, the demand for western goods that are adapted to their wants and can be had at a low cost, is very elastic. There is scarcely any limit to their power of exporting goods of high value in the west, to pay for any imports which they really care to have.

The external demand for the whole of a country's exports is seldom very urgent, and is frequently very elastic; but several countries have a rather urgent demand for British coal. Britain might pay 80s. a quarter rather than forego any large quantity of her foreign supplies of wheat: while a price, permanently set even at 15s. a quarter, would not induce her to increase very largely her importation of it to be used as human food (though she might perhaps buy it at that price to be fed to cattle and for making alcohol for industrial use). But there is no case of a country whose demand for a large part of her imports is thus rigid: every country could give up a large part of her consumption of imported products, without very great distress; and, on the other hand, she would greatly increase her consumption of foreign goods in general if they could be obtained at considerably lower real costs.

If Britain could get her imports at less real cost, she would ere long take a greatly increased quantity of nearly all of them; except only those necessaries of life, of which even her poorer classes already consume almost as much as they need. Some of the new imports would displace similar goods which she had made

for herself; and the increased cheapness of others would tempt III, VII, 4.
people to enlarged consumption of them, at the expense, perhaps,
of very different goods or services which she had previously provided for herself. The resources which had been devoted to the
home products and services, which were no longer demanded,
would be turned to producing exports to pay for the increased
imports. Such changes, if sudden and violent, would cause much
suffering in particular home industries; but, in fact, they are
generally gradual. They seldom come about on a large scale nearly
as quickly as do some of those revolutions in technique, which
supersede special varieties of skilled work; and they are *generally*
met by a slackening of the flow of new labour and capital into
an industry which is tending downwards.

The elasticity of a country's aggregate demand for foreign goods
is compounded of the elasticities of her demands for various sorts
of goods: account being taken of the time required for a tendency
towards increased demand to effectuate itself. And, turning to
the other side of the same issue, we have to resolve the aggregate
ability of a country to provide increased supplies of goods that
will be well marketable abroad, into the expansiveness and
resourcefulness of her several export industries; and their power
of applying themselves to working for the home instead of foreign
markets, if occasion should arise. Here the element of time rises
to the first rank. For a complete readjustment of supply to changed
conditions cannot always be effected until time enough has elapsed
to enable many new businesses to be set up, or old businesses
enlarged, with increased provision of expensive plant and specialized
skill: and it cannot be appropriately reduced until old plant has
fallen in value so much as to be ready to be scrapped; and
specialized skill and knowledge, that are no longer in high
request, have found refuge in other work or in rest from their
labours.

The same considerations may be put in another form, by
reference to the incidence of frontier duties, whether export or
import. The incidence of these, on nations as a whole, contains
elements other than those which relate primarily to the individuals
composing those nations: but in the main it is the aggregate of
the influences exerted on individuals. In the main it is true that

III, VII, 4. a tax on a commodity is borne by the consumer, whether at home or abroad, during the period, whether short or long, in which he is unable, or unwilling to lessen his consumption of it, or to obtain it on good terms by any other route. But the tax falls on the producers, in so far as the consumption of their produce is lessened by an increase in its cost to consumers, unless, indeed, they are unable to divert their faculties, their energies, their plant and their business connections quickly to some other profitable use.

CHAPTER VIII

INFLUENCES OF ELASTICITY OF DEMAND ON THE TERMS OF INTERNATIONAL TRADE AND ON THE INCIDENCE OF IMPORT DUTIES[1]

1. *Introductory.*

Let us suppose that, trade between the two countries E and G having been in equilibrium, there is a considerable increase in E's demand for G's goods, unaccompanied by any corresponding increase of demand on the part of G. The first result will be an increase in the amount of E's goods which her importing merchants will be able to obtain in return for each bale of G's goods. The second will be that merchants will be able and compelled to offer more of E's goods in G's markets for each G bale: their mutual competition will force them to do so. That is to say, the terms of international trade will be altered in G's favour. But how far will the movement go?

The answer depends on the relative elasticities of the demands of the two countries for each others goods. If G's demand is very responsive to a movement of the terms in her favour, then a small movement will suffice for this purpose; if not, a large one will be needed. The influence of E's increased demand in moving the rate of interchange against her (and in favour of G) will therefore be the less extensive, other things being equal, the greater be the elasticity of G's demand.

But other things cannot be taken to be equal; the result will depend partly on the elasticity of E's demand. For, in any case G will send more of her goods to E; and E will in any case not be willing to accept these without some concession from the rate (one-

---

[1] This chapter seems needed in order to develop the study of international trade in the abstract, which was set up by Ricardo and John Stuart Mill. But it has not much bearing on pressing practical problems; and it may be omitted. Readers with mathematical aptitude may get some satisfaction from the diagrammatic version of its problems which is given in Appendix J.

III, viii, 1. sixth more favourable to G than the old equilibrium rate), which she has become willing (in consequence of the recent increase in her demand) to yield in return for her old imports from G. If the elasticity of E's demand is great, she will take a considerably increased amount without demanding more than a small concession: but if her demand is inelastic, she will require a considerable concession.

Thus, in every possible combination of a large, medium, or small elasticity on the part of E's demand, with a large, medium, or small elasticity on the part of G's demand, one general rule holds. The more elastic the demand of either country, the elasticity of the demand of the other being given, the larger will be the volumes both of her exports and of her imports; but the more also will her exports be enlarged relatively to her imports; or, in other words, the less favourable to her will be the terms of trade. Thus both sides of the trade will be very greatly enlarged; if both elasticities are great. But if both are small G's exports will be increased only a little; while E's will be increased by the original sixth and a *very* little more in addition[1].

---

[1] This argument can be best presented by aid of diagrams. But it seems advisable to add here a brief statement of its results in ordinary language. We may begin with the group of cases in which G's demand is very elastic. A considerable increase in the supply of E's goods in her markets can then be absorbed without materially moving the rate of interchange against E: and a vast amount can be absorbed if E's demand is also very elastic; that is, if she is willing to accept very large quantities of G's goods at the rate, one-sixth more unfavourable to E than the old equilibrium rate, at which E is now willing to accept the old equilibrium amount. Under these conditions E's exports will increase very much, perhaps by about three-fifths: while G's will increase by perhaps a half; so that the new equilibrium rate of interchange will be about 100 of E's bales for 73 of G's. (Such a result is seen in the new equilibrium position J in Fig. 12 in Appendix J.)

If, however, G's demand remaining very elastic, E's be somewhat inelastic, she will require a greater concession in the rate of interchange to induce her to trade so largely; and therefore she will get somewhat less of G's goods than in the last result, while her own exports would be considerably less. Thus, if E's demand has but a moderate elasticity, her imports may increase only by three-tenths and her exports by seven-twentieths, giving a rate of interchange of about 75 G bales for 100 E bales. And, in the extreme case in which E's demand is very inelastic, her imports may increase only by one-sixth, and her exports by one-fifth, giving a rate of interchange of about 76 G bales for 100 E bales. (Results of these kinds are represented by the positions K and L suggested for the new equilibrium respectively in the same figure.)

Next, let us go to the opposite extreme in regard to the elasticity of G's demand, and suppose that it is very small indeed. That means that however much the supply of E's goods in her markets be increased, there will be only a small increase in the quantity of G goods that can be obtained in exchange

When the trade between E and G is in equilibrium, gold must be so distributed between them that the gold prices of E's exports in G's ports exceed their prices in E's ports only by the costs direct and indirect of transporting them, allowance being included for any taxes to be paid on the way. For, if the prices of E's goods in G's markets are above that level, merchants would be inclined to send gold from G to buy E's goods. They might, indeed, be deterred for a time from sending gold by the cost of its carriage: but, as this cost is small, some of the minor vicissitudes of trade would ere long make it worth while to export gold from G; and, the general conditions of trade remaining stable, gold would stay in E. Similarly, if the gold prices of E's goods in G's ports exceeded their prices in E's ports by less than these costs of carriage from E to G, merchants would tend to send gold instead of goods from E to G, in order to obtain G's goods. Of course, the equilibrium excess of the gold prices of G's goods in E's markets must be equal to the costs direct and indirect of sending them from G to E.

Suppose that E's demand for G's goods being inelastic, there arises a considerable increase in G's demand for E's goods, so that the terms of trade are moved against G, and a good many more of G's bales than before have to be exported in order to bring back an extra hundred of E's bales: merchants will then take gold from G to E; because they can obtain with it as many of E's bales as before. This process will continue, till the rise of prices in E caused by the increase of her currency, combined with the fall of prices in G caused by the shrinkage of the currency there, has so readjusted prices to the altered rate of interchange of bales, that E's goods sell again in G's markets and G's goods sell in E's for their several home prices together with costs of transport. Merchants will do business in terms of money at

for them. The increase will of course evoke some addition to the exports from E: but, whatever be the elasticity of E's demand, the addition will be very small, and G will export only a little more than the old equilibrium number of her bales in return for only a little more than an addition of one-sixth to E's old equilibrium exports. In this case therefore the rigidity of G's demand will thoroughly dominate the result; and variations in the elasticity of E's demand will have but little influence on it. (This group of cases is represented by U, V and W in the same figure.)

In the intermediate group of cases in which G's demand has a moderate elasticity, the results will clearly be intermediate between those in the two extreme cases. (They are represented by R, S and T in the same figure.)

III, vIII, 2 just the same rate of profits as before; and records of their profits will not disclose the fundamental change which has occurred. That change will lie below the surface of waters, that have closed above it: it will consist of an increase in the quantity of the produce of her labour and capital which G has to give in order to obtain each hundred bales of E's goods.

On the other hand, if E's demand for G's goods had been elastic so that G's increased demand could be met by exporting more of her goods without greatly burdening E's markets, and therefore without causing much change in the terms of trade: then only a slight movement of gold from G to E would have been set up, and it would have lasted only a short while. For a very little change of price levels would have sufficed to bring them into adjustment with the new terms of trade.

2. *If* E *and* G *are in exclusive trade with one another, a general tax levied by* E *either on her imports from* G *or on her exports to* G, *will diminish her imports to some extent, and her exports to a greater extent; and will thus tend to move the rate of interchange in* E's *favour.*

We pass to consider the influence which a decrease in a country's effective demand for imports exerts on the terms of her external trade: the decrease may be supposed to be caused by the imposition of a tax on her imports.

It might perhaps suffice to say that the effects of a shrinkage of E's demand for G's goods will be the converse of those of an increase. But a backward movement in organic growth is seldom quite like the previous forward movement: and the opportunity may be taken for looking from a rather different point of view at what is in effect the same problem as that already considered.

Let us first look at the general relation between import and export taxes. The considerations which can be urged for and against the levying of an import tax on a particular commodity differ widely from those appropriate to a particular export tax: and this is perhaps the origin of an opinion, which seems to pervade a good deal of economic discussion, that a general tax on all imports would have widely different effects from a general tax on all exports. In fact the two taxes would have the same effect:

provided they were evenly distributed, equal in aggregate amount, III, VIII, 2. and their proceeds were expended in the same way[1].

Suppose that an import duty is levied by E in kind, or—what is the same thing—that its proceeds are expended on an extra purchase of G's goods by E's Government in addition to those which that Government would have otherwise purchased—that action will cause the total demand for G's goods to be greater than if the proceeds of the tax had been spent on E's goods. But, exactly the same result would follow, if the proceeds of a general export tax were spent on an additional purchase by E's Government of G's goods: and in order to avoid this irrelevant disturbance, it will be best to assume that the proceeds of all of E's taxes, however assessed, are expended on E's goods. Further, we take no account of the difficulties of merchants and producers at home and abroad, whose plans may have been put out of gear by the imposition of a burden which they had not anticipated, and who, in consequence, may be glad to market some of their wares for less than the full cost of production.

Let us then suppose that trade between E and G being in equilibrium, E's Government imposes a tax on all her imports; that it amounts to one-sixth of their value, and that its proceeds are all spent by the Government at home. Then merchants must see their way to selling each bale or other consignment of the imports into E for the value of an increased amount of her goods, so that after having paid the taxes, they may still be able to export enough of those goods to cover the cost of their foreign purchases, with expenses and profits. Therefore they must stint their importations into E: the rate of interchange will move in E's favour, but it cannot move in her favour by more than a sixth. These results are, perhaps with the exception of the last, fairly obvious. Their

---

[1] It may be well to look into this more closely. Take the case of an all round merchant working from a basis in E. He lays out the equivalent of 1000 E bales on the purchase of cargo and the costs of the all round trade: these costs include hire of a ship, insurance of ship and cargo, expenses of working the ship, port dues and taxes. If these costs amount to 200 E bales, he will be able to take 800 E bales to G and bring back their equivalent in G bales. If these charges are increased to 250 bales he will bring home the equivalent which he can get for only 750 E bales in G's markets; though E's people will still have spent 1000 E bales on getting them. Thus E's effective demand will have shrunk to the same extent, whatever be the way in which this extra charge is laid on him; whether by extra cost of coal, extra dues, or extra taxes at home or abroad; provided only the extra payment required from him is taken out in E's goods and not in G's.

III, VIII, 2. proof can be reached most easily by the aid of the diagrams, which are supplied in Appendix J, Fig. 13, but they are worked out in ordinary language in the adjoining footnote[1].

It may be well to add a numerical illustration of the difference between the rate of interchange as seen from the point of view of consumers in E, and as seen from the point of view of G as a whole. We have supposed that 90,000 E bales were exchanged for 70,200 G bales before the tax: and that afterwards 78,000 E bales are sent to G in return for 62,400 of her bales. The rate of interchange between E and G as a whole will then have moved from 100 E bales for 78 G bales to 100 E bales for 80 G bales: but as E's Government has taken the equivalent of one out of every six of E bales, the consumers in E (no allowance being made for the profits of wholesale and retail dealers) will have paid in effect 91,000 E bales for the 62,400 G bales; that is at the rate of 100 E bales for about 69 G bales[2].

[1] We start from the position that, under the old conditions of trade, merchants were taking 70,200 G bales to E; and were disposing of them in E's markets on terms that enabled 90,000 E bales to go back; the costs of transport and dealing being arranged as in the preceding chapter. If now E's Government imposes a tax of one-sixth on all the imports (the tax to be paid in E's goods) the value of the tax will be 15,000 E bales; and consequently only 75,000 E bales will be returned. The result would be exactly the same if the tax were levied on E's exports: in that case also there would be only 75,000 E bales to go back. We are to inquire, on the lines of the preceding Section, how the characters of E's and G's demands respectively will influence the change in the position of the new equilibrium of trade, that results from this change in the conditions of E's demand.

In the first place, the exports of G must shrink so as to make the rate of interchange more favourable to E. For, if they were maintained at the old amount (and the case would be still stronger if they were increased), importers would obtain from E's consumers the equivalent of only as many E bales as before; and therefore, after paying the tax, would take back one-sixth less than before: and, according to our schedule, they could not market those in G with normal profits to themselves for the equivalent of those G bales which they had taken out. (It is indeed abstractly conceivable that G's demand for all of E's goods might be so extremely inelastic, that a smaller aggregate of them could be marketed in G for an equal or even larger aggregate of G's goods: but, though this "Exceptional Demand" case claims discussion from a purely theoretical point of view, the schedules on which we are working have been constructed in accordance with the belief that nothing of the kind is possible in real trade.)

Secondly, E cannot force the rate of interchange to become more favourable to her by more than a sixth. For that would imply that G goods were offered to E consumers, after the tax had been paid by the merchants, at terms more favourable to the consumers than before; and that yet those consumers refused to take over the old amount of G goods at that rate.

[2] Here occasion may be taken to guard against temptation to count twice over the gain, which E may derive from the tax. For she may appear both to turn the rate of interchange in her favour, at all events to some extent, and to

Thus, we may conclude, in regard to the exclusive trade between two countries, that if one of them (E) levies a general tax either on her imports or on her exports, the proceeds of the tax being spent by the Government mainly on her own goods and services, then she will injure the other country (G) in two ways: she will cause G's trade to shrink more or less; and she will force G to give somewhat more of her own bales in return for each hundred of E's bales which she still receives. At the same time E will injure herself in one way and benefit herself in another. She will injure herself by diminishing her trade with G, and therefore foregoing some of G's products which would have been more useful or agreeable to her people than any home products of goods or services which can be got at the same cost: for, if they had had no such superiority, the people would not have elected, as they did previously to the tax, to buy those products of G instead of home products. But, on the other hand, E will benefit herself by obtaining those of G's goods which she still receives at a rate somewhat more favourable to herself than before. Of course G's goods will be more costly to the people of E than if they had not been taxed. But they will not be made more costly (at all events by those who buy wholesale at first hand) by quite the full amount of the tax: and therefore E, regarded as a whole, Government and people being reckoned together, stands to gain something by levying the tax.

All the values and costs mentioned above are "real" values and costs; that is, they are expressed in terms of the representative bales of the country in question: but the upshot may be expressed in terms of gold prices on the assumption, made at the end of the last section, that the currencies of both E and G are based on gold; of which each possesses a stock, though neither has any gold mines in work. We start then from equilibrium, in which the goods of either country sell in the ports of the other at the gold prices which they bear at home, increased by all the expenses

throw on the foreigner some part at least of the burden of a tax, the proceeds of which accrue to her Government. But these facts do not represent two gains; they represent only one gain expressed in two ways. From the consumer's point of view the rate of interchange is affected very unfavourably: it is only when the interests of the public purse are reckoned together with the separate interests of individuals, that a movement of the rate of interchange can be shown in her favour.

III, VIII, 2. direct and indirect of the transport from one country to the other. Now E imposes taxes on her imports: merchants therefore can no longer earn their living unless they can sell G's goods to consumers in E for their gold prices in G, increased by the full money costs direct and indirect of the transport from G together with the taxes; consequently they stint their exports of G's goods, on the grounds already explained; and indeed a very little more than they would have done if they had not been able to export gold from G in lieu of some of her goods. It is to their interest to do this: because when the tax is first imposed, G's goods cost about as much in terms of gold in G as before; and, as the gold will pass E's frontiers without being taxed—this is to be assumed in accordance with general usage—they will for the time make a better business by sending gold than by sending goods. Gold will therefore continue to flow from G to E, and thereby to cause prices generally to rise in E and fall in G; until the prices of G goods delivered in E have risen relatively to their prices in G, by the full equivalent of the tax. When that result has been reached, merchants will cover their money outlays with profits; and the trade will again be in equilibrium. But this will not show that E's consumers have borne the whole burden of their taxes.

In order to obtain goods that sell for the equivalent of an ounce of gold in G, they will be compelled to pay an amount of their own money equivalent to an ounce, together with costs of transport, which now include taxes and traders' profits on them: while consumers in G will buy E goods for gold cost in E together with costs of transport, in which there are no taxes to be reckoned. But an ounce of gold will buy more G goods than before: and it will buy less E goods than before: these two changes are to the benefit of E (consumer's purses and the public purse being reckoned together) and they are to the detriment of G: the sum of them is the share of the burden of her taxes which E throws upon G. Its amount is governed by fundamental relations of international demand, which are independent of money in the long run. That is, G's share of the burden is governed by the response which E makes to the shrinkage of her supplies from G; and by the response which G makes to the consequent shrinkage of her supplies from E: i.e. on the relative elasticities of E's demand and of G's demand.

3. *Suppose that* G's *demand for* E's *goods being very*
elastic, a moderate tax is levied by E *on her imports or*
exports; it will have no very great effect on the rate of inter-
change, unless E's *demand also is elastic; but in that case the*
trade will shrink greatly.

We have now to work on the same lines, but in a reversed
direction, to those of our study (in the first section of this chapter)
of the effects of an increase in a country's demand. We start
from the basis that a tax of one-sixth levied by E on her imports,
its produce being spent on E's own goods, must move the rate of
interchange in G's disfavour, and cannot move it by a full sixth:
and we inquire what movement within these limits will suffice to
make E's goods so scarce in G's markets that G will be just willing
to accept them on terms, which E also will accept under the new
conditions for that amount of trade. It is obvious that if G's
demand is very responsive to a movement of the terms in her
disfavour, then a small movement will suffice for this purpose; if
not, a large one will be needed. The influence of the diminution
of E's demand in moving the rate of interchange in her own
favour (and against G) will therefore be the less extensive, other
things being equal, the greater be the elasticity of G's demand.

But the result will depend partly on the elasticity of E's demand.
For, in any case G will send less of her goods to E; and they will
in any case be sold in E's market at a rate somewhat more favourable to G than that (one-sixth less favourable to G than the old
equilibrium rate), at which alone E had been willing, since the
imposition of the tax, to accept her old imports from G. If the
elasticity of E's demand is great, she will considerably diminish
her imports rather than make more than a small concession: but
if her demand is inelastic, she will make a considerable concession. Thus, in every possible combination of a large, medium,
or small elasticity on the part of E's demand, with a large, medium,
or small elasticity on the part of G's demand, one general rule
holds. The more elastic the demand of either country, the elasticity
of the demand of the other being given, the smaller will be the
volumes of her exports and her imports: and the more will her
exports be diminished relatively to her imports; that is the more
favourable will be the rate of interchange to her. If the elasticity
of G's demand be great, E will in any case bear nearly the whole

III, vIII, 3. burden of her tax; but if it is small G will bear a considerable part of it. Variations in the elasticity of E's demand will cause variations in the opposite direction; and G will bear scarcely any of it if her own demand is very elastic, while that of E is not very elastic.

To put nearly the same things in another way, the elasticity of G's demand has the chief part in controlling the result of the imposition of a given tax on E's imports. If that elasticity is great, G's exports shrink much, the rate of interchange moves but little in E's favour; and only a small part of the burden of E's tax is thrown upon G, in so far as that burden is indicated by the rate of interchange: and conversely if G's elasticity is small. Some part is played also by the elasticity of E's demand. Her exports are bound to shrink by a sixth. But if her demand is very elastic, the shrinkage of E's exports in excess of that sixth will be considerable (not probably very great); and the movement of the rate of interchange in her favour is rather greater, than it would be if her demand had little elasticity.

It is, however, to be remembered that each country is likely to be injured by curtailment of any trade to which she was inclined: and that therefore, though a movement of the terms of interchange in E's favour enables her to gain at G's expense, the accompanying curtailment of E's trade may involve a heavy real loss to her: which is not mitigated by the fact that G is suffering a similar loss[1].

[1] It may be well to go a little more into detail as in the corresponding footnote in the first section; and with the same caution that all such details can be handled more thoroughly and securely, and at the same time really more easily, with the aid of diagrams, such as are supplied in regard to the present problem in Appendix J, than without such aid.

We will begin, as before, with the group of cases in which G's demand is very elastic. In this group, any movement of the rate of interchange against G will cause a relatively large diminution of her willingness to trade. The movement of the rate against her will not go very much against her; and she will therefore not bear a large share of the burden of E's taxes, whatever be the elasticity of E's demand.

Since G will send less of her goods to E, E will be forced to make some concession from the rate (one-sixth more favourable to herself than the old equilibrium rate) on which she would have insisted if G had maintained the full volume of her exports. If E's demand is very elastic, her willingness to trade will be greatly lessened by the fact that G will not consent to trade except on terms nearly as favourable to herself as the old terms; that is, except on terms more unfavourable to the consumers in E by nearly a sixth. In this case therefore G's exports will shrink very much. E's exports will shrink by rather more than a sixth, and the rate of interchange will have moved only a little in E's

But now let us consider the case in which, though G can easily III, VIII, 3. forego a considerable part of her imports, there are some of them which are almost essential to her: and first let E be supposed able to dispense easily with all of G's goods. Then a moderate tax levied by E on her imports would not reduce the supply of E's goods in G's markets so far as to call into play the urgent part of G's demand: and therefore the effects of the tax would be just the same as though G's demand were elastic throughout: that is, the trade would shrink a great deal, but the movement of its terms in E's favour would not be very great. But if the tax were gradually increased, until the shrinking of the trade touched some of G's imports which she could not easily forego, the situation would begin to change. E would gradually throw a greater and greater share of the burden of the tax on G: the receipts of E's Treasury from it might not be great, because the imports to be taxed might be small and so she might not gain very much by it.

favour. (This case is represented by the position suggested for the new equilibrium at J in Fig. 14 in Appendix J.)

If, while G's demand is still supposed to be very responsive to changes in the rate, that of E is not very responsive, then the rate of interchange will be rather more favourable to E: but the volume of her trade will be considerably less. (These results are represented by the suggested positions of new equilibrium at K for a moderate elasticity on the part of E, and at L for a small elasticity, in the same figure.)

Next let us suppose that G's demand is very inelastic: and that the stinting of the supplies of E's goods in her markets causes their value to rise so much that the diminished supply of them sells in the aggregate for the equivalent of nearly as many of G's as before. (That is, we suppose that the elasticity of her demand is but little more than unity: to suppose it to be less than unity would be to admit the Exceptional Demand case into the discussion. That case is however illustrated in Fig. 16.) E would then throw nearly the whole burden of her tax on G: for E's exports would have shrunk very much (really by rather more than a sixth), while G's exports would be diminished but little. If E's own demand were very elastic, the trade would be a little larger, and the rate of interchange would be a little more unfavourable to her, than if it were very inelastic: but the degree of her elasticity would have very little influence in comparison with that of G. (The suggested positions of equilibrium at U, V and W in Fig. 14 correspond to a low degree of elasticity on the part of G, co-existent with varying degrees on the part of E: it will be noted that they all lie close together.)

If G's demand is of considerable, but not great elasticity, the results will be intermediate between those in the two last cases. G's exports will shrink considerably: E's exports will shrink very considerably, but by a good deal less than a sixth: the rate of interchange will move in E's favour, and a considerable share of the burden of E's tax will be thrown upon G. These results hold whatever the elasticity of E's demand: but if that is great, the volume of the trade will be perceptibly larger; and the share of the burden of her tax which is thrown on G will be smaller than if E's demand has but little elasticity. (This group of results is indicated by the points R S and T in Fig. 14.)

III, VIII, 3. But ultimately, when it became so high as to deprive G of nearly the whole of those imports of which she stood in urgent need, she would suffer severe loss.

If, however, E's demand, like G's, though elastic for large quantities of her imports, were urgent and inelastic for small quantities, the effect of a continuous increase of her tax on imports (or on exports) would be different. The trade would, as before, diminish rapidly with the first stages of that increase: but would not yield much more to a further increase: and the terms of the trade would not be further modified in E's favour to any considerable extent.

Lastly, it might happen that E was under obligation to pay a heavy tribute to G; and, if the amount of that tribute covered all those imports of which G stood in urgent need, then she could not be grievously oppressed by E's tax, however heavy it was, and however elastic was E's demand even for small quantities of G's goods: the worst that could happen to G would be to forego all of those imports of which she was not in urgent need.

The special hypothesis on which we are working, in regard to the trade between E and G, excludes the possibility of any investment of capital by G in E. But, later on, we shall have to consider the fact that sparsely peopled countries have generally borrowed largely from densely peopled western countries: that as the sparsely peopled countries develop their industries, they will be able to forego without very great inconvenience nearly all their imports of manufactures; but that densely peopled countries will have an imperative need for considerable imports of food and raw material. These conditions will correspond rather closely to those of the case just discussed; densely peopled countries being represented by G, and the sparsely peopled countries by E. The tendency, already strong on the part of many sparsely peopled countries, to increase the weight of their taxes on manufactures generally, may possibly extend much further: it will make very little difference in practice whether they acted in concert or not, provided that they in fact move far in the same direction. And should this happen, the large volume of imports which western countries will probably be able to draw from sparsely peopled countries, as interest on invested capital, without being compelled to market any exports in return, will be a strong and much needed bulwark against effective oppression by III, VIII, 4. those taxes[1].

4. *Limitations of the scope of general reasoning in regard to the benefits which a country derives from her external trade.*

Ricardo's masterly treatment of *general* taxes on the trade between two countries, isolated from the rest of the world, avoids many of the difficulties which beset a realistic study of the trade relations which connect a single modern country either with the rest of the world as a whole or with any particular country in it: and this is a chief source of its efficiency.

For the effects of any tax, or other event, by which such real relations may be disturbed, are likely to be complicated by many side issues. If reckoning is made with them, the main issues are obscured: the particular trees close at hand prevent us from seeing the wood: and, if they are ignored provisionally, a partial solution is apt to be mistaken for the complete. For instance, a question may arise as to whether the commodity is the product of a partial monopoly; for in that case a tax on it, whether levied at home or abroad, is likely to make the monopolist reduce his price a little in order to avoid losing a considerable share of his extra monopoly profits. Now, nearly every producer and trader has a temporary partial monopoly in that market, or at all events in that particular part of the market, in which he has established his connection. And it may happen that one of the most important things to be said with regard to that particular tax, especially from the point of view of a short-sighted politician, is in regard to these more or less ephemeral and unsubstantial incidents. And further, if the monopolist, whether a single large business or a strongly organized cartel, is protected by high import duties against foreign producers of goods similar to its own, it may sell more cheaply abroad than at home, not merely to meet a passing emergency, but as

---

[1] Its analytical side is best seen by aid of diagram 19, Appendix J. It might be developed so as to take account of the tendency of manufactures to Increasing Return and of raw produce to Diminishing Return. But these tendencies are not in fact as broad and simple as they appear: and the application of Ricardo's rigid hypothesis to them, though seductive, collides against latent difficulties, the gravity of which increases, the more closely they are studied; and it seems therefore best to treat them directly in connection with the details of any trade in which they are severally prominent.

III, VIII, 4. a steady policy: so that its exports habitually pay less than the full cost of production. To the extent to which that is true, Ricardo's fundamental assumptions will not be strictly applicable.

Again, if the commodity is one for which the taxing country is the chief market, she may obtain it at rather less than the full equivalent of its cost of production for a longer time than she would, if those, who had provided specialized skill and plant for its production, could easily market it elsewhere. And conversely, if the commodity is one of which she is almost the sole producer, its foreign consumers must bear a great part of the burden of any tax which she may impose on its exportation.

When a customs tariff is under discussion, details such as these come to the front, and are apt to hide from view the broad influence which is exerted on the terms of a country's trade, by the relation in which the volume and eagerness of her demand for her imports in general bear to the volume and eagerness of the external demand for her exports. Ricardo's plan makes this master influence stand out in its proper proportions. It shows every import duty, and every export duty imposed by a country, as tending to move the terms of trade in her favour, because it tends to diminish the volume of trade which she is willing to do on any given terms.

Great then is the usefulness of Ricardo's method. But even greater are the evils which may arise from a crude application of its suggestions to real problems. For that simplicity which makes it helpful, makes it also deficient and even treacherous.

CHAPTER IX

TAXES ON PARTICULAR IMPORTS AND EXPORTS[1]

1. *Incidence of import duties.*

The policy of special taxes on imported goods has two sides. It obviously raises questions relating to the expediency of Government intervention in affairs of industry and trade. These questions are of broad scope: some of them are concerned with the influences which high import duties exert on the cost at which the people of the country obtain their supplies of the taxed goods, and with the consequent shrinking of the national demand for them: and these fall well within the province of economics. Others raise broad issues connected with the political and ethical relations of Government to particular interests within the nation: these issues fall to some extent within the province of the present volume. Others relate to the constructive functions of Government, as to which something is proposed to be said in a companion volume on the quality of progress in work and life, and the economic conditions favourable to it.

The effect of an import duty is felt in the first instance at the frontier. If the commodity is bulky, it may very well be imported in spite of a heavy duty, and yet be sold in other parts of the country at a rather low price. To take a strong instance, timber is sometimes almost without value on the Pacific slope, while in other parts of the United States its price responds to taxes on importations from Canada. But in countries, no part of which is far removed from a frontier suitable for importation (such as the United Kingdom and Belgium), the full effect of an import duty is felt by nearly all consumers, even of commodities as bulky as wheat.

Of course exceptional geographical causes may put a country very much at the mercy of a stronger country which lies between

---

[1] Part of this chapter is reproduced from a *Memorandum of the fiscal policy of international trade* by the present writer; which was printed by Order of the House of Commons, under the mark 321 of 1908.

III, IX, 1. it and the main movement of the world. Possibly Germany may be able to throw some part of the burden of her import duties on countries lying to the east of her. But she cannot throw on England any considerable share of the burden of her own import duties; even though there are a few chemical and other German products, which England cannot easily forego. England can always take these as her first choice: and Germany must force the way for the rest of her trade with goods which England has no special reason for obtaining from her rather than from other sources.

Again, there may be some small markets in which Britain's connections by steam-ship or otherwise give her an advantage tending towards a mitigated monopoly. But in the aggregate they count for little. There is thus no considerable exception to the rule that Britain has now to pay the burden of her own import duties.

There has, indeed, never been a country, the whole of whose exports were in such urgent demand abroad, that she could compel foreigners to pay any large part of any taxes which she imposed on her imports. But England's exports approached to it twice. Once they consisted chiefly of wool, which was indispensable to Flemish weavers. And again, in the first half of the nineteenth century, they consisted chiefly of manufactures made by steam machinery, which was not in general use anywhere else; together with tropical products, which she had special facilities for obtaining. It is possible that the rest of the world would have given twice as much of their own goods as it did give for many of them, rather than go wholly without them.

As it was, England did no doubt throw a considerable part of the burden of her taxes (import and export) on the foreign consumer: though it may be true that she made her taxes (or prohibitions of import) heavy just where they ought to have been lightest; that she thus checked that growth of the vitality of the masses of her people, which ought to have resulted from her new command over the forces of nature; and hastened the day in which she would cease to hold the unchallenged leadership in industry. But any power which she may have had of throwing a considerable part of the burden of her import duties on foreign consumers of her products has been destroyed by two inevitable causes. Her arts and resources of production have become the common property of all countries of the western world; and, in III, IX, 2. some important cases, they have been developed by others faster than by herself: meanwhile the growth of her population has made her demand for some of her imports more urgent than is the demand of any other country for any of her exports.

We are, however, now concerned with settled trade relations, and not with exceptional or temporary incidents. Of course almost every trader has opportunities of springing hard bargains upon particular customers, who have made their plans on the expectation that he would deal with them in a regular manner: but such undignified action brings its own nemesis: and it may be left out of account here.

2. *The incidence of an import duty varies with the nature of the product taxed; and of the economic conditions of the country to which it comes, as well as those of the country or countries of its origin.*

Statements as to the incidence of import duties on particular classes of goods are necessarily couched in general terms: the official definition of a class often includes some things, the demand for which would be promptly and strongly influenced by the prices at which they were on sale; together with other things, the demand for which is not very intimately dependent on their price. Even a single class of an elaborate tariff schedule may contain things, that are to be applied to different purposes, and the demands for which are governed by different conditions. For instance, machinery and other plant designed for use in industries, which happen to be exceptionally active, will be in the same class with others for which there is at the time scarcely any demand. If an import duty on the class is imposed or increased, the first group may rise in price very much; while much of the burden of the tax on the second group is thrown on the foreign producer. Again, if the same additional tax is imposed on all the woollen goods which are in the same Customs-house list, the shrewd dealer will know that some goods in the class will soon be in greater demand, and will not abate in the least the net price, after allowing for the duty at which he offers them. But he will believe that other goods are losing fashion; and he will lower their net price by perhaps the full amount of the increased tax; should he do so, his action

III, IX, 2. is likely to appear as evidence from experience that the burden of import duties falls in a great measure on the foreigner. Such cases, however, constitute only a small part of the volume of trade.

Next, we may consider the linkings up between the prices of things which are more or less "joint products" of the same process, or serve together as joint "factors of production" of one ultimate result. Good examples of this are supplied by the relations of the shipping industry to those industries whose products it carries. For instance, when an unexpected import duty is levied on a bulky commodity, shipowners are often unable immediately to readjust the supply of shipping at the ports to the diminished demand; consequently freights fall; a part of the burden of the tax is borne by the shipowner, another part by the producer, and the consumer's share of the burden is lightened somewhat.

To pass to other minor instances: when the price of wheat in Britain was raised very high, in consequence of bad harvests at home, foreign merchants often made very high profits by selling wheat here. Accordingly, McCulloch argued that prices in such years would not be increased by a moderate duty, nor reduced by its repeal or suspension; and that though the duty falls mainly on the consumer, when the price is only a little above the profitable importing price, to lower the duty when the price is very high would be to sacrifice revenue for the benefit of foreign growers and dealers[1]. Telegraphic communication and the growth of a world market for wheat have rendered this argument inapplicable to wheat now: but it suggests the explanation of cases in which, a tax having been imposed on a commodity in a market where it is in exceptionally temporary demand, the burden falls almost wholly on the foreigner. Such cases have lent undue support to the opinion that the purchaser has the upper hand of the seller; that "the seller is courtier, the buyer is king."

Of course there are some branches of trade in which the buyer and seller are on about equal terms even in regard to current bargains. This is the case in the great organized markets for grain, cotton and other commodities, which are graded and sold mechanically, without any personal contact between the actual

[1] *Taxation and Funding*, pp. 196-7.

buyer and the actual seller; and even without any knowledge, III, IX, 3. on the part of the buyer, of the particular source from which his purchases will be filled. Only a small part of a country's trade could be materially turned in her favour, even temporarily, by the sharp practice of unexpected taxation: and such practice is not consistent with her dignity nor conducive to her interest in the long run. The suddenness of the stroke may seem to be a clever piece of strategy. But good credit for steadfast dealing is a business asset of the first importance to a nation as well as to an individual. The immediate gains reaped by sharp practice would generally be bad business, even if the only people hurt by the tax were foreigners: but they are not; the injury extends to the exporting industries of the taxing countries. Ricardo's celebrated chapter on "Sudden changes in the channels of trade" is in effect an argument that even a bad system of taxation should seldom be violently subverted.

3. *A broad view of the general incidence of import duties.*

Let us suppose two countries, *E* and *G*, to trade with one another, and only with one another; and to levy no taxes on imports. The price of *E*'s goods in *G* will differ from their prices at home only by costs of transport (including costs of handling), and *vice versâ*. But now *E* puts a tax of 50 per cent. on all imports, except of course gold. The prices of *E*'s goods will still be higher in *G* than at home merely by the cost of carriage. But the prices of *G*'s goods to consumers in *E* are now bound to rise 50 per cent. relatively to their level in *G*: for, unless and until that happens, it will answer to send gold instead of goods from *G* to *E*. This rise in price of *G*'s goods in *E*, relatively to their price in *G*, takes place whatever be the urgencies of *G*'s demand for *E*'s goods, and of *E*'s demand for *G*'s goods: but it is mainly on the urgencies of these reciprocal demands that the incidence of the tax depends. The observed price movement, *taken by itself*, proves nothing conclusively.

The burden of the tax would be thrown mainly on *G* in the exceptional case, in which *G*'s demand for *E*'s goods is very urgent (and inelastic) while *E*'s demand for *G*'s goods is not. For then the tax would firstly raise the price of *G*'s goods in *E*; secondly, diminish their sales there a little; thirdly, lessen the supply of

III, ix, 3. *E*'s goods in *G* a little; and, since *G*'s demand is taken to be inelastic, any considerable check to their supply would cause each of these goods to be disposed of for a much greater quantity of the labour and general commodities of *G* than before.

Here the solution of this particular case ends, so far as essentials go. But its secondary consequences in terms of price movements should be added. Since *E*'s goods can be disposed of in *G*'s markets on such favourable terms, gold will be sent from *G* to buy them. Therefore, gold will become very plentiful in *E*; prices generally will rise there, and a rise in money wages will follow in due course. Therefore, though *G*'s goods in *E* sell for twice the price they do at home, yet their prices will not represent much more effort than before; they may not represent any more effort at all. In *G*, on the other hand, gold will have become relatively scarce, and will command more of *G*'s goods and services than before. Therefore, although *E*'s goods sell in *G* for only their price at home, together with cost of carriage, yet their real cost to *G* will be very much increased. The consumers in *E* will be nearly as well off as before, and their Government will have got the taxes mainly at the expense of *G*.

On the other hand, *E* will have to bear the burden of her own taxes in the far more probable case in which *G* is in no urgent need for her goods. For then, when the merchants slacken their deliveries of *E*'s goods in *G*, the market will be unresponsive. Each bale of *E*'s goods will bring back about as much of *G*'s as before. A day's labour in *E*, or a bale of *E*'s goods, will command about as much as before of *G*'s goods in bond, and the taxes on *G*'s goods will be paid in the main by those who consume them in *E*. In this case there will not probably be any considerable movement of gold, and the *primâ facie* suggestions of price statistics will correspond pretty closely to the actual facts.

This assumes that *E*'s demand for *G*'s goods is elastic. For the sake of completeness, however, it may be well to take an improbable case corresponding to the preceding one; but with the parts of *E* and *G* inverted: and we may even suppose *E*'s Government to spend a great part of the taxes in purchases of imported goods. Then the private consumers in *E*, being in urgent need of their old supplies of *G*'s goods, may have to force the trade, and to accept less and less of foreign goods in return for each bale of their own: so that E may ultimately have to bear even more III, IX, 3. than the whole burden of her taxes.

The two countries E and G, being taken to be shut off from all trade except with one another, it is *primâ facie* not altogether unreasonable to suppose that G's demands for E's goods are somewhat urgent; and that, therefore, the burden of the taxes will fall in a considerable measure on her. But in the real world G always has access to other markets, and therefore she will not consent to pay any of E's taxes, unless E has something like a monopoly as regards nearly all her exports; or else, from geographical or other causes, G is very much at E's mercy. It is only under very rare conditions that a country is practically the sole market for even a single product which another country has exceptional advantages for producing. A tax on such a product might indeed rest permanently on the producers; but taxes on nearly all other products would be borne almost wholly by the consumers, as soon as the producers could make arrangements for selling in other markets, either their old products, or others to which they could gradually divert their energies and resources.

This argument does not claim to apply universally. For instance, if a country is the chief purchaser of an important speciality for which a second has exceptional advantages, then an import tax on it may be borne in the main by the producer for some considerable time: this might occur in the case of a tax levied by England on Greek currants, or on some classes of heavy wines. But there is no important commodity the supply of which is in that position. We shall, however, see presently that the collective relations between those countries which are large exporters of wheat, and those which are large importers of it, tend somewhat in that direction. And, of course, if manufacturers in any country have adapted expensive plant to the needs of a particular foreign market, they may pay nearly the whole of an unexpected tax levied on their goods there; for it is better to work with but low returns on their investment than to let their plant lie idle. Conversely, if a tax on the importation of certain goods is suddenly removed, those producers, whose plant is specially adapted to those goods, may be able to add for a time nearly the whole amount of the tax to their price; and may thus reap very high profits, until

III, IX, 4. new plant is ready to meet the increased demand resulting from the cessation of the tax.

We may conclude that no country is likely to be able to throw any considerable part of the burden of her import duties on others: unless, either all her exports consist of things of which she has at least a partial monopoly; or she is the only important consumer of most of the commodities which she imports from those countries. Something will be said later on as to exceptional cases of international monopoly.

4. *When currencies are based on gold, there is some ground for the opinion that the real cost, to which a country is put in obtaining her imports by her duties on them, can be measured by the subsequent movement of her prices. But this opinion goes beyond the truth.*

It is indeed true that, as a general rule, exporters are indifferent as to the market to which they send their goods; and select that which will yield them the best price after paying all the costs: and that, if the cost of delivering any commodity in a certain market is increased by the levying of an import tax of £1 upon it, they will avoid that market until, by making the commodity scarce in that market and rather more abundant than before in other markets, they have raised its price (duty paid) in that market by at least one pound, relatively to its price in other markets in which there has been no new tax. The ultimate consumer may, therefore, be expected to have to pay this pound, together with profits on the extra capital required for moving the taxed commodity, by all the dealers through whose hands it passes on its way to him. And price statistics show that he has to do so, if he has no alternative source of supply.

This fact affords a *primâ facie* case for the conclusion that the *whole* burden of an import tax is *always* borne by the consumer. But such an inference is invalid, because it neglects the consideration that the purchasing power of money in any country is likely to be affected by its tariff policy. For taxes on certain imports into a country raise their value in that country relatively to things which are not taxed; and one of these is gold. Therefore the purchasing power of gold is generally low in a country which levies many high import duties; and when we know that a certain fiscal policy has raised the price of any given commodity to a III, IX, 4. consumer by, say, a quarter, we have not got an answer to the question how great the burden on him really is.

Of course, if the taxes affect a small portion only of the country's imports, they will not cause an appreciable substitution of gold and other untaxed imports for taxed imports: that is, they will not appreciably alter the general level of prices. The taxed commodities will cost more money to the consumer (near the frontier) by practically the full amount of the tax; and this increase of price will indicate a nearly corresponding increase of real cost, because the value of money will be but little changed.

There are also other difficulties besides that connected with changes in the purchasing power of money, which resist the endeavour to decide by direct observation what is the incidence of import duties. For instance, improvements in production and transport are constantly raising money incomes relatively to prices; and if the influence of such improvements is being felt in the same decade in which a tariff is raised, the rise in money incomes relatively to prices may be considerable; and yet it may be much less than it would have been if the tariff had not been raised. No doubt the influence of this disturbing cause can be partly eliminated by comparing the movements of incomes relatively to prices in countries in the same industrial phase, whose tariffs have not moved in the same direction. But, not to mention the difficulties of obtaining such statistics, they cannot be interpreted without taking account of the different influences which are being exerted in different countries by education, by wise and thrifty household management, and by the development of latent natural resources through the spread of railways and otherwise. A thorough study of these problems in relation to actual conditions would be an arduous undertaking, and never complete. For almost every decade brings important changes in some of these conditions.

It must suffice here to indicate general grounds for the conclusion that a country cannot expect to throw any considerable share of the burden of her tariff on other countries, unless she is in a position to dispense with a great part of the goods which she imports from them; while she is at the same time in the possession of such large and firmly established partial monopolies, that those

III, IX, 4. countries cannot easily dispense with any considerable part of their imports from her. So far as the latter condition is concerned, we have seen that England was in a strong position early in last century: but not even America is in a strong position in regard to it now; and every other country is in a weak position. No doubt the British Empire would be in a strong position, if the tariffs of its component parts could be arranged on the same general plan: but their industrial resources and their needs are so diverse, that no near approach to such a result appears possible. This matter however belongs to a later stage of our inquiry.

CHAPTER X

INCIDENCE OF TAXES ON IMPORTS AND EXPORTS

1. *The pressure of taxes on a country's exports, which are* *levied at the frontiers of other countries, increases more than in proportion to their number and intensity. Also Western Europe may possibly suffer much from import duties on manufactures, levied in countries from which she draws large supplies of raw materials and food.*

The above argument as to the incidence of a country's import duties has assumed that their pressure is not likely to extend far enough to deprive other countries of any exports of hers for which their need is urgent and their demand inelastic. This assumption implies that other countries, whose resources are similar to hers, keep their markets fairly open. Of course it is conceivable that nearly all countries, which can supply the world's demands for some group of products, might concurrently levy such high duties on their imports as very greatly to restrict their trade: in that case the supply of that group of products in world markets might be very small and inelastic. [The elasticity might conceivably be less than unity, and a stage might be reached at which a further diminution of the supply would increase the aggregate amount of the goods, for which they can be marketed[1].]

Sparsely peopled countries are seldom brought near to such a danger. For densely peopled countries will be always ready to exchange manufactures and other fine products for raw material and food; and therefore sparsely peopled countries are not at all likely to find their market for crude exports so narrowed, that they will be forced to accept very hard terms of interchange in order to procure a sufficiency of machinery, etc., to meet their more urgent needs.

Nor is this danger likely to be brought upon densely peopled countries *in the near future* by the concurrent imposition of heavy

---

[1] This case is more curious than important: but it is worked out in Appendix J, 6.

III, x, 2. import duties on manufactures by sparsely peopled countries. For many new countries are still in urgent need of capital: and they cannot afford to divert much of it from developing their abundant resources to setting up modern steel and other industries, which might absorb several hundred pounds worth of capital or more for each person to whom they give employment. Consequently, many manufactured products will long continue to be imported on a considerable scale, even into the more highly developed new countries. And, though the world is being quickly peopled up, there will long remain large areas in which there are few highly organized industries; so that their doors must be kept fairly open to many western products. The capital which has been put at their disposal by old countries is already so vast, that, even when they have become able to produce their most urgently needed manufactures for themselves, they will still be forced to export crude goods, in order to pay interest on their past borrowings.

After many years have passed, however, they may have bought back most of the securities, which have been marketed in Europe: and then those lands, which still have raw products to sell, will have the upper hand in international bargains. Acting concurrently, whether by mutual agreement or not, they might be in the possession of an unassailable monopoly; and any taxes, however oppressive, which they might impose on the products which densely peopled countries offer to them, would then be paid mainly by those countries. It is this consideration, rather than the prospect of any immediate danger, which seems to give cause for regarding with anxiety the future of densely peopled countries.

2. *Some differences between the interest of an old country and that of a new country in the development of external trade.*

There is at present a strong contrast between "old" industrial countries and those "new" countries, in which men of vigorous European race are applying advanced methods in production. An increase in the population of a Western European country adds little to their command over the most efficient apparatus, and the most advanced methods of agriculture, manufacture, and traffic: and it is likely to compel them to press manufactured products on markets of countries not yet fully developed, in order to satisfy their own ever-growing need for raw materials.

On the other hand, an increase in number of Europeans who are III, x, 2. settled in new countries, where the resources of Nature are large and those of men are small, tends to increase the prosperity of both old and new countries. Old countries gain by a broadening of the markets in which they can profitably dispose of manufactures, which are produced the more easily, the larger is the scale on which they can be marketed: and new countries gain by the resources which their external trade supplies for making great trunk roads and railroads, and for developing harbours. A great obstacle to this trade would be injurious to both old countries and new: it would deprive old countries of many comforts and some luxuries, and would make life harder: and it would deprive new countries of some comforts and many luxuries, which now brighten their lives and stimulate their thoughts. But the relatively small obstacle to such trade, which is set by costs of long distance transport, and by difficulties of communication generally, is not an unmixed evil. It is well for new countries that they are prompted to supply simple manufactures for themselves: and it is well for the world that men of vigorous and enterprising faculty are induced to spread themselves over the large areas of rich natural resources, which are as yet undeveloped.

The countries of Western Europe might of course suffer a good deal from a great increase in the taxes, already rather high, which nearly every industrial country imposes on imports of manufactures. For they might then be unable to market abroad any great quantity of those refined machines and other implements, for which there is little demand except in advanced countries; and, therefore, be somewhat restricted in the economies of production on a large scale in this specially educative group of manufactures. But their own markets would afford scope in almost every branch of such work for several large establishments: and therefore their loss under this head, might not be very great. They would give more attention to products suitable for sparsely peopled countries; which would be able to supply such crude mineral and agricultural products as they need. They would be able to draw imports of raw products as interest, etc., on external investments, without forcing exports over frontiers obstructed by heavy duties in order to pay for them.

3. *Arguments in favour of export duties on products of which a country has a monopoly have seldom much force in practice.*

In earlier times, when transport was difficult and costly, a country with large agricultural resources could often obtain an almost monopoly-price for some of her exports to a neighbouring industrial district, which had no good communication by water with other exporters of such produce. But now, an export duty on staple agricultural products is opposed by growing facilities for long distance transport, which prevent any place from maintaining a "neighbourhood monopoly" of them. Moreover, those countries which are large exporters of them, are sparsely peopled, and dependent for their own development on railways and other means of communication; and these, in their early stage, tend to yield an Increasing Return after the manner of manufacture, rather than a Diminishing Return after the manner of agriculture in a densely peopled country. Thus, even the arguments, which may be advanced from a purely abstract point of view in favour of export duties on them, seldom have much force in practice.

Many countries of the New World levy duties on nearly all their imports from the Old World; and these tend to some extent to affect the terms of their foreign trade in the same way as would general export duties; but their demand for many of these imports is so urgent that they could not afford, even if they had the power, to restrict their trade so far as to make their exports scarce in European markets: they are hindered from such action by the inadequacy of their material and human resources for many large branches of production; as well as by their obligations to pay interest to Europe for capital already supplied for the development of their land.

The stinting of the exportation of the products of particular industries, caused by special taxes on them, slightly injures home consumers of foreign goods generally; and slightly benefits other home industries that work for exportation. Export bounties (as contrasted with bounties on production for home and foreign consumption alike) are specially attractive to the industry that receives them. But their cost to the country, that gives them, is very heavy. The home consumer of the favoured goods is taxed twice: once in order to provide the bounty; and once in the price which he pays for the goods.

The influence exerted by export duties on prices is on the same lines as that exerted by import duties; but in the opposite direction. It being assumed that gold is exempt from the duties, they tend to make it profitable to substitute the export of gold for that of the things the exportation of which is taxed; until the fall of prices at home has reached far enough to enable the taxed exports to be sold profitably abroad (though in smaller quantities) after the tax has been paid. Meanwhile, the spread of the fall of prices to untaxed exports, enables them to push their way in foreign markets, and fill up the void that has been made by the decline of taxed exports: but such results never reach very far in practice. Of course export bounties on particular goods tend to promote the importation of the precious metals (except in a country which has a paper currency) and thus to raise very slightly the general level of home prices. But subtleties of this kind have little general interest.

4. *The irregularity of the immediate results of a new import duty and the evils of frequent changes of any kind in import duties, are increased by the strong reasons which particular groups of producers or traders may have for preferring a temporary lowering of their price to a sudden diminution of their sales.*

The most deepset and powerful causes of unevenness in the immediate effect of an import tax are often to be found in the widely differing lengths of time required by different industries for adjusting the processes and appliances of production to new conditions; and in varying intimacy of connection between producers, merchants and ultimate purchasers in different industries and branches of trade.

The producer does not, as a rule, set himself to obtain exactly the same rate of profit on all classes of goods, or even on the same classes of goods, in all markets or in all conditions of the same market. But he seldom accepts a price so low that it would barely remunerate him, if he only considered that particular bargain: for his business has many general expenses, which must be covered in the long run; and each transaction generally bears its share

III, x, 4. of them. In other words, the cost of production which controls value in a competitive market, relates to whole processes, rather than to particular things. In regard to the particular markets or parts of markets with which any producer or merchant has established a stable connection, whether at home or abroad, he endeavours to adjust selling price to total costs of his business in such a manner, that he shall not tempt new competitors to push their way into his peculiar market from outside, or to rise up within his markets: his purpose is so to manage his business that it will yield him, in the long run, the largest aggregate net profits, which are consistent with this condition. He derives something of a partial monopoly from the knowledge which he has of those with whom his business is chiefly transacted, and which they have of him; and from the adaptation of his plant, his staff, and the organization of his business to their special needs, habits and tastes. And therefore other men with equal capital, energy and general ability, but without these special advantages, could not make as good profits as he can, while they are selling similar things in the same markets at the same price: any more than the established business of a physician or solicitor could be worked at once with equal success by another of equal general ability and experience, but not in touch with his special clientèle. Such slight partial monopolies are inherent in all competitive businesses: and they are not unlikely to be developed into strong partial monopolies by Cartels or other regulative associations, which set themselves to maintain what they term a fair, or reasonable, price; though it may, in fact, ultimately become oppressive within the particular markets which they control.

Nothing can be predicted as to the incidence of a tax levied on a completely monopolized product, until all the special circumstances of its production and marketing are known. Some part of the burden of the tax is sure to be thrown on the monopolist; because, in so far as he raises his price, he will lose some of the sales on which he reaps his special monopoly profits; and therefore he is practically certain to avoid raising it by the full amount of the tax. But how far he will be swayed by this consideration will depend on the rigidity or elasticity of the demand for his product, and the influence which a diminution of its output will have on his total receipts and so on. And what is true of a complete monopoly, is true in a less degree of the partial and temporary III, x, 4. monopoly which each established business derives from its connections. A business will sometimes pay a considerable part of a new tax on its products rather than lessen its sales at once; in others nearly every one will put almost the whole of it on the consumer at once. And, within each industry and trade, there will be great differences between different individuals according to their varying ages, temperaments and financial strengths. The price movement caused by a first impact of such a tax will seldom be an even line: it will be broken and jagged. And almost all that can be said certainly about it is, that the total amount of the burden of the tax which will be thrown on the foreigner, will almost always be small in comparison with the harm which the sudden change inflicts on the home industries, which are directly and indirectly affected by the unexpected tax.

This general statement is however liable to some exception when a country finds that one of her imports is controlled by a foreign monopolistic giant firm, or Cartel, or other regulative association; and that its price is changed frequently and arbitrarily in such a manner as to disturb the even tenor of her own industries. A still stronger case is that of import duties designed to diminish the more mischievous forms of "dumping" foreign goods in her markets; that is of selling them temporarily at prices much below their cost of production, with or without the deliberate purpose of causing inconvenience to some of her industries. Neither experience nor general reasoning affords any good ground for supposing that such special taxes would be so managed as to effect their purpose well. The evils, to be combated, become the less grievous, the more they emerge into the light under the control of a Cartel or other semi-public association. Movements towards such a control are generally strongest in those industries, in which the natural ambition of every enterprising business man to enlarge the scope of his undertaking, is supplemented by the existence of additional efficiencies and economies, which are known to be attainable by a further increase in the size of a business that is already large. The contemplation of them urges him to extend his machinery and appliances generally beyond the limits required for meeting the probable demands for his wares within his own markets, in ordinary times: and one of his chief resources for

III, x, 4. getting rid of his surplus production will be to dump it, that is, to sell it at less than its full cost of production, in markets with which he has no established connection. By this means he advertises his business, and does something towards establishing new connections for it: meanwhile he keeps his most trusted employees together, and any excess of the price which he obtains, over that which is required to pay his out-of-pocket expenses, together with wear and tear of plant (not depreciation caused by mere lapse of time), is to the good. He may be spoiling other people's special markets against sales at a remunerative price later on: but he is not spoiling his own.

The new markets which he seeks may be at home or abroad. Home markets may be the more accessible to him: but aggressive sales in them are likely to be promptly followed by retaliation in his own special home markets: whereas any retaliation, which is incited by aggressive sales in foreign markets, is likely to be directed to the general markets of his country and not concentrated upon his own special connections.

It is, however, to be observed that dumping on a large scale has been most prominent in regard to such things as half-finished steel products, for which there is no organized market in "futures" comparable to the great cotton and grain markets; but which are yet so far standardized that a producer is not very likely to have a very strong individual interest in any one market: unless indeed it happens to be almost in contact with his own works, in which case he may be as jealous of the intrusion of his own countrymen as he is of the foreigner. For an industry which makes half-finished goods, suitable for many uses, can form new connections more easily than one which makes highly finished goods for which there is no very large market anywhere, and in regard to which each country has special requirements: this peculiarity of half-finished goods is indeed a chief cause of the predominant position which Cartels in half-finished iron and steel products have held in international trade; they have exceptional inducements towards selling more cheaply abroad than at home, and also exceptional facilities for doing so[1].

In regard to such goods, any shifting there may be of the burden of an import duty from consumer to producer is apt to come

---

[1] See my *Industry and Trade*, III, ix, x.

fitfully, as do nearly all changes that are largely under mono-   III, x, 4.
polistic control. The motives by which they are governed may be
closely reasoned; but the reasons are not always accessible to
the public, and they often appear arbitrary. And yet, though
fitful, they are organized; their details present not a jagged front
but an even front, like that of a disciplined regiment. The volume
of international trade that is thus rigidly controlled is large; and
it is increasing, though with uneven steps. The volume of trade
which is controlled by less rigid associations and understandings
is perhaps equally large, though of course no certain and definite
information is to be had with regard to it. But, though the matter
is not wholly free from dispute, it will appear that these two groups
of trade, the strictly regulated and the partially regulated, are
very much less than a half of the whole: and it seems certain that
though often despotic in regard to particular incidents, the broad
policy of the dominant groups is controlled by, more than it
controls, the multitudinous resources, contrivances and inclinations of small men. It is obvious that international dumping is
more likely when once detected, to be proclaimed aloud: it seems
probable, therefore, that domestic dumping is at least as large
in the aggregate as international, though opinions differ greatly
as to the extent of each: and it is certain that the main incentives
to dumping, and the technical problems raised by it, are substantially the same in domestic and international trade.

CHAPTER XI

IMPORT DUTIES DESIGNED TO FOSTER PARTICULAR DOMESTIC INDUSTRIES

1. *Introductory observations.*

The matters to be considered in this chapter may be regarded from two points of view. First, it may be questioned whether taxes adjusted to the purpose of directing labour and capital into industries, which claim to be of exceptional importance to a country, are likely to be beneficial, on the assumption that they will effect their purpose without inflicting on the country a cost greater than the gain to the country, which would result from the ultimate success of the policy. And secondly, it may be questioned whether this gain, if achieved, would outweigh the evils likely to be caused by the diversion of energies from large legislative and administrative work, which already presses heavily on the supreme Government of a great State and on its officials. It is proposed to say something on the second of these questions in a companion volume to the present. Here we are concerned only to inquire into the advantages and disadvantages of taxes designed to foster particular home industries, without special reference to administrative expenses which would be incurred in their collection[1].

Some of a country's industries, being inconveniently pressed by the competition of imported products which rival their own, may claim defence against this pressure by taxes on those products. Such duties are called "protective": they do protect the particular domestic industries concerned against competition which is inconvenient to them; and that is a matter of some importance to the nation as a whole. But such competition sometimes affords the only effective protection which the people generally have against unduly high prices for the products of those industries.

It is conceivable that the protection, which such taxes give, is of greater national benefit than the protection which the

[1] Something has been said in Appendices B—G of *Industry and Trade* on England's early attitude towards external trade; on the policies in regard to the trade which were enforced by the Mercantilists; and on more recent phases of international trade policy in Britain, Germany, and America.

destroy. That has perhaps been the case in regard to some taxes, III, xi, 2. which have defended nascent industries in countries, which have had but little experience in manufacture by modern methods; and but scanty supplies of free capital.

2. *Some general considerations as to the incidence of taxes on imported goods of kinds that compete with home products which are not subject to like taxes*[1].

A tax on the importation of anything which can be produced at home acts in protection of the corresponding home industry, unless it is balanced by an equivalent tax on domestic products: and if the tax is levied unequally on similar products coming from different sources, it becomes what is commonly called a Preferential tax. In either case, but more especially in the latter, political considerations are intermingled with those which are "economic" in the narrower uses of the term; and sometimes even they get the upper hand.

A tax on an imported product, which is not balanced by a corresponding tax on similar domestic products, is a differential tax: and is therefore wasteful. The objection to it does not arise, as is sometimes thought, from the fact that it is a tax on an import: on the contrary, that fact tells in its favour. It is open to objection only on the ground that it is a discriminating or differential tax. Every such tax is necessarily wasteful if it involves the diversion of demand from an easier to a more difficult source of supply, though, of course, it may have political or even indirect economic advantages which outweigh that waste. The waste may be illustrated by a simple case. Freshly quarried building stones are often soft, and can be worked roughly into shapes for their final use with but little effort. The Masons' Union at one time insisted that all the shaping work should be done at the place at which a stone was to be used, thus doubling or trebling the effort, and therefore the cost, of the rough part of the work.

That rule in effect imposed a differential tax on the most efficient method of production: and the general objection to an import duty levied on things, which can be obtained from abroad more easily than they can be produced at home, is that it raises

[1] This section is, in the main, reproduced from a contribution to *After-War Problems*, 1918, edited by Mr W. H. Dawson.

III, XI, 2. the total cost to the people of their supplies of those things, while the Revenue reaps comparatively little gain from their sacrifices. The Exchequer, with hunger but little appeased, is likely to attack other imports.

A duty on an import prejudices in some degree, not only those who desire the foreign product for any reason, but also all those who are engaged in production for export. *Other things being equal*, a diminution by £10,000 of the imports, which any merchant finds it advantageous to make into Britain, diminishes the demand for bills on other countries to the amount of about £10,000. That is to say, it tends to cause British producers for exportation, together with the shipowning and other mercantile houses associated with them, to curtail operations to the extent of about £10,000. A tax on imports, which rival the products of a British industry, doubtless stimulates the activity of that industry, enabling it to give increased employment, temporary or permanent, to the working classes and others, and increasing its command of the economies of production on a large scale. But, at the same time, it tends to diminish to about the same extent the activity of other British industries: and it narrows, temporarily or permanently, the range of the employment which they afford, and their command of the economies of production on a large scale.

The argument that taxes on a country's imports tend to alter the terms on which she obtains them, slightly in her favour, deserves more consideration: but it has been shown to be of little importance in regard to general trade, except in the case of a country nearly the whole of whose exports are without effective rivals anywhere else. It has also been shown that there are a few cases in which a great part of the burden of an import duty can be thrown on the foreigner; though they amount to very little in the aggregate[1].

When producers in one country have set themselves to cater for the special requirements of another, and to build up com-

---

[1] Of course there is no adequate basis for the argument sometimes put forward, that since merchants are not generally willing to accept a lower *net* price, after paying freights, taxes, and all other costs in one country than another; therefore consumers in a country which levies a tax on an import must pay that tax in full. For this argument neglects the fact that the general purchasing power of money in a country with high import duties is lowered by those duties; so that the real values that her people give in return for the foreign goods, which they consume, are a little lower than is suggested by the high prices which they pay.

mercial connections with it, they may go some way towards
meeting any import duty that is suddenly sprung on them, until
they have made other arrangements for utilizing their resources:
and such action may give rise to the opinion that a considerable
part of the burden of an import tax falls on the foreign producer.
Similar strategies succeed temporarily in every branch of dealing:
but they are bad business in the long run. A country, which
earned the reputation of suddenly raising particular import
duties, would find others slow to accommodate themselves to
her wants.

Another case, in which an import duty is largely thrown on a
foreign producer, is that of a particular brand of thread or the
supply of petroleum in a particular market, which yields monopoly
profits high above the normal. Such profits can be annexed, in
part at least, by the tax-collector; and his success in regard to
them is frequently quoted as affording a general argument in
favour of differential duties on imports: but the tax on such imports is not a differential tax, since there is not any efficient
substitute for them.

It is indeed sometimes argued that imported goods do not pay
their share of the general taxation of the country as home produce does; and that therefore they compete at an unfair advantage
unless they are taxed on importation. But the English manufacturer of products for exportation would pay a double set of
taxes, if the foreign products for which his goods are exchanged
had to pay a share of the general taxes of the country; while goods
which are made for home consumption pay only a single share.
For, the taxes paid on importation would have to be deducted
from the proceeds of the sale of his goods abroad, before any profit
could be realized.

3. *Britain's adoption of a liberal trade policy in the middle
of the nineteenth century*[1].

At the very time at which British statesmen were preparing
the way for uncompromising Free Trade, Britain's exports consisted to so large an extent of things of which she had some partial

---

[1] The greater part of the remainder of this chapter is reproduced from a
Memorandum on the Fiscal Policy of International Trade, by the present writer,
which was printed as a "White paper" by order of the House of Commons, under
the mark 321 of 1908.

III, xi, 3. monopoly, that she might hope then—as she cannot hope now—to throw on foreigners a considerable share of the burden of her import duties. It is further to be noted that British economists did not condemn all import duties, but only those which were levied in an inconvenient way, such as duties on raw material; or were unjust, such as those which pressed heavily on the poor; or, lastly, were *differential*. (As stated above, differential taxes are taxes levied exclusively or with special weight on commodities which are produced in certain places or by certain methods, or are imported by certain routes or in certain ships; while other commodities, capable of serving more or less well the same needs, are treated differentially, and escape the tax in whole or in part.) They objected to a differential tax that it set consumers and traders on evasions, either by substituting for the taxed commodity some other which was less serviceable, but not taxed; or by obtaining the commodity in part from some other and more costly source of supply. In so far as either of these substitutions was made, the consumer was prejudiced, and the revenue gained nothing: it was only in so far as the tax was not evaded that the revenue gained all that the consumer lost—subject to deductions for cost of collection, etc. They found that in a few exceptional cases, such as tea, coffee, tobacco, etc., there was very little evasion (unless by smuggling), and therefore little waste. But they found by a study of detail, and not by any general or *à priori* reasoning, that in the case of all commodities for which the English climate was suitable, or for which inferior substitutes could be obtained, the evasions caused by a tax were very great; the waste was in fact so great as to exceed many times the small part of the burden of the tax which could be thrown upon foreigners. They therefore advocated the abolition of all such taxes as contrary to the principle of economy in taxation; urging that the importation of goods, which can be produced at home, does not in general displace labour, but only changes the direction of employment. They recognized that any violent change is, to some extent, an evil; and there is a strong *primâ facie* possibility that if the business men of a country, when left to follow their own judgment, decide that it would be more costly to make certain goods at home, than to import them in exchange for other home-produced goods for which there is a foreign demand, their judgment is likely to be right;

provided they look far ahead and are not biased either by their III, xi, 3.
own interests, or by unwillingness to strike out new paths.

Unfortunately, however, when those in the industries, with which the imported goods compete, set themselves to persuade the public and Government that a protective import duty should be levied on them, private interests have a strategic advantage in competing with those of the public; for it is possible to point to the particular places in which additional employment would be given by the tax. It is easy to find out the particular employers and workmen whose profits and wages would be raised by it; to invite the employers to subscribe to a "campaign fund" on its behalf; and to urge both employers and employed to exert all the political influence, direct and indirect, which they possess, in putting pressure on the Legislature in their favour. Good strategy prompts that as much as possible of the argument and appeal in the special interests of any one industry should come, not from those who have a direct stake in that particular industry, but from others who have an understanding with them.

Those who cared more for the well-being of the masses of the people than for class interests or for political power, found themselves in a difficult position. For they knew that such taxes must lessen employment and lower real wages in the aggregate; and that those industries which gained by the taxes would gain at the expense of a greater aggregate loss to other industries. But yet they could not always point out the particular industries which would suffer most: while the far more numerous workers, who had nothing to gain by such taxes, had seldom any organization and were not vocal. Thus the benefits of such taxes, because easily seen and described by persons who could easily make themselves heard, were apt to count at the polling booth and even in the counsels of statesmen of upright intentions, for more than the evils. For those evils, though greater in the aggregate, were less easily seen; and they did not directly appeal to vocal classes. Fortunately for the success of Free Trade, many of the protective duties then levied were ill-chosen; they pressed on raw materials, and thus limited employment in a conspicuous way: and the evils of one of them—that which fell upon the staple food of the people—were palpable enough. But this accidental gain has somewhat diverted attention from the general argument, by which economists

III, xi, 3. proved that protective taxes lessened rather than increased the aggregate employment, wages, and profits.

The argument starts from the fact that employment in making a thing is not provided by the mere desire to have it, but by that desire combined with the appliances for making it, and the means of supporting those at work. The older economists expressed themselves badly, and laid too great stress upon the *capital stocks* of machinery, raw material, food, etc.; whereas more recent economists lay greater stress on that *net inflow* of new supplies of food, raw material, machinery, manufactured products, etc., together with personal services which constitutes the national income or dividend. This change of emphasis is very important in some connections, but not in regard to the particular point now in hand. Then, as now, the basis of economic doctrine was that the source of all wages and profits (as well as rents) was in the aggregate efficiency of national production; things obtained from foreigners in exchange for recent exports, or as interest on exports loaned in earlier years, being counted in place of the said exports.

They argued that whatever increases this total efficiency of production increases that aggregate supply of goods (of past and recent make) which affords employment and income (wages, profits, and rent) to the various classes of the nation.

Further, if goods which can be produced at home are yet imported freely from abroad, that shows that they can be got generally at less cost by making other things with which to buy them from abroad than by the direct method of making them at home. There may be exceptional cases in which goods are sold with but little attention to cost of production; and there may be other cases when a home industry is temporarily disorganized, and it is reasonable for the public to incur some sacrifice for its relief. But such cases, because exceptional and on a small scale, have little relevance to this broad issue.

Therefore a tax which puts obstacles in the way of the importation of things, which consumers prefer to buy from abroad, does not enlarge employment or raise wages; it is not in the interest of "producers." It is sure to be in the interest of *some* producers (if among producers are counted landlords and other owners of natural sources of production). But it is sure also to injure other producers more than it benefits the favoured group; because it lessens the aggregate flow of desirable things, available as a basis III, xi, 3. of employment and for distribution among the various classes of the nation.

This fundamental truth is, of course, not inconsistent with the counsel that, as the prudent husbandman puts seed-corn into the earth, so a nation should be ready to sacrifice something of present income in order to develop industries which are immature, and perhaps exposed to the competition of others which are strong. But this counsel had little application to England, because her industries were relatively mature: it will be considered later on.

The founders of our present system had to combat the objection that, though Free Trade might be for the advantage of all nations if adopted by all nations, it was a mistake to open English ports freely, unless and until foreigners would reciprocate this generosity. To that two replies were made. The first was that foreigners would certainly adopt England's policy as soon as they saw how successful it was. The events of the next few years gave some support to this hope. But it was based on a misconception of the position. It ignored the facts that protection to immature industries is a national good; and that, though this good may be bought at too great a cost, it would have been foolish for nations with immature industries to adopt England's system pure and simple.

The second answer was sufficient by itself, and was complete without a flaw. It was that if, in spite of taxes levied by other nations on her goods, she could get them in exchange for her own at less cost than she could make goods like them for herself, it was in her interest to do so. Of course, here again there might be exceptional cases. It might be possible to retaliate by taxes, a part of the burden of which would be borne by foreign consumers of English goods. But it was wisely decided not to try for such small gains.

A suggestion of more practical importance was that the remission of taxes on goods coming from any country should be made conditional on the lowering of the taxes levied by that country on English goods. This course was adopted in some cases. But it was not in harmony with that bold and large comity, on which England's leadership in industry and trade was being developed.

4. Protection to a nascent industry in a country, where capitalistic resources are scarce, is not necessarily unreasonable. But in fact the greater part of such Protection is commonly retained after the industry has already enjoyed a long and prosperous life.

Taxes on imported manufactures are convenient sources of revenue in such a country as Brazil, whose conditions make the collection of revenue over the large inland area difficult, while it can be easily collected at her ports. And a Protective tax, which helps a young industry to develop its latent strength, may be in the interest of an undeveloped country, even though the tax must inevitably do some hurt to those few of her industries which are manufacturing for exportation. For the energy developed in a few high-class progressive industries may spread over a great part of the industrial system of the country; just as an iron screen, which concentrates the whole draught of a chimney on a small part of a nascent fire, may generate an intense local heat, which spreads and pioneers the way for a broad, strong fire. But neither of these arguments applies to an old manufacturing country.

Britain's area is small relatively to her population: and coal is the only raw material, of which she exports any considerable quantity. She owes indeed much of her advantage as an exporter to the ease with which goods from all parts of the world can be used in each of her manufacturing districts. No country would lose nearly as much as she would from being unable to use foreign half-manufactures freely, unless drawbacks could be got easily; and no people, other than those of her own kindred, would resent so much the trouble and friction involved in getting petty drawbacks on small things. This is all the more important because many things which are "completely manufactured," even in the narrowest use of the term, are wanted by manufacturers for export as implements or auxiliaries of their work.

It may be admitted that there is some force in the claim that a Protective tariff is needed to aid giant businesses in establishing a complete standardization on the most advanced modern model. But many of the most important economies of production on a large scale are those which belong to a compact industrial district, such as Lancashire: for then the productions of many correlated industries for sale at home and abroad work into one another's hands.

Of course, the ultimate incidence of a tax on imported goods depends in part on the extent of the educative influence which may be brought by it to bear on the industrial classes of a nation to devote their energy to tasks, for which they have adequate resources and opportunities: but in which they nevertheless lag behind the best practice that can be found elsewhere. To the extent to which a tax effects this result, its policy cannot be judged on merely economic grounds. Occasionally it may be concluded that, *when no other means are available for bringing national resources to the aid of a particular backward industry*, a State may act wisely and rightly in subsidizing it at the expense of the population at large. When directed to this end, a tax may conceivably be for the national interest, even though it somewhat lessens for the time the material wealth possessed, or the material comfort enjoyed, by the population as a whole. But, in fact, those who can speak with the fullest knowledge on the technical side of such a question, are likely to have a strong personal interest in its receiving an answer that will increase the demand for their services: and arguments in favour of such taxes need to be scrutinized with exceptional care, even when they come from able men of the highest character.

I was so much impressed by those arguments of Carey and his followers, which had found scarcely any echo in English literature, that I went to the United States in 1875 to study the problems of national industry and international trade from the American point of view: I was prepared to learn, not indeed that the American system was applicable to England, but that it might contain ideas capable of adaptation to English conditions.

I came back convinced that a Protective policy in fact was a very different thing from a Protective policy as painted by sanguine economists, such as Carey and some of his followers, who assumed that all other people would be as upright as they knew themselves to be, and as clear-sighted as they believed themselves to be. I found that, however simple the plan on which a Protective policy started, it was drawn on irresistibly to become intricate; and to lend its chief aid to those industries which were already strong enough to do without it. In becoming intricate it became corrupt, and tended to corrupt general politics. On the whole, I thought that this moral harm far outweighed any small

III, xi, 4. net benefit which it might be capable of conferring on American industry, in the stage in which it was then.

Subsequent observation of the course of politics in America and elsewhere has strengthened this conviction. It seems to me that the policy adopted in England eighty years ago remains the best, and may probably remain the best, in spite of increasingly rapid economic change, because it is *not* a device, but the absence of any device. A device contrived to deal with any set of conditions must become obsolete when they change. The simplicity and naturalness of Free Trade—that is the absence of any device —may continue to outweigh the series of different small gains which could be obtained by any manipulation of tariffs, however scientific and astute.

We may pass to consider some of the changes which may be urged as affording a *primâ facie* case for reconsidering the fiscal policy adopted by England eighty years ago.

It is commonly charged against the English economists and statesmen of that time that they had an undue distrust of Government. They certainly did distrust Government as they knew it; but it is not certain that they were very wrong in doing so. Government at that time was, indeed, less corrupt and incapable than it had been when it evoked the wrath of Adam Smith: insomuch that he denied, not as is commonly supposed, that there were many important things which Government might undertake to do, but that it was at all likely to perform efficiently many important duties. Even after the great Reform Bill, Government remained largely under the dominion of the less enlightened and impartial members of the well-to-do classes; and it discharged very imperfectly those urgent duties which none but the Government could perform at all. There was, therefore, little to be gained by urging it to take up tasks in which private enterprise and philanthropy could make some headway.

Since then, shorthand reporting, the electric telegraph, and the improved printing press have given strength to the general movement towards higher ethical standards, which has been steadily cleansing Parliament, and invigorating Governmental departments. And, in England, this tendency has been further strengthened by the influence of Free Trade in diminishing the money value of political power—an influence which would probably have been partially reversed, if success had attended the Fair Trade move- III, xi, 4, ment of thirty years ago, or should attend the similar present movement for Tariff Reform.

The United States, Germany, and other countries have advanced rapidly in industrial efficiency; and their growing wealth has enabled them to consume very largely increased quantities of all those goods which Britain is specially expert in producing, and also to produce many goods which are serviceable to her either for direct consumption or for use in her industries: their progress has thus improved her position in many ways, while injuring it in others.

But, of course, old countries cannot in any case expect to grow as rapidly as those which are only just beginning to develop some of the best of their resources. Still less can they hope to do so if some of their own best mineral and other resources are running short. By far the larger part of whatever relative retrogression Britain may be showing, as compared with the United States and Germany, is directly traceable to their recent development of great natural resources; which had previously not been worked intensively.

The United States, indeed, present a unique combination of agricultural and mineral riches in a temperate climate, developed by a mixture of races of great energy and alertness. She possesses a good climate; and large areas, yielding generous returns to labour in the production of staple foods and textile materials, together with coal or water power, and minerals. In all these respects, excepting climate and coal, the United States is incomparably better supplied than England is; and in the earlier stages of nearly every great branch of her production, labour of a given efficiency will go much further than in England—in some cases more than twice as far. The best English ideas have nearly always been accessible to Americans. When, early in the eighteenth century, England took great pains to prevent the exportation of her best machines, the manufacturers of Europe set themselves to smuggle the machines or drawings of them out of England piecemeal and under various disguises. But the prouder Americans inquired exactly what was the operation which a machine took over from the human hand, and then devised one for themselves; and it sometimes turned out better than the English one. Foreign

III, XI, 4. trade, therefore, is not necessary to the United States. Her domestic trade is richer than that of the whole Western world was when she achieved her independence. Protection could not do her very much harm: and it is probable that the help given by her to a few industries, which really needed help, about compensated for the economic loss (but not for the moral injury) caused in other directions by her Protective policy: and in fiscal matters, as in others, the technique of her administration has been excellent.

It has been suggested above that the Protective policy, which Germany adopted, hindered rather than helped the use which she has made of the high industrial energies of a population very much greater than that of the United Kingdom. If we take coal and iron together, and remember that the very rich beds of inferior iron ore in Luxemburg and Lorraine have been rendered available for making steel by rather recent inventions; her mineral resources are seen to be rich and large. The ocean routes from her ports are indeed a little longer than those from British ports; but even in this matter there is some compensation; because her ships can make up their cargoes in convenient ports of Holland, Belgium, France, and Britain; and she has almost exclusive access to large areas of Eastern Europe which are ready to use Western goods, but are not yet ready to make such goods themselves; and she is able to send light goods to them in through railway wagons cheaply and quickly. A great part of her external trade is with these countries; and it is due to advantages which scarcely any fiscal policy could destroy.

Germany, like the United States, owes much of her strength to the large population within her own borders, among whom there is now absolute free trade. One of the chief causes which retarded her rise was the fact that Prussia, the largest and most vigorous German State, was not a compact unit, but a number of disjointed fragments divided from one another by artificial frontiers. The Zollverein, following an earlier Swiss, and a still earlier French, precedent, was one of the most important movements towards free trade that the world has ever seen. It abolished in every direction artificial hindrances to the "simple" and "natural" tendency of each man to deal with those persons who are best able to meet his wants in return for his meeting theirs.

It stopped the laborious passing of goods in bond from one III, xi, 4. Prussian "island" to another; it put an end to vexatious inquiries, and diminished the labour of custom-house officers. In short, its influence was partly in the opposite direction to that which would be exerted by the commercial federation of the British Empire; though in some respects similar to that which would be exerted by a commercial federation of all English-speaking nations, if that were possible.

Some of Germany's industries, which manufacture for export, have little occasion to use imported half-manufactures: but others are much hampered by import taxes on the things which they need. It is true that such things are not heavily taxed; but the trouble of obtaining drawbacks on foreign products, which are worked into manufactures for exportation, is so great that plans have been developed in Germany and elsewhere for setting up free-trade areas surrounding chief ports. A small free area round Hamburg docks, for instance, offers facilities for minor operations, especially those connected with transhipment for re-exportation[1].

The experience of other countries seems to show that even now there is danger if a Parliament listens to the representations of interested classes when framing its fiscal policy. Perhaps the case of Germany is the strongest, because German public officials were recognized as inferior to none in honesty of purpose; and there are probably few persons who have a higher standard of honour in private life than the "Agrarian" members of the Reichstag. But yet the methods which they, and certain powerful manufacturers, have used (both in legislation and in controlling the votes of their dependents) seem to have increased the probability that a German working-man, who takes life seriously and has a strong feeling of duty, will be an ardent Socialist.

Britain's dangers are not the same, but they are not very different. She excels all other countries in the solid strength of her Trade Unions; and perhaps her greatest danger is that they

[1] A large space in Germany's *Trade Statistics* has been occupied with the details, generally small, of imports which have been admitted free because they were to be re-exported after being finished (*Veredelungs-Verkehr*). The scheme was gradually worked out with consummate skill; but its total results have been meagre. A corresponding scheme for Britain would require a Germanic army of officials, and be very costly. It would lessen the revenue derived from taxes on imports, while yet doing little to lessen the hurt which they would inflict on her exporting industries.

III, xi, 4. be tempted to use that strength for the promotion of the interests of particular groups of workers, at the expense of wider interests, as the landowning classes did when they had the power. There is no more urgent duty incumbent on those who care for the higher as well as the material well-being of the country than to resist this temptation: and the worst method of preparing for this task is to bring back again into English politics the notion that there is plenty of money to be got by influencing votes in Parliament, and by controlling the public press.

Further, though Government is in some respects better placed for grappling with such difficulties than it was; yet, on the other hand, the amount of constructive work which the modern age is requiring from it is probably growing much faster than its power of getting through its work. This is partly because human life is larger and more complex than it was; partly because our growing knowledge and wealth and a higher standard of public duty make us ever less willing to acquiesce in grave social ills, and even in discomforts, many of which cannot be adequately handled save by the authority and force of Government. Another cause of the change seems to lie in the increased intelligence and probity of Government officials: they make us willing to take the risks of Government action in many matters, in which Adam Smith and his immediate followers would have feared that that remedy would probably be worse than the evil. Connected with such action, however, there must necessarily be openings for certain classes of employees, and also of builders, manufacturers, traders, etc., to reap money gains through Imperial or Municipal politics. Here may be found an additional reason against an intricate system of combative finance: for it would occupy much of the best time and strength of Parliament and Government; and it might tend to lower the tone of public morality: but that matter is to be considered in a later volume.

CHAPTER XII

NATIONAL CURRENCIES IN RELATION TO INTER-NATIONAL TRADE UNDER STABLE CONDITIONS[1]

1. *Introductory.*

Book I was largely occupied with the influences on a country's economic well-being which are exerted by the character of her currency. If her currency is firmly set on a sound foundation, so that its purchasing power is not liable to disturbances arising from uncertainties as to its quantity or quality; then her industry and her domestic trade are provided with a good implement for their work. Credit may even then be impaired by faulty or unfortunate ventures: but the evils thus caused are less intense and less far-reaching than they would be if the currency, in terms of which her business transactions are expressed, were distrusted.

Coins issued by open mints, which make but slight charges for converting approved metals into standard money, may be used as international currency: while for settling the balance of international transactions standard bars are often of good service. But if one country whose currency is based on gold, trades with another whose currency is based on silver, the settlement of any commercial obligation between them is apt to be impaired by changes in the relative values of the two metals. This evil was felt strongly in the later half of the nineteenth century: and, in consequence, a strong movement set in for the purpose of establishing a fixed relation between the values of the two metals[2].

2. *The exchange under stable conditions between two countries, each of which has a currency based on gold.*

Ricardo's reasoning, developed by Mill and others, cleared away many of the obscurities which formerly troubled the course of

---

[1] Part of this chapter is reproduced from evidence, submitted by the present writer in 1888, to the Royal Commission on Gold and Silver, and in 1898 to the Indian Currency Committee.

[2] The movement derived much strength, but also provoked some distrust, because many of its supporters, insisted on the adoption of the old equality of 15½ ounces of silver to one of gold, at a time when the output of the silver mines of the world was exceptionally large. (See above. I. VI, § 2.)

inquiries as to international trade in the precious metals. It is now generally recognized that, if prices measured in gold are generally higher in A than in B, there will be a small temporary bounty on exportation from B to A corresponding to this difference, which must always be small. Bills drawn in B on A will multiply, and, specie point being reached, gold will go from A to B till prices in B are as high as in A. If B hoards gold this process may be a long one, otherwise it is sure to be short.

The fluctuations of the exchanges measured in terms of gold bars (that is, of gold regarded as a commodity) are limited under ordinary circumstances to the double cost of carriage of gold. But, when measured in terms of the currencies of the two countries, the limits of these fluctuations are liable to be extended by the sum of the seigniorages (if any) charged in the two countries, and, in extreme cases by the sum of the amounts lost by wear and tear, not indeed from the average coins in circulation, but from those picked coins which are selected for the purposes of export.

Of course, even when the exchanges are at par, the trade bills on the one side need not exactly balance those on the other: for those on either side are likely to be supplemented by paper documents or telegrams representing (i) the transfer of newly borrowed capital, (ii) the repayment of business outlays and the payment of interest or profits on previous investments of capital, (iii) the drawings by absentees, who live temporarily or permanently in one country and derive their means of support from another, and (iv) the drawings of a government, which expends in one country part of the income which it derives from another. Under the first head come such items as the transfer or telegraphic sale of "international securities," that is, of securities which, whatever be the country of their origin, have a market in both A and B.

When it is said that an increase of purchasers abroad makes the exchanges unfavourable to either country, it is always tacitly implied that other things are equal; that is, either that there is meanwhile no such disturbing cause as a transfer of stock exchange securities, etc., from one country to another, or that separate allowance is made for its effects. For instance, if B should fall into political discredit, and those who had invested capital in B should want to bring it home, that would cause a premium on bills drawn on A by exporters in B. Under the second head come trade III, xii, 2. expenses of many different kinds, and especially in connection with the shipping trade. The wording of the problem is further complicated, but its substance is in no respect whatever changed, if we consider A's trade not merely with B, but with all other countries which have gold currencies.

But the true nature of the trade is often in some measure disguised by the habit, borrowed from the City, of describing the trade in the precious metals in different language from that used in describing the trade in any other commodity. If on the balance B is indebted to A, and in consequence the exchanges are "favourable" to A, merchants in B will consider what things they can send to A and sell there at a price higher than they could get by investing the same money in a bill on A, on which they have to pay a premium; in every case they must, of course, allow for cost of carriage, etc., and for interest on the time required for realising. If the premium on the bill is just equal to the cost of carriage of gold, so that it is indifferent to a merchant whether he buys a bill or sends the gold, it is said that "gold point" has been reached. But with equal appropriateness it might be said that "lead-point" is reached, or that "Egyptian-point" is reached, when the difference between the prices of lead or of Egyptian bonds in the two countries is just balanced, after allowing for the charges of transport, by the premium at which bills on A sell in B^1.

This old use of the term "favourable exchanges" is perfectly reasonable from the point of view, which prevailed when it came into use: they did really "favour" the importation of the precious metals. But from the modern point of view the conversion of the resources of a country into metallic currency is not a good thing in itself. It is good, only so far as a store of the precious metals is required, to enable the country to buy anything that she may want for cash, and therefore on favourable terms: or, which is nearly the same thing, to buy when markets are depressed, and therefore things can be bought at low prices; and to sell when markets turn the other way and prices are high. These are, of course, just those advantages which an individual trader obtains

^{1} See III, v, 5.

III, xii, 3. by having a large amount of ready purchasing power under his immediate control, either in his own keeping; or in his current account with a bank. If he is in fairly good credit, and trade is quiet, he can of course obtain advances by discounting his bills, or borrowing directly from his bank: the advantage to an individual trader of keeping a considerable stock under his immediate command is seen in disturbed times: and the same is true of the nation as a whole. Where concurrent waves of disturbed credit are moving over the "western world," the stock of inconvertible currency held by its banks and traders loses much of the power which it would otherwise possess of liquidating transactions at home by direct action, and abroad by indirect action.

On the whole the costs involved in keeping a country's currency firmly based on gold seem to be well balanced by the advantages derived from it by her industry and trade, and especially by her external trade.

3. *Influences of trade on the international distribution of the precious metals, and the purchasing power of metallic currency in each country.*

We start now from the position that the international distribution of the precious metals with open mints is such that the gold and silver values of the different commodities bear the same relations to one another all over the world, allowance being made for transport, import duties, etc. If at any time an external change, such, for instance, as new currency legislation, upsets that arrangement, then there will be a general shifting which will show itself through the exchanges: the exchanges not being the real active force, but the channel through which the real force acts. After a time there will be a new settlement, a new rate of exchange, and a new international level of prices.

The immediate effect of the imposition by a country of high duties on some of her imports is of course to incline merchants to seek other methods than the importation of those goods for discharging their obligations to her. That is, the duties would in effect give a bounty to the importation of goods which are not subject to such taxes and will be received fairly well in her markets. Gold and silver will generally find a place among these increased imports: and if her currency is based on the precious metals, they will be the most suitable goods for the purpose, partly because III, XII, 3. they can be marketed very easily[1].

In all such matters it is to be borne in mind that a country whose currency is merely based on gold, and yet does not consist in the main of gold, is liable to be greatly affected by relatively small movements of gold across her frontiers: but the fact that a small cause produces a great effect is likely to enable a small remedy to set right a great disturbance. Small movements of gold into or out of the Bank of England reserve may affect large quantities of British business: but the remedy needed for a small disturbance is likely to be small[2].

The precious metals are so distributed throughout the world, that independently of the demand for them for the purposes of hoarding and of the arts, each country has just that aggregate amount of the two metals which corresponds in value to the volume of that part of her business which the habits of her people cause her to transact by payments in coin, account being taken of the rapidity of circulation of coin, and of the absorption of

---

[1] This does not mean that no special knowledge is required for conducting trade in them to the best advantage: it means that, because they carry much value in small bulk, they can be transferred from one country to another under appropriate insurance by expert traders at low costs relatively to their values. If sent to a country in which they do not circulate as money, their value there will of course be only that of the metal which they contain: and, unless they are likely to be re-exported, that value will be reckoned on the basis of their weight; with due reference to the percentage of alloy which they contain.

[2] Before the recent great war Britain's business was firmly based on gold; but yet she used relatively little gold for the purpose, and she could easily adjust the basis of her currency to changing conditions: her position in this matter was in sharp contrast to that of India. The importance of this contrast is apt to be underrated. The following extract from an argument, submitted by the present writer to the Indian Currency Commission, 1899 (see its *Report*, Q. 1171-6), suggests reasons for the opinion that England's monetary system does not afford a good pattern for the moulding of Indian currency. "Currency is but a small part of the means of payment used in England; and under most, though not all, conditions, bank money is the main means of payment; and that is elastic. Secondly, an imperative demand for increased currency is rare in England; and, when it does occur, it is on a very small scale relatively to England's total business and resources. The importation of the amount of 10 millions of sovereigns makes an enormous difference in Lombard Street, but it is a mere nothing relatively to England's total business. Whereas, if the same difficulty arises in a country in which the main payments have to be made with currency itself, there is a need for an importation of currency, or an increase of currency, standing in some moderately high relation to the total business of the country; or, at all events, to that part of the total business of the country which is carried on on Western methods. Thirdly, England is near to other great gold markets. Fourthly, her financial houses are numerous and able." There followed a suggestion that the constitution of the German Reichsbank is adapted for imitation by India.

III, xn. 4. some quantity of the precious metals to act as the basis of a paper currency. The question what part of a country's share she takes in gold and what in silver is determined entirely by her own tastes. (If she mints them freely at a fixed ratio, it is then determined for her by Gresham's law; but just now we are not concerned with that case.)

Thus the volume of the business in each country, which requires the use of coin, is determined by her wealth and habits: the proportion between the gold and silver which she uses, whether for currency, for hoarding, or for the arts, is determined by her tastes. These conditions all the world over determine the aggregate demand for silver and the aggregate demand for gold. The aggregate supply of each metal may be taken as a fixed quantity at any time, because its annual increase is in any case but a small part of the total stock existing: but yet this is slowly modified by the annual production, that is governed by the richness of the mines on the one hand; and the value, in terms of commodities, of an ounce of the metal on the other. The value of each metal is determined by the relation in which the supply of it stands to the demand for it. The ratio between the two values thus determined is the gold price of silver.

In other words, the gold price of silver is determined by the ratio between the prices of commodities in gold and in silver countries. If any sudden discoveries of silver mines in the West, or any discarding of silver from Western currencies, disturbs the equilibrium, the silver that is not wanted in the West will go to the East; and, even if its influx into the East does not lower its value there, its efflux from the West will raise its value there, till it and the ratio which gold prices bear to silver prices are equal to one another.

4. Exact measures of the relative purchasing powers of currency in different countries are unobtainable, and even unthinkable.

It is obvious that international trade exerts no direct influence on the general level of prices in a country which has an inconvertible paper currency. But the market price of gold in terms of such a currency indicates the extent of the divergence of the value of that currency from the amount of general purchasing power which it affects to command.

All general statements as to the relations between the general III, xII, 5. levels of prices in two countries, are subject to the qualifications set out in Book I, Chapter III. The levels are necessarily estimated almost exclusively "by reference to the wholesale prices of the most important and representative of those commodities which are fairly well standardized." If the people of one country are able to select and pay for superior qualities of any commodity than can be afforded generally by the people of another, the level of prices (in terms of gold), so far as that commodity is concerned, will of course reach a higher level relatively than would be indicated by the general argument of this chapter. No simple statement can be made, which will cover all the irregularities in the relative (gold) prices of commodities in different countries: but the chief relevant considerations may be noted.

We start from the facts that, other things being equal, either an increase of the foreign demand for a country's goods, or a diminution of her demand for foreign goods will tend to bring gold to her; and therefore will tend to raise her general level of prices. Further, the prices of her imports at her frontier will be higher by their costs of carriage than in the place of their origin, and conversely the prices of her exports will be lower at her frontier than in the places of their destination by the cost of carriage. Ricardo, reasoning on this basis, which was indicated nearly two centuries ago, formulated the conclusion that "other things being equal, those countries whose exportable productions are most in demand abroad, and contain greatest value in smallest bulk; which are nearest the mines; and which have the least demand for foreign productions, are those in which prices will habitually range the highest[1]."

5. *Influences of a country's external trade on the prices of things produced by her for her own consumption.*

The main influence, which a country's trade exercises on her general prices is through the prices of her exports. These generally are governed by their money cost of production, which bears fairly settled relations to the money costs of production of the

---

[1] The phrase is taken from J. S. Mill, *Political Economy*, III, xix, 2. But the importance of proximity to the mines is not now very great; and for symmetry the phrase requires the condition that the country's chief imports should contain small value in great bulk. But these are trivial points.

III, xii, 5. things she makes for herself: because the fluidity of labour within a country tends to equalize the earnings of efforts that are similar in kind and equal in quantity in different occupations. But this tendency is not of uniform strength. It does not prevent some kinds and qualities of labour, manual and mental, from being relatively scarce and therefore relatively better remunerated in some countries than in others.

Of course, the general level of prices in a country will not necessarily rise and fall in the same proportions as do those of her exports; if the industries which produce those exports are not representative of the general body of her work in regard to method, energy and ability; or if the movement of labour, manual and mental, between various localities and groups of industries within the country, is not easy and rapid; or if many kinds of her agricultural and other bulky produce, are raised at so great a distance from her frontier, that their prices at the frontier exceed very much the average prices at which they are supplied to her own people.

Thus prices in Asia are low, in spite of the fact that her chief exports include tea, silk, spices, and other goods; which have been in great demand abroad, and have contained exceptionally high value in a given bulk. On the other hand, the chief exports of Anglo-Saxon new countries are mineral and agricultural products, which are with a few exceptions bulky in proportion to their value, and not the subjects of any specially intense demand; and yet the general level of prices in these countries is exceptionally high; and the retail prices even of their chief exports are often as high as, or even higher than, the retail prices of those very exports when delivered to the consumer in Britain from three thousand to twelve thousand miles away.

Prices in English and Continental towns are in some respects more similar than they are in an English town and rural district. In the rural districts everywhere the simpler forms of handicraft and personal service are relatively low.

Again, since it is only the wholesale prices of goods at the frontiers which are directly under the influence of foreign trade, the cost of internal transport and distribution has to be added to the general influences on the level of prices in a country. Here of course account has to be taken of the efficiency and cheapness of communication by water, road and railroad, and of organiza- III, xII, 5. tion of wholesale and retail trade within the country. The causes which raise the simpler handicrafts and personal services in Western and especially in Anglo-Saxon countries, raise also the prices that have to be paid for the simple and patient labour of which much is wanted in the retail trade. But much energy and initiative, and a high sense of the value of time, and abundance of cheap capital are needed in most branches of wholesale trade and some branches of the retail trade; and qualities which are not scarce in Anglo-Saxon countries, cannot be high-priced there. It is, no doubt, the common opinion that, on the whole, retailers charge more highly for the services which they render in those countries than elsewhere. But the Anglo-Saxon purchaser often requires a specially large, various, and quickly changed stock of goods to select from, and sometimes requires the retailers to perform various services in the way of prompt delivery of trifles, which are not demanded elsewhere. The neglect of such considerations is one side of the natural tendency to confuse a high scale of living with a high scale of prices[1].

[1] There is special interest in the following remarks made a century ago (1822) by Lowe (*State of the Nation*, pp. 164, 165); partly because his reference to the eminent riches of Holland, reminds us how recent are the high prices prevalent in Anglo-Saxon countries beyond the seas, and in Germany: though of course a large part of Germany, as of Italy, had been rich and enlightened, when England had not emerged from her early mediaeval poverty. Lowe says: "Our wish is merely to lay down the general rule, that a population dense, improved, affluent, does not necessarily render a country more expensive than one that is poor and thinly inhabited. The difference is in the mode of living, not in the price of the articles. An increase of population, by leading to an abridgment of labour, and to the transaction of business *en masse*, brings with it a despatch and an extent of accommodation; the saving from which is equal, we believe more than equal, to the enhancement in provisions attendant on augmented numbers.

It is not in towns of moderate size, however near each other, but only in the case of an overgrown capital, such as London or Paris, that the real and unavoidable expense becomes considerable. Holland and England are, it is true, dearer throughout all their provincial towns, than the rest of Europe; but that is owing partly to style of living, partly to high taxation—to the price paid by either country for the rank it has maintained in the scale of European politics. Were we to subject individual expenditure to an analysis, and to keep separate the portion of it which results from these causes, we should find that our actual prices, the purchase money of commodities at market, are not, on the whole, much greater than in other countries."

BOOK IV

FLUCTUATIONS OF INDUSTRY, TRADE AND CREDIT

CHAPTER I

A GENERAL VIEW OF CAUSES THAT AFFECTED CONTINUITY OF EMPLOYMENT IN EARLY TIMES

1. *Difficulties of transport formerly caused each district to be mainly dependent on its own harvests.*

The observations on the continuity of employment, made in the present book, are directly connected with the study of business credit in Book II. They have but little bearing on causes which govern the richness of the reward of work—a subject on which something was said in the first volume of the series, *Principles of Economics*. But those causes are the deepest concern to the student of the conditions of social well-being: and they are designed to have a prominent place in the final volume of the present series.

There is one cause of fluctuations of economic prosperity which is beyond the reach of human control. Unfavourable weather—especially at seed time or harvest—may bring grievous distress to a country, that is not in a position to import and distribute large supplies of grain from a distance. In fact, the chief causes of fluctuations of credit, industry, and trade in early times were variations of harvests, wars and plagues. Failure of a harvest generally caused the price of grain to rise more than in proportion to the short-coming of the crop; so that those who produced grain for sale were sometimes enriched by bad weather, which caused a labourer's food to consist in great measure of grain, so musty that bread made of it would not be saleable now[1].

---

[1] Some exaggerated notions as to the stability of prices in mediaeval England are attributable to a neglect of the fact that, when grain was scarce, the weight of the loaf would be lessened, while its price remained constant.

A century ago, a series of good harvests in England sometimes reduced the price of wheat so much more than they increased its quantity, that farmers could not pay their rents, and some country banks were shaken. On the other hand, after a harvest that was both wet and deficient, a labourer's weekly earnings, if spent wholly on musty bread, would hardly support himself and his family. Thus, local variations of harvests offered the chief example of the general rule that great fluctuations in price may be caused by relatively small fluctuations in the supply of a thing, the demand for a definite supply of which is very urgent; no adequate substitute being available. When heavy duties were levied on the importation of grain into Britain, its price was liable to be raised very greatly by a deficiency in her harvest: for the costs of bringing it from its chief sources of supply in central and eastern Europe were heavy.

The matter is less pressing now; for the supply of maize, which is a fairly good substitute for wheat, is large. And, what is perhaps more important, scanty harvests in a part of the Western world are supplemented by increased importations of food from a distance. Bad conditions of the crops in the Northern hemisphere are reported by telegraph in the Southern in time to increase the sowings of grain, that will be reaped during the Northern spring. But there is no similar compensating influence in regard to any depression of credit and industrial activity that spreads widely in a great industrial country. On the contrary, a considerable disturbance of industrial and commercial activity in any one Western country inevitably deprives some producers and traders in other Western countries of markets for goods, which they had designed for exportation.

Moreover, the volume of business credit increases much faster than do the numbers of the population and their wealth. The web of credit in each industrial country is closely knit; and yet it spreads widely within the country and beyond. Thus credit is already in great measure international: a large and severe shock to business anywhere is likely to cause tremors of credit in almost every part of the Western world.

This sensitiveness of each industrial country, and especially of each creditor country, to disturbances of credit in every other is, however, not an unmixed evil. It causes alert business men to

IV, I, 2. consider carefully their commitments; so that provision can be made against coming troubles, before they become heavy. The submarine telegraph has exercised a powerful influence in mitigating the intensity of fluctuations of business credit, while extending the areas over which they spread.

2. *Problems of unemployment were relatively simple when industrial skill was not highly specialized; and work in the fields often alternated with common weaving and other simple manufacturing operations.*

When agriculture was the dominant industry in western Europe, the cultivator and his employees, if he had any, used to do many things which are now regarded as belonging to other industries. They often erected buildings and made implements and clothes for themselves, and still more often repaired them; they often baked their own bread and brewed their own beer, cured their own bacon, and preserved their own fruit. Consequently there was nearly always something to be done, to which the peasant or his wife could set themselves, or the well-to-do cultivator could set his serfs or his labourers, when they had nothing to do in the fields. This subsidiary work was sometimes of so little worth that, if wages by the day had needed to be paid for it, it would have been left undone: but when a man was bound by the year, there was nothing to be said for leaving him idle. The practice of yearly hirings of agricultural labour survived in some parts of England half a century ago. But the migratory habits, which began with the great agricultural strike of 1874, caused these labourers to compare their position with that of men hired by the day. They concluded that the evils of occasional unemployment are really less than those of unwelcome constraint, at all events if some provision is made during full work for possible unemployment later on. The fisherman and the peasant farmer, in spite of bad seasons, lead happier lives than men; who, being by nature free, are compelled during even a single year to submit to the rough orders of an employer with whom they are not on good terms. So hiring by the year has almost disappeared[1].

[1] The objections of the modern wage earner to yearly hirings are set out by Webb, *Industrial Democracy*, pp. 431–3.

Eden (*The State of the Poor*, Vol. III, App. II) gives the rates of wages assessed by the year and by the day, with meat and drink and also without it, chiefly

3. *When wages were in great measure fixed by custom or authority in terms of money, operatives generally were likely to be seriously injured by a fall in the real value of the currency, however caused.*

Mankind's command over nature was increased long ago by the progress of the methods of production and transport, and by the development of powerful machinery: but a corresponding improvement in the condition of the masses of the people was delayed by the ineptitude and the selfishness of those in authority. The coins in which labourers were paid were clipped and otherwise diminished; while large transactions, especially in connection with foreign trade, were effected by agreed weights of silver, whether coined or not. When these evils had been in great measure redressed, the effective purchasing power of wages was reduced by Corn Laws, which the landowning classes made in their own interests; the rich supplies of grain which central Europe was willing to send in return for fabrics manufactured by England's new machinery, bore a heavy burden of import duties on admission at the ports, and this burden was increased by dealers' profits. Consequently the manual worker received less than his fair share of the benefits which the country derived from the masterful work of her mechanical engineers, and he was inclined to listen to those (not always disinterested) advisers, who told him that "the people," for whom Government and Parliament laboured, were the well-to-do people. He was taught by them to regard economic progress as moving backwards; and to regard a rise in prices as a source of increase in the hardships of his lot[1].

The improvements of manufacturing technique, which Britain made in advance of other countries, tended to prevent the labour cost of his food from rising as fast as it otherwise would have done, when he became largely dependent on imported supplies of grain: and, when the importation of grain was freed from Protective duties, his material well-being was seen to depend more on fluctuations of business credit than on harvests.

during Elizabeth's reign, arranged in convenient comparative tables for a great number of occupations. Additional allowance may need to be made for livery and house-room in the case of some yearly hirings; but even when this is done the figures suggest that employment for labour hired by the day, averaged not more than 60 or 70 per cent. of the working days. See also Cunningham, *Growth of English Industry and Commerce*, Ed. III, Vol. 1, p. 390.

[1] Reference may be made here to observations on successive debasements of the coinage: see above, I, v, 3.

CHAPTER II

INFLUENCES ON STABILITY OF EMPLOYMENT
EXERTED BY DEVELOPMENTS OF TECHNIQUE

1. *A fluctuation of credit directly affects a larger part of the working classes now than formerly: but they have the means of making much ampler defences against it.*

It is true that fluctuations of business credit affect a larger part of the workers now than they did in early times; and that fluctuations of employment are occasionally rather severe. But, meanwhile, there has been a rapid rise, on the average, in the total yearly wages of the employees, taking good times and bad times together. It may be said that the insurance fund against slack times is in effect given over to their charge; instead of being retained in the hands of the employer. The change works for good on the balance: it is an essential condition of rapid industrial progress[1].

Indeed the working classes in former times lacked the education, the means of locomotion, and the financial resources needed for effective combinations; except in a few industries, most of which were both highly skilled and localized. The law forbade combinations, both among employers and among employed. But masters could arrange concerted action without openly entering into a combination. And, although laws and Justices' orders with regard to wages were enforced with penalties against masters who paid, as well as against men who received, wages above the standard, they were generally ineffective against a lowering of wages below the standard[2].

[1] This consideration, together with others allied to it, is developed in the last two chapters of my *Principles of Economics*, of which the titles are "General influences of progress on value," and "Progress in relation to standards of life."

[2] Thus in 1720 the London journeymen tailors say: "If the Justices shall settle the men's wages, how is it possible that each man shall be rewarded according to his merit?" In spite of their protests an Act was passed with penalties against high wages, but none against low; with penalties against the journeyman who left his work, or would not take work when offered at the standard wages; while none were set on masters who dismissed their men abruptly. The hours of work were fixed to be from 6 a.m. to 9 p.m., with one

2. *The changefulness of modern industrial methods disturbs the relations between earnings and efficiency in different
occupations. But it increases the activity of the employer in
estimating the contributions, which his employees severally
add to the earning power of his business: and it thus tends
to redress the disturbances which it causes.*

In the modern world the chief readjustments of the remuneration of labour are associated with changes in process; which
enable some sorts of labour to make a better return relatively
to their costs than others, that had the advantage before. Almost
every change in process involves changes both in the demands for
different sorts of labour, and the relative demands for labour in
the businesses which adopt the new process and for machinery
and other plant: the change is nearly always in favour of the steel
hand, and against the human hand.

But there is no such general rule in regard to the competition
for employment between different grades of labour: for the semi-
automatic machinery, which is characteristic of the modern age,
is tended in some cases by labour which is more skilled, and in
others by labour which is less skilled, than that which is displaced.
But machinery is itself the embodiment of labour, and business
enterprise, arranged with forethought and sustained by more or
less patient waiting for its result.

Thus a chief part of the work of the alert employer is to consider whether he can increase the earning power of his business
by substituting a process which will make use of certain classes

hour for dinner, though the men averred that these hours caused their health and
especially their sight to fail at 40. (See Galton's *Tailoring Trade*, pp. 1–22.)
 Skilled tailors were not as powerful as valets, sedan chair men, and other
domestic servants who were apt to tyrannize over their fashionable masters and
mistresses at about this time. They were better able to take care of themselves
than most other wage earners: and yet their incessant complaints of unemployment show that they contributed their share to Gee's estimate made
about this time that "we have above a million of people in the three nations
destitute of work." (*Discourse of Trade*, ch. XXIX. The estimate was implicitly
endorsed a little later in the well-informed *Essay on the causes of the decline of
the foreign trade*, p. 248, of McCulloch's reprint.) This estimate, as the context
shows, does not refer to exceptional times: and, after allowance has been made
for some exaggeration, it confirms the suggestions made by records of child
labour, of practical slavery in the mines, and of vagrancy. All of these imply
that life was very hard for the workers in the first half of the eighteenth
century; though wealth was then growing faster than population, and the era
of machine industry had not begun.

IV, II. 2. of plant and labour for another process; which makes use of other classes of plant and labour, together perhaps with some of those which he used before. If his new requirements can be satisfied from plant and labour, the market values of which are fairly settled by prolonged, steady experience, he can estimate beforehand the advantages of the new process.

The changes, which he desires, may be such as could only be made on a large scale: as, for instance, the substitution of "power" (whether generated by water or heat, whether acting directly or after transmutation) for hand-power in a certain factory; and in that case there would be a certain element of uncertainty and risk in the change. Such breaches of continuity are however inevitable, both in production and consumption, if we regard the action of single individuals. There will always be trades in which small businesses are most economically conducted without steam or other power: and in businesses, which inevitably use it, there will always be a continuous stream of intermediate businesses on the margin, at which it is just becoming profitable to make use of it. Even in large establishments, in which steam is already in use, there will always be some things done by hand which are done by steam power elsewhere; and so on.

Thus the adaptation of means to ends (estimated by their money measures) is more nearly perfect in regard to the whole of an industry than it is in regard to an individual business, especially to a relatively small business which needs expensive plant. And the adjustment of remuneration to personal efficiency tends to be more and more a broad adjustment, extending over the chief national industries: because mechanical methods, which are more or less universal in character, are spreading their dominion in every direction; and the importance of mere manual skill is almost everywhere yielding to that of the qualities, that make for general efficiency, when aided by fingers of steel that are almost unerring. Alert employers, in industries, that are apparently wide apart, are simultaneously considering enlargements of old processes or introductions of new processes that will draw directly or indirectly on the kindred supplies of labour.

Thus, while competition acts steadily and directly in the direction of equalizing the remuneration which can be obtained by the same energy and steadfastness in each horizontal stratum; it also acts constantly, though indirectly, in establishing even relations between the remunerations to be got in different strata. If by accidental scarcity, or an exceptional tactical skill, the members of any one stratum were generally receiving remunerations disproportionately high relatively to their faculties; then large changes in process, for which modern invention is ever giving occasion, would be so moulded as to give an even increasing scope for the work of other strata, to the exclusion of that which was disproportionately high-priced.

Thus, the various strata of the employed class are continually competing with one another for employment over a great part, though not over the whole, of the field of industry. They do not compete for the same tasks as a rule: but they do habitually compete for employment in making the same product by different processes; or in making products which subserve practically the same purposes. This competition is in addition to the incessant rise of members of the lower strata to a position of effective direct competition for employment in higher grade work; and to the less frequent falling of members of a higher grade to the necessity of seeking employment in the work of a lower grade. On the whole it may be concluded that the money values, which market competition assigns to different services, differ in important respects from their true social values: but yet the work, which it does within these limits, is very thorough.

In spite of many failures, it has a strong claim on our respect because it grapples with great difficulties which have been ignored by the brilliant but over-bold imaginations of the propounders of large schemes for a social order that affords very little place to rights of private property. It tends with marvellous power so to assort employees among various industries, and among various businesses in each industry, that every man is employed on that work to which his personal efficiency is most appropriate. For where the assortment is bad, the employer cannot afford to pay for that part of the operative's faculty, which is not turned to full account at his present work: and the operative may reasonably expect to improve his position by seeking work in another business in which his faculty may be turned to better account.

3. *The aggregation of workers in factories causes inter-ruptions of employment to be more conspicuous than they would be, if work generally were done in cottages, as it was in earlier times*[1].

The present writer spent a winter some years ago at Palermo. The mediaeval traditions of industry went on there; and everything that one reads about with regard to the clientèle of the well-to-do houses among the working men in the Middle Ages one found in Palermo then. If one had tried to collect statistics of want of employment, one would probably have found next to none. Scarcely anybody was thrown out of regular employment because scarcely anybody was in it. But the average employment of the handicraftsman in Palermo was probably seldom as great as in the east end of London in depressed times; and the average annual earnings were probably not a quarter as high. Of course, in certain cases, hirings were made for the year, during which the employer was practically bound to give some sort of sustenance to the employee. But, when that system prevailed, the employee in return often gave up so much of his freedom that it might be questioned whether he was completely a free man.

Objections may be raised in this connection as to the sufficiency to our returns of want of employment. On the other hand, it may be urged that when people work at their own homes one cannot prove that they are thrown out of employment, because the irregularity of their employment is the rule and not the exception. If they have no work to-day they may have it to-morrow; if they are in work to-day, they have no reason for supposing that they will be to-morrow. Now those people were in the same condition as the majority of people in the mediaeval times—they took a job when it came to them: they consequently never were "out of employment"; there was nothing to get into the newspapers. When a factory with 5000 hands works half time or closes its door the fact is telegraphed all over England: while if 5000 people each working in his own home, get a little less steady employment than before there is nothing to attract attention, at all events outside of their immediate neighbourhood.

In this connection, it may be noted that, when the range of

---

[1] Much of this section is reproduced from evidence submitted to the Royal Commission on Gold and Silver in 1888; Questions 9816, 7.

skilled industry is increasing, there may be a fall in the rates of IV, II, 3. wages in many employments, at the same time that the average rate of wages of all the wage receivers taken together tends to rise. Suppose, for instance, that some time ago skilled labour had 40s. and unskilled labour 16s.; but at that time the unskilled labourers were twice as numerous as the skilled. Suppose that after a time there is a fall in the wages of every trade; that the skilled wages fall to 36s., and the unskilled wages to 15s.: but that, meanwhile, the number of skilled increases till it is twice as great as that of the unskilled: the apparent result will have been a fall of wages. But the real result will be that the wages, which were on the average 24s. in the former period, have risen to 29s. in the latter. If therefore it is true that the ranks of skilled industry have increased in anything like as great a proportion as the ranks of unionists, it is probable that the common estimates that have been given of the rise of the average wages in the working classes are below the truth.

Of course, when prices are falling, everybody who undertakes a business risk is likely to have his risk turn out worse than if prices were rising. When a fall of prices sets in, many business men strike: that is, they say, " We will not keep our mills running full time," or "We will go out of business." But after they have struck for a little while they recognize that, although they may lose money by working their mills, they would lose more money by not working them. They may indeed manage to get a combination to check production of one particular article, and artificially raise its price; and thus they may gain at the expense of the community. But such schemes have never lasted on a large scale for a long time: after a little while it is found that running half-time is less profitable than running full time.

A few men may refuse to go on with their businesses: and some great works have been completely closed, and never re-opened. But these are exceptional cases, due to exceptional causes. As a rule when closed they are sold to new men, who, purchasing them at a comparatively low rate, have all the benefit of the past fall of prices, and are able to go on, and make profits. Therefore strong evidence is needed to prove that a fall of prices diminishes the productiveness of industry, except during a relatively short transitional period.

IV, II, 4.   4. *Technical progress is responsible for the temporary unemployment of some small classes of workers. Its injuries are small in comparison with the benefit that mankind derives from it: but they call for careful study; and for remedy, where that can be found.*

The causes which make particular classes of goods liable to exceptionally great variations of demand are of several different kinds. Seasonal variations can be in great measure anticipated: though an exceptionally cold, or an exceptionally warm, winter, may cause the prices of house coals, and of certain classes of clothing, to vary a good deal from their normal costs of production. On the other hand, the demands for particular sorts of fashion goods are in great measure fostered artificially by particular groups of dealers in touch with manufacturers[1].

An advance of technique is frequently accompanied by temporary dislocations of employment. Its benefits are likely to be many times as great as the harm which it works: but that harm needs to be taken seriously, and kept within as narrow limits as possible. This seems to be a matter in which ill-considered action is likely to do more harm than good; but in which much net good may result from thorough thought and vigilant forethought.

Industrial progress involves change: perfect stability of industry or trade indicates low vitality, even in occupations, whose general character is but little modified from one generation to another. Almost every such change improves the prospects of some branches of industry and of some kinds of industrial faculty. Therefore, the conditions of industry and trade would be likely to fluctuate a little from year to year, and from generation to generation, throughout the whole western world. This is a sign of weakness and a source of weakness. But its main cause is to be found in that development of common international interests in industry and trade, which has played an important part in the rapid progress of mankind during the last hundred years. Later stages of that progress may be expected to increase the power of thoughtful men so to anticipate the future that means may be

---

[1] Rumour says that many a fashion in dress has been planned at a meeting in Paris of representatives of leading dealers and manufacturers: and that materials adapted to the coming fashion are already on many looms, before any anticipation of it has percolated through to the public; or even to the great body of manufacturers and traders, who are interested in the matter.

fitly adapted to coming needs and business credit may develop more steadily and surely. For the present, however, reckoning must be made with the probability that some credits will be granted, not wisely but too well, by leaders of finance, as well as by the less instructed public, to business ventures that are somewhat lacking in administrative capacity, or in foresight. Even if wars and other extraneous evils do not greatly hinder the development of industry and trade, fluctuations in the rate of progress seem likely to continue. Such fluctuations are likely to be the result of variations in many diverse influences: the normal periods of these variations are likely to differ; and therefore a fluctuation of general prosperity, which is due to their combined action, is not likely to present a very clear outline. These matters, however, belong more properly to a volume which is designed to supplement *Principles of Economics*, *Industry and Trade*, as well as the present volume. Attention may be directed to the able and suggestive study of them in Part VI of Professor Pigou's *Economics of welfare*. An interesting study of fluctuations in a country, whose currency normally rests on a basis other than gold, will be found in *The future of Exchange*, by Professor H. Stanley Jevons.

CHAPTER III

RELATIONS OF THE MONEY-MARKET TO FLUCTUATIONS OF INDUSTRY AND TRADE

1. *The gradual growth of organized markets for capital to be invested in business developments.*

Every great "undertaking" needs great "enterprise": these two terms have drifted somewhat apart; but their origins are near together. And, though the mastery of mechanical routine takes an even larger place in a business that needs a vast durable plant: yet its permanent success, even in mere money-making, generally requires the guidance of a few minds with a faculty of imagination; as well as of many, that are persistent in the orderly development of details. For great progress can be attained only by bold daring; and security may be purchased at too high a cost. Where no considerable risks are run, there can be no great progress[1].

In a bold, enterprising country, such as England has long been, great risks are habitually taken. As children will vie with one another to see which can snatch the finest piece of seaweed from the sand, and yet just escape the coming billow; so even those business men, who are not of a reckless temperament, do not always draw off from exciting speculations at the first sign of approaching disasters. The years, nay, the months, just before credit breaks are often those in which the highest and the quickest profits are to be made by alert financiers, who can deftly pluck the prize, and get out of the reach of danger just in time. It has been well said that "the state of trade revolves apparently in an established cycle. First we find it in a state of quiescence—next, improvement—growing confidence—prosperity—excitement—overtrading—convulsion—pressure—stagnation—distress—ending again in quiescence[2]."

---

[1] Some origins of present economic problems are discussed in Book I of *Industry and Trade*, with reference in chapters III and IV to the qualities that are required for and developed in the processes of massive manufacture.

[2] *Reflections...on the causes and consequences of the pressure on the Money Market*, 1837, by Lord Overstone, reprinted in 1857 and edited by McCulloch. Lord Overstone took a leading part in the movement for the stringent regulation of the issue of paper currency, which resulted in the Act of 1844.

The recent history of fluctuations of general credit shows much variety of detail, but a close uniformity of general outline. In the ascending phase, credit has been given somewhat boldly, and even to men whose business capacity has not been proved. For, at such times a man may gain a profit on nearly every transaction, even though he has brought no special knowledge or ability to bear on it; and his success may probably tempt others, of like capacity with himself, to buy speculatively. If he is quick to get out of his ventures, he probably makes a profit. But his sales hasten a fall of prices, which must have come in the course of time. Though the fall is likely to be slight at first; yet each downward movement impairs the confidence which had caused the rise of prices, and is still giving them some support. The fall of a lighted match on some thing that smoulders has often started a disastrous panic in a crowded theatre.

2. *The area, over which a fluctuation of business enterprise and industrial activity commonly extends has widened; and it is widening.*

While the scale of fluctuations of credit has increased, some progress has been made in the tasks of forecasting them, and of making preparations against them. They occupied a part of the attention of mediaeval Gilds and Trading Companies: but only in quite recent times has the study of them been brought up to a high level of efficiency. Powerful businesses, as well as many newspapers, are now served by highly trained business correspondents in numerous centres; whose duty it is to report fully by post on broad gradual movements: they send telegrams, sometimes in cypher, in relation to matters that are of special interest to their principals. Meanwhile the collection of detailed information has been organized by both general and special newspapers, aided by telegraph and telephone: and thus the producing and distributing centres for each important class of goods are united, almost as completely as were the individual producers and traders in Manchester or Leeds or Lyons in earlier times.

This extension of the areas, over which fluctuations of industry and trade spread, is mainly due to two causes; which are indeed closely connected with one another. The first is the increase in the size of the ordinary business unit: and the second is the

IV, III, 2. rapidity and cheapness of modern communications by land, water and air. The ownership of the means of production and transport is now distributed among a larger proportion of the population than formerly, in spite of the fact that the number of businesses engaged in production and transport is much smaller relatively to the population than it used to be. The securities of many large businesses are quoted on the Stock Exchange; and these prices fluctuate in accordance with broad changes affecting credit in general, as well as those which are peculiar to individual undertakings.

The general tendency of fluctuations of credit to become international was strengthened long ago by increased intercourse among the chief centres of industry and trade. Recent improvements in the means of communication have in great measure unified large business interests in many countries; while instantaneous electrical intercourse by land, sea, and air is making the whole western world one in regard to such intelligence as is of most concern to operators on great stock exchanges. This tendency has increased vastly in strength during recent years; but was strong before the age of steam and electricity.

Of course it seldom happens that the imports of one country (A) from another (B) exactly balance her exports to B: some of the obligations of each to the other are likely, in any case, to be discharged by the transfer of bills on other countries. But suppose that A is an old country, most of whose natural resources are fully developed, while B is a new country (such as Australia), whose natural resources are large relatively to her population; or, an old country, like Russia or India, whose resources are large relatively to the capital at her command. In such a case A is likely to accept payment for a considerable part of her exports to B in the form of stock exchange securities: some of these are likely to represent public debts, for which B's Government is responsible: while others are issued by private trading companies. Meanwhile, many a bank, especially if it has offices in an old country and in a new, transfers much command over capital, received from the public in the old country to be employed on its own responsibility in the new. By these and similar means, nearly the whole free capital of the world is made available for developing the richest natural resources of the world.

3. *The ordinary course of a fluctuation of commercial* IV, III, 3.
credit[1].

An improvement of credit may have its rise in the opening out
of foreign markets after a war, in a good harvest, or in some other
definite change: but more often it arises from the mere passing
away of old causes of distrust, which had had their origin in some
previous misfortune or mismanagement. Whatever its origin, when
once begun it tends to grow. Bankers lend more by book credits:
and, if they are issuers of notes, they increase their issues. Other
business men trust their customers readily: bills of exchange
multiply: new undertakings are started: orders are given to
builders and manufacturers: orders are given for additional
machinery and other plant. At first the movement may be slight,
but it gains strength as it grows.

Producers find that the demand for their goods is increasing;
they expect to sell at a profit, and are willing to pay good prices
for the prompt delivery of what they want. Employers compete
with one another for labour; wages rise; and the employed in
spending their wages increase the demand for all kinds of commodities. New public and private Companies are started to take
advantage of the promising openings which show themselves
among the general activity. Thus the desire to buy and the willingness to pay increased prices grow together; Credit is ever more
confident; bankers and others lend more freely; the instruments
of credit multiply: prices, wages and profits go on rising: there
is a general rise in the incomes of those engaged in trade: they
spend freely, increase the demand for goods and raise prices still
higher. Many speculators seeing the rise, and thinking it will continue, buy goods with the expectation of selling them at a profit.
At such a time a man, who has only a few hundred pounds, can
often borrow from bankers and others the means of buying many
thousand pounds' worth of goods; and every one who thus enters
into the market as a buyer, adds to the upward tendency of prices,
whether he buys with his own or with borrowed money.

This movement goes on for some time, till at last an enormous
amount of trading is being carried on by credit and with borrowed
money. Old firms are borrowing in order to extend their business;

[1] Much of this Section is reproduced from *Economics of Industry* by the
present writer and his wife, published in 1879.

IV, III, 3. new firms are borrowing in order to start their business, and
speculators are borrowing in order to buy and hold goods: trade
is in a dangerous condition. Those whose business it is to lend
money are among the first to read the signs of the times; and they
begin to think about contracting their loans. But they cannot do
this without much disturbing trade. If they had been more chary
of lending at an earlier stage, they would simply have prevented
some new business from being undertaken; but when it is once
undertaken, it cannot be abandoned without a loss of much of the
capital that has been invested in it. Trading companies of all kinds
have borrowed vast sums with which they have begun to open
mines, and build docks and ships and ironworks and factories;
prices being high they do not get much building done for their
outlay, and though they are not yet ready to reap profits on their
investment, they have to come again into the market to borrow
more capital. The lenders of capital already wish to contract their
loans; and the demand for more loans raises the rate of interest
very high. Distrust increases, those who have lent become eager
to secure themselves: and refuse to renew their loans on easy or
even on any terms. Some speculators have to sell goods in order
to pay their debts; and by so doing they check the rise of prices.
This check makes all other speculators anxious, and many rush
in to sell. For a man, who has borrowed money at interest to buy
goods, may be ruined if he holds them a long time, even while their
price remains stationary: he is almost sure to be ruined if he holds
them while their price falls. When a large speculator fails, his
failure may cause that of others who have lent their credit to him;
and their failure again that of others. Many of those who fail may
be really "sound": that is, their assets may exceed their debts.
But though a man is sound, some untoward event, such as the
failure of others who are known to be indebted to him, may make
his creditors suspect him. They may be able to demand immediate
payment from him, while he cannot collect quickly what is owing
to him; and the market being disturbed he is distrusted; he cannot
borrow, and he fails. As credit by growing makes itself grow, so
when distrust has taken the place of confidence, failure and panic
breed panic and failure. The commercial storm leaves its path
strewn with ruin. When it is over there is a calm, but a dull heavy
calm. Those who have saved themselves are in no mood to venture

again: companies, whose success is doubtful, are wound up, and new companies cannot be formed. Coal, iron, and the other materials fall in price as rapidly as they rose.

When the credit and business activities of a country are in the ascending phase, her market becomes a good one to sell in, and a bad one to buy in; and the exchanges become increasingly unfavourable to her; till at last they reach specie point, and the exportation of the precious metals becomes profitable. It foreshadows a fall of prices: people generally, and especially bankers, become anxious. Everyone takes alarm on his account, partly because he knows that others are taking alarm on theirs. His creditors are so far a little more likely to demand payment than before, and his debtors a little less certain to be ready with it. An adverse movement of the exchanges is often both a symptom and a cause of a slackening of the flow of credit. If not handled well, the ebb of credit may gather force and become a torrent: the greater had been the piling up of waters in the ascending flow of credit, the greater the violence of the ebb.

The immediate *occasion* of a commercial crisis has often been a few business failures, that would have been unimportant if the solid framework of business had not been overlaid by much rather loose credit: but the real *cause* of the crisis was not to be found in those small failures. It lay in the slender hold which much credit at the time had on solid foundations.

4. *Tendency of fluctuations of credit and industrial activity to become international.*

The transfer of international stock exchange securities, which results automatically from the natural tendency of such securities to fall in value in a stringent money market, is an instance of the rule that a high rate of interest induces people in general and speculators in particular to reduce their holdings of all marketable things for which they have not an immediate need. For instance, high rates of interest and discount in England increase the charges to which Englishmen are put who hold stocks of cotton or wheat or copper with borrowed money; and thus it lowers (other things being equal) the prices of cotton, wheat, copper, etc. in England relatively to other countries. This may possibly cause a little exportation of these commodities to other countries; and probably

IV, III, 4. will cause some cargoes of them with uncertain destination, or even provisionally destined for England, to be diverted by telegraphic orders to their ports. And every such movement would diminish the power of drawing on the part of other countries against England, and would make the exchanges less unfavourable to her.

In the same way a rise in the rates of discount and interest makes English speculators unwilling to hold large amounts of stock exchange securities; the price of these consequently tends downwards in English markets and such of them as are international in character are promptly sold by telegraph or otherwise in markets in which their price has not fallen.

But this is not all. Commodities are not held speculatively except in anticipation of a rise of price. But stock exchange securities yield a direct income independently of any such rise. Securities, therefore, are held semi-speculatively under a less confident belief that their price will rise than would be necessary in the case of commodities that yielded no income themselves; and consequently a slight increase in the profits so made by the uses of money in other ways will turn the balance of advantage against the continued holding of a larger volume of securities than of commodities. Finally, they are perfectly "graded," and can be described exactly, so that the purchaser does not need to see them before final delivery; their direct cost of transport is nominal; the risk of loss in transport is very small, and some of them can even be replaced if lost; and lastly the demand for them is elastic, and the power which foreign markets have of absorbing them is very great.

To sum up: Bankers' drafts and other financial paper have recently grown into importance relatively to commercial bills as means of transferring the temporary use of capital from one country to another. There has been a great increase in the transfer of stock exchange securities by post, and of the command over them by telegraph: and the power of all these three agencies has been very much increased by the improvement of postal communications and especially by the telegraph. Even commercial bills, though smaller in volume relatively to the aggregate of business transactions than they used to be, have gained so much in strength from the new facilities of communication that though their power has diminished relatively, it is absolutely greater now than ever

IV, III, 4.

before. And all these agencies taken together can operate so promptly in every way, that in spite of the vast oscillations of modern business, no western country can remain under pressure for any considerable time, while others have ready capital to spare, and she has not lost their confidence.

The international money market obtains ever more solidarity: the rates of discount, the prices of securities, and the prices of easily portable commodities vary in different countries less and less from their mean international level; and the exchanges are seldom allowed to move from par so far and so long as to cause any considerable futile movement of the precious metal: that is, a movement which is occasioned by a mere want of balance of immediate international claims, and would therefore be likely to need to be effaced by an opposite movement when these particular claims have been adjusted. Thus, the trade, which England carries on with the various countries of the world, is in fact welded into one whole: she balances her indebtedness, not with each other country separately, but with them all together. If her prompt claims on (say) New Zealand run a little short of New Zealand's claims on her, a small turn of the exchanges in favour of New Zealand and against England, brings at once into play excess of prompt claims which England has on other countries, sometimes enabling them to act directly, sometimes working round through a third and perhaps fourth and fifth money market. Thus, unless England is really short of prompt claims on the world as a whole, her exchanges with New Zealand are not likely to become very unfavourable to her. Various accidents, especially shocks to commercial or political credit, may cause a sharp divergence between her exchanges with different countries. But in placid times, England's exchanges with the chief gold-using countries of the Continent, tend to move together: and though the connection is less close, the same is in a great measure true of her exchanges with the gold-using countries of the rest of the world.

CHAPTER IV

RELATIONS OF THE MONEY-MARKET TO FLUCTUA-
TIONS OF INDUSTRY AND TRADE, CONTINUED

1. *Some variations in the rate of interest obtainable for the use of capital (with good security) correspond to changes in the prospects of high profits to be obtained in the development of industries new and old: others correspond to variations in the supply of capital, relatively to the development of existing enterprises, and the inception of others.*

Interest is commonly taken to be the percentage on a loan which a borrower pays for a period of the loan, generally a year: a high rate of interest always indicates strong demand for the loan of capital. This demand may be the result of lasting general distress; but it is more often the result of expectations, whether well founded or not, that general prosperity is likely to be high. It is sometimes caused by a prospect of great gains to be probably derived from the use of capital in existing businesses or in new enterprises. And it is sometimes caused by the discovery that the provision of capital, made from some important enterprises, has been inadequate; insomuch that more must be risked, or else much must be lost. The rate of interest often rises rather high, under the influence of hope, in an ascending phase of industrial and commercial activity and prosperity: but it seldom rises very high for that reason. On the other hand, it may be raised to a vast height by fears that commercial or political disturbances may soon restrict the operations of credit; and thus impel many people to strengthen their own positions by calling in all payments due to them, which are within their control.

Commercial distrust tends to fluctuate more or less in ten-year periods. Political distrust knows no law. The price of the British National Debt, bearing 3 per cent. interest, touched 97 in 1792; it fell below 48 in 1797 and in 1798. It fluctuated between 53 and 65 in the year of Waterloo; it touched 97 in 1824, but fell to 75 during the troubles of 1825.

2. Discount on a bill is a deduction of interest from the amount written on its face. Its elasticity and ease of adaptation to the circumstances of each particular advance enable it to play a chief part in the quick adjustment of free capital to the demand for it.

The rate of discount is distinguished on the Money Market, for practical reasons, from the rate of interest on short loans: but it will be sufficient here to consider only those conditions which are common to both. The rate of interest for long loans is governed on the one side by the needs of businesses for capital to carry them through the undertakings which they have in hand, or in view; and, on the other side by the amount of capital which is not as yet specialized or "fixed" in any particular use. This amount is in effect the excess of recent aggregate production over the corresponding consumption of wealth; together with the amount of new wealth, which has already been given over to productive uses, but is not yet distinctly specialized to any one. The rates of interest for short periods, and of discount, are of course often changed at short intervals, in accordance with fluctuations in the general activity of the markets and their confidence as to the prosperity of the near future[1].

It is obvious[2] that the mean rate of discount must be much under the influence of the mean rate of interest for long loans; which is determined by the extent and the richness of the field for the investment of capital on the one hand, and on the other by the amount of capital seeking investment. If the amount of capital has been increasing fast, then, in spite of a great widening of the field of investment, it forces down the rate of discount. The fall in the rate of discount so caused fails to stimulate speculation, because it has been itself caused by the difficulty of finding good openings for speculative investment: this difficulty may be due in part to the fear that prices will go on falling.

---

[1] As is well known, interest at 1 per cent. for a quarter of a year is at a rather higher rate than 4 per cent. for a year. For instance, £10,000 lent for three months on the 1st of January would become £10,100 on the 1st of April; £10,201 at the rate of 1 per cent. for a second three months; a very little more than £10,303 after a third three months; and rather more than £10,406 at the end of the year. Differences of this kind are not worth considering in ordinary business: but they demand notice in transactions involving large sums of money.

[2] This paragraph is reproduced from evidence submitted to the Gold and Silver Commission, 1887–8, Question 9686.

IV, IV, 2. Equilibrium is found at that rate of interest for long loans (and
the corresponding rate of discount for short loans) which equates
supply and demand.

Again, the influx of a good deal of bullion into the city is likely
to lower the rate of discount. This does not increase the amount
of capital, in the strictest sense of the word: it does not increase
the amount of building materials, machinery, etc. But it does
increase the amount of command over capital which is in the hands
of those whose business it is to lend to speculative enterprise.
Having this extra supply, lenders lower still more the rate, which
they charge for loans; and they keep on lowering it till a point is
reached at which the demand will carry off the larger supply.
When this has been done, there is more capital in the hands of
speculative investors, who come on the markets for goods as
buyers, and so raise prices. Further, the influx of bullion will
have caused people to expect a rise of prices, and, therefore, to
be more inclined to borrow for speculative investments. Thus it
may not be necessary to lower the rate of discount very much.
The increased demand for loans will meet the increased supply
half way; and, after a time, may outrun it, causing a rise in the
rate of discount. But, as this rise will be merely an incident in
a series of changes which put more command over capital in the
hands of speculative investors, it will go with an increased demand
for goods and a continued rise of prices.

This appears to be the way in which an extra supply of the
precious metals will bring prices up. Having been raised, they will
be sustained. For, the methods of business remaining stationary,
if a man with an income of £1000 keeps on the average £12 in his
pocket; and if there is more currency in the country, so that his
share is increased from £12 to £14: then what was formerly bought
by £12, will now be sold at £14. Thus higher prices are sustained
by an increase in the amount of cash on hand, which a person
cares to keep. This amount depends upon the habits of business
in his particular rank of life, together with his individual peculiarities: if they are not changed, any increase in the amount of
currency which falls to his share will raise proportionately prices
so far as he is concerned.

Speaking generally then, it may be said that a rise in the rate
of discount is caused by an increase in the desire of some of those

who use capital to borrow; or by a decrease in the willingness of some of those, who are in control of capital, to lend. The first commonly indicates increased confidence, and perhaps increased prosperity; the latter generally indicates the opposite. Looking at the special case of the effect of an increase in currency on the rate of discount in the western world, the cycle seems to be this. The new currency, or the increase of currency, goes, not to private persons, but to the banking centres; and, therefore, it increases the willingness of lenders to lend in the first instance, and lowers the rate of discount. But it afterwards raises prices: and therefore it tends to increase discount. This latter movement is cumulative. The loans to one man make him a good customer for others at good prices, and make them therefore eager to borrow: that makes them good customers; and so the movement grows. Thus, a fall in the purchasing power of money tends, after a while, to raise the rate of discount and the rate of interest on long investments[1].

The history of variations in the current rate of discount seems to indicate, as might be expected *à priori*; first, that rates of discount will generally be higher when prices are rising than when they are falling, because the borrowers will be eager for loans: and secondly, that they will generally be higher during periods of high prices, than in periods of low prices; not because one is the cause of the other, but because both are the results from the same cause—the prevalence of a confident spirit in the business world.

Those periods are, however, liable to be broken by cyclones of distrust, and such cyclones raise discount for a time to the very highest levels of all. They are accompanied by falling prices, followed by falling rates of discount. A change in the rate of discount is indeed the ripple of a wave on the surface: the average level of the rate is governed by the rate of interest which can be got for the investment of capital: and this is being lowered by the rapid and steady growth of things, the actual excess of production over consumption. If destructive wars could be stayed, the rate of interest on secure investments would fall far. Labour might then

---

[1] Loans for short periods are often obtained at exorbitant rates of interest from professional money lenders: but a trusted customer can obtain such a loan easily from his bank, and at a very low rate. Much the greater part of such loans are however obtained by discounting a bill not yet due. In former times, a bill frequently passed from one hand to another, being endorsed by every one who handled it: all such signatories being of course responsible for it in their order.

IV, IV, 3. be equipped with powerful appliances, and yet retain by far the greater part of the value, which is added to raw material by the joint operations of labour and capital.

To conclude: the rate of interest is governed by the average profitableness of business in general: fluctuations of the market rate of discount about the average rate of interest are governed by a great variety of passing incidents in the general course of business. The rate at which the Bank of England discounts first-class bills controls in great measure the general rates of discount for bills of various classes: that rate influences the course of business at large, partly because it reflects the general character of current business.

3. *Prompt action by the Bank of England in regard to the rate of discount often checks unreasonable expansions of credit; which might otherwise grow, after the manner of a fall of snow on a steep mountain side.*

It is a matter of common experience that even a temporary stringency of the money market materially affects stock exchange prices: this result is apt to be thought natural; but it calls for some explanation. The rate for stock exchange loans, like all others, is quoted *per annum*; and if this rises 2 per cent. the charge for a fortnightly loan needed for carrying over to the next account rises less than a tenth of 1 per cent.: and it is not *prima facie* reasonable that in consequence securities should fall in price by much more than one-tenth per cent., as in fact they frequently do.

Of course fluctuations of prices in the market are caused mainly by fluctuations in relative strength and eagerness of bulls and bears in the market; stocks in the hands of steady investors take little or no immediate part in the play. Prices stiffen if, when the account day comes, the amount of loose stock ready to be delivered is small relatively to that which the bulls are ready to carry, and *vice versa.* Some bulls and some bears are sure to be on the margin of doubt whether to continue or not, and both will watch the rate of discount. If the loose surplus of loanable money in Lombard Street is small, and carrying over rates are stiff, a few bulls will elect to close out, and avoid these stiff rates: so they will pay or receive differences, according as prices are lower or higher than when they bought; and their demand will have ceased. On the other hand

a few bears, forecasting this tendency, will have increased hopes IV, IV, 3.
that prices will move in their favour, and will be inclined to
continue their offers by carrying them to the next account instead
of settling at this account. These movements may be small: but
they are apt to act like a falling stone on a steep hill-side covered
with loose snow. The stone gathers a little snow, the snowball
gathers more snow; and ultimately there is big movement, which,
under exceptional conditions, becomes an avalanche. Similarly the
little fluctuation in price started by the action of these few people,
who were before on the margin of doubt, and therefore liable to be
influenced by a small cause, will act on the opinions of others
and thus be magnified. If the market happen to be in a nervous,
hysterical condition, even so slight a cause as a small rise in the
rate of discount may initiate a stock exchange avalanche, or panic.

In ordinary times, cool heads predominate among professional
speculators. They distinguish between those stringencies of the
money market which may probably foreshadow worse things to
come, and those which are in the normal course of events: for
instance, they expect a temporary stringency caused by the withdrawal of money from the city to the country in harvest time;
and find profit in the undue significance which the amateurs attribute to the consequent movement on the Exchange. But the
ordinary professional is himself at a like disadvantage relatively
to great financiers in anticipating those wayward moods of the
money market that conform to no rule: for indeed those moods
are themselves largely fashioned by the great operators.

For instance, the temporary withdrawal of a comparatively
small sum of gold from the central reserve in the Bank of England
acts appreciably on discount, and therefore on the power which
the market has of carrying stocks, and therefore on their price.
A moderate force applied to the regulating value can bring into
play great forces, whose action can be exploited for the benefit
of those who know of it beforehand, because they have contrived
it. Such manoeuvres are indeed difficult in any country, the basis
of whose currency is an estuary of the vast international ocean
of gold. But they are easy, where the currency is isolated;
especially when it consists of inconvertible paper[1].

---

[1] In recent years, since silver has ceased to be a chief medium of large transactions, it has been easy to act upon the small margin of silver that has been

4. *Tentative suggestions as to directions, on which organized effort may possibly work, with the purpose of diminishing
fluctuations of employment, without slackening the advance
of industrial technique*[1].

Economic institutions are the products of human nature, and
cannot change much faster than human nature changes. Education, the raising of our moral and religious ideals, and the growths
of printing press and telegraph have indeed affected English
human nature: and many things, which economists rightly considered impossible thirty years ago, are possible now. The rate
of change is increasing constantly and rapidly: and we may be
tempted to speculate boldly for the future. But we have to act
for the present; and to take human nature, not as it may be,
but as it is.

There are some causes of discontinuity of labour which we cannot
remedy, such as bad harvests; and some which we should not wish
to remedy, such as new inventions. Almost every invention does
some partial harm; and, as the rate of invention increases, so this
harm increases. But it yields a large net surplus of good; and
those, who reap the good, may be expected to bestow some of it
to shield those on whom the harm falls.

Those causes of discontinuity which lie within our scope, and
are remediable, are chiefly connected in some way or other with
the want of knowledge; but there is one which is wilful: it is
fashion. Until a little while ago only the rich could change their
clothing at the capricious order of their dressmakers: but now all
classes do it. The histories of the alpaca trade, the lace trade, the
straw hat trade, the ribbon trade, and a multitude of others, tell
of bursts of feverish activity alternating with deadening idleness.

Forced interruption to labour is a grievous evil. Those, whose
livelihood is secure, gain physical and mental health from happy

fluid in the market at any time. To lower or raise its gold price for a time by a
twentieth was not a very difficult task: and since all securities, the income from
which was payable in silver, followed suit for a time at least, there was scope
for risking a little in the silver market, and making large gains in stocks. Illustrations of this kind might be multiplied: but enough has been said to emphasize
the enormous power of those who can sow the seeds of a great change in values
in one field of speculation, and reap the harvest in remote fields where they
alone look for it.

[1] This section and the next are based on an Appendix, contributed by the
present writer, to the *Report of the Industrial Remuneration Conference*, 1899.

and well-spent holidays. But want of work, with long continued IV, IV, 4.
anxiety, consumes a man's best strength without any return. His
wife becomes thin; and his children get, as it were, a nasty notch
in their lives, which is perhaps never quite overgrown.

In backward countries irregular employment is, so to speak, the
rule: as it was in England in earlier days; and as it is even now
with some artisans, who work on their own account. Because it is
the rule, very little is heard about it: and, thanks to the breadth
of her markets and the freedom of her trade, she suffers less from
it than most other nations.

Better and more widely diffused knowledge is a remedy for that
excessive confidence which causes a violent expansion of credit
and rise of prices; and it is also a remedy for that excessive distrust
that follows. One of the chief sources of disturbance is the action
of the general public in providing funds for joint-stock companies.
Having insufficient technical knowledge, many of them trust just
where they should not: they swell the demand for building materials
and machinery and other things, just at the time at which far-
sighted people with special knowledge detect coming danger, and
this reacts on other trades. With every expansion and contraction
of credit prices rise and fall. This change of prices presses heavily
even on those who kept themselves as far as possible from the
uncertainties of trade, and increases in many ways the intensity
of commercial fluctuations. For just when private traders and
public companies are most inclined to reckless ventures, the interest which they have to pay on borrowed capital represents an
exceptionally small purchasing power, because prices are high.
And in the opposite phase, when their resources are crippled by
the stagnation of business, the lowness of prices compels them to
sacrifice a much greater amount of real wealth in order to pay their
interest. When traders are rejoicing in high prices, debenture and
mortgage holders and other creditors are depressed; and when the
pendulum swings the other way, traders, already depressed, pay
an exceptionally heavy toll to their creditors. This evil might be
lessened by the adoption of the plan, already indicated[1], of making
long-term contracts in Official units of general purchasing power,
instead of in currency.

[1] See Book I, I, § 3.

5. *Concluding observations.*

The sagacity and public spirit of the leading minds both among employers and employed are increasing fast. But, while human nature is what it is, they are not likely to be so unselfish as never to curtail production, when they can benefit themselves by doing it, though at a great cost to others.

It is true that a committee of able business men in the country, representing not one trade interest but many, might conceivably give counsel by which the traders might regulate themselves. A committee somewhat of this kind does meet once a week in the Bank of England parlour; and it occasionally gives pregnant hints to the public: but that is only incidental to its proper business. It is conceivable that a body of able disinterested men, with a wide range of business knowledge, may ultimately be able to issue predictions of trade storm and of trade weather generally, that might have an appreciable effect in rendering the employment of industry more steady and continuous. But a committee, that was not of natural growth, would not be very likely to succeed.

When considering how such a committee might come together, our thoughts naturally turn to the hopes of co-operative federation. The obstacles to the management of the more difficult kinds of business on the co-operative principle are great; but any piece of solid work that is done on the co-operative plan is a great good. It helps in many different ways to brighten the future of England's industrial life, and for one thing can scarcely fail to diminish forced interruptions of work.

The highest ranks of industry are not those which have the softest hands or wear the neatest coats. They are those which make the most use of high and rare faculties. A working-man may do better for his son by fitting him to become a responsible foreman, than if he makes him a second-rate clerk or school-master: the foreman will probably do the higher work, and rightly get the higher wages. The more there are of men, who are fit to rise to the higher posts in the management of business, the greater will be the competition for the aid of ordinary labour, and the higher will be the average level of wages.

The chief remedy, then, for low wages is better education. School education makes the mind elastic, ready to take in new ideas, and able to communicate freely with others. But what IV, IV. 5. makes one man really higher than another is a vigorous, straight-forward character. The work of true education must be in great part done by parents: they have the best opportunities for teaching their children to feel rightly, to act strongly, and to spend wisely.

The aim of social endeavour must be to increase the numbers of those who are capable of the more difficult work of the world, and to diminish the number of those who can do only unintelligent work, or who perhaps cannot even do that. The age of chivalry is not over: we are learning how dependent the possibilities of leading a noble life are on physical and moral surroundings. However great may be our distrust of forcible socialism, we are rapidly getting to feel that no one can lay his head on his pillow at peace with himself, who is not giving something of his time and his substance to diminish the number of the outcasts of society; and to increase yet further the number of those who can earn a reasonable income, and thus have the opportunity of living a noble life.

APPENDIX A[1]

NOTES ON THE EVOLUTION OF MONEY

1. *A convenient medium of exchange was needed even in early times for bargains between different family groups, and between tribes into which such groups expanded.*

Egyptian bas-reliefs suggest that the *individual* man of the present time is not very much more capable, physically and intellectually, than were many of his ancestors thousands of years ago[2]. But in the modern age men *collectively* are able to compel Nature so to work in their service that the average material well-being of a vast population is far higher than was possible formerly, even when Nature's resources were very large and generous relatively to the population. This result is due mainly to organization, combined with the foresight, which induces people to make provision for their own future; and to a complex of motives which leads each generation to make provisions of a durable kind, that will yield much of their fruit in distant times. Despotic power, moved by the desire to be remembered long, and aided by subtle knowledge of engineering and astronomy, produced the pyramids. But the application of increasing command over Nature to the improvement of the conditions of the life of the masses of the people made very little progress till quite recent times.

What improvement there was, resulted mainly from an increase in the freedom of movement and of industrial occupation, under the protection of improving social order. The breaking up of old traditions no doubt destroyed some defences, with which custom had covered the conditions of the "inferior" orders of the people. Some of its immediate effects were injurious: but it was a necessary step towards their liberation from servile or semi-servile conditions. Its chief instrument was the substitution of values expressed in terms of money for obligations expressed in terms of custom.

This money-instrument worked harshly in some directions, but

---

[1] This Appendix is attached to Book I, Chapter I.
[2] This notion was impressed on me by my father in the British Museum seventy years ago.

no alternative for it, which could have extended throughout APP. A, 2. the people, seems to be suggested by history. Great ruling classes have indeed controlled the affairs of nations by organized military force: but effective freedom could be attained by the main body of any nation, only on the condition that everyone could dispose of his goods and services to whoever was able and willing to give a return, that met his particular requirements and tastes.

2. *Even at times, when the relations between different individuals and different classes were largely regulated by custom and by force, free bargaining prevailed at fairs; and need arose there for a "current" medium of exchange.*

Gibbon, following closely on Aristotle's lead, and in accordance with eighteenth century notions as to early deliberate Social Contracts, said that money and letters were invented, the one to express our wants and our property, and the other to express our ideas; both, "by giving a more active energy to the powers and passions of human nature, have contributed to multiply the objects they were designed to represent." We now know that primitive folk do not form large purposes in advance and pursue them on set plans: their appliances are not invented, but grow gradually by imperceptible steps.

The exchange of goods began long before the rights of possession of an individual had been clearly and fully marked off from those of the family, or village, or tribe. Things were given and others received in return; and help was lent by one man to another, with the understanding that its equivalent would be rendered on occasion. But the notion of a definite measurement of give and take, whether in regard to exchanges that were completed in a single transaction, or to the return for past aid in the form of labour or goods (advanced "on credit," to use a modern phrase) emerged but slowly[1].

[1] The backwoodsmen who cleared away the virgin forests of Eastern America, invoked one another's help for rolling heavy logs. But, keen bargainers as they were by nature, they did not measure exactly the work involved in each roll: a general sense of fairness and good fellowship sufficed in place of detailed records of services rendered; and at a later date "honour among thieves" enabled log-rolling to work smoothly among those who combined to plunder the people for the benefit now of one special interest and now of another. More definite obligations might be incurred in a similar way. One man might lend to another a quantity of grain, to be returned with increase perhaps after the next harvest; or the use of a horse or a canoe for an expedition to be requited by a definite quantity of a like service later: and so on.

Accordingly it has been argued with some show of reason that, though the uses of a modern currency are larger and freer in domestic trade than in foreign trade, yet the early origins of money were in a sort of international trade which made its appearance at the periodical meetings of neighbouring clans for trade. At such meetings, which were akin to fairs, barter dominated; there being no place as a rule for credit: but it was supplemented by the use of some things of trifling nature which were used as media of exchange[1].

Among pastoral and agricultural peoples with abundant territory the first place was taken by cattle (or in some places by reindeer, buffaloes and other live-stock); because they transported themselves; and, though the individual perished, the stock could be maintained permanently: it yielded an income and was a source of increase of *capital*—a term which is said to be derived from *caput* or head of live stock. And when land became scarce in a more settled civilization, symbolic representations of cattle, impressed upon strips of leather were used as currency: thus foreshadowing the credit value of the inconvertible paper currency of later days[2].

---

[1] Thus furs, hides, specified weights of leather, pieces of cloth and mats of customary size and quality; blocks of dried fish, tobacco, salt, sugar and wax; almonds, dates, cocoanuts and even eggs have been used as money: so also have javelins, spear heads, copper, knives, etc. Much silver is even now stored up in the bangles and other simple ornaments of the needy Hindoo: and the impulsive American Indians are patient enough to get together great quantities of United States coin, among other things, to be used as personal ornaments.

A summary of the varieties of material used as money in primitive civilizations is given by Wagner, *Socialoekonomische Theorie des Geldes*, II, C. The recrudescence of "natural" money in the American colonies under the combined influences of close contact with the natives, of poverty in the precious metals, and of bad management of their banks and paper currency, are well told in Sumner's *History of American Currency*: see also Weeden's *Economic History of New England*. Devices for keeping up the standard of legal tender tobacco money in Virginia are described in White's *Money and Banking*, ch. I.

[2] Prof. Ridgeway has shown that the first unit of weight over the whole basin of the Mediterranean and eastwards to India was that of a piece of gold, of such a size that it represented what had been up to that time the chief customary unit, viz. the value of a standard ox or cow. And this gold unit seems to have been the parent of modern metallic currencies. It would seem, moreover, that a standard ox unit of gold was everywhere of nearly the same size, a little larger than our sovereign; and that it nowhere contained less than 120 and nowhere more than 140 grains of gold. He attributes this coincidence to frequent and easy traffic along various trade routes which united the shores of the Atlantic and the Indian Ocean.

Again, sometimes a commodity, which had satisfied the chief requirements

To conclude. The varieties and vicissitudes of primitive currencies are full of romantic interest; and they throw much light on the permanence of certain elements in human nature, as well as on the plasticity of the institutions in which those permanent elements take effect. The use of a thing as a general *medium of exchange*— and this is the primary function of money—grew up without conscious purpose. Its position could not be strong unless it satisfied some general want as a commodity for solid service or for ornament; and no great increase in its quantity could be made without considerable effort. Each of these conditions contains a latent element of confidence, trust or "credit" that a man's neighbours would act in the future as in the past. Little doubt as to such permanence ever obtrudes itself on the primitive, unanalytical mind: but none the less is it true that a thing could not obtain vogue as a medium of exchange, unless people generally had a quiet and perhaps almost unconscious expectation that it would not suffer any considerable loss of prestige during the period, whether short or long, of its stay in their possession.

As industry and trade developed, an even more urgent need developed for the coordination of one set of media of exchange that were suitable for large dealings, and of another set that were suitable for small dealings: that need was best met by coins, some made of rare metals and others of common metals. No quite satisfactory material has yet been found for currency of very small denominations. Paper has been tried by some impoverished Governments: but it would really be an expensive currency, if so constantly renewed as to be kept clean; and it has become offensive when allowed to be dirty. As a substitute for bronze Jevons has suggested steel, stamped by very powerful machinery, and then

---

of a medium of exchange, was superseded by inferior substitutes, which degenerated till they resembled a discredited inconvertible paper currency. Thus some fish-hooks, used as currency by fishermen on the shores of the Pacific, were frequently lost, or worn out; and therefore they could not fall in value much below their cost of production, which was considerable: and as their production was open they could not rise much above it. But after a while their use as currency spread inland; and, being handled by people who could not judge their merits, inferior specimens of them found vogue: and the deterioration continued till all the remaining hooks were used in fishing: their place was taken by useless pieces of bent wire, and the low cost of making such things ultimately governed the value of the currency. The observations in *The Wealth of Nations* on "the origin of money" are modern in tone. They are well supplemented by notes in Cannan's edition.

APP. A, 3. hardened and protected from rust. Some such suggestion as this might perhaps be combined with a provision that all coins of less value than, say, six pence should be made of base metal; and be of such sizes and shapes as can be conveniently distinguished in the dark. Some should be oval, others perhaps square or hexagonal with blunted corners. None should be either much larger or much smaller than a shilling.

3. *Services rendered even by crude forms of money.*

Money needs to be durable, in so far as it serves the purpose of complex trade; for that is likely to take a long time in completing its round of exchanges: cubes of salt for instance have done a good deal of exchange work in some primitive markets. But the handling of such things in any considerable quantity is cumbrous: so the right to receive a certain number of cubes would be transferred from one person to another. To speak more generally, as soon as a thing became recognized as sure to be available in exchange for other things in any place, it became a primitive sort of money: and values would come to be expressed in terms of it, even where a mere title to it was given in exchange for some commodity: after a time arrangements might grow up for lessening the actual transfer of the cubes. The seller of a horse having a right, say, to fifty cubes of salt—salt would be likely to be of high value relatively to horses under primitive conditions—might transfer his rights to the cubes to various persons, from whom he desired to obtain other things. That is, cubes of salt would be on their way to become primitive money. It seems certain that the use of money often came into vogue somewhat in this way.

The advantages which any one such crude money had over its rivals might be slight at first. But every step in advance would increase the pace at which it drew away from all competition, and became established in use as current money. For every one would be willing to accept it in exchange, even though he had no direct use for it; because he knew that others would do the same, and for the same reason.

In times when custom and tradition rule, even a crude "money" of so variable a character as beaver skins, will develop a well understood price list for ordinary commodities; and many such lists have been preserved. (It is to be noted that a price list for

200 commodities would need but 200 entries: a list of rates of APP. A, 4. barter would need 39,800 entries)[1].

Sometimes a medium of exchange, in which customary and other values had been reckoned, passed out of existence without leaving any substitute which claimed to fill its place and spoilt its fair name. If then its vogue had been great, its name might be used as a money of account, in which prices were wrangled about, and ultimately settled; the actual payment being made in the things that were "current" at that time and place, as media of exchange[2].

4. *Uncertainties of trade by barter between two individuals*[3].

Let us consider the case of two individuals engaged in barter. A has, say a basket of apples, B a basket of nuts; A wants some nuts, B wants some apples. The satisfaction which B would get from one apple would perhaps outweigh that which he would lose by parting with 12 nuts; while the satisfaction which A would get from perhaps three nuts would outweigh that which he would lose by parting with one apple. The exchange will be started somewhere between these two rates: but if it goes on gradually, every apple that A loses will increase the marginal utility of apples to him and make him more unwilling to part with any more: while every additional nut that he gets will lower the marginal utility of nuts to him and diminish his eagerness for more: and *vice versâ* with B. At last A's eagerness for nuts relatively to apples will no longer exceed B's; and exchange will cease, because any terms that the one is willing to propose would be disadvantageous to the other. Up to this point exchange has increased the satisfaction on both

---

[1] See Ridgeway. *Origin of Currency*, chap. II, and Schurtz, *Entstehungs Geschichte Geldes*, chap. XVI.

[2] Moneys of account seem to have been common in many stages of civilization. Thus the shilling was for many centuries simply a parcel of pence, though accounts were generally rendered in shillings: each represented at first four or five pence, and ultimately twelve pence. In like manner the rouble was a money of account consisting of 100 copecks, and not a coin, till the time of Peter the Great.

On the other hand the once common guinea is a money of account now. And Tyrolese peasants still often render accounts in Gulden and Kreutzers, though for several years such accounts have had no legal validity. Again in the Philippine islands prices are quoted in reales and quartos, though no such coins exist now. (Kemmerer, *Money and Prices*, p. 276 n.)

[3] This section reproduces Appendix F of the present writer's *Principles of Economics*.

sides, but it can do so no further. Equilibrium has been attained; but really it is not *the* equilibrium, it is *an* accidental equilibrium.

There is, however, one equilibrium rate of exchange which has some sort of right to be called the true equilibrium rate, because if once hit upon it would be adhered to throughout. It is clear that if very many nuts were to be given throughout for an apple, *B* would be willing to do but little business; while if but very few were to be given, *A* would be willing to do but little. There must be some intermediate rate at which they would be willing to do business to the same extent. Suppose that this rate is six nuts for an apple; and that *A* is willing to give eight apples for 48 nuts, while *B* is willing to receive eight apples at that rate; but that *A* would not be willing to give a ninth apple for another six nuts while *B* would not be willing to give another six nuts for a ninth apple. This is then the true position of equilibrium; but there is no reason to suppose that it will be reached in practice.

Suppose, for instance, that *A*'s basket had originally 20 apples in it and *B*'s 100 nuts, and that *A* at starting induced *B* to believe that he does not care much to have any nuts; and so manages to barter four apples for 40 nuts, and afterwards two more for 17 nuts, and afterwards one more for eight. Equilibrium may now have been reached, there may be no further exchange which is advantageous to both. *A* has 65 nuts and does not care to give another apple even for eight; while *B*, having only 35 nuts, sets a high value on them, and will not give as many as eight for another apple.

On the other hand, if *B* had been the more skilful in bargaining he might have perhaps induced *A* to give six apples for 15 nuts, and then two more for seven. *A* has now given up eight apples and got 22 nuts: if the terms at starting had been six nuts for an apple and he had got 48 nuts for his eight apples, he would not have given up another apple for even seven nuts; but having so few nuts he is anxious to get more and is willing to give two more apples in exchange for eight nuts, and then two more for nine nuts and then one more for five; and then again equilibrium may be reached; for *B*, having 13 apples and 56 nuts, does not perhaps care to give more than five nuts for an apple, and *A* may be unwilling to give up one of his few remaining apples for less than six.

In both these cases the exchange would have increased the APP. A, 4. satisfaction of both as far as it went; and when it ceased, no further exchange would have been possible which would not have diminished the satisfaction of at least one of them. In each case an equilibrium rate would have been reached; but it would be an arbitrary equilibrium.

Next suppose that there are a hundred people in a similar position to that of A, each with about 20 apples, and the same desire for nuts as A; and an equal number on the other side similarly situated to the original B. Then the acutest bargainers in the market would probably be some of them on A's side, some of them on B's; and whether there was free communication throughout the market or not, the mean of the bargains would not be so likely to differ very widely from the rate of six nuts for an apple as in the case of barter between two people. But yet there would be no such strong probability of its adhering very closely to that rate, as we saw was the case in the corn-market. It would be quite possible for those on the A side to get in varying degrees the better of those on the B side in bargaining, so that after a time 6500 nuts might have been exchanged for 700 apples; and then those on the A side, having so many nuts, might be unwilling to do any more trade except at the rate of at least eight nuts for an apple, while those on the B side, having only 35 nuts apiece left on the average, might probably refuse to part with any more at that rate. On the other hand, the B's might have got in various degrees the better of the A's in bargaining, with the result that after a time 1300 apples had been exchanged for only 4400 nuts: the B's having then 1300 apples and 5600 nuts, might be unwilling to offer more than five nuts for an apple, while the A's, having only seven apples apiece left on the average, might decline that rate. In the one case equilibrium would be found at a rate of eight nuts for an apple, and in the other at the rate of five nuts. In each case *an* equilibrium would be attained, but not *the* equilibrium[1].

This uncertainty of the ultimate position of equilibrium does not depend on the fact that one commodity is being bartered for another instead of being sold for money. It results from our being obliged to regard the marginal utilities of both commodities as

[1] Precise versions of these arguments are to be found in Note XII of the Mathematical Appendix to my *Principles of Economics*.

APP. A, 4. varying. And indeed if we had supposed that it was a nut-growing district, and that all the traders on both sides had large stores of nuts, while only the A's had apples, then the exchange of a few handfuls of nuts would not visibly affect their stores, or change appreciably the "marginal utility" of nuts: that is, the intensity of the desire for more nuts, on the part of people who would have bought more nuts, if they could have been obtained on more favourable terms. In that case the bargaining would resemble in all fundamentals the buying and selling in an ordinary corn market. The real distinction then between the theory of buying and selling and that of barter is that in the former it generally is, and in the latter it generally is not, right to assume that the marginal utility of one of the things dealt with is practically constant.

It may be objected that in a nut country, nuts would perhaps be used almost as money; and that in fact this is almost implied in the case just discussed. No doubt it is so: and here we find an illustration of the general rule that if a commodity is in general use, under such conditions that its (marginal) utility to anyone who takes or gives it in exchange is not much affected by small transactions in it, then that commodity is so far well suited to act as a medium of exchange, and discharge the simpler functions of money for the small business of a primitive community.

APPENDIX B[1]

SOME DIFFICULTIES CONNECTED WITH
STATISTICS OF PRICES

1. *Price statistics relating to recent times cover less ground than is covered by the impressions of an experienced business man or householder: but their definiteness gives facilities for criticism, and affords protection against grave errors.*

The progress of economic science depends largely on the stock of trustworthy and appropriate statistics at its command. Some of these are supplied by individual students, often in concert with Statistical Societies. But much of the work, required in order to obtain the foundations of statistical conclusions, is of a semi-mechanical character: and it can only be done by the organized efforts of large staffs of workers, for which the resources of Government are often needed. Consequently the chief material on which statistical science works, consists of information, which various Governments have required for administrative purposes; or considered it their duty to organize in the interests of the nation. Much helpful material is collected also by trade organizations for their own uses: and statistical societies are rendering great services to progress by the guidance, encouragement and subsidies which they accord to private investigations. It may be admitted that in estimating the extent of changes in the effective purchasing power of money, as in many other complex economic problems, statistical measurements stand at some disadvantage relatively to careful judgments of experienced persons. Each of these authorities has a weak side: but, when they supplement one another, they are strong.

A dominant statistical fact is likely to have but a narrow scope: for otherwise it could not be definite. Being definite, it is open to criticism and correction; and therein lies its main strength. Statistical statements, that have stood this test, have a greater certainty *within their limits* than is likely to belong to the decision even of a capable judge of the matter. These limits are generally

---

[1] This Appendix is associated with I, II and III.

APP. B, 1. narrow, but they are obvious: an erroneous statistical estimate, or inference, in regard to a matter of general interest, incites and challenges the production of figures inconsistent with it. The absence of any challenge generally affords reason for believing that it is in accord with wide experience.

A second point in their favour is that, being definite, they can generally be collected by officials: even by such as are not specially endowed with insight and well balanced minds. A third point in their favour is that each set of figures can generally be compared with others of similar scope relating to different places: international comparisons and co-operation are here of high value. A fourth point is that, being definite, much of the work, required to be done on them, can be effected by calculating machines, animate or inanimate. Thus statistical records are chief aids in the guidance of present conduct by the experience of the past.

The definiteness of a statistical fact is, however, sometimes found to rest on unsound foundations. For instance, statistics of the mortality from various diseases in pest times are of great interest: but modern science appears to have found that the diagnoses, on which they were based, often lacked both precision and certitude. Such errors are being rapidly diminished by the progress of knowledge. But that very progress is throwing increasing doubt on the possibility of attributing any event to a single cause. The more an event is studied, the larger is generally the number of causes, by which it is seen to have been influenced: and there is seldom an easy and decisive means of isolating the influence of any one cause. The chief statistical method for this purpose is the comparison of variations from time to time (generally from year to year) of two things between which a causal connection seems likely. This method probably has an important future; but its difficulties are greater than appears at first sight[1].

[1] Its negative results are often decisive: as when mortality statistics shattered the old dictum that "a warm yule-tide makes a fat kirk-yard." It was found that, though the warmth encouraged some young and middle-aged persons to neglect precautions with fatal results, this increase of mortality was outweighed by a decrease among the aged.

Some approach to unanimity on doubtful matters is indeed often reached by discussion, and under the influence of gregarious instincts. How rare would be nearly unanimous verdicts in doubtful cases without such aid, may be shown by an extreme illustration:—If 32 persons, acting independently, and without any knowledge of A or B, guess which of them is the taller, the chance that they will all agree is only one in five thousand millions (see Bowley, l.c. p. 271).

2. *Weaknesses in series of averaged prices extending over considerable periods, commonly called Arithmetical Index Numbers.*

The weighted arithmetical index number for any year represents the total money cost, in each succeeding year on its list, of the purchases of each group of commodities to the same amount as was assumed for the basal year, for which the total cost of the purchases of each was set at 100. If this total shows an average of, say, 115, the general level of prices is inferred to have risen 15 per cent. above that in the basal year: it is thus an item in a list of "index numbers."

Unfortunately any peculiarities, which have belonged to the basal year, are likely to distort the whole of the list: and a considerable alteration in the general character of the list may be made by merely changing the basal year. This disadvantage has however proved to be less than might have been expected *à priori*.

Other faults of the arithmetical index number are its tendencies to cause the rise of a price by a certain percentage to count for more than the fall by the same percentage of a similar price: and to take no account of the fact that the pressure, which the rise of price of a thing would exert on the resources of the purchaser, would be mitigated by his curtailing his purchases of that thing; accompanied possibly by an extension of his purchases of other things, which had become relatively cheaper. In consequence, an arithmetical index number always shows a higher level of prices at any year, relatively to the basal year for prices, than would have been shown if that year had been taken as the basal year for prices and the calculation had been worked backwards, the list of commodities and their weights remaining unchanged[1].

---

[1] For instance, suppose that an index number is made out on the basis of prices in year A; and that in a rather distant year B it is found that in the interval one-half of the prices had doubled and the other half had fallen by one-half: in such a case it might reasonably be said that the average level of prices had not changed. But the index numbers would show 200 for the first half, and 50 for the second half; giving an average of 125. If now we put B prices at 100 throughout and work backwards to the A prices, the index number for A will appear to be 125: so that by starting from A and then working backwards from B to A we should have raised the index number from 100 to over 156. These difficulties are discussed in *The Economic Journal*, 1896, 7, by the late Prof. Pierson, and Prof. Edgeworth.

This matter would not be of very great importance if a single price list were made out continuously on one basis. But historical records are not adequate for this purpose, except in regard to staple grains and a few other things: a general price-list, that is adapted to the conditions of one age, cannot fit well those of another. Therefore opinions as to broad changes in general prices throughout several centuries are apt to be derived from an almost automatic piecing together cumulatively of impressions gained in regard to individual periods, each of which has been closely studied: and in each of these, rises in price have counted for more than falls in price. The cumulative effect of such distortions of view may perhaps have been considerable, though no great error was introduced at any one stage[1].

3. *When a rise in an index number is mainly due to scarcity of some luxuries, and of other commodities for which substitutes are available, the effective rise of prices is likely to be much less than is indicated by the index number.*

The preceding observations suggest that, large and important as are the uses of weighted arithmetical index numbers, they have their limitations. For they implicitly assume that the proportionate distribution of expenditure among the several groups of commodities concerned would remain constant, in spite of changes in their relative prices: so that the weights to be attached to them remained constant. But, in fact, the consumption of things that have risen in price will have diminished.

Some increase in the consumption of those which have fallen in price is also to be expected; but that result is not certain. For, if those which have risen in price are absolute necessaries, or even almost indispensable, the total expenditure on them is likely to increase: and the consumption of things which are not essential may diminish, in spite of the fact that their prices have fallen. In this case the effective purchasing power of people's incomes will have fallen, while the index number shows no change.

[1] It might be well that some historian, well versed in the details of particular commodities in successive ages, should work a series of index numbers backwards: that is, his basal year should be the last, instead of the first, for each group. His results, when combined with others obtained in the ordinary way, would afford much instruction to the economist, and to the historian.

Some of the influences of progress on the prices of various leading commodities, with special reference to the purchasing power of wages, have been noted in my *Principles*, VI, XII, §§ 5–7.

On the other hand it might happen that most of those things which were indispensable had fallen in price; while good substitutes for those, that had risen in price, were accessible at nearly equal prices: in that case, an unchanged index number would correspond to a considerable increase in the actual purchasing power of money[1].

This class of consideration is apt to be overlooked; but it is important. For a choice of commodities may be fairly representative under ordinary conditions; and yet it may be misleading, if it has included only one of several things that can satisfy the same need fairly well, and that one has varied in price more than the others. The results, which it suggests, need to be corrected by allowances for the shifting of consumption from things of which the price was relatively high, to others which were in greater relative abundance[2].

If it should ever be thought worth while to give much trouble to the matter, index numbers might be made much more nearly representative of real changes in the purchasing power of money, by the plan of grouping together all the chief kinds of things that satisfy nearly the same wants, and weighting each kind according to the extent to which it enters into general consumption, under varying conditions of relative prices. If at any time one kind, A, had risen in price, while another B had fallen; then account should be taken of the fact that the relative weights allotted to A and B in the basal year were not valid for the currrent year. The weight allotted to A should be lowered and multiplied into A's increased price: and that allotted to B should be raised, and multiplied into its diminished price. By this means index numbers would be made to represent changes in the average price, at which each

[1] For instance, suppose that a man's total expenditure of £600 before the change had been divided equally between two groups of things A and B: but the prices in group A have doubled, while those in group B have halved. He finds in group B some things that will serve his purpose nearly as well as some in group A: so he shifts £100 of the expenditure from A to B, giving £400 to B and £200 to A. He gets therefore only as much of the A goods as he could previously have got for £100. But with the £400 spent on B he gets as much as he could have got with £800 at the old prices: i.e. he gets £900 worth in all; or half as much again as before.

[2] The *Labour Gazette* for October 1917, p. 359, showed an increase in a weighted index number for articles of food of 97 per cent. over its amount in July 1914: but added that, if it had been so arranged as to omit eggs, to substitute margarine for butter, and to halve the consumption assigned to fish and sugar, the 97 per cent. would have been reduced to 56.

particular kind of want is satisfied, more closely than they do now.

4. *Further cautions regarding the use of arithmetical index numbers.*

When it is important to compare the general levels of prices in two particular years closely, the comparison should be made twice over, starting once from either end; and to take the mean of the results. This device almost completely destroys the possible influence of one flaw of the arithmetical index number: and it has this further advantage that if the two results do not differ widely, we know that an index number proceeding from either base will give fairly trustworthy results for years, intermediate in general economic conditions between those two years[1].

If only one calculation is made, the starting point or basis should be so chosen from a year (or the average of a group of years) in which both the quantities of commodities consumed and their prices are at about an average level for the period. That is, as a rule, the basis should be sought near the middle of the period. It may happen that the year, which is most normal as regards prices, is not the same as that which is the most normal as regards quantities: and then the prices should be equated to 100 for the first of these years and the weights should be taken from the second. Or again the weights may be estimated over the average of the whole period[2].

---

[1] This was done by Prof. Flux (see *Quarterly Journal of Economics*, 1907, p. 616) in regard to Mr Sauerbeck's and the *Economist's* index numbers. The results were satisfactory on the whole. In no case was there a greater divergence than 6 per cent. between the results obtained by working forwards and backwards. See also his paper read before the Royal Statistical Society in January, 1921.

[2] Thus Giffen, in his official studies of changes in the real volume of imports and exports, took 1861 as the basal year for prices and 1875 for weights. The more elaborate plan of taking the weights from estimates for a considerable number of years is well exemplified in the report of the Committee of the British Association in 1888 on *Variations in the Value of the Monetary standard*, which was drafted by Giffen. The Report contains instructive comparisons of index numbers for the same period on different bases: and the appendix to it, by Prof. Edgeworth, is an important study of the more abstract and general aspects of the problem of index numbers. The central table of the Report is reproduced in Prof. Bowley's *Elements of Statistics*, Chap. IX. The study of means of measuring the general purchasing power of money has been carried far in America, especially by Professors Fisher and Kemmerer; attention being given to contrivances for stabilizing the dollar, or otherwise setting up an official standard that may serve as the basis for long-term obligations.

The chief defence against large errors in estimates of changes APP. B, 5. in the purchasing power of money is however to be found in the great number of such estimates: for casual errors—that is, errors that are not caused by faults in the method of working—are almost certain to correct one another. This fact indeed is the main bulwark of mere mechanical industry in statistics.

There is further comfort in the fact that errors in weighting, which are likely to be more extensive than errors in prices, are also less mischievous. For while every error in price enters in full into the final result, an error in weight enters only in so far as it affects a commodity the price of which has moved away from the average. An error in the weight of a commodity, the price of which is near the average, has very little effect[1].

5. *The advantages and the difficulties of Geometric index numbers.*

The chief rival to the Arithmetical Mean is the Geometric Mean: and a little must be said about it, partly because the great authority of Jevons is in its favour. It requires the use of logarithmic tables or of logarithmic paper: but its general principle can be explained simply. The first step towards it is to ascertain, in regard to each of the n groups of the commodities, selected for discussion, the ratio which its price in a given year bore to its price in the basal year. These ratios are multiplied together: and the nth root of the product, is the geometric index number for that year[2].

---

[1] The shots fired at a target are, as a rule, more widely scattered towards its extremities than near the centre. If there has been no bias in the wind or in the shooting, an unbiassed selection of prices will give a majority in the neighbourhood of the centre. That is to say, the chance is great that a moderate error in a weight causes only a small error in the result.

For special purposes, it is sometimes desirable to trace variations of a particular price not absolutely, but in comparison with the variations of average prices. This is effected by Table VIII on "Proportional variations of prices" in Jevons' *Investigations in currency and finance*: and more luminously, though less easily, by showing the price movements of each group of commodities, by a curve on a page, on which the movements of general prices are represented by a secondary curve: this is done by Schmidt, *Bewegung der Waren-preise*.

[2] The weakness of this mean may be indicated by its application to an extreme case. It happened once that a mountain village engaged in toy making brought its sawdust from a saw-mill down the valley. But after a while it had its own saw-mill, and the miller was glad to be saved the trouble of burning the sawdust; so he gave it away. And then, an adherent of the geometrical method, who had made out a local index number, including sawdust among other commodities, found that his average of local prices had fallen to zero; and it remained

APP. B, 5.   The geometric mean has this seeming advantage over the arithmetical; that, if we have once decided what weights to attach to the several commodities, we may then base our index numbers on the prices of any year that is convenient; the comparative results will be identical with those which we should have obtained by taking any other year as a base: but this consistency is in fact attained by an unconscious manipulation of the weights of the several commodities considered[1].

In regard to small variations of prices the results given by the arithmetical and the geometric methods are nearly alike. And they correspond closely to realities; because they deal with price movements too small to modify greatly the distribution of people's resources among different things: thus their common assumptions that weights are unchanged, cause no great error. But neither has any great value in regard to large changes: and they are also alike open to the charge, already made, that they are limited almost exclusively to raw commodities; and are therefore unable to take account of the vast and rapid increase in the real purchasing power of money, that is effected by the increasing economy and efficiency of the processes of manufacture.

To conclude:—in selecting representative commodities for an index number, those which are liable to great variation are to be avoided generally. Of course a thing might possibly be truly representative of a class, so important as to claim recognition, all of which moved with it. But except in the emergencies of war time,

fixed there. Graphic uses of the geometric mean may be facilitated by logarithmic paper, as is done by Jevons in his *Investigations in currency and finance*.

[1] The point has little practical importance: but it is of some interest. The indications made by the geometric mean represent what would actually happen if the total amount of money spent on each commodity remained constant, however its price varied (*i.e.* if the elasticity of demand for it were unity, so that every fall in price evoked an equal proportionate increase in consumption). Let us take p and p' to be the prices of commodity A in, say, the years 1850 and 1900: while q and q' are the corresponding prices for another commodity, B. Let m and n be the weights attached to A and B respectively: these weights represent the amounts spent on them: and by hypothesis are constant. Then the weighted geometric index number for 1900 starting from 1850 as basis is $\left(\dfrac{p'}{p}\right)^{\frac{m}{m+n}} \times \left(\dfrac{q'}{q}\right)^{\frac{n}{m+n}}$; and the weighted geometric index number for 1850 starting from the basis 1900 is $\left(\dfrac{p}{p'}\right)^{\frac{m}{m+n}} \times \left(\dfrac{q}{q'}\right)^{\frac{n}{m+n}}$: the fact that these two quantities are the inverse of one another indicates that consistent results are obtained by this method from the same date, whatever be the basal year.

or famine, this seems almost impossible: and index numbers should leave exceptional times to be studied by other methods. Save in such times, the things, which represent classes important enough to have a place in an index number, are seldom liable to extreme variations of price. And the indications of index numbers, as commonly constructed, are in the main trustworthy; not because their principles are logically perfect, but because they are in fact handled with discretion[1].

[1] It may be worth while to indicate the vagaries of which an ill-made index number is capable by an extreme instance. A, B and C are three things, the standard unit of each of which at the basal year costs £216. After an interval, fashion causes C to yield place to a rival, and its value falls almost to nothing, the others remaining nearly stationary. The result is that, whether the index numbers are weighted or not, the arithmetical mean falls to something under £150: while the geometric mean falls prodigiously. Suppose, on the other hand, that C remains in strong demand, but is almost inaccessible: then all the means, arithmetical and geometric, weighted and unweighted, but especially the un-weighted, rise vastly. So disorder is threatened till C is ejected from the index-list. The "Harmonic" mean is more free from reproach: but its methods are too intricate and laborious for common use.

APPENDIX C[1]

DIAGRAMMATIC NOTE ON A METALLIC CURRENCY

1. *An abstract version, in diagrammatic form, of the general relations among* (1) *the demand for gold in an isolated country,* (2) *the stock of it,* (3) *its current value, and consequent tendencies to modify the rate of its production.*

The general relations between the demand, supply, value and cost of production of gold, indicated towards the end of I, IV, § 1, can be thrown without great violence into a form suitable for presentation as a diagrammatic picture. This does not claim to add anything to the reasonings there advanced: but it makes an appeal to the eye, which has some advantages. The scene of the problem may best be taken to be an isolated country, having gold mines of her own[2].

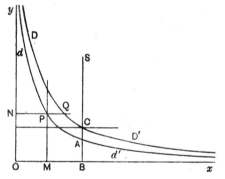

The diagram is not drawn on the same plan as those which are commonly used to represent the relations of demand and supply for ordinary commodities, the stock of which is seldom very large relatively to the annual production. For in those diagrams, the amount demanded and the amount supplied represent the rates of the flow of demand and supply respectively. But in this diagram, the demand curves represent the stocks of gold which would

---

[1] This Appendix is attached to Chapter IV of Book I.

[2] It might, of course, be taken to be the whole of a world which had a single currency, and uniform conditions of production and currency. But a single standard of purchasing power in such a world could not easily be conceived: unless climate and conditions of life were nearly the same in all parts of it.

probably be appropriated to the several uses of currency and the industrial arts, at various values per ounce of gold, sufficient time having been allowed for the necessary adjustments to be made. Supply is therefore shown by a vertical straight line representing a given aggregate stock of gold.

Let then an inch measured along Ox represent a stock of gold amounting to ten million ounces: and let an inch measured along Oy represent a value for each ounce of gold equivalent to that of ten bushels of wheat.

If the aggregate amount of wealth, over which the people of a country choose to keep command in the form of currency, is equal in value to a hundred million bushels of wheat: then the demand curve dd' for gold as currency will be such that if any point P, be taken on it, and PM drawn down perpendicular to Ox, PM will represent the number of bushels of wheat for which an ounce of gold exchanges: and its length will be ascertained by dividing a hundred million bushels by the number of ounces of gold represented by OM. Thus when PM is half an inch, representing five bushels of wheat, OM will be two inches, representing twenty million ounces of gold: when PM is two inches, representing twenty bushels of wheat, OM will be half of an inch, representing five million ounces of gold. (Thus the area of the quadrangle of which OM and MP are two sides will always be half a square inch. This is the well-known property of a rectangular hyperbola the curve that presents demand of elasticity uniformly equal to one; which may be called the *Constant Outlay* curve.

Let us further suppose that the stock of gold is ten million ounces, all devoted to currency uses: it is represented by OB, an inch measured along Ox. Let us draw BS vertically through B, cutting dd' in A: BA is then an inch representing ten bushels of wheat as the value of an ounce of gold on that supposition.

Next let us suppose that the ten million ounces of gold are not exclusively used as currency, but that some part of them is absorbed by the industrial arts. Through P draw PN parallel to Ox to meet Oy in N, and produce NP to Q so that PQ represents the number of ounces that will be used in the arts at the value ON. Then NQ represents the total number of ounces demanded at the value ON for currency and for the arts together, and the locus of Q is the composite demand curve representing the DD', the total demand for gold.

DD' meets the supply curve *SS'* representing a fixed stock of ten million ounces in *C*, and *CEF* having been drawn perpendicular to *Oy* to cut *DD'* in *C*, we see that if the stock of gold were ten million ounces equilibrium would be found where *EC* were used as currency and *CB* were used in the arts, at the value of *OE* pounds of wheat for each ounce of gold, to whichever of the two uses it is devoted. As the figure is drawn, rather less than four million ounces of gold will be used in the arts, and rather more than six millions in currency; each ounce of gold being equal in value to about sixteen bushels of wheat.

Next, let us adhere to the above suppositions as to the demands for gold for each of the two uses, but suppose that the stock of gold is twenty million ounces, instead of ten, and draw *S*, *S'*, parallel to *Oy*, but one inch from it instead of half an inch. Let *S*, *S'*, cut *DD'* in *G* and draw *GHK* horizontally to cut *dd'* in *H* and meet *Oy* in *K*: then *KH* gold will be used as gold, and *GK* in the industrial arts at the value *OK* wheat for an ounce of gold. That is, as the figure is drawn, about nine million ounces will be used in the arts, and eleven million as currency: and each ounce will have the value of about nine bushels of wheat.

The diagram of course does not claim to *prove* anything. Its sole purpose is to aid in visualizing the manner in which, the total stock of gold in the world being assumed to have remained at a given amount long enough for its distribution between currency and other uses to have been adjusted fairly well; the value of general purchasing power of the gold will tend to be such, that the amount of gold which the industrial arts will absorb at that value together with the amount for which there will be demand for use as currency at that value, will equal the total available stock.

Since gold is in fact an international commodity, the causes, that govern the relations between the composite demand for it and the composite supply of it, are complex in detail: but their general character is the same as in the case of an isolated country[1].

---

[1] The familiar method, on which the composite demand for a thing is made up, is illustrated by diagrams in my *Principles*, III, IV, 2: and the manner in which a composite demand, operating conjointly with a total supply (whether simple or composite), governs price is illustrated in the same Volume, V, VI, 4. The supply curve for gold would, however, need to represent a nearly fixed stock, rather than an annual flow; and it would therefore be a nearly vertical line. The representative currency-demand curve for gold would be a rectangular hyperbola.

APPENDIX D[1]

INTEREST ON CAPITAL AND PROFITS
ON USES OF CAPITAL

1. *The interest charged on loans, that are not fully secured,* APP. D, 1.
includes some insurance against risks ; together with some
remuneration of work, of a kind to call for discretion and the
power of judging rightly men and affairs.

The "interest" of which we speak when we say that it is the
earnings of capital simply, or the reward of waiting simply, is
Net interest: but what commonly passes by the name of Interest,
includes other elements besides this: it may be called *Gross*
interest. These additional elements are the more important, the
lower and more rudimentary the state of commercial security and
of the organization of credit. Thus, for instance, in mediaeval
times, when a prince wanted to forestall some of his future revenues,
he borrowed perhaps a thousand ounces of silver, and undertook
to pay back thirteen hundred at the end of a year. There was, however, no perfect security that he would fulfil the promise; and
perhaps the lender would have been willing to exchange that
promise for an absolute certainty of receiving twelve hundred, or
less, at the end of the year. In that case, while the nominal rate
at which the loan was made was 50 per cent., the real rate was
much less.

The necessity for making this allowance for insurance against
risk is obvious, and is not often overlooked. But it is less
obvious that every loan causes some trouble to the lender; that
when, from the nature of the case, the loan involves considerable
risk, a great deal of trouble has often to be taken to keep these
risks as small as possible; and that then a great part of what
appears to the borrower as interest, is, from the point of view of
the lender, earnings of management of a troublesome business.
A pawnbroker's business involves next to no risk, but his loans

---

[1] This Appendix, is attached to Book II, Chapter I. It rehearses some
elementary considerations, which will be regarded as superfluous by many
readers, but yet seem to be needed for completeness. They are reproduced from
Principles of Economics, Book VI, Chapters VII and VIII.

APP. D, 1. are generally made at the rate of 25 per cent. per annum, or more;
the greater part of which is really earnings of management of a
troublesome business. Or, to take a more extreme case, there are
men in London and Paris and probably elsewhere who make a
living by lending money to costermongers: the money is often lent
at the beginning of the day for the purchase of fruit, etc., and
returned at the end of the day, when the sales are over, at a profit
of 10 per cent.; there is little risk in the trade, and the money is
seldom lost. Now a farthing invested at 10 per cent. a day would
amount to a billion pounds at the end of a year. But no one can
become rich by lending to costermongers; because no one can lend
much in this way. The so-called interest on the loans really consists
almost entirely of earnings of a kind of work for which few
capitalists have a taste[1].

The price then that the borrower has to pay for the loan of
capital, and which he regards as interest, is from the point of
view of the lender more properly to be regarded as profits: for
it includes insurance against risks which are often very heavy,
and earnings of management for the task, which is often very
arduous, of keeping those risks as small as possible. Variations
in the nature of these risks and of the task of management will
of course occasion corresponding variations in the gross interest,
so called, that is paid for the use of money. The tendency of competition is therefore not towards equalizing this gross interest: on
the contrary, the more thoroughly lenders and borrowers understand their business, the more certainly will some classes of
borrowers obtain loans at a lower rate than others.

This distinction between net interest and that gross interest
which in fact includes some compensation for risk-taking needs
to be set out more fully. Both include what may be described as
the *trade risks* of the particular business, to which reference is
made. These trade risks arise from fluctuations in the markets
for raw materials and finished goods, from unforeseen changes of
fashion, from new inventions, from the incursion of new and
powerful rivals into their respective neighbourhoods, and so on.
But there is another set of risks, the burden of which has to

---

[1] Of course the division between earnings of management and expenses in the
form of salaries varies with the size of a business; this point will be considered
further in the next Section

be borne by the man working with borrowed capital, and not by APP. D, 1. the other: we may call them *personal risks*. For he who lends capital to be used by another for trade purposes, has to charge a high interest as insurance against the chances of some flaw or deficiency in the borrower's personal character or ability. The borrower may be less able than he appears, less energetic, or less honest. He has not the same inducements, as a man working with his own capital has, to look failure straight in the face, and withdraw from a speculative enterprise as soon as it shows signs of going against him. On the contrary, should his standard of honour not be high, he may be not very keen of sight as to his losses. For if he withdraws at once, he will have lost all he has of his own; and if he allows the speculation to run on, any additional loss will fall on his creditors; and any gain will come to himself. Many creditors lose through semi-fraudulent inertness of this kind on the part of their debtors. A few lose through deliberate fraud: the debtor for instance may conceal in subtle ways the property, that is really his creditors', until his bankruptcy is over, and he has entered on a new business career: he can bring gradually into play his secret reserve funds without exciting over-much suspicion.

The price then that the borrower has to pay for the loan of capital, and which he regards as interest, is from the point of view of the lender more properly to be regarded as profits: for it includes insurance against risks, which are often very heavy; and earnings of management for the task (which is often very arduous) of keeping those risks as small as possible. Variations in the nature of these risks and of the task of management will of course occasion corresponding variations in the gross interest, so called, which is paid for the use of money. The tendency of competition is therefore not towards equalizing this gross interest: on the contrary, the more thoroughly lenders and borrowers understand their business, the more certainly will some classes of loans be granted at lower rates than others.

It is true that if any of the investments is on a small scale, and few people know much about it, the flow of capital may be slow. One person, for instance, may be paying 6 per cent. on a small mortgage, while his neighbour is paying 5 per cent. on a mortgage which offers no better security. But, in all large affairs, the rate of net interest (so far as it can be disentangled from the other

APP. D, 1.] eléments of profits) is nearly the same all over England. And further, the divergencies between the average rates of net interest in different countries of the Western World are rapidly diminishing, as a result of the general growth of intercourse; and especially of the fact that the leading capitalists of all these countries hold large quantities of stock exchange securities: for these yield the same revenue, and are sold at practically the same price on the same day all over the world.

Various causes make the supply of capital for immediate use much larger relatively to the demand at some times than others: when the demand is slack, bankers and others are content with a low rate of interest, provided the security be good and they can get their money back into their own hands quickly in case of need. At such times, they are willing to lend for short periods even to borrowers, whose security is not of the first order, at a rate of interest that is not very high. For their risks of loss are much reduced by their power of refusing to renew the loan, if they notice any indication of weakness on the part of the borrower: and, since short loans on good security are fetching only a nominal price, nearly the whole of what interest they get from him is insurance against risk, and remuneration of their own trouble. But, on the other hand, such loans are not really very cheap to the borrower: they surround him by risks, to avoid which he would often be willing to pay a much higher rate of interest. For if any misfortune should injure his credit, or if a disturbance of the money market should cause a temporary scarcity of loanable capital, he may be quickly brought into great straits. Loans to traders at nominally low rates of interest, if for short periods only, do not therefore really form exceptions to the general rule just discussed.

The flow of investment of resources from their common source in production consists of two streams. The smaller consists of new additions to the accumulated stock. The larger merely replaces that which is destroyed; whether by immediate consumption, as in the case of food, fuel, etc.; by wear-and-tear, as in that of railway irons; by the lapse of time, as in that of a thatched roof or a trade directory; or by all these combined. The annual flow of this second stream is probably not less than a quarter of the total stock of capital, even in a country in which the prevailing forms of capital

are as durable as in England. It is therefore not unreasonable
to assume for the present that the owners of capital in general
have been able in the main to adapt its forms to the normal conditions of the time, so as to derive as good a *net* income from their
investments in one way as another. Only on this supposition are
we at liberty to speak of capital in general as being accumulated
under the expectation of a certain net interest which is the same
for all forms of capital.

It cannot be repeated too often that the phrase "the rate of
interest" is applicable to old investments of capital only in a very
limited sense. For instance, we may perhaps estimate that, before
the recent great war, a trade capital of seven thousand millions
was invested in the different trades of this country at about 3 per
cent. net interest. But such a method of speaking, though convenient and justifiable for many purposes, is not accurate. What
ought to be said is that, if the rate of net interest on the investments of new capital in each of those trades [*i.e.* on marginal
investments] be taken to have been about 3 per cent.; then the
aggregate net income rendered by the whole of the trade-capital
invested in the various trades was such that, if capitalized at 33
years' purchase (that is on the basis of interest at 3 per cent.), it
would have amounted to some seven thousand million pounds.
For the capital already invested in improving land and erecting
buildings, and in making railways and machinery, had its value
determined by the net income which it produced. If its prospective
income-yielding power had diminished, its value would have fallen
accordingly, and would be the capitalized value of that smaller
income after allowing for depreciation. Unsettled conditions, such
as those which have followed the recent world-war, render it impossible to make any near approach to an estimate of this kind.

It is perhaps impossible to believe that the population of this
world will ever reach a condition in which, while the institution
of private property remains as at present, the supply of capital
will be so great that no advantageous employment can be found
for some of it. We can however conceive a world, whose inhabitants
are not more unselfish than are those of our own world; but in
which the stored up accumulation of private wealth is very great,
while the advantageous uses to which it can be put are narrow.
In such a case many persons might desire to make good provision

APP. D, 2. against old age, sickness, etc.; while comparatively few were willing to mortgage the future for the benefit of the present. In that case the postponement of, and waiting for enjoyments would be an action that incurred a penalty rather than reaped a reward. By handing over his means to another to be taken care of, a person could then only expect to get a sure promise of something less, and not of something more than that which he lent; and the rate of interest would be negative.

Such a state of things is conceivable. But it is also conceivable, and almost equally probable, that people may be so anxious to work that they will undergo some penalty as a condition of obtaining leave to work. For, as deferring the consumption of some of his means is a thing which a prudent person would desire on its own account, so doing some work is generally desired on its own account by a healthy person. Political prisoners, for instance, sometimes regard it as a favour to be allowed to do a little work. We are justified in speaking of interest on capital as the commercial reward of the sacrifice involved in the waiting for the enjoyment of material resources, only because few people would save much without reward; just as we speak of wages as the commercial reward of labour, because few people would work hard without reward.

To conclude, the additional net product, which is obtained by deferring the enjoyment of the services which production can render, is paid for by interest. When the value of the net product, thus estimated, is greater than the price that has to be paid for the use of capital, the rate of interest rises: when the two balance, interest is at its equilibrium level.

2. *In a large business some earnings of management are classed as salaries; and in a small one some earnings of work are classed as profits, with the result that the rate of profits in small businesses appears to be higher relatively to that in large businesses than it really is.*

Adam Smith observed that "the head of a small business does himself much of the work which in a large business is done by salaried managers and foremen, whose earnings are deducted from the net receipts of the large business before its profits are reckoned, while the earnings of the whole of his labour are reckoned among his profits." And again, "The whole drugs which the best em- ployed apothecary in a large market-town will sell in a year may not perhaps cost him above thirty or forty pounds. Though he should sell them, therefore, for three or four hundred or a thousand per cent. profit this may frequently be no more than the reasonable wages of his labour in the only way in which he can charge them, upon the price of the drugs. The greater part of the apparent profit is real wages disguised in the garb of profit. In a small seaport town a little grocer will make forty or fifty per cent. upon a stock of a single hundred pounds, while a considerable wholesale merchant in the same place will scarce make eight or ten per cent. upon a stock of ten thousand[1]."

The greater part of the nominal inequality between the normal rates of profit per annum in small businesses and in large would indeed disappear, if the scope of the term profits were narrowed in the former case or widened in the latter, so that it included in both cases the remuneration of the same classes of services. There are some trades in which the rate of profit, rightly estimated, on large capital tends to be higher than on small, though if reckoned in the ordinary way it would appear lower. For of two businesses competing in the same trade, that with the larger capital can nearly always buy at the cheaper rate, and can avail itself of many economies in the specialization of skill and machinery and in other ways, which are out of the reach of the smaller business: while the only important special advantage, which the latter is likely to have, consists of its greater facilities for getting near its customers and consulting their individual wants. In trades in which this last advantage is not important, and especially in some manu- facturing trades in which the large firm can sell at a better price than the small one, the outgoings of the former are proportion- ately less and the incomings larger; and therefore, if profits are so reckoned as to include the same elements in both cases, the rate of profit in the former case must be higher than in the latter.

When the work of management is heavy in proportion to the capital, the normal earnings of management are of course high in proportion to the capital, and therefore the rate of profits per annum on the capital is high. The work of management may be

[1] *Wealth of Nations*, Book I, Chapter x.

heavy because it involves great mental strain in organizing and devising new methods; or because it involves great anxiety and risk: and these two things frequently go together. Individual trades have indeed peculiarities of their own, and all rules on the subject are liable to great exceptions. But the following general propositions will be found to be valid, other things being equal, and to explain many inequalities in the normal rates of profit in different trades.

First, the extent of the work of management needed in a business depends more on the amount of the circulating capital used than on that of the fixed. The rate of profit tends therefore to be low in trades in which there is a disproportionately large amount of durable plant, that requires but little trouble and attention when once it has been laid down. These trades are likely to get into the hands of joint-stock companies: the aggregate salaries of the directors and higher officials bear a very small proportion to the capital employed, in the case of railway and water companies, and, even in a more marked degree, of companies that own canals and docks and bridges.

Further, given the proportion between the fixed and circulating capital of a business; the work of management will generally be the heavier, and the rate of profits the higher, the more important the wages-bill is relatively to the cost of material and the value of the stock-in-trade.

In trades, that handle costly materials, success depends very much upon good fortune and ability in buying and selling; and the order of mind required for interpreting rightly and reducing to their proper proportions the causes that are likely to affect price is rare and can command high earnings. As a rule, a person will not enter on a risky business; unless, other things being equal, he expects to gain from it more than he would in other trades open to him, after his probable losses had been deducted from his probable gains, on a fair actuarial estimate. If there were not a positive evil in such risk, people would not pay to insurance companies premia, which they know are calculated on a scale sufficiently above the true actuarial value of the risk to cover the companies' great expenses of advertising and working, and yet to yield a surplus of net profits. Where the risks are not insured for, they must be compensated in the long run on a scale about as high

as would be required for the premia of an insurance company, if APP. D, 2.
the practical difficulties of insurance against business risks could
be overcome. And further, many of those who would be most
competent to manage difficult businesses with wisdom and enterprise, are repelled from great risks; because their own capital is
not large enough to bear great losses.

In trades in which the speculative element is not very important,
so that the work of management consists chiefly of superintendence,
the earnings of management will follow pretty closely on the
amount of work done in the business; and a very rough but convenient measure of this is found in the wages-bill. And perhaps
the least inaccurate of all the broad statements that can be made
with regard to a general tendency of profits to equality in different
trades, is that where equal capitals are employed, profits tend to
be a certain percentage per annum on the total capital, together
with a certain percentage on the wages-bill.

A manufacturer of exceptional ability and energy will apply
better methods, and perhaps better machinery than his rivals:
he will organize better the manufacturing and the marketing sides
of his business; and he will bring them into better relation to one
another. By these means he will extend his business; and therefore he will be able to take greater advantage from the specialization
both of labour and of plant. Thus he will obtain increasing return
and also increasing profit: for, if he is only one among many
producers, his increased output will not materially lower the prices
of his goods, and nearly all the benefit of his economies will accrue
to himself. If he happens to have a partial monopoly of his branch
of industry, he will so regulate his increased output, that his
monopoly profits increase.

But when such improvements are not confined to one or two
producers: when they arise from a general increase in demand
and the output which corresponds to it; or from improved methods
or machinery, that are accessible to the whole industry; or from
advances made by subsidiary industries, and increased "external"
economies generally; then the prices of the products will keep close
to a level which yields only a normal rate of profits to that class
of industry. And in the process, the industry is likely to have
passed over to a class in which the normal rate of profits is lower
than in its old class; because there is in it more uniformity and

APP. D, 2. monotony, and less mental strain than before: and, though this
is nearly the same thing in other words, because it is more
suited to joint-stock management. Thus a general increase in
the proportion which the *quantity* of product bears to the
quantity of labour and capital in an industry is likely to be
accompanied by a fall in the rate of profits; which may, from
some points of view, be regarded as a diminishing return measured
in *values*.

APPENDIX E[1]

NOTES ON THE DEVELOPMENT OF BANKING, WITH SPECIAL REFERENCE TO ENGLAND'S EXPERIENCES

1. *Early origins of banking. The enterprise of Italy and*
Holland.

The dawn of civilization seems to have brought with it some recognition of the advantages of association and organization in the custody of money and the transference of purchasing power and of credit. Traces are found, for instance, of rudimentary banks as well as joint stock trading companies, in the histories of the Chaldaeans, Egyptians and Phoenicians. In Greece, the temples of Delphi and other safe places acted as storehouses for the precious metals before the days of coinage, and in later times they lent out money for public and private purposes at interest, though they paid none themselves. Private money changers began with the task of reducing many different metallic currencies, more or less exactly, to a common unit of value; and went on to accept money on deposit, at interest, and to let it out at higher interest, permitting meanwhile drafts to be drawn on them. Roman money dealers followed in the same course; and gradually engaged in various and extensive operations of banking and bill exchanging, as the commerce of Rome grew and the relations of public finance between her and her provinces grew even faster[2].

But the influence of Roman example died out. And when trade and industry began to revive in the Middle Ages, the lessons of finance were learnt anew from the beginning. The coinage, originally ill-made, had been mutilated by ill doers; so that the task of dealing in it required special knowledge, and offered great opportunities of easy gains to men of sharp wits. For some time

[1] This Appendix is attached to Book II, Chapter III.
[2] Paper money was used in China two thousand years ago; and the fitting name of *flying money* was given there to bills of exchange at least a thousand years ago. *History of Banking in all Nations*, IV, p. 549.

A compact history of Mediaeval and Modern Banking is given in Palgrave's *Dictionary*; another beginning with early times is to be found in Conrad's *Handwörterbuch*. See also Büchsenschütz, *Besitz und Erwerb*; and Deloume, *Les manieurs d'argent à Rome*, for Greek and Roman banking.

APP. F, 2. this work, as well as the lending of money, was chiefly in the hands
of the Jews; but in about the thirteenth century it came to be
taken over by Christians, whose business competition was aided
by frequent outbursts of crude popular violence against the Jews[1].
In many countries the Lombards led the way; and foreign Christian
exchangers and money dealers were generally called Lombards
even when they were not. As time went on these private dealers
developed their businesses; and, when the arts of banking had
been developed by them, State banks were founded, especially
in Italy. But private enterprise seems always to have come before
public.

2. *The origins of many great banks are to be sought in
the operations of money changing; which were rendered
difficult by the imperfect condition of each currency. Early
uses of the term "bank-money."*

Money-changing was not an important business in a very early
stage of civilization; for long-distance travelling was rare: and a
ship, when calling at a strange port often endeavoured to make
its sales balance its purchases so that it did not need either to
bring, or to take away, much money. But later on, when trade
became more various and more highly specialized, a merchant's
sales in terms of a local currency were often either much greater
or much less than his purchases. The consequent disturbance of
this balance of trade could be most easily set right by elementary
banking expedients: and these were in effect generally those of
the money-changer. But some of the coins brought to him were
of inferior metal: and others had been grievously clipped: so that
in fact he often treated a parcel of coins in the same way as he
would miscellaneous pieces of old metal: he weighed each and
ascertained its quality roughly: giving himself of course the benefit
of any doubt; so he was rather busy and often became very rich.
Crusaders and rich travellers, especially to Rome and to Jerusalem,
consumed much on their way, though they carried little with them:
and their needs gave occupation to the money lender and the
money exchanger. The coins in general circulation had frequently
been clipped: because the arts of mintage seldom sufficed to make
the coin fit exactly the die, which was designed to certify its value:

[1] See *e.g.* d'Avenel, *Histoire des Prix*, I, pp. 106–113.

and the irregular shape of each coin tempted a money-dealer, APP. E, 2 through whose hands it passed, to cut off a little of the metal for his own benefit.

Money changing was a chief task of early banks in Italy, Germany and Holland: these privileges were often obtained in return for loans made to, or arranged for, Governments; which had large ambitions, but whose resources were narrow, even when the permanence of their hold on power was not assured.

This matter was clearly set out by Adam Smith. He said: "The earliest banks of Italy, where the name began, were finance companies...to make loans to, and float loans for, the Governments of the cities in which they were formed....After these banks had been long established, they began to do what we call banking business: but at first they never thought of it....The currency of a small State, such as Genoa or Hamburg...must be made up, in great measure, of the coins of all the neighbouring States, with which its inhabitants have continual intercourse." The money of the great mediaeval banks, being kept in good order bore an agio: "The agio of the bank of Hamburg, for example, which is said to be about 14 per cent., is the supposed difference between the good standard money of the State, and that...of neighbouring States[1]."

Here may be made a comparison between the conditions of former money markets of Amsterdam and that of London now. Each in its time has been a leader, if not the chief leader of the world's finance: and each owed much at critical periods in its history to its defence by water. Water protected the Bank of England against the armies of Napoleon, even when the best armies of the Continent went down before him; while England's army was still small: the treasures of England have been defended by the

---

[1] *Wealth of Nations*, Book IV, Chapter III, Part I. His account of the Bank of Amsterdam may be further quoted: "It received both foreign coin and the light and worn coin of the country at its intrinsic value in the good standard money of the country, deducting only so much as was necessary for defraying the expense of coinage, and the other necessary expense of management. For the value which remained, after this small deduction was made, it gave a credit in its books. This credit was called bank money, which, as it represented money exactly according to the standard of the mint, was always of the same real value, and intrinsically worth more than current money....It could be paid away by a simple transfer, without the trouble of counting, or the risk of transporting it from one place to another." The modern use of the term "bank-money" is akin to this early use.

APP. E, 3. sea: and those deposited in Amsterdam could be made difficult of access by opening the sluices and covering the land with water.

A chief task of early banks was that of remitting command over money from one place to another: and, as good standard coins were seldom to be had in either place, the task was difficult: the organization of bank money secured that the money paid out should be the equivalent of that paid in. Therefore, as Bagehot said, "the real introductory function, which deposit banks at first perform...is the supply of paper currency to the country....When a private person begins to possess a great heap of bank notes, it will soon strike him that...he is trusting the banker very much, and in return he is getting nothing. He runs the risk of loss and robbery, just as if he were hoarding coin. He would run no more risk by the failure of the bank, if he made a deposit there; and he would be free from the risk of hoarding the cash....But in the end common sense conquers. The circulation of bank notes decreases and the deposit of money with the banker increases[1]."

But England's system of banking, like her exploration of the New World, was based on Dutch, rather than Italian precedent: the Bank of Amsterdam held for a long while a position in international commerce, as prominent as the Bank of England does now.

3. *Various functions of banks in the later Middle Ages.*

In early times banks discharged on a smaller scale most of the functions of modern banks: and in addition they were responsible for the counterpart of much of the work of modern stock exchanges. They acted also as agents for potentates: and indeed a king or ruling prince could not always easily borrow directly; because people generally, and traders in money in particular, had learnt by experience that a prince who found it inconvenient to discharge a debt, which he had incurred, simply set it aside: or, as the saying goes, "threw his sword into the scale" to make up the balance of his payments against his obligations.

[1] *Lombard Street,* pp. 80–88.

Gilbart, *History of Banking* (Vol. I, p. 14, of edition of 1882) calls attention to the fact that the name "Exchange" rose from the important part which the exchange of different disordered currencies took in early business. The king's exchange at a seaport furnished foreign money to those who needed it. His house "was called the *Exchange,* from which it is probable the public structures, where merchants meet for transacting business, derive their name."

On the other hand, the Free Cities of Italy and other countries, APP. E, 3. though their public expenditure was sometimes as extravagant as that of princes, could not easily dishonour their engagements. For their power rested on their credit; and their wealth was derived mainly from trade, a reputation for honesty in public dealings was necessary for success in trade. The chief centre of England's financial business is under direct obligations to Italian initiative, as is indicated by the name of "Lombard Street" in the financial centre of London. It is recorded that "the Longobards, and other merchants and strangers of divers nations were in the habit of frequenting the street twice a day[1]."

A storehouse for grain or iron bars is but a station on the journey of commodities from the producers to the consumers. But a storehouse for metallic money can perform its chief functions without yielding up any considerable part of its contents; provided it supports the good opinion or credit of certain pieces of paper, and renders them as efficient as coins of equal denomination would be in effecting exchanges: in fact, since opinion is the offspring of opinion, they can lend this support after they have themselves ceased to exist, provided they are universally believed to exist. The credit of the Bank of Amsterdam was at its best at a time, when the solid basis of that credit had been undermined by the secret lending of its metallic stores for various public purposes. Neither the Italian banks nor the Bank of Amsterdam seem to have issued bank notes proper; that is, promises by the bank to pay on demand definite sums of money to the bearer, without requiring endorsement. This was done in Sweden in 1661[2].

---

[1] Quoted by Bisschop, *Rise of London Money Market*, p. 35; where some interesting details are given.

[2] The fraud committed by the Bank of Amsterdam in lending its deposits was without taint of private selfishness. It was not discovered till 1790. Harris (*Essay upon Money and Coins*, 1757, Part I, p. 101) implies that he suspected it: (the State, which ordered the fraud, ultimately made good the loss caused by it to the bank's customers). He observes: "Bills of undoubted credit are of great conveniency in large payments; and besides save the wear of coin. But their extent should be restrained within due bounds. Should they increase much beyond the real stock of bullion that ought to be in their stead, they would prove mischievous in two ways; by increasing in effect the quantity of circulating cash beyond its natural level; and by endangering, on a cloudy day, their own credit. But the profits to be made by lending, as I may say of credit, are temptations too strong to be resisted; and it may be questioned if any of the banks now subsisting keep exactly within the above rule, though some of them are formed upon the very model here laid down." This shrewd observation probably refers

APP. E, 4.   The beginning of the eighteenth century saw the commercial power of Holland beginning to yield to those of France and England. Both of these countries were pupils of the Dutch. But the expenditure of Louis XIV had disorganized the financial condition of France; and she suffered so much from the lack of a rich and stable middle class, that she was unable to lead the way in the scientific development of banking. The misery due to the failure of the Royal bank, founded in Paris by the Scotchman Law early in the century, caused the very name bank to be shunned in France: "it needed the lapse of almost a century, and the exercise of all the authority of the First Consul, before another institution of like privileges and styled the Bank of France could be created[1]."

4. *Beginnings of the Bank of England.*

The Low Countries and France spread the influence of Western Europe over other Continents, sometimes in advance of England. But her resources and her necessities gradually made her the chief maritime power: her people, if less quick than some others in reaching out towards new ventures, were wise in council and steadfast in purpose; and their language was extending its dominion more rapidly than any other.

At last the occasion arrived for the work: but it needed in addition a masterful organization of those financial resources which are the sinews of empire, in at least as full a measure as of war. The most important single step towards that end, though its full importance was not recognized at the time, was the foundation of the Bank of England. This Act appeared to be of but little significance. For it professed merely to "grant to their Majesties certain duties upon tonnage of ships and vessels, and upon beer ale and other liquors, for securing certain recompenses and advan-

mainly to the Bank of Amsterdam; and suggests that its failure was not a complete surprise to far-seeing people.

The Bank of Hamburg was on similar lines to that of Amsterdam, and not much less important: it always kept faithfully the bullion deposited with it. The famous *Bullion Report* of 1810 pays an interesting tribute of respect to it.

The early Swedish and German notes seem to have been certificates of deposit, corresponding rather to the "certified cheques" now sometimes used in America than to the *Recipissen* issued by the Bank of Amsterdam. These were receipts for bullion deposited; the bullion could be claimed (subject to certain conditions) on retirement of the bank credit issued against it, and on presentation of the *Recipissen*; which were in fact transferable (and divisible) pawn tickets. See Jensen and Van der Borght in *History of Banking in all Nations*, Vol. IV, pp. 211 and 394.   [1] M. des Essars in *History of Banking in all Nations*.

tages in the said Act mentioned to such persons as shall voluntarily advance [at eight per cent.] the sum of fifteen hundred thousand pounds towards carrying on the war with France." These persons, so associated, might borrow, but not in excess of the £1,200,000; and they might lend by notes of their own payable to individuals and transferable by endorsement: they were left free to decide for themselves what reserve in coin was necessary. Paterson, the founder of the bank, was well aware of the need for a good reserve: in opposition to such schemes as those of Chamberlayn and Law. He declared that so long as gold and silver were "accepted and chosen by the commercial world for the standard and measure of other effects...all credit not founded on the universal specie of gold and silver is impracticable, and can never subsist neither safely nor long." He thought the bank might perhaps "circulate their own foundation of £1,200,000 without having more than two or three hundred thousand pounds lying dead at one time or another," an estimate of the right proportion of reserve to liabilities which fits with later experience.

Presently, however, the bank was brought into great straits, partly through some carelessness as to its reserves on the part of the directors, from whom Paterson had separated; but mainly in consequence of the spasms into which commerce was thrown by the necessary but drastic remedy, which the Government was applying in 1695 for the corrupt condition of the coinage. This is the first episode in English monetary history which has been made classical by the great ability of those who took part in it; especially Locke and Newton. In opposition to the able but wrong-headed Lowndes they supported Montague's scheme for bringing back the coinage to its full value[1].

In 1697 a new charter allowed the bank to make their notes transferable without endorsement, i.e. to issue bank notes proper:

---

[1] The burden which was placed on the bank, itself an advocate of the honest policy, through being called on to use coin of full weight in the discharge of debts which it had contracted in coin of not much more than half that weight, is described in Macleod's *Banking*. That work and Rogers' *First Nine Years of the Bank of England* are good books of reference for this period: and there is still some interest in Bannister's *Life of Paterson*, especially Chapter VI; in Francis' *History of the Bank of England*, which contains a fascinating "Short Account of the Bank of England" by Michael Godfrey, Paterson's ally, and the first deputy governor in 1695; in Anderson's *History* and Macpherson's *Annals*. Macaulay's vivid account of the period is well known. Rogers gives an interesting chapter to Chamberlayn's wild scheme for a Land Bank.

APP. E, 5. and gave it *exclusive* privileges, which were developed in the
Charter of 1708 into a prohibition for any other partnership
"exceeding the number of six persons in that part of Great Britain
called England to borrow, owe, or take up any sum or sums of
money on their bills or notes payable at demand, or at a less time
than six months from the borrowing thereof." In the Charter of
1742 this clause is repeated, and described as conferring the
privilege of "exclusive banking." Each of these charters gave
certain rights of exclusive trading in return for pecuniary aid to
Government: but the renewal of the exclusive privileges of the
bank became less defensible, as the new dynasty became more
firmly settled on the throne[1].

5. *Expansion of the scope of English banking.*

Some of the exclusive privileges granted to the Bank of England
could not be maintained. For the Bank of England then had no
branches; and a London bank could not suffice for all the monetary
business of a large country.

In particular the new manufactures required good access to
banks for the transmission of payments, as well as for the granting
of credits. There was no electric telegraph: the posts were slow;
and independent travelling by relays of horses was very expensive.
Canals had indeed greatly facilitated traffic in heavy goods: but
their total mileage was small: even the best of them were apt to
be blocked by accumulations of barges at locks, and by ice. Every
centre of economic activity required at least one bank or branch
of a bank close at hand.

[1] The Stuarts had strengthened those suspicions of the commercial credit of
monarchs, which had given inordinate power to the bankers of Augsburg and
other cities. The position of William III was made more difficult by the fact that
many of his subjects regarded him as a usurper: for his debts might be ignored,
when the rightful sovereign got his own again. In a well-known passage Bishop
Burnet tells how he "had heard the Dutch often reckon up the advantages they
had from their banks; and they concluded that, as long as England continued
jealous of the Government, a bank could never be settled among us, nor gain
credit enough to support itself; and upon that they judged that the superiority
in trade must lie on their side." William's shrewdness, as well as his honesty,
induced him to lay stress on the fact that the commercial credit of a constitutional
government was that of the parliament and not the king. And the honesty and
bravery which, taking its history as a whole, have been the best part of the capital
of the Bank of England, owe much to the counsel whereby in 1701 he pressed
the House of Commons to take care of the public credit, "which cannot be
preserved but by keeping sacred that maxim that they shall never be losers who
trust to a parliamentary security."

Meanwhile the new activities of business were demanding increased facilities for the quick granting of credits, and the prompt discharge of obligations. Home-made goods were being superseded by the products of workshops and factories; and wages were being paid more in money and less in kind. Middlemen were multiplying; and both raw and finished commodities passed through more and more hands. And while the growth of manufacture was concentrating population in some parts of England, in others it was scattering the workers in search of water-power or to escape the restrictive trade regulations of the older centres. All these changes increased the need for currency in the provinces.

Meanwhile there was an equally rapid increase in the demand for loans. The old families of business men were being supplanted by new men who had risen from the ranks of artisans, or whose fathers had done so; and who wanted fresh capital at every step of their upward career. These men offered fairly good security for lenders on the spot, who were able to read their characters and watch their varying fortunes from one quarter of a year to another: but they had not good security to offer to those who had no local knowledge; and lastly, they needed the greater part of their loans in the form of currency for local use.

Of course, bills of exchange could do part of the work without the aid of any formal agencies of credit. But their scope was limited; and there remained a great opening for any paper currency issued by people known in each neighbourhood; and which everyone would accept in payment, at all events for small sums; not so much because he was certain of the permanent solvency of the issuer, as because he felt sure of quickly passing it on to his neighbours. A rich harvest was often reaped by those who could start as dealers in loans by making them chiefly in the form of their own notes or promises to pay; and by using the loans themselves as a means of getting these notes into circulation. This state of things had some striking results: it led many to think that credit is capital. They saw that whoever could put his own notes into circulation got command of capital, which he could use in his own business or lend to others; and they did not see that he was in effect turning to his own use part of the expensive machinery of trade, which had been provided at the public expense by the national metallic currency, by political security and social credit.

APP. E, 5. They did not observe that while making that machinery more efficient, he made it also more likely to break down; and that, while he reaped for himself the chief benefit from this increase in its efficiency, the chief evils from its increased instability fell upon others.

Although issue of notes had not played any part in the success of the Bank of Amsterdam, which so strongly influenced English rivalry; although it had played but a small part in the success even of the Italian banks; and although bank notes, properly so called, had but recently come into use; yet it was commonly believed that the power to issue bank notes was essential to the success of banking.

That freedom, which was a chief source of England's prosperity, brought about some strange results in the industry of banking. Thus, as late as 1802, it could be said that "a shopkeeper, being in the habit of drawing bills on London and remitting bills thither for the purposes of his own trade, would do the same for his customers and other neighbours, and having as yet possibly little or no view to the issuing of bank notes, printed 'The Bank' over his door, and engraved those words on the checks on which he drew his bills[1]."

Some of these tradesmen bankers did a solid business, and founded banks that exist to-day. Some were unfortunate. Some scarcely tried to make their way sure; for so long as they could appear to be rich, it mattered little to them whether they were wasting the property of their customers. They speculated boldly: the gains, if they were lucky, came to them. If they were unlucky,

---

[1] Thornton, *On Credit*, pp. 155, etc. He adds that in some cases such a shopkeeper would "take at interest some of the money of his neighbours, on the condition, however, that he should not be required to pay it back without notice," giving in exchange a transferable "note in which would be expressed the sum lent or deposited, the rate of interest upon it, and the time which was to intervene before payment could be demanded." But such notes would "circulate heavily," partly on account of the trouble involved in calculating their value: and therefore "some banks, wishing on the one hand to encourage the circulation of their paper, and on the other to avoid the inconvenience of a strict obligation to pay without notice, have issued notes payable after a certain time, and yet have been in regular practice of giving money for them whenever payment was demanded, and have taken no discount for the accommodation."

The Liverpool Municipality obtained in 1793 an act empowering them to issue, under certain conditions, notes of £100 and £50 payable with interest accrued: a copy of one of them is printed in an article by Prof. Gonner in the *Economic Journal* for Sept. 1896.

and a breath of doubt caused the presentation of a small parcel of their notes to reveal the emptiness of their coffers, their failure left them little worse off than they had been at starting. Meanwhile they had enjoyed life[1].

The evils of reckless trading are always apt to spread far beyond the persons immediately concerned: and in this case a good deal of such trading was based on funds obtained from people of small means. It is true that the holders of small notes did not technically lend to the bank which had issued the notes. But they exchanged things of real value, and above all their daily labour, for its promises to pay: and, when rumour attacked its credit, they made a wild stampede to exchange any of its notes which they held: their trust had been ignorant, their distrust was ignorant and fierce. Such a rush often caused a bank to fail, which might have paid them all gradually, if each had not been so eager to be paid among the first. The failure of one bank caused distrust to rage around others, and to bring down banks that were really solid; as a fire spreads from one wooden house to another, till even nearly fireproof buildings succumb in the blaze of a great conflagration. In fact panic succeeded panic at intervals of about ten years; and the attention of thoughtful people was constantly drawn to the regulation of the currency. Some of the worst of these evils had indeed been stopped by the law of 1775, which prohibited the issue of bank notes for less than £5: but out of 400 country banks existing in 1793, 300 were greatly shaken by the panic of that year, and of these 100 failed.

No doubt the natural remedy was to repeal the monopoly of the Bank of England, which prevented the formation of powerful joint stock banks throughout the country. At length the clause in the charter of the Bank of England, which had prevented the foundation in England of banking partnerships with more than six members, was scrutinized: and it was found to apply only to banks which issued their own notes payable on demand. So joint

---

[1] The history of mushroom banks of issue has some resemblances to that of the hollow local benefit clubs which have often raised and betrayed the hopes of so many of the poorer classes. But while the records of the clubs are almost unbroken tragedy, there is a good deal of comedy in the accounts, which are to be found in detailed histories of mushroom banks in England, Scotland, Ireland and other countries, especially America. See Colonel Sykes' paper on "Free Trade in Banking" in the *Statistical Journal*, Vol. xxx; and Verden's *Economic History of New England*, Chs. x and xiii.

APP. E, 6. stock banks of the type now common in England were founded.
As is well known, they have increased in number: several of them
have numerous branches, and banking facilities are thus brought
close to almost the whole population[1].

6. *Relations of the Bank of England with the British Government during the Napoleonic wars.*

For a long while before the wars with the French Republic and
Napoleon issuers of notes in England, Scotland and Ireland had
looked to the Bank of England for support in case of need; and the
possession of its notes gave an unfailing command over the means
of finally discharging debts either in London or abroad. So a
stock of them was held as a reserve by all prudent bankers. Even
in London, the private banks had found that their customers
gave a preference to Bank of England notes. Moreover, their
own notes could be easily collected and suddenly presented by
their enemies; at last the panic of 1793 confirmed them in the
resolution of quietly withdrawing their own notes.

Thus all eyes were already turned on the bank in 1797, when
the necessities of the war caused Pitt to put strong pressure on it
for aid; and this pressure, combined with renewed commercial
distrust, reduced the bullion in its coffers to less than two millions.
The only aid, which Pitt could offer it, was that of forbidding it
to pay coin or bullion in exchange for its notes. These notes
became therefore in fact, though not in name, the sole legal tender
throughout the country for considerable sums: and the rest of
the circulation rested on them as a basis.

The mechanical strength thus given to the bank was aided by
the moral strength derived from the fact that the Government
openly leant upon it; and that the fortunes of the two were almost
as closely united as they had been a century earlier. But there
was this difference. In the earlier time, the interests of the Government
were those of one party only in the nation; in the later time
the Government represented the whole nation in its struggle with
a foreign foe[2].

---

[1] Four of the largest have between them over five thousand branches in London
and elsewhere.

[2] It is, however, true that services rendered to the Government by the bank
were largely those of an intermediary. Tooke observes that the real advances
by the bank to the Government were seldom very much in excess of the balance

APP. E, 6.

The course of the war made England the centre of the world's trade; for indeed at times scarcely any ships could sail at all without license from her: and it was to English funds that impoverished nations of the continent looked for aid in their struggle against the common foe. So the bank became, in the eyes not only of England but the whole world, the centre of a vast struggle in which the predominance of economic forces became, if not really more thorough, yet certainly more obvious than ever before.

As the perils of the war increased, its directorate came to be regarded, both at home and abroad, as a committee of safety of English business generally. Unfortunately jealousy of other banks had excluded from their counsels all bankers in the narrow English sense of the word: that is, all who issued their own notes or accepted deposits against which cheques could be drawn on demand. But representatives of the great financial houses which had the largest acquaintance with the business of the world, as well as chief merchants and wholesale traders, were there to tell in advance of coming changes; and, by comparison of their several special informations, to read between the lines of the news that reached them. They might have been tempted to use their great powers for private aims: but here they were safe-guarded both by their high personal character, and by that very joint stock privilege, of the monopoly of which others were justly envious. "The numerous proprietors who choose the directors," said Thornton in 1802, "and have the power of controlling them (a power of which they have prudently forborne to make any frequent use) are men whose general stake in the country far exceeds that particular one which they have in the stock of the company[1]."

of the Government with the bank (*History*, IV, pp. 94, 7). The circulation of the bank did not often exceed £25,000,000, while the special expenditure caused by the war aggregated to about £1,100,000,000. See Lowe's *State of the English Nation*, Ch. I.

[1] He adds some interesting statistics, *On Credit*, pp. 67–9. Thirty years later the Governor of the Bank, when asked by Lord Althorp whether the directors did not purposely limit their holdings of bank stock, "believed that none of them held more than his qualification." Bagehot gives a vivid description of the young bank director, with no special knowledge of banking, who is at first a silent member of the board, but gradually learns; so that, when he attains the full prime of life and his turn comes to fill the post of governor, he has acquired almost enough special knowledge of the work to fit him fully for his supreme responsibility. (See the chapter in *Lombard Street* on "The Government of the Bank of England.")

APPENDIX F[1]

INTERNATIONAL TRADE STATISTICS

APP. F, 1.   1. *The data, of which the edifice of international trade statistics is composed, are so numerous that some of them are necessarily collected by methods too rapid and rough to ensure strict accuracy.*

Difficulties connected with the interpretation of statistics of prices have been discussed in Appendix B: its argument is continued here with special reference to international trade.

The private books of any merchant are numerical records of trade. But they are not commonly called statistics; because they are of small range; and are compiled mainly for the use of people, who can bring their own knowledge of that particular business to aid them in the interpretation of the figures. On the other hand, numerical records of the trade of a country, or of any branch of it, are called Statistics: they are compiled on a large scale; and therefore, of necessity, by more or less mechanical methods.

They are required by the student, because without them he would be thrown back on general impressions as to quantities. Now such general impressions may be trustworthy when made by a strong man with a full and direct knowledge of the chief matters in hand: but they have no considerable part to play in regard to national trade. For no one has, or conceivably can have, a direct knowledge of any great part of that trade: without such knowledge no sound judgment can be formed as to whether any particular instances are reasonably representative of the whole; and therefore every attempt, however seductive, to base general conclusions as to quantities on a study of representative instances runs the risk of serious error.

The risk would be great even if the selection of instances could be made impartially. But in fact the sources of such information are likely to be biassed, consciously or unconsciously: those, whose interests are affected, are more ready than others to give full

---

[1] This Appendix is attached to Book III, Chapters II and III

information even at considerable trouble to themselves; and, in APP. F, 1. addition to this bias of personal interest, there is sometimes the bias of a desire for striking effect. When a picture of national life is put together from travellers' notebooks, it often happens that an event is recorded because it arrests attention; and that it arrests attention because it is not representative: in so much that a chief work of subsequent careful study is to destroy conceptions, that had been based on unsound foundations. For this task there is sometimes no other recourse than the discovery by critical faculty of internal inconsistencies in the picture presented. But in matters relating to simple quantities, a partial remedy may often be found by the aid of statistics: provided that careful attention be paid not only to their liability to error; but to the even greater dangers that arise from their inability to take account of some of the most important influences that bear on almost every economic issue.

There is indeed some ground for the saying that a bad statistical error is the worst of all errors. For a statistical fact claims merely to bring to bear on the question at issue the relevant items from a number of figures: and such items are, for the greater part, collected by secondary officials in the public service or other like persons, with little or no regard to any particular purpose to which they will be applied. This claim is a half truth; and therefore more mischievous and harder to meet and deal with outright, than if it were wholly untrue. A selection of relevant items is a difficult task. An untrained student is likely to overlook some of the influences which bear strongly, though indirectly, on the matter at issue: and an unscrupulous partisan can often so select his data and so group them as to suggest false conclusions; even though every statement on which he bases them is true, as far as it goes.

The very definiteness of conclusions which are based on statistical evidence does, indeed, suggest that caution is needed for handling them. But if anyone, carelessly or of set purpose, has based a conclusion on only a one-sided selection of data, the precision of the terms which he is forced to use makes it easy for someone else to add the omitted data. Thus, while it is true that statistics lend themselves to illegitimate forms of *primâ facie* evidence; it is also true that, if the evidence has run the gauntlet of acute and well-informed criticism without material injury, it is less likely to be invalid than almost any other kind of evidence.

APP. F, 2   There is indeed little statistical evidence with regard to economic matters, that will emerge from this ordeal with a perfect record in regard to certainty and completeness. Certainty is likely to have been toned down to some measure, perhaps a slight measure, of probability; and, what appeared to be a conclusion, is found to be only the first tentative step of a long inquiry. The statistics of international trade are, however, exceptionally full, precise, and authoritative: and the uses made of them must be large, though cautious.

Statistics are indeed often powerful in the destruction of error. They seldom show precisely what share of any event is to be attributed to each of the many influences bearing upon it at the time, and in preceding years. But they often prove that a result, which has been attributed to a certain cause, cannot have been produced by it: and such destructive work is a considerable factor in scientific progress.

2. *Description of devices for bringing under the eye, almost simultaneously, statistical records relating to various economic tendencies in any specified year or group of years.*

The following suggestions are concerned with a plan for bringing to a focus some of the chief influences which may probably have affected any particular movement of industry or trade. Nearly every change, whether upwards or downwards, works good in some directions and harm in others. Some of the good appears at once and also some of the harm. But other parts of each come slowly; some three or four years later, some ten or even twenty or thirty years later. If, for instance, a Protective tariff is alternately raised and lowered at comparatively short intervals, some of the deferred effects of one set of customs duties will be seen only after that set has ceased to exist; and are therefore likely to be attributed to a subsequent set of a different character.

The difficulty in such cases may be lightened by devoting each of many similarly ruled sheets to a special group of statistical and other records for the same half century or more: and by assigning a given line in each sheet to each year of the period. The statistical records would generally be expressed as curves; and other records in short statements. Facts are the bricks out of which reason builds the edifice of knowledge. Such a system helps to give, ready to the hand of the builder, a supply of those particular bricks which he wants for any purpose. Suppose an event A happened in the year 1880, and we think it may have been due to causes B, C, D, etc.; this system will show almost in an instant what were the states of B, C, D, etc., in 1880, and the previous years. Also by calling attention to a remarkable change at about that time in some other cause, K, it may put us on the track of a causal connection that might otherwise have been overlooked. What it cannot do is to tell directly the nature of the dependence of A upon B, C, D, etc. That must be done by our reason making use of that abstract of past experience; which is, on the one side, a science; and, on the other, a practical instinct[1].

There are indeed certain limited purposes, for which the facts of each successive year may be considered in special relation to those of the group of a fixed number of years immediately preceding it, or following it, or surrounding it. The most familiar instance of this is that of tithe averages. Tithes used to vary with the prices of certain grains from year to year; and might be half as high again one year as the next. But in 1836 it was ordered that the tithe payable in 1830 should be computed on the average of the seven preceding years, 1823–9: that for 1831 to that of the years 1824–30 and so on. For instance, the tithe for 1831 would differ by only a little from the tithe for 1830 on the one hand, and from that for 1832 on the other by amounts, which would necessarily be but small. Thus the table of prices for calculating tithe charges is a "smoothed" table, and the corresponding curve is a "smoothed" curve. This plan is reasonable; because relative stability is desirable in itself, and the ability of the farmer to pay a high charge in any year is very much affected by the prices he has received for some years past.

Let us turn now to the method of smoothing tables of curves. If this is to be done mechanically, averages must be calculated for five or seven or ten, or some other fixed number of years. But

---

[1] This paragraph is part of a description given in the Jubilee Number of the *Statistical Journal*, 1885, of a book arranged by the present writer, each page of which is ruled with a hundred lines to represent a century. Reference has already been made to it at the end of Appendix G of *Industry and Trade*, in connection with the difficulties of interpreting statistical evidence as to the influence of a high tariff (or other causes) on the prosperity of a country.

APP. F, 3. where the figures for each separate year are set out in a curve, they themselves generally suggest that in some parts of the period under investigation only a few years should be grouped together and in others many: and a curve drawn with a free hand through the points representing the figures for the several years is often found to present a truer picture of the whole movement than a curve smoothed on any fixed rule[1].

3. *Changes in the trade and economic conditions of any one country are likely to be caused in great measure by changes in other countries: and several years often elapse between a change and its chief effects. Therefore statistics, relating to any country and year, need to be interpreted by a broad study of other countries and other years.*

Attention has already been called to the fact that when examining the changes in the courses of any country's trade one must resist the temptation to seek the explanation mainly in circumstances directly affecting her own industries. In some cases the influences that would be overlooked on this route are much more important than those to which almost exclusive attention is given.

For instance, about a century ago Britain's industries, and internal means of communication, were changing rapidly, while those of other countries were relatively stationary: and during several decades the history of the foreign trade of almost every country of western Europe had to concern itself with the industrial conditions of Britain, as much as, or perhaps more than, with those of the country in question. The conditions of British industry are now changing as fast as ever: but those of some of the chief countries with which she deals are changing faster than hers.

We shall presently find that these considerations are of special

---

[1] For instance, the general price index number fell from 95 in 1846 to 74 in 1848; and, after remaining at about that level for three years, it rose from 78 in 1852 to 102 in 1855. The sudden fall was due to a combination of causes:— railway panic in England, good harvests, great reduction of import duties of corn into England, etc.: the low level was maintained for three years by bad commercial credit at home, and political troubles abroad. The great rise between 1852 and 1854 was due to the influx of the new gold, bad harvests, the Crimean War, etc. The freehand curve, by its abruptness in this particular place, suggests that the fall and the rise must each have been due to a consilience of powerful causes acting in the same direction. But the smoothed curve implies that there was a nearly steady, slow swing of prices downwards from 1838 to 1847 followed by a gradual swing upwards to 1859: a suggestion which is absurdly false.

importance in relation to fluctuations of credit and commerce APP. F, 3. which are increasingly apt to spread from one country to several others, and even in some cases over the whole of the industrial world: the telegraph causes the pulses of one country to synchronize with those of another, nearly as do the beats of a group of clocks that are connected electrically. But other movements are slow, and spread very slowly from one country to another.

This brings us to the observation that one of the most difficult tasks of the historian, whatever be his special field of work, is the estimation of the period by which the effect of a cause lingers behind that cause. On the broad ocean the tidal wave lies not under the moon but is "retarded" so as to be some hours behind it: and in long broken seas the high tide at any time may be due to the increased attractions of the moon (and sun) twenty or thirty hours earlier. A similar retardation is specially large and uncertain in many branches of economic history: but the very precision of statistical data offers temptations to a popular treatment of them in which dangers of this kind are ignored. The student may, as we have seen, derive assistance in guarding against such dangers from certain mechanical devices.

International trade is so much under the influence of the cycle of the seasons that a calendar year is almost always the best unit of time in regard to it. But commercial fluctuations need to be studied in connection with those of credit; and in regard to them the unit of time must not be longer than a month; for, when monthly records of a credit crisis are averaged into yearly, the most instructive features of the crisis are apt to be blurred out of sight.

For similar reasons averages ranging over long periods frequently obscure the most instructive causes of changes in the volume, the character and the courses of trade. No doubt such averages serve the good purpose of submerging out of sight many transient disturbing influences, such as those of irregular harvests and of fluctuations of credit: and statistical tables representing averages for, say, five or ten years are helpful in conjunction with tables or curves representing movements from year to year. When, therefore, we are considering the aggregate effect that has been produced on the volume of a country's trade (or anything else) by the continuous progress of slow changes, it is better to compare

APP. F, 3. her average trade for the last decade with that of an earlier decade, than to compare her trade for a single recent year with that for a single earlier year. But such a comparison does not enable us, it is not very likely even to help us, to consider what part of that aggregate effect is to be assigned to each of the many broad changes that have contributed to the result.

Slight disturbances may conveniently be hidden from view by "smoothed" statistical tables (or curves) in which the figure (or point) set down against each year represents the average of (say) the decade of which it is the end (or the middle). But in regard to large disturbances such as those of the Franco-German war, or the South African war, this method is apt to suggest a continuity of movement, which has no existence; and to bear in one undiscriminating result the effects of many causes of diverse character, and needing different methods of study. It may be of service so long as the smoothed tables or curves are carefully subordinated to those which represent changes from year to year. But when isolated, it is most misleading, and incompatible with a sound and careful study of the history of trade.

It may be concluded that several years, sometimes few and sometimes many, may be grouped together for study in connection with any particular problem: but there is no uniform rule which can be applied profitably for general purposes: and, unless handled with great care, averages relating to several years are apt to conceal, rather than to make manifest, the true causes by which the course of events has been shaped.

Figures, representing changes in the aggregate external trade of a country, have an important place in a study of the forces which control broad international relations. But attention is often directed to the mutual influences which are exerted on each other by the development of a country's industries, and by changes in her external trade; and in such studies, statistics *per capita* of the population are the most useful generally; and especially when they are used for comparisons of her economic conditions with those of other countries.

APPENDIX G

TRADE AMONG COUNTRIES WHOSE CURRENCIES REST ON DISSIMILAR BASES[1]

1. *Trade of a country whose currency is based on a precious metal, with one which has an inconvertible paper currency.*

The question whether any one thing, such as lead, can exercise any important influence in adjusting the balance of trade, depends partly on its portability and partly on the extent of the market which it finds in either country. The power of gold for this purpose is therefore of primary importance between two countries, each of which has a gold currency, for gold has in each a practically unlimited market. But its influence would be much weaker if one of the countries had a paper currency or a silver currency.

Let us consider the trade between two such countries, say England and Russia. Gold prices in England and rouble prices in Russia are determined by the work which the currency has to do in either country on the one hand and the volume of that currency on the other. And when trade is in equilibrium, the gold price of the rouble will be fixed at the ratio which gold prices in England bear to rouble prices in Russia. For, suppose that it were not at this level, but were, say, below it: that is, suppose the number of roubles which exchanged for £1 to be increased above the ratio which the goods that were priced at £1 in England bore to those which were priced at a rouble in Russia, allowance being made for transport. Then exporters from Russia would sell their goods for gold which, when converted into roubles, would give them more than ordinary trade profits; while importers into Russia would lose money, if they sold their bills on Russia at the current rate of exchange. The immediate result would be that these importers would refuse to sell at that price, but would prefer to buy Russian goods and bring them back. Exporters' bills in

---

[1] This Appendix is attached to Book III, Chap. v. Its first section is reproduced from the present writer's evidence before the Gold and Silver Commission in January, 1880, Q. 10,226. Much official information on subsequent developments of the currency policies of the chief countries of the world will be found in Appendices to Prof. Kirkaldy's *British Finance*, 1914–1921.

APP. G, 1. Russia would therefore be without any market at the old rate, and their value, or, in other words, the rouble price of the sovereign, would fall quickly. That is, the gold price of the rouble would rise until it was equal to the ratio in which gold prices in England stand to rouble prices in Russia. In the same way it can be proved that the gold price of roubles cannot be in equilibrium above this level; and therefore that in equilibrium it must be at this level.

Next, suppose that the trade being in equilibrium, there is a sudden fall in the gold value of the rouble due to some extraneous cause, as, for instance, political apprehensions. To put the case in the strongest way, let us suppose that these apprehensions are not shared in Russia; and that at first there is no depreciation of the rouble in Russia, and no rise of rouble prices there. Russian exporters will then expect to sell at an unchanged gold price, and to convert that gold price into a greater number of roubles, and thus to make abnormally high profits. All those, therefore, who were in doubt whether to export or not, will do so in order to gain the anticipated bounty from the exchanges. There will be a flutter of increased exportation from Russia. The excessive supply of Russian exports in the English market may lower their price there a little. But this bounty on exportation from Russia can last only until Russian exporters try to dispose of their bills; the moment they do that they will find that since a bill for £100 will give the means of purchasing only as many English commodities as before; and since by the hypothesis there is no depreciation of the rouble in Russia, these can only be sold for as many roubles as before, and no one will continue to pay a premium for the bill; the gold price of the rouble will adjust itself almost instantaneously to the ratio which gold prices bear to rouble prices.

Different suppositions may be made as to the causes of the fall in the gold value of the rouble, but it will be found that by similar routes we get in all cases to the same result, namely, that a fall in the gold price of the rouble cannot give any permanent stimulus to importation from Russia, because it must almost instantaneously accommodate itself to the ratio which gold prices bear to silver prices. But of course this does not exclude disturbances of the Russian exchanges due to fluctuations in the relative supplies of importers' and exporters' bills and other international obligations.

Such disturbances may, as we have seen, occur among countries with gold currencies. A bounty on exporters' bills in a country may be caused by excessive importation on the part of her merchants; or by her lending to other countries: or, which is more probable in such a case as that of Russia, through other nations withdrawing some of the capital which they have lent to her. It is worth while to remark that this last event is especially likely to happen when political distrust has lowered the price of the rouble.

This fact is perhaps accountable for much of the popular belief that a fall in the value of the rouble gives a permanent bounty to Russian exporters generally. For people see that a fall of the gold price of the rouble is accompanied by a prolonged bounty on exportation from Russia; and think the first event is the cause of the other. But the real cause in this case is a general distrust of Russia's economic future, which makes investors desire to withdraw their capital from Russia; at the same time that it makes the price of the rouble fall, and so long as they are withdrawing capital, the exchanges must necessarily be such as to give a general bounty on exportation from Russia.

2. *Exchanges between countries, whose currencies rest on different metallic bases*[1].

The trade between England and a country which has a silver currency, say India, differs from the preceding case, only in consequence of the fact that silver is an exportable commodity, and roubles are not; and, therefore, while the gold value of the rouble adapts itself almost instantaneously to the ratio which the gold prices of goods bear to their rouble prices (allowance being made for carriage), the adjustment is liable to be delayed in the case of the rupee. For whereas Russian exporters can generally make no use of their bills on England except to buy with them (or to sell them to others who want to buy) commodities in the English market whose gold price has not altered, it is otherwise with Indian exporters. If silver has fallen in value in England and not

---

[1] This section is reproduced from evidence submitted by the present writer to the Indian Currency Committee in January, 1899, Q. 11,770–11,775. Some of the historical diagrams which were shown in support of the statistical arguments advanced in the evidence will be found in the Report of the Committee.

APP. G, 2. in India, Indian exporters to England will use their bills on England to buy (directly or indirectly) silver for importation into India; and so long as this state of things lasts there will be a steady flow of silver to India. During the whole of this process there will be a bounty on the exportation of goods from India; and, therefore, it is interesting to inquire how long it will last.

It must, however, be admitted that a fall in the gold price of silver may cause Englishmen to distrust Indian securities, public and private. This will lead them to withdraw capital from India, or at least to check their lendings to India; and this will diminish the number of bills which India is able to draw on England, and thus give a premium to the bills of exporters from India. But, as in the parallel case relating to Russia, we may put aside a disturbance arising from this cause as extraneous to our main investigation. And if this be put aside we shall find that the premium cannot last long.

Those who hold the contrary opinion generally insist that as custom forbids silver prices to change in India, they must be taken as a fixed point, and we must expect any change in the gold price of silver to cause a parallel change in the gold prices of commodities in the western world. (It may be true that the force of custom in India is much less than is generally supposed, but in order that this argument may not be taken in the flank by an attack on this point, we may for the present assume that their premises are correct.)

Supposing that the flow of silver to India will not appreciably affect the purchasing power of silver there, it is clear that the flow of silver will go on, until either the gold price of commodities has fallen in the English market or the gold price of silver has risen there; or, lastly, that there has been a little of each of these changes; with the effect of making the gold price of silver again equal to the ratio which the gold prices of goods in England bear to the rupee prices of goods in India (allowance being made for carriage).

The interests of the Government of India in a rise or fall of the rate of the exchange between London and India are complex. A fall in the value of the rupee as compared with the English pound, which is caused by a rise in the value of the sovereign, the rupee being stationary, would be quite different as regards the interest of India, from the effects of a similar fall caused by a fall in the purchasing power of the rupee, the sovereign remaining stationary. Therefore, it is best to take the two parts separately. The permanent interest of the Indian Government in the value of the rupee is limited to its fixed land dues. In respect of the importance of those dues, it is unique among great governments conducted on Western principles. Its permanent interest in the value of the sovereign is limited to its debts in gold. Next, as to interests which are not perpetually fixed, but yet are very firmly rooted, it has a very heavy interest in the value of the rupee extending over perhaps 15 years or a little more—the average remaining life of the non-permanent leases. It has also a sub-permanent interest in taxes; because, though it equitably can raise those so as to take its share of the growing wealth of the country, its freedom of action is practically limited by the necessity for going rather more slowly and in a rather less aggressive manner in the East than is possible in the West. Lastly, it has an interest as an employer of European labour, in the ratio between the rupee and the sovereign, independent of their absolute values; that is in the rate of exchange. If they both rose equally, or both fell equally, these difficulties would be small.

As regards railways, these difficulties are, perhaps, less than appears. For it is scarcely possible for a railway ever to have fixed upon the ideally right charges, and the number of cases in which any railway would lose much by deliberately lowering its charges is small. Thus it seems that the indirect lowering which arises from a fall in the value of the rupee, has not been so great an evil to the railways as is sometimes supposed. As regards the prices of stores and railway plant, the Indian Government has no interest in the value either of the rupee or of the sovereign, in addition to the considerations already mentioned; because it buys them as a trader, and gives commodities for commodities.

These difficulties are in themselves considerable, but the main importance of most of them arises from their bearing on the central difficulty of the position of the Indian Government, which is not directly connected with either the rupee or the sovereign, and would remain if the whole world had the same currency. This difficulty is that the immense increase in the wealth and prosperity of the Western world, which began in the second third of last

APP. G, 2. century, and has gone on at an ever-increasing pace since then, has made the resources at the command of the Western Governments beyond all comparison greater than any known before. These resources are spent on civil government and on military preparations. The administration of law, education, and sanitation are more thorough and more costly in terms of labour, and far more costly in terms of commodities, than they were. Military expenditure has grown perhaps even faster.

APPENDIX H[1]

RELATIONS OF INTERNATIONAL VALUES
TO COMPARATIVE COSTS

1. *Differences between the relations of value in domestic* APP. H, 1.
and in international trade.

Values in domestic trade are governed by the general relations
of demand and supply. Effective demand depends on the available
purchasing power of those who desire a thing, and the strength
of their desire for it. Supply depends broadly on the relation,
which demand bears to the costs of production for all parts of
the product; and, among others, for those which are at the margin
of the profitable application of labour and capital to the production
in question. The margin itself governs nothing: its position is
governed simultaneously with value by the broad forces of demand
and supply. But the manner in which those forces control value
can best be studied at the margin.

For indeed, as Ricardo said, cost would have no influence on
value, if it had no influence on supply. Therefore the margin
at which supply is in peril of shrinking under the influence of
cost is the best place for studying that influence. Desire for
a commodity influences its value by influencing the eagerness
of purchasers for it at a given value. Therefore the margin,
at which increased or diminished demand causes movement in
price and in supply, is the best point for studying the influence
of demand[2].

These considerations need to be reckoned with in a study of
international values: but in their case there are two (or, if several
countries come into the account, then several) sets of margins to
be dealt with, instead of one. Thus, if E and G are two countries

---

[1] This Appendix is attached to Book III, Chap. VI. Its reasoning is necessarily
rather difficult.
[2] No doubt movement is a process requiring time: and therefore the depth
and content of the margin, over which movement may best be studied in relation
to a problem of value, varies with the period of time to which the problem relates.
This raises questions at once difficult and important; but they have little bearing
on the matter immediately in hand. Something is said about them in my
Principles of Economics, Book V, especially Chapter VIII.

APP. H, 2. trading exclusively with one another, their trade is in equilibrium when goods of each of many classes are imported into E from G up to the limit (or "margin") at which the demand for that class only just suffices to send back goods to G, which can be marketed in G on terms sufficiently good to make the trade profitable. This implies that E goods of each of many kinds are pushed on G markets up to that margin, at which the demand for them just suffices to enable corresponding G goods to be sent back in return for them: and similarly in regard to G's exports.

Similarly, G goods of each of many kinds are produced for exportation to E up to that margin at which their costs (including those of transport) are just covered by the net receipts, that are got from the importation of the E goods, in exchange for which they can be marketed in G and conversely.

2. *The essential features of the problem of international trade (and especially its relations to comparative rather than absolute costs) are most clearly seen when international transport is supposed to involve no considerable cost: as in the case of two neighbouring islands with different natural or acquired advantages for production.*

It was pointed out a century ago that the labour of men's hands, as distinguished from that of their brains, is entirely given to moving things. The fisherman and the coal-miner obviously do nothing but move things. The farmer causes wheat to grow; but his direct part in the work consists only in so moving the ground, the manure, and the seed that they will be in suitable positions for nature's forces to act upon them. It is therefore true in a certain sense that, if all visible movements could be made without cost, the only labour costs of production would be those of thinking.

But without any such extreme assumption as this, we may proceed on Ricardo's lines, and suppose that E and G are neighbouring islands which trade with one another, the goods being carried at public expense to the extent of one half by either island; and thus the cost of transport is eliminated from the trading account: the peoples, however, are supposed to be intolerant of one another's customs, and to refuse to migrate from one island to the other. The real cost of production of each commodity in each island is taken to be constant; though differences of soil, climate, agricultural and mineral resources cause many differences in APP. H, 2. the relative costs of various commodities in the two islands. Differences in the skill required for different occupations, and in the amount of capital by which each man's labour needs to be assisted, are neglected (or else the values of the several classes of labour and stocks of capital are expressed in terms of the value of labour of a standard efficiency), so that the real cost of production of any commodity in either island can be regarded as proportional to the amount of the standard labour of that island. Also, transport being gratuitous, the relative values of different things would of course remain generally the same in the two islands: if a quarter of oats and a hundredweight of sugar were of equal value in one island, they would be of equal value also in the other[1].

At starting we may simplify our problem by supposing that the portable products of the two islands can be divided into seven broad groups of commodities, $P, Q, \ldots V$, arranged in descending order of E's advantages for their production relatively to G's. Thus, let the labour of *ten men* in E produce as much as that of

$$
\begin{array}{ccc}
16 \text{ in } G & \text{in regard to} & P \\
12 \quad ,, & ,, & Q \\
11 \quad ,, & ,, & R \\
10 \quad ,, & ,, & S \\
9 \quad ,, & ,, & T \\
8 \quad ,, & ,, & U \\
6 \quad ,, & ,, & V \\
\end{array}
$$

Let us consider various possible positions of the equilibrium of trade between E and G. We may suppose that E's demand for U and V, in the production of which G has great relative advantage, is broad and intense; and that G's exports of these goods enable G to satisfy nearly all her needs in regard to P, Q, R and S. Then U and V will be made only in G; while P, Q, R and S will be made only in E; and T will be made in both countries.

---

[1] Assumptions such as these are made quietly by Ricardo: he took for granted that his readers would supply them.

Of course an increase in the external demand for manufactured goods is likely to develop new economies in their production; and therefore to increase the ease with which they can be marketed abroad: while an increase in the demand for raw produce might require intensive cultivation, which would yield less than proportionate returns to increased application of labour and capital

APP. H, 2.   What is the relation of international costs thus set up? It is that the (portable) product of nine days of G labour exchanges (costs of carriage being neglected), throughout both islands for the product of ten days of E labour; or, as we may say for shortness, a G day is equivalent to ten-ninths of an E day.

That this must be so is obvious. For if the quantity of U made in G in a day could be marketed for more than ten-ninths of the product of an E day, its exports would be pushed, in place of those of T; and thus equilibrium would be reached on terms that made a G day equivalent to ten-ninths of an E day. And this rate would be maintained, although E's demand for U and V continued to increase, till she supplied all G's needs for T as well as for P, Q, R and S.

If her demand went still further, a new level would be set up. For, her demand for V being great, she had probably supplied all the P, Q, R, S and T which G would take at the rate of ten-ninths of one of her day's products for one of G's: and, if her demand still increased, she would be forced to offer more and more favourable terms. In return for a day's product of G's labour she would have to give, first nine-eighths of one of her own, then eight-sevenths, than seven-sixths, then six-fifths: and at last five-fourths, $i.e.$ ten-eighths, which is the proportion of the labour cost of U in E to that in G. At that point a new, relatively settled, equilibrium would be found; and from that time forward, E's demand might continue to increase without further altering the rate of interchange. The rate would then remain fixed at the comparative cost of U in E and G; unless indeed E ceased to import U altogether: then V would set the rate of interchange at ten E days for six of G's.

Exactly the same process, in the opposite direction, would be worked out; if G's demand for E's goods P, Q and R had increased instead of E's for U and V. The first step would then be that G would supply all E's needs in regard to T, as well as U and V: after which the level would be set by S; and then a G day would be equivalent to no more than an E day. If the process continued, S would be made exclusively in G. If the process went yet further, G would begin to send R to E; and a G day would be equivalent only to ten-elevenths of an E day: and so on.

It is only for the sake of simplicity that the portable products of E and G are arranged as a staircase of seven high steps, each spreading wide. If they had been arranged into many hundreds of groups, corresponding to small successive changes in the relative advantages of the two islands, the nature of the problem would not have greatly changed; but its wording would have been more complex. The group which, under any given conditions of international demand and supply, was just on the margin of being sent from E to G instead of from G to E (or *vice versâ*), would have been a very small one: and therefore the stage during which a G day was held equivalent to ten-ninths or ten-elevenths or any other portion of an E day, would have been very short. The neighbouring goods on either side of this neutral group would have been liable to a change in their direction of movement from E to G or from G to E, owing to some trifling fluctuation of the relations of international demand and supply such as might be due to vagaries of harvests, fashion, or credit; or to inventions or developments of improved processes; or even to some slight change in the *rapport* between individual traders or producers in one country or both. As has been noted in Book III, much of the cross trade of similar commodities between neighbouring countries in the same industrial phase is due to causes of this class.

3. *The preceding argument, continued with reference to possible differences in energy and ability between the two races.*

So far nothing has been said as to the relative industrial efficiencies of the inhabitants of the two islands: the argument is valid whatever they may be. In any case the trade—at all events so far as its direct effects are concerned—is beneficial to both islands.

But now let us assume that the efficiency of the representative worker in E is the same as in G. On this supposition there would be a premium on migration from E to G, when the level of international values was being set by T or U: when it was being set by R or Q there would be a premium on migration from G to E: and in all these cases the resistance to international migration, so far as it reached, would maintain the contrast between international and domestic trade. But this contrast would vanish when the standard was being set by S: for then there would be no premium on migration.

APP. H, 4.   Suppose, however, the standard of efficiency in E to be greater by a tenth than in G: then the fact that as much of R could be produced by ten days' labour in E as by eleven in G would shew that E's natural advantages for the production of R were just equal to those of G: and, in that case, when R (and not S) was setting the level for international values, labour in E would command just the same amount of E and of G products as would labour of equal energy and ability in G. That is, there would be no premium on migration either way, and the distribution of industries would be the same as if E and G were adjacent parts of the same country. [This of course refers only to direct results. A person who migrates to a country in which the standard of energy is higher than in his own, sometimes rises part of the way at least towards that higher standard, and earns more than if he had stayed at home.]

We may conclude that if transport were gratuitous; then, under the other assumptions made above provisionally in order to simplify the problem, international values would be definitely governed by comparative costs of production; taken in conjunction with the comparative volumes of the demand by each country for those goods for which the other had the greater relative advantages. But, if E and G had been parts of the same country, and labour and capital migrated quite freely over the whole of it, they would thus have tended to be so distributed between different parts of it, that supply would have pressed against demand in regard to every commodity, in such a way that the fruit of one day's labour exchanged (under steady market conditions) for the fruit of any other of equal efficiency which had equal assistance from capital.

4. *The same argument continued, account being taken of the cost of international transport.*

These pictures, presenting the relations between comparative costs and international values, lose their clearness of outline when account is taken of the cost of international transport. This may be sufficiently illustrated by abandoning the supposition that the costs of transport between the islands are defrayed out of public revenues; by supposing that every merchant defrays the cost of his own trade in the ordinary way, and by discussing over again the first case considered in this argument.

In that case, E supplied the needs of both islands in regard to P, Q, R and S; G supplied the needs of both in regard to U and V; while T was made in both islands. The merchants, on finding that they have to pay their own costs of transport, will strike out of their trading lists those of the T goods, that are not light and of small volume in proportion to their value; and also those of the S, R and U goods, which are distinctly heavy or bulky in proportion to their value; and even some Q, P and V goods that are excessively heavy in proportion to their value. If the goods thus struck out are of about equal aggregate value on the two sides of the trade, the terms of interchange are likely to remain nearly as before: but the details of the trade will be much changed.

Transport has now to be reckoned as an industry, taking its place among the groups $P, Q \dots V$, like any other. Perhaps, indeed, various parts of it may be regarded as separate industries; just as may happen with different branches of any manufacture: that is, such part of the transport, as is suitable for wooden sailing ships, may go into a group showing a differential advantage for one country, while steam traffic may show a differential advantage for the other.

Let us begin by supposing that one half of this trade is worked from E, and the other from G: so that there is no balance of payment due on either side for "invisible" transport and trading services. The increased expensiveness of U goods to consumers in E and of Q goods to consumers in G, resulting from the new costs of transport, will have reduced the consumption on either side to amounts for which the desire is more eager than before (marginal .utility being greater): the reduction may possibly, though not very probably, be about equal on either side. Suppose as a result that the trade is just remunerative when U goods, that cost 800,000 standard days' labour in G (with proportionate aid from capital), are exchanged for Q goods that cost 900,000 days' labour in E: also that the cost of transport, etc., is 10 per cent. either way, equally divided between the two countries: so that, in the total, 880,000 days' labour from G are exchanged for 990,000 days' labour from E; *i.e.* in the ratio of eight to nine.

If the trade had been compressed within narrow limits, as it

APP. H, 4. could have been by an eighteenth century monopolistic trading company, it might have been made to yield very high profits. But, being open, it is carried to that margin at which it yields merely normal profits: and at that margin the relation of comparative costs to international values is seen.

Similar results are reached at the margins of other branches of trade: the terms of interchange at all such margins being kept approximately uniform by the freedom of producers in general to make for export as many goods of such kinds as they please; and of merchants and shipowners to engage in what branches of trade they please; (at all events in so far as the restrictive tendencies of cartels and rings may be left out of account).

Complications will of course arise in matters of detail, such as the partial dependence of the margin of the profitable exportation of heavy goods on the supply of suitable return cargoes at the port of delivery; and again the relations between export and import merchants: but such matters need not be discussed here.

It is, however, to be noted that if the greater part of the transport were worked by merchants and shipowners resident in E, the transport industry would constitute an important addition to those groups P, Q, etc., from which E's chief exports were derived. The growth of the transport industry would then have the same effect on the terms of trade, as would a large development in E of manufacture or mining for exportation.

Thus, when costs of transport are reckoned as part of the costs of production of goods destined for foreign use, the general bearing of Ricardo's doctrine with regard to the relations between comparative costs, international demand, and international values remains unchanged. But he seems to have been certainly right in holding that the general outline of those relations was seen most clearly when costs of transport were provisionally ignored[1].

[1] Sidgwick, observing that under Ricardo's and Mill's provisional assumptions, the relative exchange values of any two commodities would be the same in the two countries, concluded that they had made a grave error in supposing that the relative immobility of labour and capital between different countries was the basis of the chief characteristics of international values. In opposition to them he held that the peculiarity of international trade really lies in the fact that the exchange value of one of E's imports relatively to one of her exports is greater in E than in G by the double cost of transport. But in fact this is equally true of the relative values of coal and slates in a place that is near to a slate quarry and a place in the same country that is near to some coal mines. He says: "There are various causes of economic gain through trade between

distant places. The peculiarity of the theoretical determination of the values of the products of such trade depends primarily not on the imperfect mobility of labour, but on the cost of carriage." He urges that if England and Spain exchange cloth for wine, they might probably both grow corn (or any other commodity that was suitable to both climates and conformed to the law of Diminishing Return) even though transport were costless; and that then "the values of both wine and cloth relatively to corn...must be as much determined by cost of production as the values of home commodities are." But he adds in a footnote that "it does not follow that the wine and cloth will exchange for each other in proportion to their respective costs; since, if (as Mill supposes) labour and capital are imperfectly mobile, the cost of producing corn may be different in the two countries." (The references for these passages are p. xiv of Contents, and pp. 213, 4.) The phrase "respective costs" is ambiguous; and it may be so interpreted as to bring the footnote into harmony with the Ricardian doctrine. But however it be interpreted, his charge against that doctrine seems to be unfounded. A further answer to his charge is suggested by Prof. Edgeworth, *Economic Journal*, vol. IV, p. 621.

APPENDIX J[1]

GRAPHICAL PRESENTATION OF SOME PROBLEMS OF INTERNATIONAL TRADE

1. *Conditions that govern the shapes of curves, designed to represent various relations of demand and supply in international trade; and their relations to international values.*

The schedules given in III, VI, are repeated here, and taken as our starting-point: it is not necessary to repeat the explanation there given of the gradual rise of the numbers in column (2) and the gradual fall of those in column (4): but of course the explanation belongs to the present diagrams, as much as to the columns of figures.

(1)	Terms on which E is willing to trade		Terms on which G is willing to trade	
	(2)	(3)	(4)	(5)
Number of E bales	Rates in G bales per hundred E bales at which E will part with those in (1)	Total number of G bales which E is willing to take for those in (1)	Rate in G bales per hundred E bales at which G will buy those in (1)	Total number of G bales which G is willing to give for those in (1)
10,000	10	1,000	230	23,000
20,000	20	4,000	175	35,000
30,000	30	9,000	143	42,900
40,000	35	14,000	122	48,800
50,000	40	20,000	108	54,000
60,000	46	27,600	95	57,000
70,000	55	38,500	86	60,200
80,000	68	54,400	$82\frac{1}{2}$	66,600
90,000	78	70,200	78	70,200
100,000	83	83,000	76	76,000
110,000	86	94,600	$74\frac{1}{2}$	81,950
120,000	$88\frac{1}{2}$	106,200	$73\frac{3}{4}$	88,500

[1] This Appendix is attached to Book III, Chapter VIII. Much of it had been designed to form part of an Appendix to a volume on International Trade, on which a good deal of work was done, chiefly between 1869 and 1873. Somewhat later dates attach to attempts to assign definite measures, in abstract theory at least, to the elasticity of national demand; and to the total direct net benefit of a country's foreign trade to her. Subject to these exceptions, the main body of the present Appendix is reproduced with but little change in substance from that part of the MSS. which was privately printed and circulated among economists at home and abroad in 1879.

Some of the diagrams contained in this Appendix were reproduced, with my permission, by Prof. Pantaleoni in his *Principii de Economia Pura*, 1889, subsequently translated into English. In 1889 also appeared Auspitz and Lieben's

To represent these schedules graphically, let distances along Ox APP. J, 2. represent E bales on the scale 100,000 bales to (say) an inch: and let distances along Oy represent G bales on the same scale. Let OE, which may be called E's curve, be drawn to represent the terms on which E is willing to trade. Thus, if P be a point moving along it and PM be drawn always perpendicular to Ox, then, as OM represents successively the numbers in column (1), PM will represent the corresponding numbers in column (3). Thus,

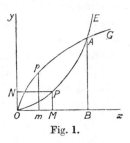

Fig. 1.

when OM is half an inch, representing 50,000 E bales, PM will be two-tenths of an inch representing 20,000 G bales. When P arrives at A, the distance of P from Oy will be nine-tenths of an inch representing 90,000 E bales; and its distance from Ox will be a little over fourteen-tenths of an inch, representing 70,200 G bales.

Similarly, let OG, G's curve, be drawn to represent the terms on which G is willing to trade. Thus, if p move along OG, and pm be drawn always perpendicular to Ox, then, when Om represents the successive numbers in column (4), mp will represent the corresponding numbers in column (5). When Om is six-tenths of an inch, representing 30,000 E bales, pm will be about eight and a half-tenths of an inch, representing 42,900 G bales. And when p arrives at A, Om and pm will be respectively equal to OM and PM. The point of intersection of OE and OG may be called *the equilibrium point*.

2. *Graphical representation of the elasticity of international demand under various normal conditions.*

Proposition I. Every statement as to the shape which it is possible for OE to assume, has corresponding to it a similar statement as to the shape which it is possible for OG to assume; but wherever Ox occurs in the former statement, Oy will occur in the latter, and *vice versâ*; whenever reference is made to a horizontal

powerful *Theorie des Preises*, in which use is made of diagrams similar to mine, which they had constructed independently. See a generous note by Dr Lieben in the *Zeitschrift fuer Volkswirtschaft*, Vol. VII. Reference may also be made to Prof. Edgeworth's excellent series of articles in the *Economic Journal*, and to Sir H. H. Cunynghame's *Geometrical Political Economy*.

APP. J, 2. straight line in the former case, there must be made reference in the latter to a vertical straight line; and *vice versâ*. Let a diagram relating to *OE* be drawn on thin paper, and held up to the light with the reverse side towards the eye, and *Oy* pointing towards the right, so as to serve as a new *Ox*; while the old *Ox* serves as the new *Oy*: then any demonstration with regard to *OE* will apply *verbatim* to *OG*, which may be supposed to have various shapes while the shape of *OE* is normal.

The case in which the shapes of *OE* and *OG* are both abnormal corresponds to problems which might conceivably arise, if two monopolists were in exclusive trade with one another; and therefore a little is said about it at the end of this Appendix; but it does not appear to have any bearing on the real problems of international trade. For the present the shape of *OG* is supposed to be normal.

The possible limits of variation of the shapes of two curves are the same: but in any particular case the two curves are likely to differ widely. For instance, if *E* has some important exports which are nearly indispensable to *G*, while *G* has none which are nearly indispensable to *E*, then *OG* will be nearly vertical in the neighbourhood of *O*; but *OE* will not be nearly horizontal in the neighbourhood of *O*. This case is represented in Fig. 2.

That figure, like the first, represents ordinary (or "normal") conditions of international trade, in which neither country is in

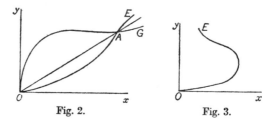

Fig. 2.   Fig. 3.

urgent need of the greater part of her imports from the other; and the demand of each is very elastic in the neighbourhood of the equilibrium point. As has been stated in III, vIII, this class of conditions is the only one which has any great bearing on the actual problems of modern international trade. For in fact a country, whose exports are in high demand on a large scale anywhere, can obtain imports of corresponding value from anywhere else: so long at least as the international market for bills of exchange, and other instruments of credit, is in full work.

But, there is another class, that of Exceptional Demand, in which the markets of a country for foreign wares may be so inelastic as to be completely glutted by moderate supplies; in so much that any further increase of the supplies, forced on the market, will compel them to be sold for a diminished aggregate return. It is illustrated by the shape of OE in Fig. 3.

Under the ordinary conditions of actual trade OE cannot bend round far enough to be vertical; and OG cannot bend round far enough to become horizontal. This may be put more shortly by aid of a *definition*, which will be useful for other purposes: Whatever portion of a curve lies in such a direction that a point, which moves along it so as to recede from Ox, recedes also from Oy; that portion of the curve is said to be *inclined positively*. Conversely, whenever a portion of a curve lies in such a direction that a point which moves along it so as to recede from Ox approaches Oy; that portion of the curve is said to be *inclined negatively*.

Hence we get:—

Proposition II. In the Normal Demand class (but not in the Exceptional Demand class) each of the curves is inclined positively throughout its whole length.

In the Exceptional Supply class, the size of an E bale is supposed to be capable of quick and great increase, as a consequence of a very great increase in the economies of production by E, which is inherent in an increase of her export trade. And in that case G might conceivably be willing to take an increased number of E's bales at a rate of interchange that moved nominally against her; for their nominal movement might be consistent with her obtaining an increased quantity of goods that she desired in exchange for a unit-product of her own labour and capital. But this class is so widely removed from all practical possibilities and uses, that it may be ignored at present, though it is considered at the end of this Appendix.

Proposition III. In the Normal and Exceptional Demand classes, if P be a point moving along OE, and PM drawn perpendicular to Ox, every increase in PM is accompanied by an increase

APP. J, 2. in the ratio of *PM* to *OM*; and therefore in the angle *POM*[1]. Therefore:—

Proposition IV. In the Normal and Exceptional Demand classes, if *P* be any point in *OE*, every point in that portion of *OE* which is between *O* and *P* must lie below the straight line *OP*; and every point in the remaining portion of *OE* must lie above the straight line *OP* produced. Similarly, if *p* be any point in *OG*, every point in that portion of *OG* which is between *O* and *P* must lie to the left of the line *Op*, and every point in the remaining portion of *OG* must lie to the right of the straight line *Op* produced. Hence it follows that neither of the curves can cut twice any straight line through *O*.

We know that if the number of *G* bales offered for sale in *E* is very small, it will be disposed of on terms advantageous to *G*. Thus, where *PM* is small, the ratio of *PM* to *OM* is small: and a point moving from *O* along *OE* will keep at first close to *Ox*. So a point moving from *O* along *OG* will keep at first close to *Oy*. Therefore:

Proposition V. In the Normal and Exceptional Demand classes, that portion of *OE*, which is adjacent to *O*, lies below the corresponding portion of *OG*.

Under given conditions, the total purchasing power which any particular number of *G* bales can be disposed of in *E* is known: and so also is the number of *E* bales which can be produced for that total purchasing power. Therefore *OE* cannot bend downwards towards *Ox* after the manner of the curve in Fig. 4. For if it did, it would imply that *AB* bales from *G* are just capable of being sold for the expenses of producing *OB* bales

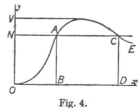

Fig. 4.

from *E*: and also *CD* bales from *G* (which is the same as *AB* bales from *G*) are just capable of being sold for the expenses of producing *OD* bales from *E*. But this is impossible. Thus we obtain a proposition that is of universal application; and not dependent, as the last two were, on Proposition III:—

[1] Of course the terms on which *E* obtains her imports, when the *OA* of her bales are being exchanged for *AB* bales from *G*, is measured mathematically by tan *AOB*: and those, at which *G* gets hers, by cot *AOB*.

Proposition VI. OE cannot be cut more than once by a horizontal line in any case. Similarly, OG cannot be cut more than once by a vertical line.

Let us next investigate the laws which bind the curves if they belong to the Normal class, but not if they belong to Exceptional Demand class. For the Normal class, but not for the Exceptional Demand class, it is assumed that every increase in the number of G bales offered for sale annually in E increases the total proceeds of the sale, and consequently increases the number of E bales that are exported in exchange for them. That is to say: if from N, any point in Oy, NP be drawn at right angles to Oy to meet the curve OE in P, then the greater be ON the greater also is NP.

But in the Exceptional Demand class, represented in Fig. 4, as M moves from O along Ox, though the increase in ON is at first accompanied by an increase in NP; yet when M arrives at a certain point (V in Fig. 4) the distance of the curve from Ox ceases to increase, and begins to diminish, so that the curve bends round towards Oy. These and corresponding results for OG may be stated thus:

Proposition VII. In the Normal class OE cannot cut the same vertical line more than once: but it may in the Exceptional Demand class. So in the Normal class OG cannot cut the same horizontal line more than once; but it may in the Exceptional Demand class.

If A be a point of intersection of the curves as in Fig. 1, then AE must lie entirely above OA produced (by Proposition IV); and AG must lie entirely to the right of OA produced: consequently AE and AG cannot cut again. Nor can AE cut the portion of OG which lies between O and A. For by Proposition VI the portion of OG between O and A must lie entirely to the left of a vertical straight line through A; and by Proposition VII AE must lie entirely to the right of this straight line. Similarly, AG cannot cut the portion of OE which lies between O and A. Therefore OE and OG cannot meet except in O and A. Thus we get:

Proposition VIII. In the Normal class OE and OG cannot cut one another in more than one point (besides O): but they may conceivably do so in the Exceptional Demand class.

As, however, the Normal class is the only one which has any

APP. J, 2. real importance, the discussion of multiple intersections may be postponed a little.

If T lay to the left of O, then OP produced would cut OE again, which is contrary to Proposition IV. Therefore, though the curve may bend back a little towards OP (*i.e.* it may have points of contrary flexure); yet it cannot bend back so far that the tangent at any point beyond P becomes parallel to OP. Thus the tangent

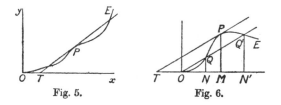

Fig. 5.   Fig. 6.

at P in Fig. 5, cuts OE twice; but T is to the right of O. On the other hand Fig. 6 shows an impossible shape for OE. For the bending backwards near P is carried so far that T is to the left of O; and, OQQ' being drawn parallel to PT cuts OE in Q and Q': thus the curve represents E as willing to purchase $Q'N'$ bales at less favourable terms to herself than PM, though $Q'N'$ is less than PM, which is impossible. Hence we reach:—

Proposition IX. In the Normal and Exceptional Demand case, if PT the tangent at P any point on OE cut Ox in T, T must lie to the right of O: and in the Normal case it must lie between O and the foot of the perpendicular from P on Ox.

If the elasticity of E's demand at any point be unity, then OE must at that point be vertical. For a small movement of the rate of interchange in her favour (indicated by an increase in the angle xOP) would cause her to increase her purchases exactly in the same proportion: that is, after getting the more favourable rate, she would return exactly the same amount of her goods as before.

If OE belong to the Exceptional Demand class, it may bend round through the vertical, so that a point moving upwards along it, after moving away from Ox returns towards it. If P be in this part of the curve, T will lie to the right of M; and, if T moves off to infinity, so that the curve has become parallel to xO, that will indicate that there is no elasticity: *i.e.* no increase in the favourableness of the rate to E will induce her to increase her purchases of G's goods. These considerations afford general evidence for the first part of the next Proposition. The second part of it needs a mathematical demonstration:—

Proposition X. Let the tangent at any point P on OE cut Ox in T; then the elasticity of E's demand indicated at P is indefinitely great, if the angle OPT is indefinitely small. The elasticity indicated diminishes as that angle increases: it is equal to unity if T coincides with M: and when, in the Exceptional Demand case, T moves off to the right of M, the elasticity indicated dwindles to nothing. The elasticity of demand indicated is equal to OM divided by OT[1].

[1] The following is a geometrical proof that e, the elasticity of E's demand represented by the curve at P, $= \dfrac{OM}{OT}$: T being the point at which the tangent at P cuts Ox. The proof applies to both Fig. 7 and Fig. 8, in which e is respectively greater and less than one: and therefore in which T is respectively to the lef and the right of M.

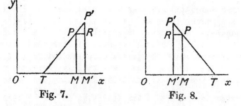

Fig. 7.   Fig. 8.

Let P, P' be consecutive points on E's demand curve. Then PP' is virtually the tangent at P, and $\dfrac{P'R}{PM}$ is the *proportionate* change in E's purchases due to a small actual change in the terms of trade (or, as we may say, to a small lowering of the real price which she pays), from $\dfrac{OM}{PM}$ to $\dfrac{OM'}{P'M'}$.

Now
$$\frac{OM}{PM} - \frac{OM'}{P'M'} = \frac{OM.P'R - PM.MM'}{PM^2} = \frac{(OM-TM)\,P'R}{PM^2},$$

or
$$\frac{P'R.OT}{PM^2};$$

since
$$\frac{MM'}{P'R} = \frac{TM}{PM},$$

and therefore
$$MM'.PM = TM.P'R.$$

The *proportionate* change in the price paid by E is therefore
$$\frac{P'R.OT}{PM^2} \div \frac{OM}{PM} = \frac{P'R.OT}{OM.PM}.$$

Therefore e, which is the proportionate change in E's purchase of G's goods, divided by the proportionate change in the terms of trade,
$$= \frac{P'R}{PM} \div \frac{P'R.OT}{OM.PM} = \frac{OM}{OT}.$$

The differential calculus yields a shorter cut to such results. Thus, if (k, y,

3. *The net benefit which a country derives from her foreign trade, under artificially simplified conditions, represented graphically.*

A graphical representation of G's trading surplus described above (III, VI, 4), and subject to the limitations there noticed,

be the coordinates of P, the *proportionate* change in the favourableness to E of the terms of trade on passing from (x, y) to $(x + \Delta x, y + \Delta y)$ is

$$-\Delta \frac{x}{y} \div \frac{x}{y} = -\frac{y\Delta x - x\Delta y}{y^2} \times \frac{y}{x} = \frac{\Delta y}{xy}\left(x - y\frac{\Delta x}{y}\right),$$

$$\therefore e = \frac{\Delta y}{y} \div \left(x - y\frac{\Delta x}{\Delta y}\right)\frac{\Delta y}{xy} = \frac{x}{x - y\dfrac{\Delta x}{\Delta y}} = \frac{OM}{OT}.$$

Integrating the equation

$$\left(x - y\frac{dx}{dy}\right)e = x,$$

on the supposition that e is constant, we get

$$y^{e-1} = cx^e.$$

It is to be understood that the supposition of an elasticity that is even approximately constant, cannot reasonably be made in relation to amounts of trade either much smaller or much larger than that of the time and under the circumstances in view. Similar limitations apply to nearly all mathematical and diagrammatic illustrations of any part of economic theory.

If e be infinite, the curve becomes a straight line passing through O. If $e = 1$ it becomes $x =$ a constant, if $e = 0$ it becomes $y =$ constant: in accordance with previous results. It may be noted that, since $\dfrac{d}{dy}\left(\dfrac{y}{x}\right)$ must be positive, therefore $x - y\dfrac{dy}{dx}$, *i.e.* OT, must be positive; and thus Proposition IX is deduced direct from Proposition II.

Next, let e' represent the elasticity of E's willingness to extend her sales, instead of her purchases. This bears some analogy to "elasticity of supply" in domestic values (compare my *Principles*, V, XII, 1): but that has special relation to the influences of Diminishing and Increasing Supply; the seller being supposed to receive money, which has an approximately constant marginal utility for him. The dominant factor, in this case of E's willingness to push sales, is the varying marginal utility of the goods which she receives in exchange for them. There is no suggestion that her exports generally show a marked tendency to either Diminishing or Increasing Return. The result now sought belongs to a large class, which seems at present to have no practical bearing; but which, if kept on the shelf ready for use, may be of service in some unexpected way:

$$e' : e = \frac{\Delta x}{x} : \frac{\Delta y}{y}, \qquad \therefore e' = \frac{y}{x\dfrac{dy}{dx} - y}.$$

Integrating this, on the supposition that e' is constant, we get

$$y^{e'} = Cx^{e'+1}.$$

If $e' = \infty$ we get as before a straight line through O; if $e' = 1$, we get a parabola of which Oy is the axis; if $e' = 0$, we get a straight line parallel to Oy; these results are reasonable in themselves.

is given in Fig. 9. A is the exchange-point, G is giving up AB (70,200) bales in return for OB (90,000) E bales. Draw a fixed line DR parallel to Oy and at any convenient distance from it: let it be put so that OD represents 1000 E bales. Let OA produced cut DR in K; and draw KH perpendicular to Oy.

Let OR be the tangent to OG at O. Through P, any point on OG, draw OPp to cut DR in p; and produce MP to P'; so that, M' being the point in which it cuts HK, $M'P'$ may be equal to Kp'. Then G is willing to pay for the OM'th bale from E at the rate of PM bales of her own for OM bales from E: that is, at the rate of pD bales of her own for OD bales from E. She therefore obtains a surplus on that OMth bale at the rate of Kp; which is the same as $M'P'$ for OD bales from E. Thus her surplus on that OMth bale is represented by an ODth part of $M'P'$ bales of her own.

If P, starting from O, is made to move along OG; then P' will start from U, the foot of the perpendicular drawn from R on Oy; and it will trace out a curve ending at A', the point at which BA' produced meets HK. Then the aggregate surplus or net benefit which G derives from her trade will be an ODth part of the aggregate of the lines $M'P'$ as P' passes from U to A': that is, it will be an ODth part of the area UHA'.

Draw VW parallel to Ox, so that the rectangle $VHKW$ is equal to the area UHA'. Then VH, a line of unit breadth corresponding to a single bale, will be an ODth part of the rectangle $VHKW$; and will be the representation, which

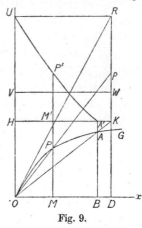

Fig. 9.

we are seeking, of G's total (direct) net or surplus benefit from the trade.

It is obvious that UHA', and therefore this surplus, will be the larger (on the understanding that the position of A is known), the more rapidly a point P moving from O along OG rises, that is the greater the angle which the tangent OR makes with Ox; and the longer P maintains a considerable distance from OA. In other words the surplus is the greater, the more urgent is G's demand for a small amount of E's goods and the more of them she can

APP. J, 4.   receive without any great movement of the rate of interchange in her favour. If, on the other hand, OG remains close to the straight line OA throughout, indicating that G does not care for even a small quantity of E's goods, at a rate much less favourable to G than that of OB bales from E for BA of her own; while her demand is so elastic that she is willing to receive large quantities at that rate: then the area UHA' will be very small, indicating that G gets very little net benefit from the trade.

4. *The stability of the equilibrium of international demand and supply on certain hypotheses, which do not diverge very widely from the normal conditions of actual trade.*

It will be convenient to have a name for the point which corresponds to the actual position of the trade between E and G at any time. If at any time OM bales be exported from E in exchange for ON G bales; and MP, NP be drawn at right angles to Ox, Oy respectively, meeting in P; then P is the *exchange-index* at that time.

We may begin by supposing that the exchange-index is not at A: but that some external disturbing force, as a war, or a bad harvest, has jerked the exchange-index to some position, such that the trade corresponding to it is not in equilibrium; and we may investigate the forces which will govern its motion.

Proposition VI states that OE cannot cut a horizontal straight line through P more than once: and that O cannot cut a vertical straight line through P more than once. We may have therefore the following definition:

A point is said to be *to the right* or *to the left* of OE, according as it is to the right or the left of the intersection of OE with a horizontal straight line through that point. And similarly a point is said to be *above* or *below OG* according as it is above or below the intersection of OG with a vertical straight line through that point.

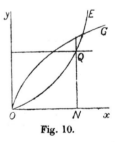

Fig. 10.

Much of the abstract theory of foreign trade may be deduced from the above propositions, together with the following:

Proposition XI. If the exchange-index be at any time to the right of OE it will tend to move to the left; if it be to the left of

OE it will tend to move to the right. Similarly, if the exchange-index be at any time above OG it will tend to move downwards; if it be below OG it will tend to move upwards.

To prove this, let the exchange-point P be to the left of OE, as in Fig. 10, and let NP produced cut OE in Q. Then since Q is a point on OE, G bales to the number of ON are capable of being disposed of annually in E in exchange for the means of producing and exporting NQ bales from E. But at the time in question ON bales from G are being imported into E, and G bales to the number only of NP are being exported in exchange for them. Consequently the trade affords abnormally high profits; and, since competition in the trade is supposed to be free, the exportation of E bales will increase. Therefore when the exchange-index is to the left of OE it will tend to move to the right. So if the exchange-point lay at P' in NQ produced, it would show that E bales were being exported at the rate of NP' annually in exchange for G bales numbering ON, which could be disposed of in E only for the expenses of producing and exporting NQ bales from G: consequently the exportation of E bales would tend to diminish, i.e. when the exchange-point is to the right of OE, it will tend to move to the left. Similar proofs apply to the second part of the proposition which relates to OG[1].

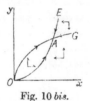

Fig. 10 *bis.*

The equilibrium at a point of intersection of OE and OG may be described as *stable*, provided that when the exchange-index strikes either of the curves in the neighbourhood of that point, the forces acting on the index tend to make it oscillate along the curve *towards* that point. In other cases the equilibrium is *unstable.*

It is obvious that if OE and OG belong to the Normal class they can cut one another in only one point (besides O); and that

---

[1] Thus the motion of the exchange-index is in every respect similar to that of a material particle moving freely under the action of forces which attract it towards OE and OG. Suppose OE to be a rigid wire which exerts attractions only in a horizontal direction and always towards the right when the particle is, according to the definition in the text, on the left of OE, and *vice versâ*. Similarly, suppose OG to be a rigid wire which exerts attractions only in a vertical direction, and always upwards when the particle is, according to the definition in the text, below OG, and *vice versâ*. Then this particle will move exactly in the same manner as does our exchange-index, so that if we chose to assign to these horizontal and vertical forces any particular laws, we should obtain a differential equation for the motion of the exchange-index.

that point represents stable equilibrium (see the arrowheads in Fig. 10 *bis*). If the curves could belong to other classes, then they might cut several times.

> 5. *A graphic version, with some extensions, of the previous study of the influences, which varying degrees of elasticity in E's and G's demands respectively exert on the change in the terms of the trade between them, that results from a general increase in E's demand for G's goods.*

Our next step is to express the problem raised in III, VIII, 1, it being understood that the curves belong to the Normal class; so that neither of them can cut twice either the same vertical line or the same horizontal line. A study of the Exceptional classes is deferred to §§ 8, 9.

We suppose then that E's demand for G's goods increases: and in consequence OE is shifted to a new position OE'. From P any point on OE draw PpM, PP' and $P'M'$ as in Fig. 11. Then P' must lie to the right of P, and p must lie below P. For the number OM' of her bales, which she will give for PM (or $P'M'$) of G bales, is greater than OM: and the number pM of G bales, which she is willing to accept in exchange for OM of hers, is less than OM. This suggests two methods of representing the change: we may say that OE is moved to the right, or that it is moved downwards. Having in view the fact that, if OE did not belong to the Normal class, it might cut the same vertical line twice, while it could not in any case cut the same horizontal line twice, there will be an advantage in speaking of OE as *moved to the right* by an increase in E's demand.

To give definiteness to the ideas we may suppose that, in consequence of an increase in the population of E, or of the cessation of a tax which she had levied on imports from G, the amount of her bales which can be commanded by any given amount of G bales has increased by one-sixth, that OM' is seven-sixths of OM.

The position is represented broadly in Fig. 11 where OE and OG are reproduced from Fig. 1. A is the old position of equilibrium. CAa is drawn horizontally through A, cutting Oy in C: Aa is one-sixth of CA. Then, on the supposition in the last section, that E's demand increases so that she will give one-sixth more of her bales than before for the old equilibrium number BA of bales

from G, a is a point on E's new demand curve OE'. Let OE' cut APP. J, 5.
OG in A'. Then A' is the new position of equilibrium: and, if the
general shape of E's new curve re-
sembles that of the old, then A' must
be about in the position shown in the
figure.

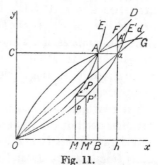

If, however, we make no assumption as to the shapes of OE or OG,
except that both are of the ordinary
or Normal class, and that they meet
in A; and if we assume with regard
to OE' only that it is like OE of the
ordinary class and that it passes

Fig. 11.

through a: then all that we can know about the position of A', is
that it lies within the area $DFad$; D and d are points on the
straight lines OA and Oa produced, and F is the point at which a
vertical line through a cuts OD. For since OE' and OG belong to
the Normal class, A' cannot lie to the left of a, nor below A: since
it is a point on OE' further from O than a is, therefore it must lie
above Oa; and since it is a point on OG further from O than A is,
therefore it must lie below OD.

In order to examine in detail the influence exerted on the
position of A' by the elasticities
of E's and G's demands, we shall
need more space. The area $DAad$
is reproduced from Fig. 11 on a
larger scale in Fig. 12, and we
may follow closely the order
observed in the text. The letters,
D, F, A, a, d have the same
significance as in Fig. 11; and
therefore DA and da, if produced
beyond the limits of the figure,
would meet in O. AG, AG' and
AG'' are continuations of G's de-

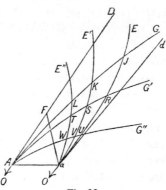

Fig. 12.

mand curve representing great, medium, and small elasticities
respectively: and aE, aE' and aE'' are similar continuations of
E's demand curve under new conditions.

First let us consider the group of results which are indicated

APP. J, 6. when G's demand is very elastic, and is represented by OG. They all show much increased exports of G's produce, since J, K and L are much above A: while the angles LOx, KOx and even JOx are not very much greater than AOx; showing that E obtains her increased supplies of G's goods without suffering any great injury in regard to the rate of interchange. Thus the great elasticity of G's demand is on the whole the predominating influence in the group of results.

The next group of results is that shown by the intersections of the three positions of E's new demand curve, with OG' representing a moderate elasticity in G's demand. The positions of R, S and T differ from one another in the same directions as do those of J, K and L; but the differences are small in amount; and on the whole they stand as a compact group in contrast to the first. Variations in the elasticity of E's demand exert a greater influence on the rate of interchange than in the former case, but a less influence on her supply of G's goods. Here therefore the character of G's demand again dominates, though not so markedly as before.

In the last group of results, on the other hand, the character of G's demand is absolutely dominant: for U, V and W, the intersections of the three positions of E's new demand curve with a curve representing a very inelastic demand on the part of G, lie close together, and close also to a. Each of them shows E to obtain but a very small increase in her supply of G's goods, while yielding up rather more than a seven-sixth of her old equilibrium exports; and therefore having to submit to a rate of interchange much less favourable than the old.

Of course the rates of interchange at J, K, L are in ascending order of favourableness to E, and unfavourableness to G; so are those at R, S, T; and at U, V, W: so also are those at W, T, L; and at V, S, K; and at U, R, T. Those at W, S and J are presumably about equal: and so are those at T and K; and so again are those at V and R.

6. *A graphic study of the influences, which varying degrees of elasticity in* E's *and* G's *demands respectively exert on the change in the terms of trade between them, that results from a general diminution in* E's *demand for* G's *goods.*

We are now to apply the diagrammatic method to the problem of the preceding section. Let P be any point on OE; draw PM

perpendicular to Ox: take a point OM' in OM such that $OM' =$ five-
sixths of OM, and draw $M'P'$ vertically equal to MP; then P'

is a point on E's new demand
curve OE'. For if PM of G's bales
are offered in E's markets they
will command OM of E's bales:
but MM' of these will be taken by
E's Government; and therefore
OM' will go back to G. Let OE'
cut OG in A'; then A' is the new
position of equilibrium; while the
tax is represented by Aa, a being
the point of intersection of a
horizontal line through A with E'.

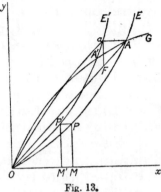

Fig. 13.

Draw OA and Oa, straight lines;
and aF vertically to OA: then A' must lie within the rectilinear
triangle OaF. For, as in the preceding case, since OG is of the
Normal class, AA' must lie within the angle OAa: and, since OE'
is of the Normal class, aA' must lie within the angle OaF.

The movement of the terms of trade in E's favour is represented by the angle AOA': and we have to inquire what are the

conditions which make that
angle large, the amount of
the tax Aa being given. It
is obvious that it will be the
greater (if we first take the
shape of OE'' for granted)
the less be the angle $A'Aa$;
that is, the less be the elasticity of G's demand in the
neighbourhood of A. And,
if we next take the shape of
OG for granted, then the
angle AOA' will be the
greater the greater be the

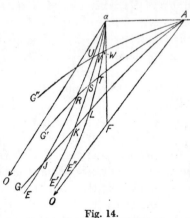

Fig. 14.

angle AaA', that is, the greater be the elasticity of E's demand.
Combining the two results, the amount of the tax being given, the
movement of the rate of interchange in G's favour will be the less, the
less be the elasticity of G's demand, and the greater be that of E's.

APP. J, 6.　　On going into detail we shall find the first of these conditions to be generally more important than the second. For this purpose the top part OAa in the figure is cut off and presented on a magnified scale in Fig. 14.

Going into detail it will be noted that AG is a part of G's curve when her demand is very elastic. It intersects aE, aE', and aE'', which are parts of E's new curve on the suppositions that her demand has great, medium and little elasticity respectively. The point J represents a very great shrinking of the exports both of E and G, the terms of trade being very little changed; and E bearing nearly the whole burden of her taxes. K and L represent much smaller shrinkages of the trade, with very slight increases in the share of the burden of the tax that is thrown on G.

That share is a good deal larger, and the shrinkage of the trade is a good deal less, in each of the cases represented by R, S and T; the points of intersection of a G curve of moderate elasticity with E curves of varying degrees of elasticity.

The third group of intersections, U, V and W, of a G curve of very small elasticity, with three E curves of varying elasticity, show scarcely any shrinkage of G's exports, but a shrinkage by nearly a sixth of E's exports; and in all of them nearly the whole burden of E's tax is seen to be thrown on G.

The rate of interchange at J, K and L are in ascending order of favourableness to E; and so are those of R, S and T: and so again are those of U, V and W.

G's exports are nearly the same for each number of the group U, V, W; and they do not differ widely between the three numbers of the second group R, S and T. E's exports shrink in every case by more than a sixth, but not by very much more than a sixth, except when her demand is very elastic.

We may next consider, as an abstract problem, the influence on the rate of interchange which would be exerted, if a tax on E's imports were levied, the whole proceeds of which were spent on G goods: or, which is the same thing, if the tax were levied in kind, and the whole of the G goods taken under it were retained by the Government; it being supposed in either case that the consumption of G goods by the Government did not subserve any purposes for which they would have been used if left in the hands of private consumers in E.

As before, let the tax amount to, say, one-sixth of the value of the imports in bond: but now (Fig. 15) take a point R on PM such that PR = one-sixth of PM. Then, if PM bales from G were imported, the Government would take PR of them, leaving only RM for private consumers. Draw Rp horizontally to cut OE in p, and draw pP'' vertically to cut a horizontal straight line through P in P''. Then P'' will be the point, which corresponds to P, on E's new demand curve OE''.

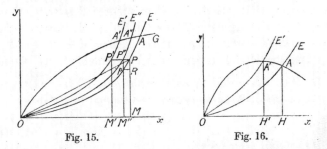

Fig. 15.   Fig. 16.

For pM'' represents the five-sixths of the PM bales from G imported into E, which will be thrown on the general market: and the curve OE indicates that they can be disposed of for OM'' of E's bales. And since, in order that private consumers may get pM'' of G's bales, pP'' must be handed over directly or indirectly free to her Government; therefore E will be prepared to offer only OM'' of her bales in return for $P''M''$ bales from G. It is obvious that P'' must lie to the left of P. But if OE' be drawn, as in Fig. 11, to represent E's demand after the imposition of a tax amounting to one-sixth of E's imports, the proceeds of the tax being spent on E's goods; and if P' be the point on OE' which corresponds to P, then P'' must lie to the right of P'. In other words, OE'' lies between OE and OE', and therefore the effects, which the tax now under discussion exerts on the terms of trade, resemble those of a smaller tax, the proceeds of which were expended in the ordinary way on E's goods[1].

---

[1] It may be well to add a formal proof of the obvious fact that P'' must lie between P and P'. Take M' on Ox such that OM' = five-sixths of OM: and draw $M'P'$ vertically to meet PP'' in P'. Then P' lies on OE': and

$$PP' = \tfrac{1}{6}OM = \tfrac{1}{6}PM \tan OPM,$$

while $$PP'' = PR \tan pPR = \tfrac{1}{6}PM \tan pPM.$$

But by Proposition IX the angle pPM must be less than the angle OPM: therefore PP'' must be less than PP'.

APP. 3. 7.   It may be well to add here a brief reference to the case in which one of the curves, that of G, belongs to the Exceptional Demand class, as in Fig. 16. The trade is supposed to be in equilibrium at A, under such conditions that E has nothing to lose and a great deal to gain by imposing a considerable tax on her imports, and her exports, sufficient to move her demand curve from the position OE to OE'. This will cause G to give $A'H'$ bales (about four-thirds as many as AH), in return for OH' bales from E (about two-thirds as many as OH): thus making each hundred E bales to exchange for about twice as many G bales as before. This gain is shared between E's Government and the consumers of G goods in E, and E's Treasury obtains revenue with little trouble for collection.

7. *Illustrations of G's vulnerability by E's import taxes, on the supposition that they reach far enough to strike a part of G's demand, which is very inelastic; and of the defence against such an attack, which E would derive from any obligations that G might have incurred to her.*

We may now develop, by aid of diagrams, the general remarks made at the end of III, VIII, 3, as to the bulwark of defence which

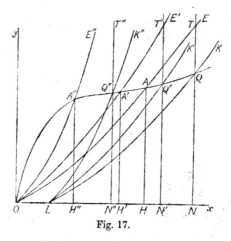

Fig. 17.

G, if in urgent need of a part of her imports, may have against a heavy tax levied by E on her imports (or exports); it being supposed that E's demand for her imports is elastic throughout.

In Fig. 17 G's demand is represented as rigid for very small quantities; and in Fig. 18 as belonging to the Exceptional class

for rather small quantities; in each curve it is elastic for quantities
in the neighbourhood of the ordinary equilibrium position.

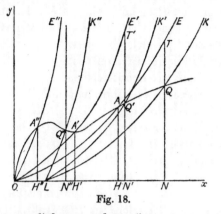

Fig. 18.

In each curve a light general tax (import or export) levied by
E proportional to the value of the trade, but not used as a means
of increasing her Government's consumption of G's goods, shifts
E's curve from OE to OE', and the equilibrium point from A
to A': while a very heavy tax of the same kind shifts E's curve
to OE'', and the equilibrium point to A''. But the first change
has comparatively little effect on the rate of interchange; for the
angle $A'OH'$ is only a little greater than the angle AOH in each
of the figures. But the heavy tax moves the rate of interchange
disastrously to G: for in Fig. 17 the angle $A''OH''$ is much greater
than the angle AOH; and in Fig. 18 it is very much greater.

The position would however have been much altered if E had
been bound to deliver annually
an amount of her goods, represented by OL, to G, as interest
and profits on investments of
capital in various ways by G in
E. For then all E's demand
curves, OE, OE', and OE'' would
have been moved to the right
by a horizontal distance OL;
that is, they would have started
from L instead of from O, and
would have followed courses

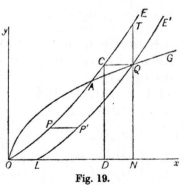

Fig. 19.

APP. J. 7. from L similar to those followed by OE, OE', and OE'' respectively from O.

To prove this, let P be any point on E's demand curve (the argument holds equally whether it be in its original position, or moved to the left by a light or a heavy import duty); from P, Fig. 19, draw PP' horizontally outwards, and equal to OL: then the locus of P' is E's composite demand curve, LE'. Let it cut OG in Q: then Q is the new equilibrium point. For let QC be drawn horizontally to meet OE; and let CD and QN be drawn perpendicular to Ox. Then because Q is on OG, QN bales from E can be sold in G's markets in return for QN bales from G: and since C is a point on OE, therefore CD of G's bales can be sold in E's markets in return for OD bales from E; while receipts for the interest, etc., due from E to G will be obtained by the delivery of DN further bales. Therefore the trade will be in equilibrium when G obtains ON bales from E for QN of hers. Had she not been fortified by the interest, etc., amounting to DN (or OL) bales from E, she would have had to pay NT bales from them; T being the point in which NQ produced meets OE.

Returning now to Figs. 17 and 18, we produce NQ to meet OE in T, and $N'Q'$ to meet OE' in T': but however far we produce $N''Q''$ it will never cut OE''. These results indicate that G's power of drawing OL bales from E, without sending any of her own in return for them, enables her to be much better supplied with E's goods, at a much more favourable rate to herself, than she would otherwise have been, in the two cases in which E levies no tax, and a light tax on her imports. And when E levies a very heavy tax on her imports, this defence enables G to obtain a greater quantity of E's goods than E would have been willing under the circumstances to spend on G's goods, even though G had offered them at a rate extravagantly unfavourable to herself; G obtains this very considerable amount OH'' of E's goods, in addition to the fixed payment, at a moderate cost to herself.

8. *Hindrances to the isolation for separate study of tendencies to* APP. J, 8.
Increasing Return to capital and labour in the production of a country's exports.

The remainder of this Appendix does not claim to have any direct bearing on the actual problems of the external trade of a real country: but it deals with cases that are included under the broad views of imaginary international trade, suggested and developed by Ricardo and J. S. Mill. And, though its direct applications are only to some theoretically conceivable issues of the trade between two isolated countries, it can be translated into terms of any sort of bargains between two bodies, neither of whom is subject to any external competition in regard to those particular bargains.

No country has ever attained leadership in manufacture for export, without previously developing manufacture on a rather large scale for domestic consumption: but the export trade affords exceptional opportunities for dealing on a large scale; and this, in its turn, tends to promote manufacture on a large scale. It is therefore not unreasonable to consider the influence which an increase in the exportation of a country's manufactures may exert on the volume of her external trade; and therefore on its terms. The export trade of Britain, in particular, has exercised a quiet but constant influence on the development of improved methods and increased economies in manufacture. As Adam Smith said, one of the chief advantages of foreign trade is that "by means of it the narrowness of the home market does not hinder the division of labour in any particular branch of art or manufacture from being carried to the highest perfection."

Such facts as these suggest, but they do not justify the assumption made in the *Exceptional Supply* case. To do that, it would be necessary to show that a great and quick fall in the cost of production is traceable to an increase in the production for exportation, independently of any influence that may be exerted by an increase in the domestic demand for those commodities which constitute the bulk of the country's exports. This has never happened, and apparently it can never happen, in regard to the general exports of any great industrial country.

Further, it has often been remarked, that in economics every event causes permanent alterations in the conditions under which future events can occur. This is the case in the physical world also to some extent, but not to nearly so great an extent. The forces that act on a pendulum in any position are practically independent of the oscillations that the pendulum has already made; and many other classes of movement in the physical world are exact copies of movements that have gone before. But every considerable movement that takes place in the moral world alters the magnitude if not the character of the forces that govern succeeding movements. And economic forces belong to the moral world in so far as they depend upon human habits and affections, upon knowledge and industrial skill.

When, for instance, any casual disturbance increases the amount of English wares of any kind that are consumed in Russia, it leaves behind it a permanent effect in an increased familiarity on the part of Russian consumers with English wares; and in this and other ways occasions permanent alterations in the circumstances of demand. An alteration of the shape of Russia's demand curve is rendered necessary by any change

APP. J, 9. which alters the amount of Russian wares that can be exported annually with the proceeds of the sale in Russia of any given amount of English wares. Consequently, every movement of the exchange-index entails some alteration in the shapes of the curves, and therefore in the forces which determine its succeeding movements. If the curves belong to the Normal or to the Exceptional Demand class, the alterations thus required are not likely to be extensive. At all events, the general character of the curves will seldom be changed: and though the positions of equilibrium may be slightly shifted; the general tenor of the reasonings that have been based on the assumption that the shapes of the curves remain rigid and unchanged, will not be thereby invalidated.

But these reasonings may be frequently invalidated if either of the curves belongs to the Exceptional Supply class. For suppose that an increase in the amount of cloth produced for exportation leads to the introduction of extensive economies. Such economies when they have once been obtained are not readily lost. Developments of mechanical appliances, of division of labour, and of organization of transport, when they have once been effected are not readily abandoned. Capital and skilled labour which have once been devoted to any particular industry, may indeed become depreciated in value, when there is a falling off in the demand for the wares which they produce; but they cannot quickly be converted to other occupations. So that for a time their competition will prevent a diminution of demand from causing an increased price of the wares[1].

9. *On the extreme hypothesis that each of two imaginary countries, in exclusive trade with one another, had an urgent demand for a small quantity of the other's goods, but could find no good use for any large quantity of them, then there might be several positions, alternately stable and unstable, of equilibrium between them.*

If OE and OG both belong to this Exceptional Demand class, they may cut one another three (or any other odd number of) times, not counting O. The first of these reached from O in either direction will be stable, the second unstable, the third stable and so on. This is most easily seen by drawing arrowheads in Fig. 20 corresponding to those drawn in Fig. 10. These show that O is a point of unstable equilibrium, A of stable, B of unstable, and C of stable. It is obvious from inspection that in order that the curves may cut more than once (not counting O) they must both belong to the Exceptional Demand class; that is, unless one of them can bend back so as to cut the same straight line through O. But a simple geometrical proof of this can be derived at once from Proposition VI.

---

[1] It is argued, in Appendix H of the present writer's *Principles of Economics* that, though there may be several intersections of a curve representing the demand for a commodity in any market, with a curve representing the supply of that commodity under a tendency to Increasing Returns; yet some inferences, which such intersections suggest, are vitiated by the fact that if the supply point moves forwards and downwards along that curve, and is then forced backwards, it will not return upwards along the old curve: it will trace out a new curve lying below that one.

The above short account is sufficient for most purposes. But perhaps it APP. J, 9. may be well to add, for the sake of completeness, a formal proposition. It is: *The equilibrium is stable at every point of intersection of OE and OG, excepting those at which both curves are inclined positively, but OG is more nearly vertical than* OE; *and excepting those at which both curves are inclined negatively, but* OG *is more nearly vertical than* OE.

This can be seen by reference to Fig. 21, where D is any point of inter-section of *OE* and *OG*. Let horizontal and vertical straight lines *TDU, VDW* be drawn as in the figure.

Firstly, let *OE* be inclined positively at *D*: let it point at *D* in the direction of the straight line *eDE*. Then will the equilibrium be stable provided that *OG* either (i) be inclined positively at *D*, but make a greater angle with the vertical than *eDE* does (pointing at *D* for instance in the direction of *gDG*): or (ii) be inclined negatively, and pointing at *D* for instance in the direction of *g'DG'*: or, in other words, provided that *OG* lie within the angles *eDW, EDV*.

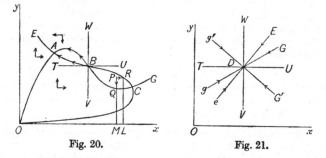

Fig. 20.   Fig. 21.

For suppose the exchange-index to strike *OE* just below *D*, then it must be below *OG*, whether *OG* lie in the direction *gD* or *g'D*; because *eD* lies below both *gD* and *g'D*: therefore it must be attracted upwards. Therefore the arrowhead on *eD* must point towards *D*. So it may be proved that the arrowhead on *DE* points towards *D*: and that the arrowheads on *gD* and *DG*, and on *g'D* and *DG* all point towards *D*. Which proves that under the stated condition *D* is a point of stable equilibrium.

In exactly the same manner it may be proved that the equilibrium at *D* will be unstable if, while *OE* lies at *D* in the direction *eDE*, *OG* is positively inclined and makes a smaller angle with the vertical than *eDE* does, and lies therefore in the angles *eDV, WDE*.

In the same manner also it may be proved that if *OE* is inclined negatively at *D*, the equilibrium at *D* is stable, unless *OG* be inclined negatively at *D* and be more nearly vertical than *OE* is: this completes the proof of the Proposition.

There is of course nothing to prevent either *OE* or *OG* from keeping close to the straight line joining *A* and *C*. In that case they might cut one another any odd number of times between the two points; and a small disturbance might suffice to move the rate of interchange from one of the many positions of stable equilibrium to the next. But all such suggestions derive their origin from the sport of the imagination rather than the observation of facts.

APP. J, 10. For they assume the total elasticity of demand of each country to be less than unity, and on the average to be less than one half, throughout a large part of its schedule. Nothing approaching to this has ever occurred in the real world: it is not inconceivable, but it is absolutely impossible[1].

In the case represented in the figure the two positions of stable equilibrium are far apart; and, if the rate of interchange were in rest at one of them, A, it would, when slightly disturbed, oscillate about A. There could be no question of its moving to C unless it were thrown far away from A by some violent disturbance. If it were so thrown away, the question whether it would return to A, or move to C would be decided by the relative strength of the various forces impelling it in various directions; and this would largely depend on the nature and permanence of the convulsive disturbances which had thrown it away from its original position[2].

Among the causes which govern the strengths of these forces, would of course be difficulty of finding sufficient labour and capital for a great increase of exports; or on the other hand the eagerness for employment of labour and capital, which might be thrown out of gear by a check to the export trade. They would be specially liable to be influenced by the disturbance in question: but, except in so far as thus influenced, they would necessarily have been reckoned in at their full strength; and may not be counted again[3].

10. *Diagrams representing the case of Exceptional Supply, in which the exports of a country show strong general tendencies to Increasing Return, are deprived of practical interest by the inapplicability of the Statical Method to such tendencies.*

The Exceptional Supply case has already been defined as that in which the increase in the economies of the export industries of one of the countries (which we may take to be G) consequent on an increased demand for export, may so increase the contents of the bales, which are the unit-products of her labour and capital, that the other country (E) may be willing to take an increased number of them at a rate of interchange which is nominally (though not really) less favourable to her. That is to say, the cause which

---

[1] Referring to Figs. 6 and 8, we see that if AC make angles of 45° with both Ox and Oy, the elasticity represented by it for each of the curves at a point equidistant from the two axes is $\frac{1}{2}$. At a point which is three times as distant from Ox as from Oy it is $\frac{3}{4}$ for G's demand, and $\frac{1}{4}$ for E's. If AC make any other angle with Ox, then the elasticity indicated is greater for one of the curves and less for the other than the above is.

[2] The analogy of a particle moving under the attraction of two rigid wires, as suggested in connection with Proposition XI, may help towards visualizing the problem.

[3] Mill, however, thought to find the missing key to the otherwise insoluble problem of "the indeterminateness of the rate" in the fact that a country's imports take the place of a definite quantity of similar goods, which she used to make for herself; that the quantity of exports which she can make, is governed by the amount of her labour and capital set free from making those goods. But in this he appears to have been mistaken. The goods which a country imports, are generally different in character from those, which she would provide for herself if she had no foreign trade: and much of the capital and labour required for making her exports is almost as likely to be taken from domestic provision

makes E's curve belong to the Exceptional Supply class, according to this APP. J, 10. definition, is not that the condition of her own industries is exceptional, but that the condition of the industries in the markets with which she deals is exceptional. In consequence, as a point P moves from O along Ox, the angle xOP need not continually increase, as it must in the Normal case and in the Exceptional Demand case. That is to say, Proposition III does not apply to it: nor consequently do IV, V and IX. A straight line through O may, in this case, cut the curve more than once: the portion of OE which is adjacent to O may lie below the corresponding portion of OG: and a tangent to OE may cut Ox to the left of O. The argument of section 3 as to the net benefit of the trade to a country remains valid even if her curve belongs to this class: but it is invalid if the other country's curve does. On the other hand, Propositions VI and XII are valid in regard to Exceptional Supply.

If OE belongs to the Exceptional Supply class, it may cut OG several times, even if OG belong to the Normal class, as in Fig. 23: while if OG also be an Exceptional Supply curve, the two will have larger opportunities for sportively crossing one another. If OE lie above OG in the neighbourhood of O, so that O is a point of stable equilibrium, A, the first subsequent point of intersection must be unstable: and it must be followed by an odd number of points of intersection, not an even one, as in the more natural case when A is stable.

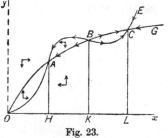

Fig. 23.

If OG belong throughout to the Exceptional Demand class, and OE to the Exceptional Supply class, they cannot easily cut twice, unless O is an unstable point. But very intricate

of goods and services which are not of a nature to be imported or exported. There is therefore no key such as Mill supposed.

But further, Mill's problem was to decide at which of all the possible positions of equilibrium trade would settle between two countries, in each of which "any given increase of cheapness produces an exactly proportional increase of consumption"; that is, in each of which the elasticity of demand is equal to unity. Whatever be the rate of interchange, E will spend a given amount of her goods, say OV in Fig. 22, on them: that is to say, her exports will amount to OV unconditionally. In like manner G's exports will reach a certain amount, say, OW unconditionally. That is, we know that E sends OV

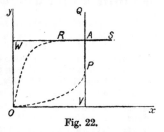

Fig. 22.

of her goods to G, and that G sends OW of her goods in return: and there is no problem to be solved at all.

Of course the conditions are impossible. It is conceivable that E's demand curve may be a vertical straight line for a part of its length, but not for all. For if it could take the position AV, that would imply that E was willing to give OV of her goods for an infinitesimal amount of G's.

APP. J, 11. results might be reached if E's demand for increased quantities of G's goods (not unit products of G's labour and capital) were of elasticity much less than one; so that if G's supply had been normal OE would have belonged to the Exceptional Demand class[1].

11. *Summary of the curious results of the imposition of general import taxes by one of two countries, trading exclusively with one another, under all conceivable conditions of reciprocal demand and supply.*

We have now to examine the effects which may be produced by the imposition of a tax on the importation of linen, into E, or any other change which pushes E's curve to the left, in cases in which the curves are not restricted to the Normal class. But before doing this it will be convenient to obtain a general notion of these results by the inspection of diagrams.

In Fig. 24 both curves belong to Class I, in Fig. 25 E's curve belongs to Class II[2]. The movement of E's curve from the position OE to the position OE' corresponds to the imposition of a small tax, the movement of it to the position OE'' corresponds to the imposition of a larger tax.

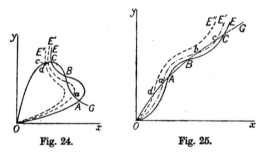

Fig. 24.　　　　　　Fig. 25.

First let us consider the results which arise if E's curve is pushed from the position OE to the position OE'. Then in both figures the exchange-index, if before the change it is at A, will after the change move to a; and, if before the change it is at C it will, after the change, move to c. It will be

---

[1] If the unit of measurement had been a certain artificially averaged quantity of each country's export goods, instead of a unit-product of her labour and capital; then those Exceptional Supply conditions, which enable G's export industries to produce at a violently reduced cost, in consequence of an increase in the export demand for their products, would affect the shape of G's curve instead of E's. It would then be OG and not OE that belonged to the Exceptional Supply class: but, that substitution having once been made, the reasoning in the text as to multiple points of intersection would apply throughout, the diagrams remaining unchanged.

The original draft of this study of exceptional cases dealt with an imaginary trade, in which the economies of production on a large scale acted so strongly and so quickly that OE and OG might take on some fantastic shapes. But in all the years that have elapsed since that study was made, I have seen no profit in the results thus reached: so they are suppressed.

[2] Henceforward "Class I" is used as an abbreviation for "Exceptional Demand class," and "Class II" for "Exceptional Supply class."

noticed that in both figures a is nearer to Oy than A is, and c nearer than C.
That is, in each of the four instances in which the exchange-index moves
from A to a or from C to c in either of the figures the amount of cloth
exported is diminished. Also the amount of linen imported into E is
diminished in three out of the four instances, but is increased in the instance
in which the exchange-index is by the change made to move from A to a
in Fig. 25. Also, if straight lines be drawn from O to A, a, C, c, the angle
cOx is greater than the angle COx, and the angle aOx is greater than the
angle AOx in both figures. That is, in each of the four instances the rate of
interchange is altered to E's advantage.

Of the above cases, that which has the greatest general interest is that
in which the exchange-index moves from A to a in Fig. 25. For in this
instance the imposition of the tax causes the rate of interchange to be
altered in E's favour to so great an extent that she obtains an increased
amount of linen in exchange for a diminished amount of cloth. A more
striking result of this class is, however, obtained when E's curve is pushed
further to the left to the position OE'''. For then the exchange-index will
move away to d, and E will obtain more than twice the old amount of linen
in exchange for less than half the old amount of cloth.

By giving a special interpretation to the curves in Fig. 26 we may cause
them to correspond closely to the actual circumstances of some important
practical problems. E may here be taken to represent England; and G
to represent Germany.

Instead of using distances along Ox to measure cloth as representative
of the whole of E's exports to G, let us use these
distances to measure only one of the wares which
E exports, viz. coal.

OE can no longer be called E's demand curve but
may be called E's coal export curve; and OG may
now be called G's demand curve for coal. OE will
now be a curve such that if any point P be taken
on it and PM drawn perpendicular to Ox, OM
represents the amount of coal which England is
willing to export annually in exchange for an amount of Germany's wares
represented by PM. So OG will now be a curve such that if any point p
be taken on it and pm drawn perpendicular to Ox, pm represents the amount
of her own wares which Germany is willing to export annually in exchange
for Om coal.

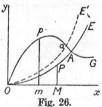

Fig. 26.

Recent history[1] shows that Germany's demand curve for coal may take
the form which is given to it in Fig. 26. But England's coal export curve
cannot belong to Class I; it cannot bend round and approach Oy. For the
amount of Germany's wares which can be bought with the proceeds of the
sale of English coal in Germany cannot be very great, and no increase of this

[1] [P.S. 1921. This refers to events which culminated in 1873. When writing
this (about 1871), I had carelessly dropped into the practice of using money as
a measure of the value of exports and imports: and the subsequent debâcle of
prices illustrates well the danger of such a course. But it seems best to let the
passage remain.]

APP. J, 11. amount that could occur would be sufficient so to increase the total supply of these wares as to glut the English market with them and cause a very great diminution in the rate at which they could be disposed of.

Looking at the figure, we see that any cause which pushed England's coal export curve to the left, from the position OE to the position OE', might cause the exchange-index to move from A to a, i.e. might cause England to obtain a larger amount of Germany's wares than before in exchange for a smaller amount of coal than before. But, as has been already remarked, although England may bring about this result by imposing a special export duty on coal, she cannot do it by imposing an import duty on German wares. For Germany's demand for English wares generally is to be classed under the Normal class. Though she cannot easily dispense with English coal, there are many other wares which she is just induced to purchase at the present rate of interchange, but which she would obtain either from her own producers or from those of some other country, if England endeavoured by imposing an import duty to alter the rate of interchange to her own advantage. In the same way it may be true that the demand curve of European nations for the finest staples of American cotton is of the character represented by OG in Fig. 23, so that America might derive immediate gain from a special export duty on these particular staples. But the burden of the import duties of America cannot be made to fall in the main on European countries, so long as a large portion of America's exports of cotton and other goods are closely run by the competition of rivals from other countries.

The cases, in which the circumstances of a small portion of the trade which one country carries on with another, correspond to the curves in Fig. 23, though by no means unimportant, are not very common. But the circumstances of the trade which any industrial group carries on with the rest of the community may very often be represented by these curves. Thus the circumstances of the demand of the community for new houses may, at certain times and places, correspond pretty closely to the shape of OG in the figure. The conditions under which the building trades are willing to dispose of their services may be represented by OE: and the claims which their Unions make, when written out in exact terms, may be such as to be rightly interpreted by the assertion that they can push this curve to the left into the position OE': and thereby obtain an increased amount of the wealth of the community at the expense of a diminished amount of their own labour.

It is in connection also with the circumstances of commerce of particular industrial groups, rather than with those of the trade between two countries, that interest attaches to the position of OE'' in Fig. 25. [It is a curious result that if in this figure the exchange-index be at C, and England's curve is pushed into the position OE'' the exchange-index will move off to d, and the trade will be nearly destroyed.]

In the present section, the curve OE' is to be taken to be the position assumed by E's demand curve after the imposition of a tax on the importation of linen into E; or some other event which diminishes E's demand for linen and pushes E's curve towards the left, but does not alter the position of G's curve. This event will, for brevity, be referred to as "the change."

The change will cause a diminution in the amount of cloth exported to Germany. In other words if the exchange-index be, before the change, in equilibrium at A, the point to which the index moves after the change, must lie on the left of A. The exchange-index is taken to be at A at the time at which England's curve assumes the position OE'. From this time the forces acting upon the index will tend to make it move towards the right or left according as it is to the left or the right of OE'. But by construction A is to the right of OE'. Therefore, if the exchange-index is at A at the time of the change it will, after the change, move from A along GO towards the left.

In the above reasoning it has not been assumed that the intersection at A was one which corresponded to stable equilibrium. Hence it results, that if OG has several points of intersection with OE and also with OE', those two sets are distributed along OG in pairs. That is, if we pass along OG from any one intersection of OG with OE to any other, we must pass through an even number (0, or 2 or 4, etc.) of intersections of OG with OE': and if we pass along OG from any one intersection of OG with OE' to any other, we pass through an even number of intersections of OG with OE. Of course an independent geometrical proof can be given of this result.

Next, let us assume that A is a point of stable equilibrium for the curves OE and OG: and that F is the point of stable equilibrium for OE' and OG to which the exchange-index moves after the change. And let us inquire what are the positions in which it is possible for F to lie. Let straight lines be drawn as in Fig. 27. That is, let the horizontal line $TA'AR$ be drawn through A cutting Oy in T and OE' in A'. Let the vertical line $HASV$ be drawn cutting Ox in H

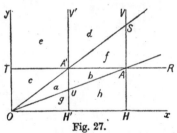

Fig. 27.

and the straight line OA' produced in V: and let the vertical line $H'UA'V'$ be drawn cutting Ox in H' and the straight line OA in U. [F is not shown on the diagram, because its movements from one part of the diagram to another are under discussion: and they could not be shown without drawing a separate diagram for each possible combination of conditions.]

We obtain then the following results:

If OG belong to the Normal class, F must lie within the triangle OAT; if to Class I, F must lie in the space $yOAV$; if to Class II, F may, so far as this condition is concerned, lie anywhere to the left of HV.

Similarly, if OE' belong to the Normal class, F must lie somewhere in the spaces $OA'H'$, $V'A'SV$; if to Class I, F must lie within the spaces $OHAA'$, $yTA'SV$; if to Class II, F may, as far as this condition is concerned, lie anywhere to the left of HV. Combining these conditions, we have:

Firstly, on the supposition that OG belongs to the Normal class:

(i) Let OE' belong to the Normal class, then F must lie within the triangle $OA'H'$ as, for instance, a;

(ii) Let OE' belong to Class I, then F may lie anywhere within the triangle OAA' as, for instance, a or b;

(iii) Let OE' belong to Class II, then F may lie anywhere within the triangle OAT as, for instance, a, b or c.

Secondly, on the supposition that OG belongs to Class I:

(i) Let OE' belong to the Normal class, then F may lie anywhere within the spaces $OA'H'$, $V'A'SV$; as, for instance, a or d;

(ii) Let OE' belong to Class I, then F may lie anywhere within the spaces $OA'A$, $yTA'SV$, as, for instance, a, b, d or e;

(iii) Let OE' belong to Class II, then F may lie anywhere within the space $yOAV$, as, for instance, a, b, c, d, e or f.

Thirdly, on the supposition that OG belongs to Class II:

(i) Let OE belong to the Normal class, then F may lie anywhere within the spaces $OA'H'$, $V'A'SV$, as, for instance, a, d or g;

(ii) Let OE belong to Class I, then F may lie anywhere within the spaces $OHAA'$, $yTA'SV$, as, for instance, a, b, d, e, g or h;

(iii) Let OE belong to Class II, then F may lie anywhere to the left of HV, as a, b, c, d, e, f, g or h.

These results cannot be recapitulated in a short Proposition, but they may be conveniently displayed thus:

OE' Normal lies in $\angle\ OA'H'$			OG Normal lies in $\angle\ OAT$		
„ Class I	„	$OA'A$	„ Class I	„	OAS
„ Class II	„	$OH'A$ or $OA'T$	„ Class II	„	OAS or OAH.

If OG belongs to Class	While OE belongs to Class	F may move to the points
Normal	Normal	a
—	I	a or b
—	II	a, b or c
I	Normal	a or d
—	I	a, b, d or e
—	II	a, b, c, d, e or f
II	Normal	a, d or g
—	I	a, b, d, e, g or h
—	II	a, b, c, d, e, f, g or h

The amount of cloth exported from E is diminished in every case. The rate of interchange is altered in E's favour in every case in which G's curve belongs to the Normal class or to Class I. The amount of linen is diminished in every case in which G's curve belongs to the Normal class. Positions c and f can be reached only when E's curve belongs to Class II; positions g and h only when G's curve belongs to Class II.

INDEX

[References under each heading are arranged generally in numerical order: but when the chief discussion of a subject is concentrated in a single place, that place is mentioned first.]

Adam Smith, on migration 3–4, 109; on price of labour 3 n., 22; changes in local interests since his time 10–11; his genius 41 n.; on the value of money 47 n.; on Joint Stock banks 85; and the purpose of his *Wealth of Nations* 108; on the Bank of Amsterdam 147 n., 297; his fear of Government intervention 220, 224; on "origin of money" 267 n.; on advantages of foreign trade 351

Adjusted mean 29 n.

"Alternative-metallism" 62, 64

Anderson's history of Commerce 90 n., 118, 301 n.

"Arithmetical index numbers" 26–7; weaknesses of 275–6, 278–9

Ashley, Sir W. 118 n.

Auspitz and Lieben 330–1 n.

Bacon, on banks 81

Bagehot, on unit of purchasing power 21 n.; on joint-stock and private banks 85; on early forms of banking 298; on Bank of England directors 307 n.

"Balance of trade" 130

"Bales" as representative of a country's products 157, 161

Bank 81; of Amsterdam 15 n., 297–300, 304; of Hamburg 297, 300 n.

Banking, functions of 14–15, 81–2; deposit 15 n.; in relation to early forms of trade and manufacture 71–2, 295–300; and note issue 72, 298–300; development of British 81–5, 300–307; history of during 19th century 87–8; private and joint stock 85–8; in Greece and Rome 295; in Italy 296–7

Bank of England, as the bank of bankers 83–5; and Act of 1844 84 n.; printing of its notes 49 n.; effects of its prompt action on the rate of discount 258–9; foundation of 300–1; its *exclusive* privileges 301–2; charter of 1697 301, of 1708 302, of 1742 302; owed much to counsel of William III 302 n.; during the Napoleonic wars 306–7

Bank money 15, 297 n.

Bank notes, their relation to currency 13; origin and early history of 298–300, 304

Bannister, life of Paterson 301 n.

Baring, Alexander, on uncoined gold and silver as a basis for paper money 67

Barter, inconveniencies of 269–71; equilibrium rate in 270

Beames' *Lex Mercatoria* 70 n.

Beissel 54 n.

Bills of Exchange, their relation to Currency 14–15; economy effected by 140–4; history of 141 n., 142; "roundabout" operations of 143; "fictitious" 141; "long" and "short" 147–8; value of 148–9; called in China *"flying money"* 295 n.

Bimetallism or "fixed-ratio mintage" 62–4, 225; likely to become "alternative-metallism" 62

Bisschop, on Rise of London Money Market 299

Bosanquet, Charles, on the organization of banking in London 83 n.

Bosanquet, J. W. on bills of exchange 142 n.

Boulton, his massive production of accurate coins 55 n.

Bounties, on exports 204–5; in relation to import duties 228; which are due to an inconvertible paper currency 316–17; and to dissimilar metallic currencies 217–320

Bowley, Prof., on comparison of British and German trade 116 n.; on statistical method 274 n., 278 n.

Bread, change in its quality during last century 34; and in the weight of the loaf in mediaeval England 234 n.

British, system of currency 57–9; sovereign, its prestige in international finance 57–8; foreign trade 113; and German trade compared 116 n.; external trade 118–29; in 17th and 18th centuries 118–19; changes in it since 1850 119–20; export trade 121–6; trade smaller and less important than it appears 126–9; imports and exports

CAMBRIDGE: PRINTED BY J. B. PEACE, M.A., AT THE UNIVERSITY PRESS